Praise for
We Are Not Meant to Die

"*We Are Not Meant to Die* is an innovative and practical guide for health optimization and a major contribution to the science of longevity. Within its pages, you will find the keys to optimizing your health, managing stress, and choosing life."

— Kenneth R Pelletier, PhD, MD, Clinical Professor of Medicine, Medical consultant to the World Health Organization, Founding Board Member of the American Board of Integrative Medicine (ABOIM), and bestselling author of *Mind as Healer, Mind as Slayer* and *Change Your Genes, Change Your Life*

Gerald Epstein's teachings have always been, and will always be a safe path to healing, integration, and wholeness for anyone, regardless of their religion or belief system. Whenever the soul reads, sees, or hears The Truth, it doesn't matter who you are or what your religious orientation is, for the Heart says "A-Men." I say "A-Men to *We Are Not Meant to Die: How to Choose Life in Every Moment*" and I'm confident your soul will too!

— Paul Chek, founder of Chek Institute for Holistic Health Studies. Founder of Spirit Gym and the Spirit Gym with Paul Chek podcast

Gerald and Rachel Epstein have created a masterpiece. They have brought the ancient holistic spiritual practice of mental imagery into our modern world. It is a must-read for anyone wanting to deepen their spiritual growth, heal their physical and emotional issues, open their hearts, and prepare their souls for transformation and freedom.

— Penny Price Lavin, filmmaker of *The Healing Field: Exploring Energy & Consciousness,* and author of *The Healing Field: Exceptional Healing Practices to Change Your Life.*

Dr Gerald Epstein juxtaposes ancient texts about longevity (Methuselah lived 969 years) and Eternal Life (Enoch ascended to heaven in his mortal body) with modern research into slowing down and even reversing the aging process. He poses the question: Have we been programmed to believe that death is inevitable? Certainly, modern scientists are putting their thinking minds and resources into trying to prove the opposite. Dr Jerry (as he was familiarly called) reminds us that longevity is a healing process, an alignment to the true ecology of God's dream – that allows our bodies to live longer, healthier lives. To enable this alignment, he reminds us of the spiritual laws that guide us towards this goal: the Ten Commandments, the Three Virtues, and the Seven Divine Forces. He then leads us through a series of profound imagery exercises to have us experience rising above ourselves and above time into blissful oneness. This book is his final opus and gift to us before he passed into timelessness, reminding us that it is our choice to break through to what the texts tell us can be a world where death does not exist. Beautifully co-authored and brought to life by Rachel Epstein, it is a book you will want to read.

— Catherine Shainberg, PhD, author of *Kabbalah and the Power of Dreaming* and the *Kabbalah of Light*

In these pages, you'll discover Dr Jerry Epstein's rare gift of alchemy, transforming complex ideas into illuminating insights, delivered with his characteristic warmth, wisdom, and humor. His unique ability to weave both the practical and esoteric elements of life into a coherent, vibrant whole has profoundly influenced not only my personal life but that of my work with clients and graduate clinical students, so much so that they would often joke, "We're almost done, and you haven't mentioned Jerry yet!" (frankly, current modalities could learn a lot from Jerry). Through this book, you can experience the same enlightening perspective that has guided many others. As you engage with his words, you'll find yourself drawn into a rich tapestry of imagery and understanding rooted in his deep sense of what it means to be an awake human today.

— Randy Kasper PhD, LCSW, BCD, Professor, California State University. Recipient of Imagery International's Person of the Year.

Dr Jerry Epstein was probably the wisest man we have ever had the privilege of knowing and calling our friend. He was always pushing the boundaries of ultimate truth in his work as a psychiatrist, in his books, his lectures, and in his private interactions with us. It is, therefore, not surprising to us that his final book is his bravest, insightful, and thought-provoking. It is also his most audacious and provocative, expressing in its title and its pages the declarative sentence and rational, reasonable supporting text that we all long to read, written by the wisest man we have ever known. As science gets closer and closer to understanding the mechanics of death from "natural causes," the suspicion arises that perhaps the story of Methuselah living for nine hundred plus years may one day soon join the many other biblical stories once thought to be mythical or allegorical but found to be true. Our set of "junk genes" (Google it!) may one day be found to be part of the physical mechanism enabling long life that can be "switched on" by the concepts and techniques contained in *We Are Not Meant to Die*.

— Amy Zerner & Monte Farber, authors of *The Intuition Oracle* and *The Vision Board Oracle*

Gerald Epstein, MD was an inspiring, innovative psychiatrist who increased our understanding of the mind-body unity. In this lucid, newly posthumously published book, he draws on Jewish spirituality and other traditions to enhance our mental and physical well-being with guided activities and lessons from his healing practice.

— Edward Hoffman, PhD, author of, *Paths to Happiness: 50 Ways to Add Joy to Your Life Every Day*

I met Jerry around 1992 and read and studied all of his books, audio programs, and most of his publications, in addition to taking classes and doing clinical supervisions under him for five years. This final book is an exceptional synthesis — and evolution — of all of his prior work that lays out piece-by-piece Western spiritual healing practices. Within, you will find conceptual components first seen in his *Studies in Non-Deterministic Psychology;* approach to dreams and the 'invisible reality' seen in his *Waking Dream Therapy;* plenty of new imagery exercises akin to those in *Healing Visualizations,* geared specifically to create transformative shifts; *and* a spiritual direction as seen in all of Jerry's works but emphasized in *Climbing Jacob's Ladder* and *Kabbalah for Inner Peace.* Like *Healing Into Immortality,* this book offers a comprehensive approach to the healing arts of the Western spiritual tradition but offers important additional nuances laying out Jerry's own evolutionary thought. Despite its complex material, it is simple and easy to read.

— Oleg Reznik, MD, author of *Mystical Poetry of Colette Aboulker-Muscat and Reflections of Her Student* and *Secrets of Medical Decision Making*

In this book, Dr. Jerry Epstein, a Jewish mystic teacher, offers a very profound and radical idea, "We do not need to die!" He then presents extremely practical advice and specific methods for living a holy existence, emphasis on the "whole" of "holy." Through personal stories and teachings from the great masters of many traditions, he makes his case, urging us to let go of beliefs that bring pain and suffering and embrace the life force of spiritual light from within. Whether or not you believe you are going to die, you will learn a great deal from Dr. Jerry's wisdom.

— Alan Levin, LSW, author of *Crossing the Boundary: Stories of Jewish Leaders of other Spiritual Paths*

We Are Not *Meant* to Die

BOOKS AND AUDIO RECORDINGS

Healing Visualizations
Creating Health Through Imagery

Natural Laws of Self-Healing
Harnessing Your Inner Imaging Power to
Restore Health and Reach Spirit (audio)

The Phoenix Process
One Minute a Day to Longevity, Health & Well-Being (audio)

Emotional Mastery
Life Transformation Through Higher Consciousness (audio)

Healing into Immortality
A New Spiritual Medicine of Healing Stories and Imagery

Kabbalah for Inner Peace
Imagery and Insight to Guide You Through Your Day

Climbing Jacob's Ladder
Finding Spiritual Freedom Through the Stories of the Bible

The Encyclopedia of Mental Imagery
Colette Aboulker-Muscat's 2,100 Visualization Exercises for
Personal Development, Healing, and Self-Knowledge

Waking Dream Therapy
Unlocking the Secrets of Self Through
Dreams and Imagination

Studies in Non-Deterministic Psychology

Reversing the Trauma of War
PTSD Help for Veterans, Active Duty Personnel and Their Families

We Are Not *Meant* to Die

HOW TO CHOOSE LIFE
IN EVERY MOMENT

Dr. Gerald Epstein, MD
and Rachel Epstein, LAc

ACMI PRESS
New York

We Are Not *Meant* to Die
How to Choose Life in Every Moment

Copyright © 2025 by Rachel Epstein

All rights reserved. No part of this work may be reproduced or utilized in any form or by any means, electronic or mechanical, including the Internet, photocopying, microfilming, recording, or by an information storage and retrieval system, without permission in writing from the publisher.

This book is not intended as a substitute for medical advice of physicians. The reader should consult a physician in matters relating to his or her health and particularly in respect to any symptoms that may require diagnosis or medical attention.

Publisher's Cataloging-in-Publication Data
Names: Epstein, Gerald, 1935-2019, author. | Epstein, Rachel, 1957-, author.
Title: We are not meant to die : how to choose life in every moment / Dr. Gerald Epstein, MD and Rachel Epstein, LAc.
Description: Includes bibliographical references and index. | New York, NY: ACMI Press, 2025.
Identifiers: LCCN: 2024948269 | ISBN: 978-1-883148-32-4 (hardcover) | 978-1-883148-30-0 (paperback) | 978-1-883148-31-7 (epub)
Subjects: LCSH Longevity. | Aging. | Self-care, Health. | Conduct of life. | Meaning (Philosophy) | Self-realization. | BISAC BODY, MIND & SPIRIT / Healing / General | SELF HELP / Spiritual | HEALTH & FITNESS / Longevity
Classification: LCC RA776.75 .E77 2025 | DDC 613.2--dc23

Printed in USA
First edition, 2025
ACMI Press, Inc.
351 East 84th Street, Suite 10D
New York, New York 10028
Tel: (646) 269-4742
www.acmipress.org

To our teachers who brought us
closer to Truth and Love
And
To our readers may they find this book
helpful on their Life Path

The universe is an endless
source of creative life force.

It is there for us to partake of its energy and be
constantly filled with its life-giving power.

This book is designed to teach each of us
how to tap into that endless flow.

Contents

Illustrations 10
Acknowledgments 11
Introduction..15
Instructions for Practicing Mental Imagery 24

SECTION I
Gerald Epstein's Medicine System (GEMS)
Ingredients for Everlasting Life

Chapter I	Buddha Was Correct, and What We Can Do About It 29	
Chapter II	My Spiritual Journey 39	
Chapter III	The Two Trees of Eden: Entropy and Ectropy 47	
Chapter IV	What IS Spiritual Science? 67	
Chapter V	Laws of Longevity: A Spiritual Perspective 84	
Chapter VI	GEMS: A New Sacred Health-Care Model 94	

SECTION II
The Death Plan: How Death Works

Chapter VII	Theater of Life	111
Chapter VIII	The Physiology of Death: The False Emergency State	120
Chapter IX	The Social Errors of Living: The Death Plan	139

SECTION III
The Life Plan: Laws of Detachment and Practices of Ectropy

Chapter X:	Developing Spiritual Awareness	185
	The Alliance: A Love Relationship with God	187
	Will: The Force of Life	189
	Remembering: Restoring Ourselves to Wholeness	189
	Watching: Observing the Inner Terrorists	196
	Reversing: The Way to Self-Organization and Eternal Life	202
Chapter XI	The Seven Divine Forces	204
	Will: Engine of Change, Creative Force, Life Force	205
	Love: Unconditional Feeling	208
	Faith: Unconditional Action	215
	Intuition: Unconditional Thought	228
	Imagination: Unconditional Language	232
	Hope: Perpetuation of Life	236
	Light: Diving Away the Darkness	238

Contents

Chapter XII	Reversing: Practices of Detachment	242
	The Ten Commandments: The Gift of the Laws of Love and Community	244
	The Laws	251
	The Three Virtues: Overcoming the Laws of the Jungle	296
	Concentration Without Effort: Living Without Goals	310
	Thinking by Analogy: Intuitional Thinking	321
	Mental Imagery: A New Way of Self-Healing	329
	Prayer: Conversing with God	341
	The Yes or No Phenomenon: Resolving Doubt	345
	Grammar of Self: Reversing the Trap of Linear Time	355
	Stopping Exercises: Visa to Freedom	364
	Gratuitousness: Emulating God	369
Chapter XIII	Health-Care Reform — Health-Care Reformers	371

SECTION IV
Future Vision: From Here to Eternity

Chapter XIV	Becoming an Imaginaut: Imagery for Discovering Eternal Life	381
Chapter XV	The Great Sabbath of the Earth and Beyond	423
Glossary		431
Index		437
About the Authors		447

Illustrations

The Family Tree 21
The Spiral: Symbol of Self Organization 52
Spirit Births Matter... 68
1. Spirit to Matter: 7 Divine Forces 79
Diagram I: The 5 Dimensions of Experience........................ 84
Diagram II: Heart Ailment Example 86
Diagram III: Miriam (Moses's Sister) 88
From Disorder to Order (Thinking, Feeling, Acting)......... 97
Diagram IV: Sheila (Example of Chronic Emotional Condition) ... 102
Diagram V: Paula (Example of Acute Physical Condition) 104
Theater of Life I — Fragmented Life → Integrated Life 111
Theater of Life II — Fragmented Life 112
Theater of Life III — Integrated Life..................................... 117
The Physiology of Death 125
Death Plan 143
The Mechanism of Illness: How it Works............................. 155
Enslavements = Idolatries Chart 173
Forgetting, Sleep, and Death 190
2. Spirit to Matter: 7 Divine Forces 205
Dark and Light Currents of: Will 207
Tree of Life 242
Life Plan: 10 Laws, 3 Virtues, and 7 Forces 244
Ten Laws Tablet 245
Charting Ten Laws Example 293
Charting Ten Laws Template 295
Stop and Go.. 366
Seventh Cervical Vertebra 407

Acknowledgments

To my honored parents, Max and Celia Epstein, for giving me life.

To my beloved brothers Ezra, Myron, and especially Sandy, who taught me how to be a "good kid."

To my former friend Alan Konigsberg, who opened my eyes to the reality of ESP and kept me belly-laughing for ten years through those depressive adolescent years and beyond.

To my ex-wife Perle Besserman, who showed me the door to spiritual life that started me on my life journey of spiritual quest.

To my analyst Isidor Silbermann, who became a dear friend. He was a voice of reason and a ballast in my life.

To my beloved teacher and spiritual guide Mme. Colette Aboulker-Muscat, who took me on a journey that celebrated life and showed me the wonders of Imagination. She made me understand "normal."

To those other inspirational teachers I had the serendipity to come to know, either personally or through their work: Philo of Alexandria,

We Are Not Meant to Die

Dr. Medard Boss, Henri Corbin, Dr. Robert Rhondell Gibson, Valentin Tomberg, Paul Watzlawick, and Frederick Weinreb, all of whom came along after Colette and attuned me to expand and enlarge my vision, consciousness, and awareness.

From all of them I learned to grow up and become a "mensch."

To those longtime friends: Dan Singer, Colin Greer, Rozy Fox, Elizabeth Barrett, Shatay Trigère, Stephanie Berger, Lisa Broderick, Holly Jaffe, Lucia Pires, Jack Victor, Brendan Elliott, and so many others too numerous to name, and who know who they are.

To all the students who stayed the course to join me on this odyssey and persevere with me. They are too numerous to mention for fear of leaving someone out. But they know who they are, without question. They are forever in my heart.

A special shout-out of thanks and gratitude to Shatay Trigère, who graced these pages with her illustrations. They have helped to clarify many salient points of understanding on which this book rests.

To Carol Shookhoff, typist supreme, who was able to navigate the highways and byways of this manuscript.

To Harris Dienstfrey, a great editor who provided valuable insights into this book's organization.

To the readers of the manuscript: Barbara Delage, Nance Guilmartin, Rick Jarow, and Amy Kruvant for their invaluable input as pre-publication readers of this book.

And then there is last and first my dearest beloved wife, without whom this book could not have been written. She is my helpmate, loving all-around pillar of life, partner, true friend, fellow traveler, spiritual companion, mother of my beloved children Sarah and Max. Her name is Rachel (the lamb of God).

—Jerry

Acknowledgments

To my parents of blessed memory, Jean and Morty Blumenthal, who provided me with a loving home, endless support, and a deep well of Jewish spirituality that I draw on daily.

To my two gems, Sarah and Max, whose hearts "I carry in my heart, always!"

To my sister Celia, of blessed memory, who helped "grow me up."

To all my dear friends and family who have been true pillars of support and love through the years.

To the American Institute for mental Imagery (AIMI) Board Members and students, who trusted in me to carry on Jerry's life's work.

To my assistant, Julia Machina for her fine editing and midwifing of this book from the last stages of labor to birth; and Stephanie Berger, Sarah Epstein, and Shatay Trigère who helped me to the finish line.

To Matthew and Joan Greenblatt for their patience, loving care, and attention they brought to the design of this book.

To the teachers, healers, shamans, and spiritual masters I have had the privilege to learn from directly including Werner Ehrhard, Muktananda, Harry Palmer, Mark Seem, Jack Coddington, and Mehrdad Noorani; and indirectly, S. N. Goenka, Medard Boss, Valentin Tomberg, and Meister Eckhart.

To my spiritual teachers that continue to teach me from beyond the thin veil that separates this world from the next: Colette Aboulker-Muscat and Robert Rhondell Gibson.

And lastly, to Jerry, my most beloved spiritual partner, husband, and teacher par excellence, who walked in ancient fields of wisdom with me for 30 years and whose love is stronger than death.

—Rachel

We Are Not *Meant* to Die

Introduction

THIS IS A BOOK ABOUT LIFE AND DEATH. *We Are Not Meant to Die* presents a new evolutionary system of medicine built around holiness, where love, faith, health, and hope reside. [1] I call this model of medicine GEMS. It provides a new education between our everyday health, our social relationships, and our spiritual life. It prescribes essential remedies to make the necessary corrections in ourselves to bring harmony and order back into our lives, all of which promotes our longevity.

From early on we find ourselves in an existential tension between life and death. We are indoctrinated to believe we all die — that death is inevitable. Consequently, a deep angst pervades us as the specter of death hangs over our heads like a dark cloud. On the other hand, we are not given any information about the possibility that also exists of

---

[1] Throughout the book "I" refers to Gerald Epstein

ongoing, endless life – that life is inevitable! This book aims to educate you about this possibility. I present a LIFE PATH and delineate what it is and how it works, including how to choose it throughout your daily life. Constantly choosing this LIFE PATH naturally leads to an enhanced quality of life, an extended life span, and the possibility of eternal life; that is living eternally to complete a trinity of body, soul, and spirit, here on earth.

We Are Not Meant to Die is built on the perennial wisdom of the Western monotheistic spiritual tradition and focuses squarely on how each of us can actively engage in mental processes linked to a spiritual value system to prolong our lives. I also briefly recap some of the pertinent physiological and biological findings that corroborate the possibility of extended longevity flowing into the possibility of uninterrupted life — the aim of the Western spiritual tradition and the GEMS system of health. The origin of the name GEMS, the Gerald Epstein Medicine System, came from my father, Max Epstein. At my bar mitzvah, my father concluded his speech by alluding to his four sons, saying that we all together were GEMS — <u>G</u>erald, <u>E</u>zra, <u>M</u>yron, and <u>S</u>andy. Who knew what would grow from that seed?

The evolution of this model began over 40 years ago at my first meeting in Jerusalem with Mme. Colette Aboulker-Muscat, who became my teacher in this direction of healing. This book is the fruit of decades of my clinical practice, study, and research of the techniques and methods I have discovered or learned from Colette and other great spiritual masters of the West. When I first met Colette, I thought I was enrolling in a course of study to reconcile Eastern meditative practices with Western therapeutics; instead, Colette taught me how to live fully, presenting me with an almost entirely forgotten Western spiritual therapeutic path of healing. To this day, I continue to explore and revel in this Western spiritual path. Eventually I came upon the teachings of other Western wisdom keepers: Philo of Alexandria, Val-

Introduction

entin Tomberg, Dr. Robert Rondell Gibson, Frederick Weinreb, Prof. Henri Corbin, Dr. Paul Watzlawick, and Dr. Medard Boss.

Why this book now? Over 30 years ago, in the late 1980s, I spoke to my then-editor at Bantam Books, Leslie Meredith, about doing a book focusing on Western spirituality for Bantam's New Age imprint. My now classic book *Healing Visualizations* had just been published, and I wanted to explore the core of the Western tradition, namely, preserving life in an uninterrupted, sustained way. Leslie nixed the idea, believing it was ahead of its time, and maybe something to consider at the turn of the century. Well, it seems the time is ripe now. Our world is in a deep upheaval. Climate change seems more extreme with each passing year. Governments are going through upheavals, and the global economic system is in disarray, with gross inequalities ever widening. In these profoundly disturbed times, do we not need HOPE? That we can individually and collectively choose a Life Path? I propose that in these pages you will learn how to make contact with your life-preserving self and those universal life-giving forces available to all of us. Learning ways to contact our life-giving power gives us hope for now and for the future of ongoing life.

In choosing to take the excursion presented in this book, we may find there is a way out of the chains imposed on us by a world committed to the inevitability of death and where social strife and perpetual war are the order of the day. Life is not a closed circle of birth and death, an endless wheel of birth and death built only on entropy, the gradual decline into disorder, breakdown, and decay. Even natural scientists who subscribe to this worldview are seeking and proposing a natural scientific rationale for extreme longevity/immortality.

The possibilities for longevity and beyond such biological life is the central core of the Western spiritual tradition that appears to have been revealed directly and disseminated widely. That is, it has always been an open secret, though not really addressed seriously until now both in biology and spiritual life. The writings and speaking of spiritual traditions are always meant as concrete facts, never as metaphor. These are revealed truths, though in everyday life they are difficult for many of us to swallow. In spite of the ongoing resistance with which spiritual truths have been met in the man-made world, penetrating inroads have been made, especially in the last 40 years, beginning with the Vietnam War era, which opened the door to greater awareness of worldwide spiritual practices.

Now that substantial ground has been broken along these lines, death can be met head on. In the words from 1 Corinthians 15:26, "The last enemy to be destroyed is death" (NIV). I can easily imagine that almost everyone, spiritually oriented or not, can accept no "truth" other than that death is inevitable. Case seems closed. No! Case open! In this book I offer a rationale and evidence supporting this spiritual message.

In a sense, it's peculiar to explain this proposition. The western tradition describes overcoming death, and as such, there is nothing either to debate or contend. This is not an unusual sentiment: Every spiritual or esoteric way has its own principles, facts, and practices, which you either accept or dismiss as not worth stepping into.

Knowing the pitfalls of venturing into the turbulent waters of possible public scorn and ridicule, I nonetheless possess enough reason and faith to share this work — which may be a most precious gift of that hope alluded to above.

The aim of this book and my life's mission is to provide a spiritual health-care education that reverses what we have all been taught and subjected to in the usual channels of "health" education. In essence, GEMS brings spiritual life down to earth and shows how it is applied to our mundane daily problems and the travails that all impact our health and well-being. The sacred supplies ways for us to reverse — that is, to turn around — our usual habits of thoughts, behaviors, and feelings to

Introduction

free us from the grip of death. This approach takes us beyond the conventional medical system. The word *educate* comes from the language root that also gives rise to the word *doctor*. In these pages you will find the tools you need to become your own doctor/healer and to teach this healing way to others.

The book presents many practices; all are easy to learn and apply. You are invited to use and experiment with any that appeal to you. As you begin integrating the tools and steps, you may find life taking new turns not met before and recognize a new dimension of living called "spiritual."

GEMS is an organic, self-organizing internal system of health and wholeness. It brings *together* our PHYSICAL, EMOTIONAL, MENTAL, SOCIAL, AND MORAL/SPIRITUAL lived experience at each moment. It is actually a return to the ancient Western model recast in a new light that embraces the knowledge that an invisible spiritual realm surrounds our material world of existence. We are born of two natures: material and spiritual. These exist side by side. We grow up with both of these together. The spiritual part of ourselves is not taught in our general secular or parochial education, yet the spiritual world exists. It is analogous to the dark side of the moon, invisible and as yet unknown to us. The bright side of the moon can be likened to our material natures: that which can be perceived and explored. The dark, or spiritual, side can also be perceived and explored. The tools for this exploration are the meat and potatoes of this book. In doing so, though, our material nature is not neglected — it is addressed and works hand in hand with the spiritual one. The infinite spiritual reality informs our everyday material reality that is limited to and bound by time and space. For the past four centuries or so, Western science has been enthralled with the material world, searching out and dissecting its hidden mysteries. In the process, it has been forgotten that we are fundamentally interconnected in the matrix of life on this planet, to our fellow humans and to the invisible realities.

Before the rupture in Western thinking took place in the seventeenth century, our forefathers perceived the world with quite a different consciousness from ours. They did not experience a separation between their consciousness and the world around them, or between each other. The worldview of the ancient, medieval, and renaissance world was a unity, spirit and matter were entwined. After the "Enlightenment," we began to detach ourselves from the world and each other. We split our universe in two: into the physical (all that could be directly perceived by our five senses) and the nonphysical (that which is not directly apprehensible by our sense). Physical became synonymous with objective, and nonphysical with subjective. Physical also became equated with body and all things quantifiable, subjective with mind and unreality. Spiritual and invisible realms fell into the latter category.

Through personal experience and experimentation, I have discovered the truth of subjective reality, or more precisely, subjective realities. Imagination, mental imagery, dreams, reveries, hallucinations, spiritual visions – these are all subjective realities. They cannot be physically measured. They can't be quantified physically. The have qualities that can't be calculated. This book is designed to help you train your mind in a new way, to reeducate your bodymind as a whole so that you can live in a new, healthful way that is in harmony with your true nature and the world around you.

The word *science* means *to know*. And just as there is natural science (e.g., biology, physics, chemistry), there is a spiritual science. As a spiritual manual, this book provides a framework for expanding our knowledge of the existence of this invisible reality. At the same time, it sets out to deepen our ability to experience this spiritual dimension. It shows us how the invisible world exists everywhere around us and plays a direct role in shaping our lives, if we permit it. Through this connection, we can restore ourselves to health and lengthen our life

Introduction

span. In so doing, we simultaneously repair and restore our social, environmental community, attaining peace on earth and goodwill toward all. But this cannot be accomplished without the Holy. Holiness is synonymous with morality and spirituality.

GEMS introduces this new level of healing, which is absent in the framework of conventional therapeutic interventions — that of the holy or moral dimension as a significant key for living. Why is living a moral, spiritual life connected to health? The etymological or word origin of the word *holy* comes from the Germanic root *kailo*. This root is the parent, and all words derived from it are its children. They in turn are siblings to each other. The words arising from *kailo* are: whole, heal, health and *holy*.

As soon as I discovered this, I understood that there can be no model of health without considering our wholeness, which is tantamount to healing and must include the holy. Bearing all this in mind — and given my decades-long investigation and practice of spiritual life and its therapeutic applications — I knew I had within me the makings of GEMS: a genuine wholistic system of healthcare and healing that includes the holy/spiritual dimension. In contrast to the conventional medical model, a *science of disease* that affects human beings, GEMS introduces the *art and science of becoming a whole human being*.

Love and law are the pillars of holiness upon which GEMS is built. Love is the divine power sent to us that is "strong as death," as King Solomon stated 3,000 years ago (Song of Songs 8:6, JPS). Alone, love binds small groups together. Law — and by law I mean the cosmic laws of the Ten Commandments — or calls to action allow us to live harmoniously in larger communities, nationally and globally. I call these laws our *Spiritual Constitution*. Love, the ten cosmic laws, and other practices described later are all practices of healing. We are meant to love both Invisible Reality and our neighbors here on earth, not to disparage and dismiss the former, nor to subjugate and extort the latter through violence and hate. This is the new evolutionary course for us — to become conscious and develop conscience. Love and cosmic law — the ten sacred precepts — put an end to war, hatred, violence, and enslavement, or the major ingredients for dying. Perhaps the need for the ten sacred precepts will dissolve as we jointly mature into loving beings. For now, understanding how we can concretely apply these precepts in meaningful and creative ways in our personal life is part of the practices and a key to our health.

In this new way, each of us can find our way back to our inner Eden, the realm of truth, inner peace, harmony, wholeness, and bliss. This shift in consciousness brings about a shift in our very physiology to preserve and extend life. When we bring the body into order, we simultaneously bring order to the soul (the infused essence of spirit we are born with housed within the body) — a reunion of both our natures, visible and invisible. I have witnessed it operate in my own life as well as in the lives of many patients, seekers, and students I have worked with over the years. Through your own personal experimentation with these practices, you too become a seeker of knowledge, engaged in discovering truth for yourself.

This thesis is derived from the wisdom of the spiritual traditions of monotheism. It emphasizes our purpose in living to become free through the exercise of our free will and choice while developing a loving relationship with the Divine above and our neighbors here below.

The fact of the matter is that we have been asked to *choose* the Life or Death Path ever since we were old enough to comprehend the exis-

Introduction

tence of such a choice. The asking is framed in Deuteronomy 30:15,19 where the Lord God sets before us life and death, good and evil, blessings and curses, and asks us to choose, and not so subtly, recommends we choose life so we and our descendants may live.

These passages set me on the course of my deep exploration of eternal life, which has become my life's mission.

The book is divided into four sections:
(1) Appetizer: Introducing the spiritual platform upon which the book is built.
(2) Soup: Defining the world of everyday life that leads to the inevitability of death, what I term the Death Plan.
(3) Entrée: The main meal, providing the tools and steps to take to reverse the inevitability of death, what I term the Life Plan.
(4) Dessert: A trove of imagery exercises to create wholeness and healing that lead to the possibilities of resurrection and everlasting life, and my vision of things to come.

In accounting for the social, moral, and spiritual aspects of health, I recollect Shakespeare's statement that "all the world's a stage and we are merely the players." Out of this comment I envisioned GEMS functioning as a Theater of Life. Now the stage is set to give you your ticket to enter this theater, to become the actor on stage, and much more as we begin the journey together.

Instructions for Practicing Mental Imagery

One important tool for healing and change is mental imagery. Short imagery exercises are scattered throughout the book, and Chapter XIV is devoted exclusively to imagery for discovering eternal life.

To take up this practice, only three things are required: (1) Sit up straight in a chair, preferably one with arms. Do not cross your feet, legs, hands, or arms. Place your feet flat on the floor, with your arms resting on the arms of the chair (if the chair has no arms, place your hands palms down on your thighs). (2) Close your eyes to blot out external distractions. This helps to turn your senses inward to discover this new subjective reality presenting itself to you in the language of image. (3) Breathe out long, slow exhalations and then brief or normal inhalations.

Most imagery exercises begin with the words "Close your eyes and breathe out and in three times slowly." This is a shorthand for the instruction to breathe out full respiratory cycles of long, slow exhalations through the mouth and short or brief inhalations through the nose for three rounds of "out and in" breathing. By focusing on an exhalation first, we are able to quickly reach a relaxed state to ready ourselves for the imagery exercise.

When doing imagery, you want to engage *all* your senses, not just your visual capacity, thus many exercises ask you to see, (physically) sense, and (emotionally) feel the imagery. Sometimes the instructions ask you to "experience" the imag-

Introduction

ery. This is a shortening of the statement "become one with the experience of..." or "experience together."

Generally, imagery exercises are practiced three times a day: in the morning (on rising), in the evening (at sundown), and before bed. Most imagery exercises take only a few seconds to do (short-handed in the book as "some seconds"). While it is true that people's internal rhythms differ, most imagery in this book is not intended to take longer than 30 seconds to a minute. The longer you dwell in the image, the more the logical mind seeps in cutting the imagery experience. To see a video on how to sit and breathe when you practice imagery go to the American Institute of Mental Imagery's website: https://aimi.us/resources/.

Finally, I've noted the sources of the imagery exercises in parenthesis after the title if I did not create them.

We Are Not *Meant* to Die

SECTION I

Gerald Epstein's Medicine System (GEMS)

Ingredients for Everlasting Life

We Are Not *Meant* to Die

"In the New Wave of Consciousness descending on us,
steps such as those described in these pages
add a meaningful dimension of liberation,
putting us in charge of where life takes us."

CHAPTER I

Buddha Was Correct, and What We Can Do About It

IN BEGINNING A BOOK ABOUT LIFE, DEATH, LONGEVITY, and eternal life through a Western spiritual inquiry, I want to start off with the Buddha. He said something whose truth echoes universally through all spiritual traditions: basically that "Suffering in life is inevitable, the source of which is *attachment*." The ultimate suffering culminates in death.

What you are about to read reveals some existing possibilities for the continuation of life and *for ending death*, as many valiant individuals over the millennia have championed — and some have demonstrated. But more significant for us to explore and experiment with as open-minded readers is our singular attachment to death and our unquestioned belief that death is inevitable.

Almost everyone believes that death is inevitable. The thrust of this book is to consider whether there may be a viable contrary belief that is acceptable. I introduce my thesis by framing four fundamental

questions to be answered and expanded.
1. Since suffering is attachment, can we *reverse* our propensity for making attachments, thereby reversing suffering and with it reverse our attachment to death?
2. Does the most powerful statement in the Bible — "I set before you this day life and death. Choose life so you and your descendants may live" (Deut. 30:19) — provide an *option* to not choose death and our attachment to the Death Path, but to choose an attachment to the Life Path?
3. Does the second most powerful statement in the Bible — "Love is strong as death" (Song of Songs 8:6) — provide an antidote to counteract death?
4. Can we use everyday life experiences as a means to the freedom we are yearning for?

In truth, we all have to find out these answers for ourselves through experimentation to discover what is true. These four questions provide a starting point and a means for discovering and coming up with your own answers freely found.

To begin with, releasing our attachments is pivotal. The hardest detachment is that connected to family life. Attachments to loved ones (even to hated ones) make the idea of separating from them most painful. We are conditioned to attach. That is the way of the world. In families, there are warmhearted attachments and coldhearted ones. The former are loving and caring, the latter quite the opposite. However, regardless of how open or closed the heart, feelings for family run deep.

The monotheistic Western spiritual tradition seeks to master our conflicted social experience and form an alliance with Invisible Reality. This path chooses to plunge into the stream of social existence at every moment. We face the world of attachment and by direct action toward it, rather than withdrawal from it, we accept it but do not get caught up in its swirling sea of temptations and intimidations, threats and promises, that draw us down into the "agitated" sea of the "electrical field of death."[2] Facing the source of suffering and acting to distance ourselves from it is an enriching task well worth taking on. We aim to shift the urge for power in the service of control to another sort of power, that in the service of freedom: We freely let others be free. We do "unto" others as we would do to ourselves and would want others to likewise reciprocate.

Stepping away from the family orbit, with its misdirected errors, habits, and beliefs, needs to be done for the sake of attuning to spiritual awareness. The art of detachment may take us into some form of exile for a time, which might include friends and colleagues, while we are breaking from the error-filled world surrounding us. Then, when we return to the family in a new way, we can provide a new model for the family to follow, sharing and helping everyone to come into order.

However, the outer "exile" is mirrored by an *inner* one in which we undertake the spiritual practices for health described in these pages. They present a clear picture of what to do to depart from the absurdity and bondage of the man-made world of critical judgments, standards, and ideals, including cherished ideals of "self-improvement." We exit from the grip of the natural laws of the struggle for existence to discover a new set of principles — *the laws of collaboration:* love, sharing, caring, giving — a much-needed transfusion of health-giving new blood to the world.

Take a look at the Bible. All the great (male) masters went into some form of exile to escape the enslaving conditioning that prevails in the man-made world. Moses is a prime example — he goes into

---

[2] Anonymous, *Meditations on the Tarot: A Journey into Christian Hermeticism* (Amity, NY: Amity House, 1985), p. 310.

exile then returns to the people he is to lead. We are here to master the task set before us. We have been given the gift of mental strength to accomplish the challenge. We have the gifts of will, purpose, and reason to leap over the hurdle. We have the gift of imagination to find new directions and possibilities. We have been given the gift of life to pursue the purpose for which we have been put here.

Here is another example of how the laws of detachment work. A young couple came to visit my teacher, Colette. She complained to Colette of a longstanding disturbance involving her husband, who would come home in the evening, take his coat off, and throw it on the living room floor. He did the same with his jacket, shirt, tie, and shoes, then he would plop himself down in a chair and begin to read. She felt angry and aggravated. She was never able to "get him to change this habit and stop making a mess in the living room." Colette responded: "What does this have to do with you?" Suddenly, a light went off for this young lady (much like the light bulb of inspiration you see in comic books). She had a revelation. She realized at that instant that she was not a slave; she did not need to have her mood determined by what someone else said, did, thought, or felt. This applies to all of us. Attachment to someone else in the manner just mentioned is an act of enslavement — but we are born free, not meant to be slaves. Recall what Buddha said about life being attachment/suffering. Attachment and enslavement, this time–space continuum in which we live, equal each other. She recognized at that moment that she was not a slave, she was free. From that moment on, she changed her attitude and feelings toward his behavior into one of acceptance. They came back to their house in California, and she carried over what she had realized in Jerusalem. She detached. Within a week, he stopped his behavior without her saying a word. She simply created a new space, a space of freedom where he had the opportunity to be free, to create something new in his habit.

Buddha Was Correct, and What We Can Do about It

Here is an example from my practice: Judy, a student, calls and says she has the feeling of a nodule at the back of her throat that has been there for almost a month and doesn't seem to be getting better. When I inquired as to what feelings may be accompanying this physical experience, she mentioned she had been feeling sad. I asked her then what or who she was feeling *down in the mouth* about, a vernacular statement representing the reflection, also called analogy, between the somatic sensation, the feeling state, and the social disturbance, expressing colloquially how the body speaks to us in its own language. Everything is communicating as language and grammar. The body speaks a language in its somatic way. Reading the reflections and relationships between things is called "thinking by analogy." Learning this new way of spiritual thinking, to be described later, will come with practice.

I asked her when the distress began; she responded by saying that her middle adult daughter wanted to come and visit her, but not if the younger sister was to be there at the same time. She had been aware these two "children" had incurred a rift, severing their relationship. She was sad about the situation, wanted to say something to them, held back, *swallowed* it, and it became stuck in her throat, the reflection of the social disturbance and her response somatically — of the conflict.

I reminded her of Buddha's statement: Human suffering is inevitable; the source of this suffering is attachment. She immediately pinpointed the attachment — an ideal she was holding on to concerning how families are *supposed* to be united, loving, and friendly toward each other. There you go. **We hold attachments to human-devised ideals, standards, and norms for ourselves and others to which we all aspire.** Does this make sense? Standards are artificial measurements applied to physical objects such as nuts, bolts, tire treads, drill bits, and so on. This mechanical approach has been applied to human functioning. However, human beings aren't mere physical objects. The goal of standards for machines is to homogenize them so those standards can apply to all machines of a certain type for use throughout the world. So, too, standards for humans are applied through various forms of early miseducation and conditioning to homogenize us to the point where we end up treating one another as machines. If we routinely accept and follow the standards, if we attach ourselves to standards, we are human robots, with the result that we become slaves to those masters who want to control us. Through detachment we help ourselves to become human and put ourselves on the path of life. As for Judy, the nodule disappeared through our covering this ground in our short session together.

***

In the New Wave of Consciousness descending on us, steps such as those described in these pages add a meaningful dimension of liberation, putting us in charge of where life takes us.

The original spirituality of the West was a nomadic one. A full-scale delivery of this spiritual path is to be found in the impressive book *Nomadic Spirituality* by Morris Berman. In line with this understanding is the recognition that the meaning of the word *Hebrew* means passing through, coming from somewhere else. A former teacher of my ex-wife was a renowned Kabbalist in Jerusalem named Rabbi Zvi Yehuda Kook. It turned out one day that the Rabbi received a wealthy visitor from abroad. That Rabbi Kook's abode was simple would be an overstatement: His digs consisted of an entrance foyer, small bathroom, small kitchen, small bedroom, and his receiving space, a smallish living room with a threadbare couch, wooden table and chairs, linoleum on the floor, an overhead light, and a couple of walls lined with books. Like my teacher Colette, money in any form was not permitted to be given, taken, or exchanged.

The wealthy man was ushered in, feeling awed to meet this Rabbi of such renown. Once seated, and getting his bearings, the man looked around. After surveying the scene, he said to Rabbi Kook, "Where is your furniture?" Rabbi Kook shot back, "Where's yours?" The man was momentarily shocked, then responded, after pulling himself together, "I have none, I'm just a tourist here." Rabbi Kook responded, "So am I."

A more familiar example of the nomad in Western spirituality is to be found in the tarot in the person of the Fool, depicted as a kind of hobo walking on the road, carrying a stick with all his possessions in a bag tied up over his shoulder. His clothes are simple, and a dog is nipping at his pant leg, creating a tear in the fabric.

What has all this to do with taking charge of our life, liberation, and self-healing? The Fool is an archetype — archetype itself meaning a way of living our time in the world, who embodies all of the above elements coherently brought together as one piece. Obviously, the Fool is independent, free of the constraints of the mass-conscious value system rooted in material possession, acquisition, ownership, and eventually greed. As a liberated being he travels unencumbered, having to find and develop his own means to health and wholeness as an ongoing, continuous practice. He is not bothered by the dog of desire and conventional social mores trying to injure and control him. He lives by the ancient adage stated in Proverbs: "What is wisdom in God's eyes is folly in men's eyes; what is wisdom in men's eyes is folly in God's."

As troubadours of life taking the freedom road, dislodging ourselves from attachments to the "I'm missing something, gotta have it" world, we feel obliged to take it upon ourselves to give ourselves placebos as a healing gift, while ridding ourselves of nocebos at the same time.

What are placebo and nocebo? Placebo means to please. Nocebo means to do harm. To please is to give ourselves something bringing the possibility for healing and an experience of health, wholeness, and, as we shall see, the potential for holiness.

Bonnie, a young woman, was grieving over the loss of her dog, whom she regarded as a precious friend. She was undecided about getting another pet. When she spoke of her beloved pet, her eyes welled up with tears. I asked her what was the opposite of the sadness she said she was feeling. "Happiness," she responded. "What is the image of happiness?" I asked her. She discovered a small, spunky yellow-haired dog scampering around. She broke into a smile and felt the sadness lifting.

What do we have here? A physical response of a smile, relief of sad feelings, and the image of a spunky yellow dog of happiness, all bolstering the belief that sadness can be overcome by the new belief condensed as one word, *happiness*. That, folks, is a placebo. She gave herself a placebo. The nocebo of chronic sadness is *reflected* physiologically in lowered immune function. Chronic sadness is also a violation of the sixth sacred law against murder, as it is on a continuum of self-murder that includes moroseness, somberness, pouting on the one end and depression and suicide on the other. She reversed the habit via a mental act, and sadness was replaced by optimism and a feeling of happiness. Really, there is no healing without the inclusion of placebos. It is a function of choosing life, an intimate part of our endless participation in the stream of life. The beauty of the process is her self-discovery — now she has at hand her own ability to change the course of life direction by knowingly participating directly in that change. As the healer, I provided the catalyst for that process without crossing any boundary to intrude on her healing.

Some may come out with a nocebo like "It seems too simple for it to be real and true." Please don't let us hornswoggle ourselves by claiming the techniques and methods are "too simple." Spiritual life and its practices are made to be simple; the "I gotta have it" world is one of endless complications. The aim of spiritual life is to move toward voluntary simplicity. The simpler the life, the less strain put on our physiology with its concomitant conservation of energy.

What can be a simpler technique than closing your eyes and imaging? Or meditating cross-legged, counting your breaths while gazing at the tip of your nose? Does the system of life force that we are respond immediately to the instructions given by imaginal reality? The answer is yes, and the wealth of imagery research over the past 50 years attests to this phenomenon.

It seems that becoming the Fool is a key to our everlasting being. Becoming a "wise guy," a "made" man in the "I gotta have it" world is certainly a ticket to early extinction. These latter fools, hoodwinked by attachment, are ripe for an education the spiritual life gives.

As the song goes, "Only fools fall in love." Changing lust to love, we become a Fool in love with our Source and all who are fellow lovers. We become the ones we have been waiting for, as the ancient Hopi saying goes. Every placebo we give ourselves is an act of self-love, and Love overturns death, as King Solomon noted in Song of Songs 8.6. The nocebo is our necessary painful reminder to reverse course and to give ourselves a dose of love.

On the next page is an imagery exercise to help us detach. For instructions on how to practice imaging, see Page 24.

IMAGERY EXERCISE

ROOM OF DETACHMENT: FOR BECOMING FREE
(adapted from Francis Clifton)

Do every morning for one week, each time for "some seconds."

Sit up straight in a chair with uncrossed arms and legs. Close your eyes. Breathe out and in three times, counting backwards from 3 to 1, each out breath being a new number. At 1, imagine yourself in your room of attachments. Look around. Experience your feelings. At your right there is a door. Breathe out one time and go through that door to the next room. Look around to see who and what attachments are there. Experience the feelings. Breathe out one time. See a door to your right. Go through it and look around, seeing what attachments remain. Continue the exercise, going through each door and successive room, one by one, until you come to your room of detachment. What do you see, feel, and physically sense there? Keep what you discover and now know for yourself. Breathe out and open your eyes.

To summarize: There is a Life Path and a Death Path, as is clearly stated in the life–death option of Deuteronomy. This option allows us a redemptive chance to reverse the error of choosing from the tree of death, as occurred in the Garden of Eden, a foundational event that is the start of our journey.

Before expanding and expounding upon these most significant points on which our life depends, let me first describe some of my journey that has led to the sober revelations that have come to me.

CHAPTER II

My Spiritual Journey

LET ME TELL YOU A LITTLE ABOUT MYSELF and how I came to the understandings in this book.

It's 1942. At age six, I wandered into a small room on the third floor of my 14-room house in Brooklyn, New York. There I discovered two wall hangings of Egyptian hieroglyphs! I was enthralled by them, but never asked what they were doing in a conservative Jewish household until I asked Mom shortly before her death in 1990. She told me they were a gift from a family friend who visited Egypt in 1938 on a professional mission and brought them back.

It was about that time that I began reading every fairy tale I could get my hands on. Mom bought me many fairy-tale books over a four-year period, till I was 11. She understood my penchant and passion for them. I knew, even then, predating Harry Potter, the value and reality of magic. I found out later on, when I started my journey into the realm of imagination and imagery therapeutics, that fairy tales were the way of communicating sacred spiritual knowledge and wisdom in a way that could go undetected by the authorities in Europe, who could inflict serious punishment on those publishing "heretical" works espousing spiritual doctrine.

Since I've come to understand that *nothing* happens by chance, I realized in retrospect that I was being directed to a life dedicated to the world of imagination and all its derivative and allied functions.

It is 1953. I am in my first year of college at Dickinson College in Carlisle, Pennsylvania, 20 miles west of Harrisburg, the state capital. I wasn't altogether sure then where I was heading as a life direction. I noticed that the psychology department was offering students the opportunity to take an aptitude test. I took it, and it showed that the top career to consider for myself was to be an undertaker! There it was — my first exposure to looking at death. In retrospect, it made sense.

My academic life took over in college and on into med school. I was primarily focused on and absorbed by the workings of the mind, not yet understanding the direct relationship between it and hieroglyphs, fairy tales, imagery. I minored in psychology in college and had a direction-changing experience there. A fraternity brother named Gary Spero spoke to me of his being in psychoanalysis at age 14. At that time, analysis was becoming all the rage, enjoying a postwar boom of interest in the 1950s. He suggested I read a book called *Man Against Himself* by Karl Menninger. That did it. I decided immediately to become a psychoanalyst and a mind explorer.

Ken Pelletier wrote a book years ago called *Mind as Healer, Mind as Slayer*. That title is absolutely true. Mind is the source of all our gains and losses. It is at the top of the pyramid. Mind is consciousness. My teacher referred to God as "the Absolute One Mind (AOM)." Her definition of mind: "The channel of communication between invisible and visible realities." Mind is registered in us as mental experience.

It was 1962. Alan Konigsberg (Woody Allen) and I were sitting on a park bench somewhere near the Jefferson Hotel in Washington, D.C., where we were staying. I had come down from New York to visit my friend, who was performing as a stand-up comic at a D.C. club. I always appreciated his humor, actually finding him funnier in personal life than on stage or, later, in movies. Another and lesser known side of his life is his psychic ability. Throughout our teenage years, we did experiments together in hypnosis, ESP, and mental magic. As a late teenager, Woody was going to volunteer as a subject for the American Psychical Research Society but thought better of it.

Our conversation was about the direction of our lives (the next night he went to visit a female astrologer at another hotel who told him of his impending ascent to movie fame). Woody told me that my life direction would be to focus on and investigate death. At the time, I was moving from medical internship into first-year psychiatric residency at Kings County Hospital in Brooklyn, New York. Given where I was in my career path and because I had a passion for and dedication to the function of mind and mental life, I found his comment interesting, if not mildly shocking. Some years later, an astrologer I befriended named Jerome Rainville told me that my zodiac sign was Scorpio — the sign concerned with death and the underworld.

For the next ten years, I worked toward fulfilling my aspiration to become a psychoanalyst, and I graduated from the New York Psychoanalytic Institute in 1972. During this time, I was drafted into the army for two years, ending up as a major, the highest-ranking medical officer in the military who was in non-career status.

In the spring of 1974, I was blessed by an illuminative experience in which I became a being of light, experiencing my own "lightness of being." I was in Jerusalem as a visiting professor teaching psychiatry and law at Hadassah Hospital. The subject was of real interest to me and had led to cofounding the *Journal of Psychiatry & Law* in 1973 with my friend and attorney Howard Nashel. I was editor-in-chief

We Are Not *Meant* to Die!

until 1986. While in Jerusalem with my ex-wife Perle Besserman (now a Zen teacher), we discovered a Zen center run by a Japanese *roshi* or headmaster. We were both interested in Eastern thought and practice, so we continued meditating at the center, where we met a young man named Serge. He told me that he had been in a three-year psychoanalysis without much success, but that here in Jerusalem he had met a therapist with whom he succeeded in clearing up longstanding depression in just four meetings through a process I had never heard of called *mental imagery*. Being a practicing psychoanalyst, I scoffed at first that he could make such rapid change. Eventually he introduced me to his "therapist," Mme. Colette Aboulker-Muscat. That encounter became the most significant turning point of my life. I was then 38 years old.

In my initial encounter with Colette, I shared, in a sudden flash of insight, that Freud presented the rule of free association — the cornerstone in conducting a psychoanalysis — as an image. In a paper he wrote in 1912 called "On Beginning the Analysis," he told young analysts giving the free association "rule" to tell patients to *imagine* they were traveling on a train and to report to the analyst what they saw passing by in the countryside. I was shocked to see right then he gave the "rule" of free association as an image. Colette then looked at me and asked, "In what direction does a train go?" I was stunned. Direction of trains? What does that have to do with anything? Anyway, I had to answer. My mind started racing. All the trains I knew went in a horizontal direction, except the trains in Switzerland and Machu Picchu that went vertically. I was sweating. What to do? Anxiety mounting, with sweating hands I was clutching the arms of the chair, tilted back on two legs. Finally, the tension was too great. I needed a release. I ventured to say, tentatively, "Most often, not infrequently, trains generally go like this." I thrusted my arm straight forward in front of me (horizontally). Whew, what a relief. Again, Colette looked squarely at me, didn't say anything, then lifted her right arm straight up (vertically) and said, "And if we change the axis?" With that I became illuminated. I became light, a being of light. Jerry disappeared. There was only light! When I came back to my senses, as it were, my initial thoughts were: "I'm no longer a psychiatrist, psychoanalyst, physician. There's a truth here I must follow no matter the cost." Colette saw my face and said, "You find this interesting?!" I said, "You bet." She asked if I wanted to learn more. I said, "Of course." She told me to come back the next morning at 8 a.m. to begin.

And begin I did, becoming an apprentice to this Algerian Jewish master teacher for seven years. Going back and forth to Jerusalem 13 times in those seven years for varying periods of time ranging from three weeks to three months. This apprenticeship birthed over 40 years of unfolding of education and revelation, and a practice centered on mental imagery, birthing books, research, and the American Institute for Mental Imagery (AIMI), a training center for health-care professionals and an adult educational center for the public.

It's 1997. A gentleman named F.M. 2030, suffering from prostate cancer, came to see me. When I asked him how he came by such a moniker, he said he went through an official name change and this was his legal name. Surprised as you are by this name, wait till you hear his occupation: He was a futurist. Like Alvin Toffler and Faith Popcorn, he traveled the globe in search of cutting-edge research taking place in all fields of study. By cataloging these trends, these futurists were able to predict rather successfully what would be forthcoming culturally. F.M. 2030 told me he had written a successful book in the 1960s indicating what we could expect in the 1990s and was now on the trail of the coming millennium. He said that if we could come into the year 2010 in good health, we automatically would be given another 20 years of life. Then in 2030 (his name), we would be able to select the number of years we would want to live — indefinite numbers if we wished — and this was the reason for his name selection.

We Are Not *Meant* to Die!

It's 1999. I received a newsletter called *Demographics*. How it got to me I shall never know. I had no subscription to it, nor had I ever heard of it. God works in mysterious ways. In this newsletter there was an article by a recent former head of the U.S. Census Bureau in which she stated that if we reached age 65 by the year 2000 in good health, we would be given another 20 years of life automatically! Shades of F.M. 2030.

Well, here we are now, more conscious than ever of the possibility of longevity. Natural health care is gaining ever-increasing acceptance; people are more motivated to take care of their bodies. Life expectancy is extended; we are living longer. There are studies extant of many of us living normally to over 100 years of age. Investigator Dan Beuttner described the "Blue Zones," areas of the world where many, many people are over 100 years of age. There are five zones: one in the East (Okinawa) and four in the West (Icaria, Greece; Sardinia; Nicoya, Costa Rica; Loma Linda, California). Beuttner discovered five elements common to all these societies. These are: 1) strong religious beliefs; 2) geniality; 3) decisive action; 4) open-mindedness; and 5) no concern about money. In my research into the subject, I found three more to add to my social/spiritual factors: 6) having some meaningful relationship (one or more); 7) ability to bear loss; and 8) the ability to laugh.

And now, more than 60 years after my occupational test, here is a work dedicated to the exploration of death and life. By studying death, I've come upon a deeper understanding of life. After all, becoming a medical doctor puts one squarely in front of life and death in an exquisitely intense way. Now, instead of becoming an undertaker, I have embarked on undertaking a deep examination of life and how to preserve it. Spiritual values and the purposes of living are at the core.

For me, the existential experience of life that we are all addressing, knowingly or unknowingly, is facing life and death. We ask ourselves the famous statement posed by Shakespeare through the character of

Hamlet: "To be or not to be, that is the question" in other terms. One of the ways we ask is What is the purpose of living? It is a fundamental spiritual inquiry. In my studies of spiritual life, I've come to recognize a number of seminal purposes along these lines. The ones framed below are essential starting points that actually propel those at the crossroad of their lives — and everyone reaches at least one such crossroad in life — who are dissatisfied with what their current life is offering them; they are searching along with those already committed to taking this journey:

PURPOSE OF LIVING

1) Discover who I am; where I am; what's going on here in this game of life.
2) Free our self from the enslavements that we have allowed to dominate our lives from without and within by detaching from unrestrained desires to acquire material gain.
3) Become our own authority, a law unto our self.
4) Become a mature human being: considerate, harmless, contributory, gratuitous, loving, truthful, divinely inspired, and humane.
5) Become a servant of God.
6) Climb the ladder of self-mastery by reuniting our two inborn natures: body and soul.
7) Make union with the One.

These purposes naturally meld into one another. As we appropriate one, the others come along seamlessly.

My spiritual way distinguishes itself from the pursuit of material life by its value system and stated purpose(s) of and for living. The values that seekers of spirit hold most dear are a firm commitment to attachment to Invisible Reality as a partner through life. The relationship to material life is weighed proportionately against the high values placed on invisible experience and awareness of invisible partners surrounding self. Generally speaking, the thrust is toward living simply, voluntarily: having food on the table, a roof overhead, clothes on our back, some means of transportation at hand. Material life becomes subsumed under the umbrella of spiritual awareness, attention, and activism.

CHAPTER III

The Two Trees of Eden: Entropy and Ectropy

"He will swallow up death forever; And the Lord God will wipe away tears from off all faces."
—Isaiah 25:8.

LIFE IS A CONSTANT FLOW OF MOVEMENT, a source of ceaseless creation, never-ending, everlasting. It is early conditioning and miseducation that prod us not to adapt to this ever-changingness of life. Instead, we are urged to cling, to hold onto the familiar, *attach* to what has been, and consequently we do not adapt to the flow of change. We get stuck in time, lose our physical, emotional, and mental flexibility, and become rigid. This rigidity is a precursor to death, the ceasing of movement altogether, both biologically and physiologically, according to medical science.

But is this how to define death? Is it merely what generally passes for the definition in conventional medical science as the cessation of physical life? It can't be the case, because medical and other natural sciences do not understand fully what life is. They define life not only as a random, chance event happening here on Earth, but also simply as a biological event having a beginning in the womb at some point in time and proceeding until a final breath is taken and/or the heartbeat stops at another point in time. However, spiritually speaking there is no such thing as a finality called death. Life is an ongoing function of force and energy given us by God, who has no relationship to linear time and is not bounded by its constraints or merely a physical component of consciousness.

Yes, some biologists do believe the human life span can be extended greatly. Longevity reflects a possible long-lasting stream of existence for our biological organism here in the linear time–three-dimensional space continuum defined as physical existence. Given this understanding, it is correct and appropriate to speak about longevity biologically. Most natural scientists do not conceive of an endless biological life span, although the ostensible aim of natural science and conventional medicine is to extend life, perhaps even in theory to the point of overcoming death.

What spiritual scientists have always understood, certainly from the Western perspective, and actually echoed in the Indian epic the *Bhagavad Gita*, is that our consciousness is endlessly ongoing, irrespective of biology. This is particularly so given that consciousness, known as soul, is an individually infused essence of Spirit instilled, installed, and housed in the physical body as a life force called *bios*. This infused essence nourishes the body and receives nourishment in return until such time as the body can no longer furnish a suitable habitat. When that moment arrives, the individual is considered to be physically dead. *Bios* is released when the physical body can no longer carry out this biological life function.

The focus of spiritual science is not on biological existence, which it doesn't dispute. It is not that the biological being is unimportant, but the focus is on the uninterrupted flow of life in us, *both* soul and matter. It is necessary for spiritual science to evaluate what gives life to life, not only in the visible world of matter, but also in the invisible world not subject to natural science investigation. These life-giving forces — for example, morality, faith, love — are not subject to reduction to quantitative counts or numbers. As humans, we keep tending to the precious gift of life in all its dimensions in this habitat ceded to us by the will of the Eternal One. We are expected to maintain our life force, to realize that truly *the opposite of life is life*, and to refuse to acquiesce to the lure of death. We are not to mistake quantity — the physical body — for the be-all and end-all of life. Rather, the body is a receptacle housing the most precious force in the universe bestowed on us, wherein resides the faith, hope and love of the Divine.

Yes, the house is precious too. We need to continue making the house habitable for its tenant — the soul force — to continue residing there. The means are at hand for doing so. Modern medicine and other nonmedical health-care options — in particular, nutrition, exercise, environmental awareness — are contributing to longevity. However, these alone are not enough. To ensure our everlasting flow of life, we add the ingredient of God/Spirit — transmitted through mind, filtered through heart, conveyed to brain, sent from there everywhere via the stream of life force reflected materially as blood — to replenish the physical system. Through care of the body and soul, we reverse the *entropy* of physical death to the *ectropy* of never-ending life.

Our Western tradition frames never-ending life as the presence of the Tree of Life located in the Edenic Garden. But there is another tree, the Tree of Death, that of the knowledge of good and evil. God cautioned Adam to stay away from the fruit of that tree "lest you die." God seems to mean don't elevate the Tree of Death to the level of the Tree of Life. It's beneath where you are in your quest for life eternal.

The Tree of Life reveals our relationship to Divinity, the relationship between invisible essence and visible existence. This relationship holds and is the key to longevity and immortality — to both linear time-bound quantity and to everlasting life. The exploration and experience of this relationship, freed from linear time, and its partner, the grip of death, is called spirituality.

The Tree of Death reveals our relationship to time–space reality, what is termed the world of duality. Death is a function of linear time, finite end points, and three-dimensional space, which has boundaries and limits defining it. An inherent property of death is finiteness — a finality that carries with it the properties of decay and decomposition. Breakdown is an irrevocable property of time–space to which we are subject by virtue of living in this particular existence. We are born into this dual world of opposites, and with it what in material science is called entropy, leading to the ultimate fate we all meet…death.

Entropy is a standing feature of all physical objects, meaning that any object, defined as something having boundaries and limits, is subject to decay, breakdown, and decomposition. All dissipative systems are closed systems, as no new energy can enter them to give them greater life. In fact, entropy applies to *all* systems in our material time–space world. We can see this in the economic, medical, and educational areas, for example. Most of these institutions are in flux, going through an entropic phase. It remains to be seen what new forms will emerge out of these ashes.

Human beings presumably are not exempt from the law of entropy either, since the "logical" conception of human existence is that eventually all of us *have* to die. It's "impossible" for it to be otherwise, since everyone dies! This seemingly simple assertion drones on incessantly, even though the direction of natural scientific endeavor is to prolong life as much as possible.

The spiritual truth is that life is an open system, an evolutionary spiral built on the reverse of entropy, which is called ectropy. Ectropy exists as an open system of self-organization. The prefix *ect* means a radiating outward, a spiral opening where we are able to receive this universal life energy. Ectropy is the "self-organizing" principle of the

The Two Trees of Eden: Entropy and Ectropy

world germane to all sciences, spiritual or not. By definition, a creative open system has no end point, having an unlimited fount of energy at its disposal termed *zoe* in the Western lexicon.

It came to me first through the work of Dr. Henri Atlan, professor of biophysics at Paris Medical School, then at Hadassah Medical School in Jerusalem. This was followed by the work of Ilya Prigogine, a Belgian biophysicist who won the Nobel Prize in chemistry for self-organizing systems detailed in a book called *The Self-Organizing Universe* by Eric Jantsch. Their works describe a rhythmical pulsation of self-organization in the universe applicable to many systems here on Earth, be they biological, political, medical, cognitive, in the natural world, and so forth.

Dr. Atlan, in his groundbreaking paper "On the Creativity and Reversibility of Time,"[3] describes the flip side of entropy — something above and beyond time that stops and reverses time. This phenomenon is above and beyond linear time and not even connected to time as we understand it, invoking systems of greater organization and complexity that are not subject to the natural function of entropy.

The premier biological analogy of this potential for self-organization is reproduction — how we come into life. Dr. Atlan cited human pregnancy, the woman being the bearer of self-organization expressed by birth of a child. How does this work?

Recalling the One who is without end, having no entropic function operational in Eden, creates life here. How? By creating two — the ovum and sperm cells. These two marry to create one cell that plants itself in the wall of the uterus, where it multiplies into two — it is not divided or split into two, as biology would have us believe — and continues to multiply exponentially until it becomes 60 trillion unified into one human being from embryo to fetus to recognizable birthed

---
[3] Henri Atlan. "On the Creativity and Reversibility of Time." *Shefa Quarterly: A Journal of Jewish Thought and Study* I, No. 2 (Autumn 1977): 40–54.

human. This is an exquisite example of ectropic self-organization that actually precedes birth into the world where entropy then begins and disorganization becomes a potential. Dr. Atlan called gestation an instance of the reversibility and creativity of time rolled up into one package.

This means *we are born with the possibility for entropy and ectropy,* the option to choose life or death! Hence the extraordinary statement in Deuteronomy 30 to either *choose* life or death. That means we can choose to become at one with that open system of life force denoted by the symbol of the spiral, the opening of the closed circle of death. *We can become an open system!* This is what makes us unique. As open systems have no end point, so do we have the possibility of no end. *We don't have to die!* The endless life-giving energy of the universe is then able to incessantly pour its influx into us, creating constant renewal and regeneration of our physical organization.

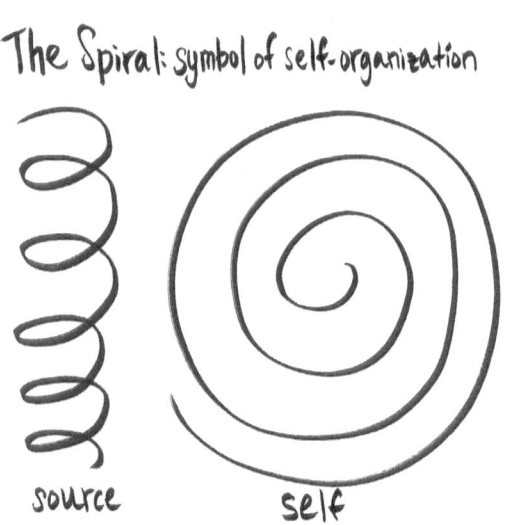

The monotheistic spiritual understanding of this phenomenon is revealed in God, who stands above the cycles of linear time and nature. Thus while God sets in motion the coming and going of the seasons, the cycles of human development from birth to death, God has transcended above these time-bound occurrences, broken free from the wheel of the eternal return of the closed circle of linear time–three-dimensional space.

We realize ectropy by actively bringing the timeless–spaceless

The Two Trees of Eden: Entropy and Ectropy

essence into our time-bound, material existence to become a unified being, no longer torn apart by conflict and maladies. Here boy and soul are reunited to become one again — as we were at birth.

The "dualistic," "dialectical" structure of language shows us that we cannot speak about one thing without tacitly implying the other. This point — this phenomenon — is of no small matter, for it actually exists for us as real and true. For instance: You can't say someone is "short" unless you know and understand "tall," or "he is thin" unless you know and understand "fat." You can't know the reality and truth of entropy, or its possibility, unless you know and understand the reality and truth of the existence of ectropy. The latter offers the possibility and option for the inevitability of life, if, to repeat, we so choose. Remember: "I set before you...life and death...choose!"

Duality shows itself in the ordinary world of opposites: good or bad, right or wrong, rich or poor, pretty or ugly, normal or abnormal, big or little, clean or dirty, smart or stupid — it goes on ad infinitum. These opposites are all "fictional," man-made, more or less abstract standards.

So while we recognize that we live in a world of duality, we seek to relegate duality to its proper use in managing physical objects and technology — not in setting our moral direction or compass of life.

When Eve mistook the serpent's voice to be at the level of God's, she became seduced and stupefied by it, thus giving them equal value. Otherwise, why pay attention to the voice of a lesser being? So what did the serpent impart into Eve's ear? The message that she was incomplete, she was not whole, she didn't have it all, she was lacking something — but she *could* have it all by eating from the tree of duality called the tree of "good and evil." Now caught in the illusional cycle of insufficiency and self-improvement, she and all of us wear ourselves out listening to the inner and outer serpentine voices, the constant chatter of "not good enough," "there is always more." I call this wearing-out "the physiology of death" and these inner voices "the inner terrorists" (covered in the Death Plan section). This trick, to eat the fruit of the Tree of Death, promises immortality and the power and perfection of God. We wear ourselves out striving after this illusion. Its illusory promise that it can provide our earthly perfection — pleasure in our daily material life and peace and tranquility in our inner life — can never come to fruition.

In the legendary, mythological description of Creation (mythology here meaning messages of spiritual truths, reflected in historical unfolding), the habitation of life on Earth ends up with the creation of us. We came to live in a world of perfection already prepared for our descent into it. This means we are included in the perfection of Creation. As such, we are the tree that is the fruit of Divine Will. We are the Tree of Life. We need no second tree to make us whole. We need nothing to be added to us, nor can anyone nor anything subtract anything from us. We are complete in ourselves. But we don't know it.

The trick played on us by the dark forces of destruction and death gives us the impression that we are not enough or sufficient. We have been conditioned to believe that we need to be added on to by the world through others' flattery, compliments, and adoration. Alternatively, we are intimidated by the world through others' threatening to take away love or life in whole or in part, setting up conditions or demands for us to fulfill to get that love or to save our life. Are you kidding me?! It is impossible for anyone or anything on this earth to add to or subtract from us. We are the tree that is fruit...the Tree of Life. If we are imperfect or feeling less than or insufficient, then we have touched and eaten from the tree of death and duality. This tree bears the fake fruit of insufficiency, feeling less than, incomplete, and not whole.

Eve paid attention to the serpent, the operator of the game, rather than to the game or trick he was playing. We have individually suffered by falling for the charming motivational speaker, leader, or dynamic personality whose seductions and intimidations purvey fear or fortune

The Two Trees of Eden: Entropy and Ectropy

by offering pseudo-truths. We haven't seen behind their facades the "games" that have in reality spawned untruths. (These games are unveiled in Chapter IX, which describes the Errors of Living.)

The story of the Garden, Adam and Eve, the snake, the two trees, and the ultimate eviction from Eden leads us to thank Eve for birthing civilization as a setting where all the Adams and Eves — us — of this world have an opportunity for redemption by correcting the errors of misperception of the value of the voice of the serpent. In other words, we can play the trump card to turn back to eternal life.

Eating from the Tree of Death that makes and bears fruit, we aim to perfect the world and ourselves, prompting us to develop a world of multiplicity, productivity, and profitability — where we live by the credo of more, better, different! This endless greed factor can never be satiated. Ultimately, we find ourselves enslaved to our produced mental misconceptions and produced material goods.

In the esoteric Western tradition, the serpent's challenge was an existential "bombshell" presented to Adam and Eve by God to test their love and faith. Passing the test gives them entrée to another world and a consciousness beyond Eden. They (we) failed, as everyone here on Earth knows well. They (we) were quickly dispatched to this "lower" world where we reside with death.

In God's everlasting mercy and love, humanity — collectively and individually — has been given another chance for redemption. The task involves the incredible tension existing here between life and death. The tension is a necessity, a condition we find at birth. We are constantly faced with following the call of the Tree of Death, to attach to the luscious fruits it bears and to the rewards it promises by doing so. On the other hand is the call of the Tree of Life, guarded scrupulously by cherubim with flashing swords and by other various barriers made difficult for us to overcome. Yet it calls us to it, again testing our love and faith to remain steadfast to our God-like gratuitous self:

sacrificing, renouncing, and detaching from our desire to be king of the world through usurping God's knowledge and power.

The two calls come from different directions: The Tree of Death calls us to go out there in the world and trust that the external world around us holds the key to happiness, liberation, freedom, and self-actualization; the Tree of Life calls us to turn inward to discover through self-knowing and actualizing those very same possibilities of self-realization, individuation, wisdom, knowledge, and understanding. The choice is before us constantly: the road less or more traveled; the narrow or wide gate; the razor's edge or the smooth track of hedonistic pleasure. The reason everyone now dies — physically — is that we choose the Death Path. Nowhere in ordinary education of any sort, from earliest life on, are we taught how to choose the Life Path, much less taught its value — or even the possibility. Here in these pages lies the new education, conveying what has always been available but suppressed, obscured, or veiled: the key to restoring Edenic consciousness, the spiritual meaning and purpose of life. Am I saying that I believe we can live forever? Am I saying that the new education in this book tells us how? Yes. And yes.

One of the great gifts bestowed on us is that we are given the ability to choose the road to either ectropy or entropy. This choice is stated in Deuteronomy 30, in, as I wrote earlier, the most powerful statement of the Western wisdom tradition, where God says we can choose the path of the Life or Death; the path of Truth or Falsehood: "I set before you this day life and death. Choose life so that you and your descendants may live."

Death is life gone awry. Death is "the most awful event." Life is the most wonderful event. If death is a "natural" part of life, why is it so stated that we have, or need, a choice? As this powerful statement indicates, it is not normal to die. "Natural," yes. "Normal," no. That we have been conditioned to believe in death's normal inevitability, yes.

The Two Trees of Eden: Entropy and Ectropy

Rabbi Adin Steinsaltz, in an essay called "Death Thou Shall Be Defeated,"[4] cites direct Hebraic sources corroborating his thesis, that life is to be everlasting. Of course in the relative, dualistic world, debate and doubts will always be raised. Nevertheless, this is the core of monotheistic prophetic spirituality. Here is an excerpt from his essay:

> The basic attitude of Judaism to death, it is said, was ushered in with Adam's [and Eve's] expulsion from the Garden of Eden, is that it is not a natural, inevitable phenomenon. Death is life diseased, distorted, perverted, diverted from the flow of holiness, which is identified with life. So, side by side with a stoic submission to death, there is a stubborn battle against it on the physical and cosmic hand. The world's worst defect is seen to be death, whose representation is Satan. The remedy is faith in the resurrection. Ultimately, "death and evil" — and the one is tantamount to the other — are dismissed as ephemeral. They are not part of the true essence of the world, and, as the revered Rabbi Abraham Isaac Kook[5] emphasized in his worship, man should not accept the premise that death will always emerge the victor.
>
> In the combat of life against death, of being against nonbeing, Judaism manifests disbelief in the persistence of death and maintains that it is a temporary obstacle that can and will be overcome. Our sages, prophesizing a world in which there will be no more death, wrote: "We are getting closer and closer to a world in which we shall be able to vanquish death, in which we shall be above and beyond death." (pp. 194–195)

---

[4] Adin Steinsaltz, "Death Shall Be Defeated," in *Strife of the Spirit* (Northvale, NJ: Jason Aronson, 1988), 192–95.

[5] Father of Rabbi Zvi Yehuda Kook mentioned previously.

We Are Not *Meant* to Die

The central view of Western spirituality is based on two concrete realities that have persisted from its inception: 1) resurrection — the return of the dead to life; 2) eternal life — the ongoing continuance of life, where there is no death.

Now, if a poll were to be taken as to whether one would like to live a greatly extended life or forever, I would venture to say the majority would feel negatively about or repelled by the idea of eternal life. What I have encountered are answers based in not wanting to extend life when in pain or otherwise suffering, life where senses are dimmed, locomotion curtailed, and interest in the world around one diminished. Death here is viewed as relief from the misery of old age. Rightfully so, I would agree. Death can be a welcome visitor for the travails of life.

On the other hand, imagine a life where everyone is ready to accept life as eternal, a life free of suffering, misery, pain, disease, and eventually death; a life absent of violence, murder, and hatred. As the death world does exist, so must a life world. This is what Steinsaltz is getting at, echoed in various ways by luminaries throughout the millennia. We can't have a death world without a life one, a truth muffled by the cacophonous noise of this world. This death world — a man-made one — is full of noise, unclear communication, and disorder, as well as some chaotic elements. That life world is a God-made one, full of revelation, beauty, truth (especially truth), love (especially love), faith, peace, and overall bliss. Why would one not want to opt for living in that world? That's what Eden was/is — a world we can restore as a home for ourselves, a world where there is no death, only life. *We Are Not Meant to Die* is about restoring our life to a beautiful, blissful Garden of Eden. That is what life in this world has to teach us, not in spite of our suffering, but because of it. We get to bliss by going through the pain, not by avoiding pain.

First and foremost of the other luminaries who have shared Rabbi Steinsaltz's view is God. The Jewish service on the Day of Atonement constantly asserts that the Divine wants no one to die and wants to restore the dead to life. Now, this is a particularly hard act to follow. But, there have been those who, having a revelatory or illuminative experience mirroring, sensing, feeling in and through the heart, being in the thrall of love and knowing God, felt moved to give witness to the possibility of life evermore. Here, in chronological order from earliest times to our contemporary age, are some examples:

- King Solomon: "Love Is Strong as Death" (Song of Songs 8:6).
- The Book of the Prophet Isaiah: "He will swallow up death forever" (25:8).
- The Book of the Prophet Ezekiel: Upon instruction from God Ezekiel delivers an incantation (chant) in the Valley of the Bones to those selfsame bones. They are returned to life. (37:1–11). A resurrection occurs.
- Jesus Christ: Bearing the "good news" that death can be overcome (John 3:16).
- Maimonides: "Belief in the Resurrection of the Dead." Repeated in every synagogue in the morning service as part of the recitation of the 13 cardinal principles of Judaism.[6]
- Hafiz, a Poet Laureate of Islam: "How fascinating the idea of death can be. Too bad, though, because it just isn't true."[7]
- John Donne, English poet: His poem entitled "Death Thou Shalt Die."
- Teilhard de Chardin, 19th- to 20th-century French theologian and mystic: "Death is the last enemy to be destroyed."[8]

---

[6] 13th Article of Faith in Judaism. See http://www.religionfacts.com/thirteen-articles-judaism

[7] Daniel Ladinsky. *A Year with Hafiz: Daily Contemplations* (New York: Penguin Books, 2011), p. 285.

[8] Teilhard de Chardin, *The Future of Man*, trans. N. Denny (London, 1964), p. 309.

We Are Not *Meant* to Die

- Dr. Henri Aboulker, French neurosurgeon and father of my teacher Colette Aboulker-Muscat: Author of an unpublished manuscript promoting immortality.

The fact of long life finds an early expression in the Bible, in the Book of Genesis, particularly where the lineage from Adam to Noah is laid out. Methuselah is the longest-lived person mentioned in the Hebrew Bible. The son of Enoch, and a grandfather of Noah, he lived 969 years (Gen. 5:27). He reportedly died seven days before the flood. By the way, Enoch, who "walked with God," never actually died but was taken by God (Gen. 5:24). Noah himself lived to 927 years.

By the way, the ancient Chinese tradition was no stranger to immortality either. In fact, the Chinese were active proponents of it. They designated three components of a spiritual practice that lead the practitioner toward it: dedication, morality, and sacrifice. Along with the spiritual dimension, they advocated the use of a special plant called lingzhi (reishi), a fungus still used today to boost immunity and promote longevity.

However, with the advent of a materialist world view of the past several centuries, the spiritual worldview was eroded. Even theologians, who saw the facts of resurrection and immortality staring at them from the pages of their own scriptures, lent their weight against it. Forget that Christianity begins with the resurrection of the Master some 2,000 years ago, or that every Jew at morning prayers in synagogue affirms a belief in resurrection. None of this was taken seriously. Not until now, and from an unlikely source: materialist science, in a form called "cloning." In recent times these scientists have succeeded in "resurrecting" dead animals such as dogs, cats, bulls, and sheep[9] by

---

[9] Yoichiro Hoshino, Noboru Hayashi, Shunji Taniguchi, Naohiko Kobayashi, Kenji Sakai, Tsuyoshi Otani, Akira Iritani, Kazuhiro Saek, "Resurrection of a Bull by Cloning from Organs Frozen Without Cryoprotectant in a −80°C Freezer for a Decade," *Plos*

cloning, taking bone cells from them and reproducing replicas.

Why bone cells? The Western tradition long understood that bones never die even though the physical body disintegrates after death. The living marrow of those bones contains DNA, the primordial protein of life, the nuclear seed around which viable life forms. In Hebrew, the word *etzem* (phonetic of the Hebrew) translates as *self, essence, bone*, meaning the essence of the self is in the bone(s).

Interestingly, Gloria Gronowicz, PhD, a former biologist at the University of Connecticut, devised a rigorous experiment testing the efficacy of Therapeutic Touch, a form of energy healing by placing hands one-quarter of an inch above the affected area of the body. She took healthy human bone cells and placed them into one of three groups of petri dishes: a group that received Therapeutic Touch treatment, a group that received sham treatment, and a group that received no treatment. The group of bone cells that received treatment from trained Therapeutic Touch practitioners showed a significant increase in DNA synthesis and mineralization than the other untreated healthy bone cell groups. They grew more quickly and absorbed calcium at a faster rate.

Dr. Gronowicz also tested Therapeutic Touch on osteosarcoma-derived cell lines (cancerous bone cells). Again, she had three groups of petri dishes. Here she found that the cancerous bone cells that were treated with Therapeutic Touch actually *decreased* differentiation and mineralization. In other words, the treatment weakened the cancerous cells, curbing their out-of-control growth and their ability to absorb calcium. These experiments prove that our minds, trained and directed, can effect changes in the life force of in vitro cells.[10]

One Journal, January 8, 2009. https://doi.org/10.1371/journal.pone.0004142. See also https://viagenpets.com/ for cloning house pets.

[10] G. A. Gronowicz. A. Jhaveri, L. W. Clarke, M. S. Aronow, T. H. Smith, J. Altern. "Therapeutic Touch Stimulates the Proliferation of Human Cells in Culture."

Currently the biological, neuroscientific, and medical communities have weighed in in no uncertain terms, and unwittingly at that, on the side of spiritual doctrine. Let's chronicle a few of these scientific discoveries:

(1) The FoxO gene: In animal and human research, the master gene has been discovered and called FoxO. This gene has the capacity to give orders to the chromosomes to remain alive and not wear out. More specifically, there is a cap at the end of each chromosome strand called a "telomere." As we age, these telomeres begin to decay. The FoxO gene can order the telomere to reverse this process, to reverse the decay. When this happens, aging stops and is reversed! Ronald DePinho, PhD, is a biologist who has succeeded in reversing the aging process in mice by exactly the method just described.[11]

More recently, researchers at Stanford University School of Medicine have developed a new procedure to increase the length of human telomeres. This increases the number of times cells are able to "divide," essentially making cells many years younger.

(2) The British biologist Aubrey de Grey[12] has dedicated his work to longevity studies, and opines that he sees no reason why we

---

Complement Med. 2008 Apr; 14(3): 233–39. doi: 10.1089/acm.2007.7163. PMID: 18370579; E. Monzillo and G. Gronowicz. "New Insights on Therapeutic Touch: A Discussion of Experimental Methodology and Design That Resulted in Significant Effects on Normal Human Cells and Osteosarcoma." *Explore* (NY), 2011 Jan–Feb;7(1): 44-51. doi: 10.1016/j.explore.2010.10.001. PubMed PMID: 21194672.

[11] Ergün Sahin and Ronald A. DePinho. "Linking Functional Decline of Telomeres, Mitochondria and Stem Cells During Ageing." *Nature* 464.7288 (2010): 520–528. https://www.ncbi.nlm.nih.gov/pmc/articles/PMC3733214/. Accessed August 13, 2018.

[12] Original cofounder of the SENS Foundation and founder of the LEV foundation.

should not be living at least 1,000 years. He focuses on making repairs to a portion of the human cell that produces energy — the mitochondria, which converts sugar from a stored form called Adenosine triphosphate, or ATP, to its released form called Adenosine diphosphate, or ADP. His investigations in biology and those of his adherents in biology are attempting to find ways to keep this energy system "forever" alive. He proposes that if that succeeds, he will have taken the next logical step to support his hypothesis. Having an unending supply of biological energy available means our bodies can sustain life for these 1,000 years of longevity.[13] This theory, including how the activation process could be installed, was initially heavily (an understatement) criticized by biologists. Finally, a panel of eight scientists from around the U.S. met at MIT to evaluate this theory.[14] The scientists spent considerable time dissecting this theory and came to the unanimous conclusion that they could find no flaw in the supposition. Many biologists have now come over to this camp. Ray Kurzweil, former Google engineer and supporter of the SENS Research Foundation that De Grey cofounded, believes that this research could lead humans

---

[13] Aubrey de Grey, D.N.J. "The Singularity and the Methuselarity: Similarities and Differences." *Studies in Health Technology and Informatics* series, ebook Vol. 149: *Strategy for the Future of Health* (2009), pp. 195–202.

[14] Interestingly, in scientific terms, a theory is considered proved if a contrary hypothesis can be claimed to negate the theory. Many years ago, a group of philosophers and psychoanalysts convened at New York University to discuss the validity of the major thesis of psychoanalysis to see if it had scientific validity. They chose to look at the Oedipus complex (the child wanting to murder the parent of the same sex in order to have the opposite parent; for the girl, it is called the Electra complex). The analysts held the Oedipus complex as universal and inviolable. The philosophers, wanting to test the validity of this proposition, asked what someone would look like who did not appear to have an Oedipus complex. The analysts responded by becoming enraged that such a proposition could be raised, no less entertained, and stormed out of the meeting.

to achieve immortality as soon as 2030[15]. While these advancements in research are exciting, without ecological security and resolving our moral obligation to care for our environment in a systemic and heartfelt way, physical immortality will be meaningless.

(3) From the medical establishment has come the development of organs taken from other humans, even animals, scraping off all the cells and creating what's called a "ghost organ." Cells scraped from your own organ are grafted onto the surface of this organ, where these new cells reproduce, giving you a fresh organ that can be surgically implanted in your body to replace the decayed one. These medical researchers foresee that in the coming years, sooner rather than later, there will be laboratories throughout the U.S. filled with these organs ready to be used on call, thus making it possible to extend organ life indefinitely.

(4) Stem cell replacement. This is a process of taking embryonic cells from one's bones, inserting them back into the body wherever needed, and growing them into the organ required in that area. According to the NIH, stem cells, when directed to differentiate into specific cell types, could be a renewable source of replacement cells and tissues to treat diseases and injuries, including macular degeneration, spinal cord trauma, stroke, burns, heart disease, diabetes, osteoarthritis, and rheumatoid

---

[15] Danny D'Cruze. "Ex-Google engineer says humans will achieve immortality in 7 years; here's how netizens reacted." *Business Today*. (2023): https://www.businesstoday.in/technology/news/story/ex-google-engineer-says-humans-will-achieve-immortality-in-7-years-heres-how-netizens-reacted-375766-2023-04-03. Accessed June 16, 2023.

arthritis.[16] Again, this is a process that would help extend life indefinitely.

What I understand from the above, is that scientists have devised, or are devising, a means to develop a virtual you and me. This virtual you and me will be able to carry out the functions we do. I think that's how it works. You can see the report on this phenomenon that appeared on the public television series *Nova*, entitled "Can We Live Forever?" which aired January 26, 2011. At any rate, I sure do hope this virtual being is more computer savvy than I am.

(5) Experiments reported by the HeartMath Institute of California report that adults were able to change their chromosomes by an effort of will through focusing on a belief about affecting their chromosomes. Another experiment, this time conducted on children, had the same outcome. The significance of these findings is that according to genetic scientists, genes — which have chromosomes — are the determiners of our lives. They are our hereditary element that's not subject to any influence. Further, certain genes are irreversible determiners of biological and psychological maladies. The accepted "fact" is that certain conditions such as heart disease, cancer, schizophrenia, and many, many more are hereditary. Once the claim "it's hereditary" is asserted, the reaction is that the situation is always "hopeless." The HeartMath experiments suggest otherwise, and that extended life is possible for people with "hopeless" "hereditary" conditions.

---

[16] http://stemcells.nih.gov/info/basics/pages/basics6.aspx, NIH website, accessed October 27, 2015.

Genes in themselves cannot alone be the determining factor in the emergence of disease.[17]

---

[17] Rollin McCraty, PhD, Mike Atkinson, Dana Tomasino, B.A. *Modulation of DNA Conformation by Heart-Focused Intention*, HeartMath Research Center, Institute of HeartMath, Publication No. 03-008, Boulder Creek, CA, 2003.

CHAPTER IV

What IS Spiritual Science?

SCIENCE MEANS "TO KNOW." Just as there are principles and knowledge of natural science, there are principles and knowing of spiritual science. This science gives rise to an understanding and knowing of how the Invisible Reality works. This approach is in sharp contrast to the approach of natural or materialistic science, itself posing another way to know. How that knowledge is derived creates differing points of view. Knowledge is based on the evidence of our senses, which are perceptually directed toward either the outer material world as the starting point (the approach in natural science) or the inner subjective reality as the starting point (the approach of spiritual science, sometimes called revelatory or intuitive science). The former places emphasis on what is physically measurable, quantifiable, and calculable in the objects detected in the time–space world around us. In contradistinction to this quantitative approach is the qualitative one, which begins from perceptions focused toward qualitative, unmeasurable, invisible realities that birth our measurable time–space world. The governing principle of this metaphysical proposition is rendered in this Spirit→Matter diagram:

The first two components represent the qualitative dimension and the latter two the quantitative manifestations. Energy and matter can be observed and measured outwardly; spirit and force are realized inwardly. For conversational purposes — hard as it is to put this wisdom into words — we might term the qualitative elements the inner forum of consciousness and the quantitative elements the outer forum of consciousness. Simply put, the invisible realm births the visible realm that we experience as our time-space "reality." What we conceive and perceive births our experiences here on Earth.[18]

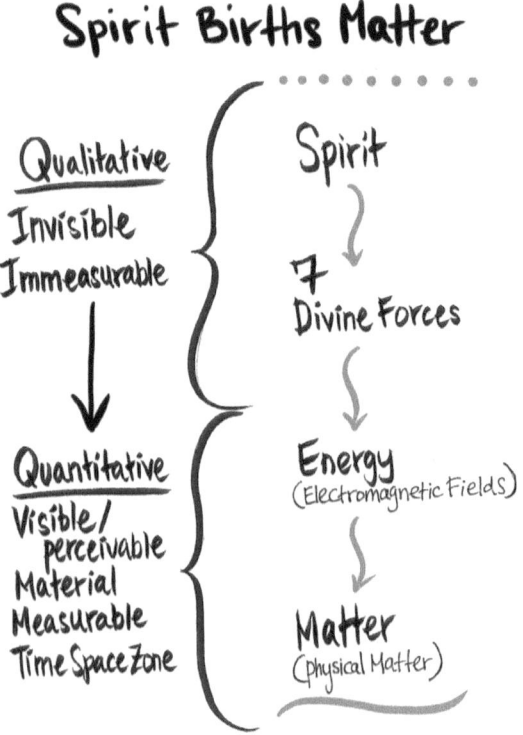

The Neter Principle

The principle of this movement from the unseen to the seen, from the invisible to the visible, was expressed in ancient Egyptian wisdom as the "Neter Principle." The function/quality of something is birthed as

---

[18] Epstein, G. (2010). *Healing into immortality: A new spiritual medicine of healing stories and imagery*. ACMI Press.

What Is Spiritual Science?

a quantitative, measurable *form to fulfill that function*. For example: The possibility/function/quality of seeing is birthed as eyes. The same goes for smelling and every other function we can think of. So it is that the invisible births the visible. The function births the form. The quality gives rise to quantity. Inner creates outer. That's magic. Isn't that what happened when God created the world? The first book of the Bible — the Book of Genesis or Origins — begins with the genesis of the world where the All elects to create a form constructed in six days. The genesis or origin is then where it — the world as we know it — all started. The rest of the story — in Genesis and the subsequent holy books that followed through the entirety of the Bible onward into the New Testament — speaks to the unfoldment of the forms thus created in their essential spheres of human behavior: physical, emotional, mental, social, moral.

Let me clarify. The Neter Principle is one of the influences of invisibility in our lives. It supplies that missing piece that keeps a lid on our understanding of that which guides our destiny — the Invisible Reality.

To understand how Neter works, it is not necessary to dismiss the reality of physiological and biological functioning of our body. Yes, the *process* of seeing takes place through the eye (of course other senses allow blind people to "see" through these other channels). Yes, light rays reflect from the object looked at, pour through the pupil onto the retina, off to the optic nerve, and so forth. The physical eye serves the physical function of seeing. We are in agreement. Neter points us to the *source* that has birthed the eye! Those who stop at material explanation (and we were all educated at the outset of our lives this way) say "We see *because* we have eyes." The physical is placed at the forefront of our "knowing." Neter says "the *possibility* (potential, qualitative existence) for seeing gives birth, or births, the eyes." Once eyes are birthed, the process of seeing physiologically is set in motion.

In spiritual science, we understand that what is perceived and conceived in the inner forum gives birth to what we experience and perceive in the outer forum. Our beliefs and conceptions become our created realities and experiences. "What is conceived in us is birthed through us." In short, the inside creates our outside life.

After all, we are co-creators, made in God's image and likeness, following the prescriptive description of how creation came into being in the first chapter of Genesis. Material science, on the other hand, looks at its genesis from the other direction, starting with matter as the birther, leading to the discovery of energy and usually stopping there.[19] The fundamental error of modern psychology and material science is that your outside creates your inside; that your outside experiences create who you are and your beliefs, your past creates your present, that the experiences that happen to you in your life are responsible for what you become. However, in current times, quantum physicists are probing further, seeking to extend the boundaries of the quantitative model to expand into invisible regions of Force and Spirit ("invisible" here is equated to "quality"). Each process, be it Spirit downward or Matter upward, is a genuine attempt at achieving knowing. The final proof of the pudding lies in each of us determining which direction bears fruit for life rather than thorns or thistles, to paraphrase the famous saying of the Master of Christianity. It is of interest to note that quantum physicists have now empirically demonstrated that what doesn't appear to be physically present, or "nothing," has an effect on matter. If that is the case, I would think that these physicists would need to drop the term "quantum" from their field of study. Quantum refers to a numerical thing and is not appropriate to that which is no thing. The latter is no longer physics, in fact, because physics is a science of things.

---

[19] This is the construction of a Tower of Babel, built from the ground up to supplant spiritual understanding that starts from the top down to Earth.

What Is Spiritual Science?

Permanent vs. Impermanent Reality

Our life here on Earth is presented to us as a paradox, where we attempt to make permanent what is absolutely impermanent in the ever-changing impermanency of time–space reality.

Early on in our life, incorrect conditioning together with miseducation push us to make this uncertain world that is changing before us, literally moment to moment, become certain. To reinforce the false-certainty principle, we are driven to make the future that is definitely uncertain, certain. In this attempt we are conditioned to focus on outcomes, results, end points, conclusions, consequences, and goals. In doing so, we also tend (1) to hang on to fixed ideas, thoughts, beliefs, feelings, opinions, habits, ideologies, and the like internally, and (2) to hang on to material possessions of many sorts in the external world around us. We may call all of these "attachments" that come and go endlessly. The going is experienced as separation, parting, loss, and death, with their consequent effects on us physically, emotionally, mentally, socially, and behaviorally. We are called on to adapt to the consequences of these losses and transition from one set of circumstances to another. Our ability to do so successfully or not depends on our resilience, flexibility, and mutability. The first adaptation occurs in the transition from womb to birth. There we are in our primordial non-disturbed state — lolling about in the amniotic fluid in the uterus, free of cares, no conflicts. Suddenly we are thrown out and into a severely disturbed environment, the human world. Once there we need to adapt to this cacophony of inputs and come to terms with the loss of that Edenic environment we once knew that leaves us with a trace memory of that paradise together with a yearning to return there. We go throughout life facing loss, transitions, adaptations. How we handle these three experiences happening as a unit, or independently, impacts our health, well-being, and longevity. When we insist on holding on to the illusion of fixity in an unfixed, ever-changing world, we are setting ourselves up for a fall, for a hit to our physiology and biology that creates entropy and, ultimately, death.

So it is the impermanent reality, rightly so, that is the world of death, where it reigns supreme. However, there is a permanent reality — that of the invisible world, full of invisible beings, spirits of various sorts, those on earth who have since departed, as well as an aspect of this reality called "soul" that exists within us and around us — that needs our nurturing. This permanent reality is ceaseless, endless, without boundaries, full of never-ending life force, energy, love, always here to lend assistance to us. It is fixed and unchanging. A forever friend. It provides a continuous unfoldment, self-organization, greater complexity, expansion, and, thereby eternal life and no death.

To sum up, a paradox forms from the foregoing: Accept without question the inevitability of death, or integrate the permanent reality. No need to try and make the impermanent reality a permanent reality. By accepting impermanence without fear and leaving it at that, we can then turn our attention to permanent reality that is the soul, spirit world. Here we come to accept the inevitability of life that may likely motivate us to change our pattern of living to embrace a new pattern featuring our taking the path of life. As we practice this Life Path, we take ourselves out of the grip of the transitory time–space–death world and reunite body and soul to become a "Spiritual Body of Light." We build this body of light, or resurrective body, by correcting our social and spiritual errors of living. With each correction, the soul, bit by bit, provides the light of transformation to our (physical, emotional, mental) body. My teacher Colette called this process "climbing the ladder of self-mastery," where we become people of conscience and conscious beings of light. The "final" unification occurs when the reunited body and soul joins Spirit (the Absolute) to form a spiritual trinity of eternal life. Colette described this final unification as leaping across the abyss that separates the "waters of the heights" (pure spirit) from the "waters

What Is Spiritual Science?

below" (Genesis 1: 6), where we live.

Here are some notions that may help orient you more quickly to the concepts of monotheistic spiritual science. A number of them are contrasts, some are straight definitions.

— **Invisible Reality:** All spiritual traditions of the world posit an invisible reality that births the visible reality. What is the makeup of this invisible reality that has no immediate tangibility? First, we experience invisibility as a local phenomenon within our personal awareness of our emotional and mental life. While not material, emotional and mental phenomena can be measured. These measurements give us a peripheral sense of these events but are not the same as the events. For example, measuring brainwave states points to a recognition of the existence of the state but is not to be confused with or as the state. Likewise, depression and anxiety scales give an objective sense of these mood and emotional disturbances but are not the same.

The Invisible Reality has no special location. It encompasses that vast realm of existence within which humans reside. This includes the soul; the worlds of imagination; the world of invisible beings such as angels and spirits: universal consciousness, which is conveniently termed "God." All of this invisible reality exists all the time and is experientially knowable to us.

— **God:** God is a term derived from Norse or Icelandic literature. While not inherent in Western Mediterranean spirituality, it has become a convenient catchword to designate a wide variety of terms signifying sacred reality. Some of them are: Spirit, Invisible Reality, divinity, Absolute One Mind, All, Ancient of Days, Great Exchange Being, Supreme Lord, consciousness, Supernal Light.

In my understanding, God is at once being and consciousness — analogous to the definition of light as discovered in physics to be simultaneously both wave and particle — dubbed a "wavicle." This light, investigated in different fields of physics, mirrors Divine Light as it filters down into human existence.

This wavicle, as defined in quantum physics, represents two distinct experiences: the wave is nonmeasurable, existing outside time, while the particle reflects an element of matter measurable in this time-space reality in our relative world. When the invisible wave meets the visible particle, they exist as one.[20]

— **God-made and man-made:** In the Monotheistic tradition, there are two worlds: God-made and man-made. The latter has been grafted onto the former by our design. As we are made in God's image, we are, like God, co-creators of our world. We have been given free will and choice by dint of birth so we are free to build upon the days of God's creation. The man-made world is full of standards, ideals, and judgments and games.

— **Games:** In the everyday world there are a plethora of games. Games are competitions where there are winners and losers, rules, officials, and penalties. Ordinarily we think of games as referring to sports like baseball, football, etc. But we also engage in "games" in many other areas of life, such as the theology game (good- bad, right-wrong), political games (winners are in power, losers are out of power); big business (winners are rich; losers are poor), medical arts (normal or abnormal) and the natural sciences (real-unreal), beauty game (pretty-ugly) promulgated by advertising. In each of the aforementioned institutional games, we can opt in or opt out from engaging in them. In choosing to play the game, we accept to play by their rules with many promised rewards of pleasure and comfort if we play along.

— **Divine Providence vs. Chance:** Most people in the West believe that chance is the fundamental reality. That the universe, although

---

[20] Amit Goswami, PhD, "Love, Death and the Meaning of Life," *Atlantis Rising*, No. 122, March/April 2017, pp. 46, 72; *The Everything Answer Book: How Quantum Science Explains Love, Death and the Meaning of Life* (Charlottesville: Hampton Books, 2017).

perhaps ultimately determined, is in its moment-to-moment workings an inchoate, disordered mass, random and unpredictable that can perpetrate on us, at any random moment, some awful consequence, such as illness. Chance is the cause of all events in a world where God does not and cannot exist. Along with this comes the notion that there cannot be an invisible reality and that we are fundamentally habituated, enslaved, mechanical beings who operate in a determined manner, according to fixed cause and effect laws; in essence we are at the mercy of luck. From this perspective, our job as human beings is to try to put this physical and social universe under our control to prevent its randomness and wild unpredictability from affecting us. This belief holds that with enough knowledge at our command, we can put the universe under our dominion and that we can control, even own, the forces of nature. Thus, trying to gain power and control the future become all important. In contrast, Spiritual Science posits that the universe is ordered operating according to a divine plan (providence). Human beings are born with free will and have the choice to co-create their own reality for themselves.

And even if outer events are seemingly not changeable, we always have the choice of how we respond to the world by choosing our inner state of being and by shifting our beliefs. Beliefs are always open to change. How does this work? Within invisibility reside will, beliefs, and images — and all of them are not subject to measurement. Operationally, our will births our beliefs (ideas, concepts) that birth images (inner sensory perceptions) that in turn birth our physical world of experience that is quantifiable and subject to measurement.

To ascribe to chance denies God and the influence of Invisible Reality. By doing so there is no door open to further investigation to learn about ourselves or to take steps to correct our errors, as GEMS educates us to do.

— **Holy:** God's world is termed holy, sacred, spiritual. It's of the instant (the closest time word I could think of) and exists without conditions or attachments. It is a holy realm.

— The term "holy" is related not only to whole, health, and healing through their common etymological Germanic root — *kailo* — but also to the consecration of the seventh day of creation, the Sabbath, when God rested and ceased creating. The seventh day is the zone of "no time." In Hebrew, the sacred language of the Western monotheistic tradition, holy also means "separate," a phenomenon that stands at the heart of this book and all the practices connected with extended and eternal life. By these practices we separate ourselves from the tentacles of future and past time. As we do this we become holy. The explication of holy in full flower awaits further reading — and surprises.

— **In the World But Not of the World:** Another important distinction for understanding spiritual awareness is *in* the world but not *of* the world: "In the world" relates squarely to participating in the world in a holy way. "Of the world" is to live here according to the general value systems of a society that is living not by these shared holy values but by its man-made ones. The great masters on Earth, past and present, have sought to make clear the unholiness pervading the world in which we live. By separating from the value system and mores enmeshed in man-made authorship, we separate from the death world reigning supreme in the material or man-made world. As we separate, we never forget the material. Rather, by separating we are able to bring a spiritually based healing, therapeutic impulse to bear on the material world, providing service to stem suffering and create a foundational value system based on love, divine law, cooperation, conservation, collaboration, and conversation, while thereby putting an end to conflict and controversy and, by extension, war. We remain then *in* the world, but not *of* it. A spiritual life brings us to this place.

— **Vertical and Horizontal Worlds:** The God-made world is often envisioned or perceived as a *vertical* one. We all know this. When we appeal to God or pray or rejoice, our gaze goes heavenward (the celestial term for skyward). As we tread Earth, weighed down physically by terrestrial gravity, we approach each other on a *horizontal* plane. The vertical world is the invisible one connected to the element air. The horizontal world is denoted by the element earth, the material area. Spiritual practice is a self-reflective one, where the vertical realm and its ceaseless creative force and power influence the visible. We are then bringing verticality into the horizontal dimension, so we are living *in* but not *of* the world.

— **Essence to Existence Model:** This is another name for the birthing process of Spirit to Matter. It describes the preeminent 5,000-year-old system of spiritual understanding of the connection between the vertical and the horizontal, the invisible and the visible realities.

This birthing process is acausal — outside of time and space, beyond the habitual understanding that something physical causes something physical to happen, rather than something invisible causing or birthing something visible.

— **GEMS Model:** When we apply the essence to existence model to health care, we have GEMS. (Essence/Invisible → Existence/Visible Model)

Subjective experiences (essence) gleaned through inwardly conceived and perceived processes — such as imagination, will, and belief — permit us to actively take charge of everyday life (existence), bringing with it many, many beneficial rewards. These experiences are not materially based and cannot be directly measured, calculated, or quantified. We do, however, call on them to become our primary resource for healing, continuous health, longevity, and beyond.

— **Spiritual Symbols of the Meeting of Vertical and Horizontal Realities:** Both Christianity and Judaism adopted ancient symbols of spiritual origin for the organization of their religious institutions. The cross, the adopted symbol of Christianity, condenses movement of the vertical as it is brought to bear on the horizontal. The ↓ = vertical, the → = horizontal. In Christian esoteric wisdom, the crossing point of vertical and horizontal came to look like this:

☦

In Christianity the crossing point is called the Chosen One, or Jesus, the catalyst for universal love to become birthed in the horizontal — on Earth. The center of that crossing point is termed the "sacred heart" of the Master, the storehouse of love.

While both Christian and Judaic wisdom traditions share a common transcendent source known as monotheism = one God, Judaism does not subscribe to an idea of a "chosen one," but rather to a "chosen people." The Judaic concern was that a chosen one could become a source of idolatry, identifying a single incarnated individual as being God. In the monotheistic framework, both traditions are embraced. We are individually chosen to reflect Godliness — Moses, Abraham, Sarah, Jesus, and Mary come to mind — while we all as a "chosen people" have a purpose to eventually become beings of light and to join that light with the Light of God/Spirit.

Given the Judaic preference for steering clear of extolling individual chosenness, Judaism utilized a symbol that didn't point to a human being and chose instead a six-pointed star, a hexagram consisting of two overlapping (reversed) triangles.

The triangles taken alone and also intersecting become the following symbols: △ is the symbol of fire, ▽ water, ⍫ earth, △ air— the four fundamental elements of creation here on Earth. The star also symbolized the great spiritual law of "As above, so below" — that the horizontal world of matter is a mirror of the vertical world of spirit.

— **"As Above, So Below"**: The direction we apply to the movement of spirit to matter (essence to existence) is ↓ <u>vertical</u>, from above to below. The great spiritual hermetic summation of the process of essence to existence is known in the Western wisdom thus: "As above, so below. And that which is below does honor to that which is above." In spiritual science, not only does the invisible birth or conceive the visible but the physical reflects or mirrors the immaterial. Thus, we are made in the image of God and are reflections of God; we bear a likeness to God but are not the same as God. Analogy is yet another word for mirroring. In analogy, two things share points of likeness but are not the same and so have points of dissimilarity as well. In later chapters we will take up how this mirrored reflective quality plays out in our health and in our social relationships. We will also learn how to begin to read the analogies in our lives.

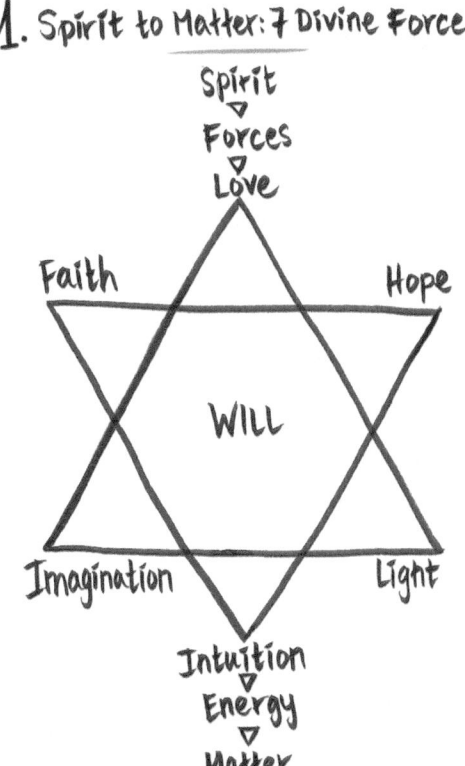

—The Seven Forces: God (the uncreated Spirit) puts forth seven nourishing forces — Light, Love, Faith, Hope, Intuition, Imagination, and Will. Diagrammatically they could be displayed thus, in two overlapping triangles:

The center is *Will*, the Light of Truth. When Moses asked God who S/He was, the answer came back: "I AM THAT I AM," "I WILL BE THAT I WILL BE," or, paraphrased (by me): "'I AM' IS THE TRUTH."

Here in the world of measurable, created matter, our physical body registers the influence of the forces of Spirit as "*InvisibleVisible* Unity" or unity of body and soul. It is indivisible, One Awareness manifesting in and through us, creating a unitary system between the two realities: invisible and visible. I emphasize here two realities parallel to each other, interacting with each other. We will explore these spiritual forces in Chapter XI.

— **Mind, Brain, and Heart:** These seven forces (which include images and intuitive messages) travel to us through the inner informational superhighway called *Mind*. Mind is the channel of communication between invisible and visible reality that makes these forces perceptible to us. These qualitative, immeasurable forces are filtered at first through the heart and then sent brain-ward. The ancients referred to this function as the "intelligence of the heart." Love, Imagination, Faith, Hope, Intuition, and Will are all facets of this intelligence filtered through the heart. The heart is the central organ of the body. From a spiritual perspective, the brain is a limb of the heart. The brain is the seat of verbal, cognitive, discursive thought, which is important. However, this thinking serves the heart. We cannot think without the heart, as it is the activating principle of thought, and we think either warmheartedly or coldheartedly. It can never be any other way! This ongoing dance of communication between the physical heart and the brain has been researched extensively for over more than 30 years, starting in 1958 with the husband-and-wife investigative team of John and Beatrice Lacey.[21]

***

---

[21] Sam A. Rosenfeld, *Conversations Between Heart and Brain*. Rockville, MD: Dept. of Health, Education, and Welfare, National Institute of Mental Health, Division of Scientific and Public Information, Mental Health Studies and Reports Branch, 1977–1978.

What Is Spiritual Science?

GEMS, a new *unitary* model of medicine/health care, naturally emerges from this understanding of Spiritual Science. It reverses the conventional medical approach: It posits an invisible (immaterial/spiritual) cause for imbalances in life rather than citing physical causes as the source. In this new model, disturbances are incurred from our errors made with regard to violating, breaking, or not abiding by the spiritual laws governing our life here on Earth that in turn birth our social errors of living that in turn birth our everyday life problems. The Ten Commandments, the Three Virtues, and the Seven Divine Forces are prescriptions for correcting our errors of attachment. *Stated another way, our basic errors are rooted in the tapestry of the social/moral existence by which all humans interact with each other*. When we come into order here, we simultaneously come into order and harmony physically and the course of physical disorder and disharmony eases.

This univision approach to life realizes itself in terms of our balance, order, clarity, wisdom, knowledge, and understanding. Assessing whatever disturbance manifests in our system is gleaned by this larger scope of understanding to help us put the pieces of our lives, the dismembered fragments, back into the mosaic, the order, and balance of life.

As might have been discerned at this point, the most powerful force available to us by virtue of birth (and I really mean virtue in its pure sense, as we are born virtuous or with the potential to become virtuous) is our mental capacity. Every possibility for longevity and beyond presented in this book begins and ends with a mental process. To reiterate: By no means are these processes to be considered as residing in the brain. Mental does not mean brain. Rather, it means those qualitative functions (e.g., to dream, to imagine, to watch, to intuit) are immeasurably filtered at first through the heart and then sent brainward.

Love — or not — for our fellow humans is played out through the binding forces of the Ten Laws/Commandments. They are *all* life-preserving, self-organizing forces that reinforce the love we hold for Spirit, neighbors, and self. Being awake to the laws operating constantly in our daily activities fills us evermore with love and is reflected in our biological being.

It is surely a fact that love increases immune function. A study was conducted at Harvard by David McClelland in the 1980s where 40 students were shown a film of violence. During the viewing, swabs of saliva were taken from the mouth of the students to measure IGA (immunoglobulin) function. Across the board, the tests showed a lowering of IGA level. Afterward, a film of Mother Teresa administering to the poor in India was shown. Again swabs were taken. In the first instance, the students expressed distress at the violence presented. In the second instance, 20 of the students were overtly disparaging and mocking of Mother Teresa's work, while the other 20 praised her activity. Yet the IGA measures of all the students went up regardless of whether they approved or were critical of what they were viewing.[22]

Our mental functions, emotional responses, behaviors, and the intelligent use of thinking (e.g., thinking in the present, thinking analogically) are important personal factors that contribute mightily to longevity. Their importance is highlighted by recognizing that each of them stimulates the natural healing resources within us. When we experience this, we begin to trust our own authority and independence. The spiritually based health-care practices we take on become major agents responsible for healing. In adopting these practices, we start to realize the incredible living power that is us. After all, we are created as reflections of God, imbued with all knowledge, wisdom, and understanding. God wouldn't want it any other way. Actually, we have

---

[22] David C. McClelland and Carol Kirshnit, "The Effect of Motivational Arousal through Films on Salivary Immunoglobulin A," *Psychology & Health* 2:1 (1988), 31-52. DOI: 10.1080/08870448808400343)

What Is Spiritual Science?

been miseducated and conditioned to believe we lack this inherent wisdom and knowledge. We look to external input for the answers. There indeed may be outer resources available to help us along, but the tradition states unequivocally that we should go first to ourselves. We owe it to ourselves to do so. We are going to learn here how to do this.

Bringing to light the possibilities we have for taking charge of ourselves can only bring soft winds of change and hope, not to mention the cost-effective result. It costs nothing — no energy drain — to work on self. What we use inwardly not only affects our state of health but also benefits our relationships in both the outward everyday actional life and inward holy world.

CHAPTER V

Laws of Longevity: A Spiritual Perspective

LONG LIFE IS NOT ONLY A BIOLOGICAL phenomenon, it is also a social, emotional, mental, moral/spiritual one. When taking this view, we cannot talk of the quantity of life without examining the quality of life and the qualitative factors involved in extended living. In fact, quantity and quality are inextricably intertwined. Their inter-digitation and interrelationship are never neglected in the wholistic view presented in these pages.

The art of living long includes qualitative and quantitative, spiritual and material, which requires realizing the connections, reverberations, and reflections that go on all the time throughout our human system. When you think, the physical body is responding simultaneously. When you are in doubt mentally, the body suffers an ailment, reflecting this same doubt.

The sacred system is a whole one operating organically as such at each moment, unfolding our life story in its own unique way, different from everyone else's. We are each individual — undivided wholes — separate but at the same time united as one under the skin. We are one integrated unity, yet distinctly different from each other, but all part of one fabric governed by the Absolute One Mind.

As I suggested earlier, the GEMS model of health and well-being from which I work centers on a two-pronged approach: (1) recognizing the influence of the invisible, subjective reality (or essence) on human existence and (2) understanding the definite connection of invisible with visible reality. The invisible axis has been called by the less precise term "mindbody." This term should never be hyphenated as the mentalphysical interact synergistically, one side representing "invisiblesubjective reality," the other "physicalobjective reality."

It is this first prong that brings us to a greater focus on long life physically and biologically. It's pretty well recognized now how mentalphysical are in mutual process, each exerting influence on the other. A wealth of research evidence attests to both the upside and downside of physiological changes associated with emotional shifts. Examples of this relationship include my two research studies (both conducted with Dr. Ulas Kaplan at James Madison University in Harrisonburg, Virginia, with invaluable consultation with Dr. Anne Sullivan-Smith of Wayne State University, Detroit, Michigan School of Nursing) showing how mental imagery definitively strengthens heart rate coherence and variability, both signs of health. Here, a mental process is significantly reflected in a physical one.[23]

Another example is a research study on the effects of treatment of asthma with mental imagery that I conducted with Dr. Elizabeth Barrett, Professor Emerita of the Hunter School of Nursing (New York City) at Lenox Hill Hospital, New York. Here nearly 50 percent of the patients were able either to stop medications altogether or to substantially reduce them without deterioration of their respiratory functioning after one session of mental imagery education.[24] These studies are just two examples of the plethora of research studies showing the mindbody connection. Let's apply the GEMS Dimensions of Experience to heart ailments,

Diagram II: Heart Ailment Example

The 5 dimensions of experience

The experience is simultaneous and synchronous, analogous and correlative.

---

[23] Ulas Kaplan, Ed.D., Gerald N. Epstein, MD, and Anne Sullivan Smith, PhD, R.N., "Microdevelopment of Daily Well-Being Through Mental Imagery Practice." *Imagination, Cognition and Personality* 34(1): 73–96. First published online Oct. 2014; print issue published Sept. 2014. https://doi.org/10.2190/IC.34.1.f.; Ulas Kaplan, Ed.D., and Gerald N. Epstein, MD, "Psychophysiological Coherence as a Function of Mental Imagery Practice." *Imagination, Cognition and Personality* 31(4): 97–312. First published online June 2012. https://doi.org/10.2190/IC.31.4.d.

[24] Gerald N. Epstein, James P. Halper, Elizabeth Ann Manhart Barrett, Carole Birdsall, Monnie McGee, Kim P. Baron, and Stephen Lowenstein. "A Pilot Study of Mind-Body Changes in Adults with Asthma Who Practice Mental Imagery." *Alternative Therapies in Health and Medicine* 10(4)(2004): 66–71.

one of the most common causes of death. The physical heart ailment is reflected in the other four spheres of experience, as shown in Diagram II.

The heart is the seat of love. Emotionally, being heartsick, having heartache, eating your heart out, all have their roots in the arena of love. Physically, heart ailments such as chest pain, cardiac arrythmia's, coronary artery disease and heart attack speak to issues of love. In the social dimension, we may experience being spurned, jilted, divorced, isolated, or heartbroken. In the spiritual/moral dimension we often idolize the other, becoming enslaved in the relationship. Becoming aware of the connections between the physical and these other dimensions brings relief and helps the healing process, that in turn can direct the flow from illness to well-being. In my clinical experience I have found again and again that using mental imagery has not only yielded insight into these connections but has speeded up the healing process as well.

My book *Healing Visualizations* describes the biomental connection to 80 ailments and recounts many instances of healing physical disorders through mental imagery. Such current results validate the truth of the ancient model of health care dating back 4,000 or 5,000 years.

The ancient health-care system was wholistic. That is, it portrayed a model incorporating and integrating all the related aspects of the etymological root from the Germanic root "*kailo,*" which, as I indicated earlier, gives rise to the terms *heal, health, whole, holy.* Therefore, there could be no health without taking into account the holy. All healing, bringing us into wholeness, was/is dependent on the inclusion of holiness. The ancients recognized the intricate relationship of biology and spirit. In the Western system that meant making contact with the Great Exchange Being. An instance of this contact and the first written example of how Spirit was brought to bear for healing appears in the Torah,

Diagram III: Miriam (Moses' Sister)
The 5 dimensions of experience

The experience is simultaneous and synchronous, analogous and correlative.

when Moses's sister Miriam is stricken with leprosy, or some sort of "white" skin disorder, after she chastises Moses for neglecting his family in order to attend to the needs of the flock under his guardianship responsible for 600,000 plus strong.

I believe this to be the first historically recorded instance of the social-mental-emotional-physical-moral relationship.

Miriam is clearly angry at Moses. The anger is *reflected* physically by the eruption of the skin disorder deemed by modern interpretation to be leprosy, a prevalent ailment of that time — a toxic response we refer to in the GEMS model as a cleansing reaction, an attempt by the body to remove the offending poisons. She is physically, emotionally, mentally, socially disturbed. She feels rubbed the wrong way — offended by Moses's tending too much to the needs of the group while neglecting the needs of his family. This behavior was getting "under her skin." Alongside the feeling is the moral issue of anger connected usually to the sixth spiritual law — don't murder. Other laws coinciding with anger are the second — setting oneself up as an idol, becoming self-inflated and vain — as well as the ninth law, to not speak ill of another. In this kind of circumstance, we can easily feel insulted when our puffed-upness, the cock-of-the-walk state, is disturbed. She wishes to change Moses into her ideal of what he should be as a leader. In her attachment to this ideal, she is becoming imbalanced physiologically, emotionally, socially, etc.

Moses is well aware of his sister's plight, great healer that he was, and intones five words, the shortest prayer known in recorded history: "God, please heal her, please." His prayer is answered. Miriam is instantly healed. This vignette is a lesson to all of us about the healing power of prayer.[25]

The upshot of this model is that humans constantly reflect their existence in the world as whole beings, functioning physically, emotionally, mentally, socially, and morally/spiritually at every instant. There can never be a separation along the continuum of these five dimensions, which reflects a person's "isness" at every moment of their life experience. To live is to restore "wholeness" (my term) to ourselves.

Establishing these correspondences between the five dimensions of experience immediately catapults us into a state of unity, thereby becoming open to a resource of endless sustenance and healing possibility through a life force infusing our existence, calling us to wholeness and healing. That is exactly what Moses did in uttering his prayer. And it is exactly what the function of prayer is: to call on Spirit to come to our assistance in this life. We are asking Spirit to bring Life to life. In other words, holiness is an integral part of the healing process. By opening up to the holy — that is, to health and wholeness — we become an open system, a receptacle for the reservoir of life force for which there can never be drought. (By the way, according to the Bible, Moses lived to 120.)

Long and eternal life is the push against the entropic, disintegrative effects associated with the flow of linear time. This resistance falls directly in line with the universal law influencing life on Earth. The law that says that every initiative that we undertake must incur a resistance pushing against it, leading to a new result, creation, or form. Therefore,

---

[25] To this end I highly recommend the three books on prayer by Larry Dossey, MD

the disintegrative movement of linear time/aging incurs a resistance of anti-aging, producing a form of healthier individuals cognizant of what must be done to maintain health and ever-increasingly aware of what provides healthy living, resulting in longevity. We see this movement toward "healthier" happening now societally.

At present it is impossible to know where increased life span will take us. That is, how long is longevity? Mr. F.M. 2030 thought we could name the time for each of us in 2030. What I do know is that living in a healthy manner individually reflects itself in a healthier society. In turn, healthy societies fashion a different attitude to life, in which individuals pursue a course of realizing how precious life is. That's what the thrust toward longevity creates inwardly as a propellant toward and rejuvenation of the possibility of eternal life. As we begin to appreciate the holiness of life and the necessity to preserve it, this impulse will take hold in larger and larger measure throughout the world. I think these days are coming, if not already upon us.

The prophet Isaiah describes the advent of a framework in which longevity and eternal life would come to exist. Isaiah's famous words are often paraphrased so: "The lion shall lie down with the lamb [the end of predatory life on all levels], swords shall be beaten into ploughshares [constructive, nutritional, beneficial activity for all will replace the murderous impulse], neither shall we know war anymore [the end of the madness of licensed, wholesale murder]" (Isaiah 1:6, 2:4). Here the prophetic words convey in logical terms the end of the downward cycle of evolution highlighted by the Darwinian ideas of natural selection and survival of the fittest, conveniently used by the predatory world as a rationale to prey upon and enslave the ones who are "not fit." Isaiah's vision, coupled with the new increase of life expectancy, bespeaks an upward turn on the evolutionary wheel where concern for the welfare of self is balanced with concern for the welfare of others as well, in a communal global sense, where freedom for self and others

Laws of Longevity: A Spiritual Perspective

becomes our highest-priority value.

Addressing the meaning of an illness, not just the physical symptoms, can bring about healing. In the following example I use an imagery process called the "one-minute life repair"[26] to facilitate healing:

A middle-aged man complained of bursitis, inflammation of the bursa, in his left shoulder, which had been bothering him for months. It started when someone he deeply loved and respected betrayed him. He realized, on reflection, that he wanted to "smash" or punch the betrayer violently. The bursitis reflected the resistance in himself of committing such an act. He could hardly lift his arm from his side. Taking aspirin gave him the only relief he could find. When I asked him to tell me the opposite of bursitis, he said "rejuvenation" (reflecting how he was feeling about recognizing some signs of aging). "What image is connected to rejuvenation?" I asked. Closing his eyes, he replied, "A field of lilies. Very beautiful." I said, "Feel that rejuvenation and get a physical sensation, if one comes." A faint smile crossed his lips. I said to him to say, "Bursitis, be gone!" and to see it skipping away, disappearing into the horizon. Then to say, "Thank you" and breathe out and open his eyes. He opened his eyes, tested his arm and was able to lift it away from his side without pain. We did the exercise again at his request. Again, the same response. I told him to repeat the process whenever he was aware of experiencing the difficulty until it was resolved to his satisfaction.

A young woman in her mid-30s was experiencing sciatic pain running down her left leg. I asked her who was the "pain in the ass" that she wanted to kick. She absorbed the shocking question for a moment, then replied her brother, with whom she was in conflict at the time. She responded that the reverse of pain was "no pain." With eyes closed,

---

[26] See Gerald Epstein, *The Phoenix Process: One Minute a Day to Longevity, Health and Well-Being* (Nightingale-Conat, 2007), 6-CD set.

she saw emptiness, felt immediate relief of pain, said, "Pain be gone," and saw pain skipping away from her and disappearing. Saying "Thank you," she opened her eyes. The pain has not returned.

A woman in her mid-40s was suffering from chronic eczema. She engaged in the one-minute life repair, following the way outlined here. Carrying out this exercise over the ensuing week, she observed her face clearing up considerably. After one week she met a circumstance that incurred anger she could not express — a chronic characteristic. Voilà, an eruption — perhaps volcanic — broke out on her face. She recognized the connection immediately. By doing this, she finally was able to begin reversing a lifetime habit and to find a reasonable expression of what she was feeling, able to come to an understanding compatible with the individual in this case with whom she was in conflict. After working with imagery and learning to speak up and curb her anger, she was able to reduce the medications she had been taking for the condition substantially.

The point here: Longevity is not simply a matter of only physically based interventions, valuable as they are. Other considerations need to be taken into account for overall healing to occur and be sustained. As healing falls into place, so does self-organization and life extension, in the process of energy conservation. With it comes a feeling of being open, lighter, pain-free, optimistic, happier, glad to be alive, and, often, loving. The laws of longevity and eternal life birth a new awareness of recognizing these relationships — indispensable for maintaining longevity — while at the same time preventing physical deterioration. This new conscious awareness makes taking personal responsibility for our health a priority, a viable possibility, and a meaningful value. While it is not an overnight phenomenon in most instances — there's no magic bullet here — this shift is nonetheless taking place, perceived in incremental steps. It is certainly valuable as well. That awakening to natural health-care measures — including nutrition, exercise like yoga, herbs, homeopathy, and environmental preservation — constitutes a wonderful start to creating a healthy direction to life.

It has occurred to me how awareness of the importance of health is fueled ironically by the excesses brought about by the greed and avarice of societies influenced adversely by the value system of an institution like big business, promoting avarice and greed as primary values. "Greed is good," says Gordon Gecko in the film *Wall Street*. Greed is an unsustainable and destructive value. Its influence can be observed in the worldwide plagues of obesity (a greed for food, based in part, in a fear of destitution) and drug addiction (a greed, based in part, for sensory pleasure, seeking a shortcut to freedom). It commonly takes such excesses to bring us to our senses and then to implement some more balanced response.

Longevity has the meaning of extending life in time. To most people this means merely a delay in the eventual death that overcomes us. However, I think we should look at longevity in the opposite way — as the antechamber to an ever-increasing longevity, leading to an eternal one. Surely if the body can maintain its freshness and resilience, it gives us pause to wonder: "Why can't this resilience continue indefinitely?" It is certainly a legitimate question and a reasonable inquiry.

In sum: Longevity exists. It is accompanied by physical anti-aging interventions that have rational grounds for working biologically and have been shown to work in different parts of the world. What I add to perpetuate the process are those other necessary spiritually based social ingredients.

CHAPTER VI

GEMS: A New Sacred Health-Care Model

*"No problem can be solved from the same level
of consciousness that created it."*
—Albert Einstein

HOLINESS IS THE PIECE MISSING FROM MEDICINE. Without it a whole picture of human existence and human functioning cannot exist. Without it we are left in the rut of focusing squarely only on the physical expression of illness. This is the science of disease model, not a science of whole human beings who are ill. GEMS is a science and practice of becoming a whole human being. This singular focus on disease cannot and has not to date made any significant dent in the cure or healing (they are two different functions) of chronic ailments. The current model is not equipped to deal with the overwhelming incidence of morbidity (sickness) afflicting our highly modernized industrialized society. To fulfill our humanness, our wholeness, healing, and health, we can't pin our hopes only on a "science of disease" that misses the point about facing life and death, as they are the overarching existential question of everyone's life. Such questions cannot possibly be answered by a limited field such as modern medicine, preoccupied as it is by a science of disease (just take a look at the current ICD, the International Classification of Disease, containing 55,000 different unique codes for injuries, diseases and causes of death) rather than by a "science of man" — a phrase first used by a former physician, Robert Rhondell Gibson.

Once we consider the whole human being, we have left the domain of modern medicine in its main sense, alluded to above, and its derivative sciences of psychology, chiropractic, osteopathy, plus all those sundry methods looking closely only at the "science of disease."

The science and practice of becoming a whole human being is an all-inclusive, integrative system that addresses the wholeness of our being here on Earth and includes not only our physical presence but also our emotional, mental, social, and moral/holy qualities not immediately available to study by the criteria applied from the standards that govern the "scientific method." This method is solely concerned with investigating the material, mechanistic, calculable, and measurable world of things that reside in linear-time three-dimensional-space. There is more to life than just the physical.

In short, there is a huge missing piece in the shortsighted paradigm of modern medicine and other forms of therapeutics. An expanded and new paradigm is required, and to this end I have attempted to fill the vacuum built on the root *kailo*, together with the ancient spiritual principles and practices of our Western heritage and a bit of Shakespearean wisdom.

In alignment with the thrust and theme of this book, I have established a "new" unified model of health care: GEMS. It is predicated on an ancient sacred model that existed as a science of human beings and a "science of human becoming" (a term first used, to my knowledge, by Rosemarie Parse, R.N., PhD).

In contrast, the current conventional science of disease medical system relegates the whole human being to bystander status in favor of a diseased organ and the microorganism that causes such pathology.

GEMS brings together two avenues of understanding and wisdom: health and holy. The health part applies practical therapeutic interventions drawn from traditional health-care techniques based in spiritual principles. The holy part provides the educative arm, showing how the sacred works in our everyday lives. It is used to explain how illness happens that prevents us from coming into wholeness and healing where we may discover our true spiritual Self and how to become aware of our real purposes for living. Without the latter, we are left to repeat over and over again in our lives the suffering occurring in its manifold ways that besets us in life as it sets in seemingly after birth.

GEMS is a *whole health* system of treatment, maintenance of health, and prevention of illness. It is also a whole health system that addresses the *whole* human being in all the five critical dimensions of living, *happening simultaneously* at each moment. We have not been trained, nor educated, to see in this way, nor to see to ourselves in this manner. Rather, we have been educated to think consecutively and sequentially, that is, one thing follows another in a pattern of cause-and-effect thinking, in parts that need to be fitted together instead of thinking in wholes (*kailo*) where everything is occurring together as one.

As this "new" way of understanding takes hold in us, it doesn't necessarily replace the conventional model. But it does put the latter in a different context than we are used to. The conventional model can use powerful technological tools for investigating complaints and symptoms of physical distress and ascertaining discovered facts through its testing.[27] Once those are known, GEMS can step in to discover the emotional, mental, social/relational/environmental, and

---

[27] There are other ways of knowing outside modern medical technology. For example, Chinese medicine where pulse and tongue diagnosis is used.

GEMS: A New Sacred Health-Care Model

moral/spiritual connections for a *whole* picture to emerge. When these are uncovered, we are able to introduce corrections to repair the disturbances within them. Applying GEMS, we make these corrections in our thinking, feeling, and behavior (instinctual action), as these are our three fundamental modes of expression of how we live as a whole human being in everyday life (see illustration).

Through this GEMS practice, we reunite as one body and soul. GEMS brings us together as a whole, unitary individual: united in body and soul; in thinking, feeling, behaving; in how we express this unity through five dimensions of lived experience — all guided by an invisible reality.

Another note of interest, especially to me, is that psychiatry would have headed to introducing these other four dimensions had the field not allowed itself to be waylaid by the pressure of the physical medicine system. In succumbing to the need to be accepted, psychiatry shifted from a deep exploration of mental life to a poor Cinderella stepsister of modern medicine, based in pharmacology. In becoming materially focused, it lost its possibility of reaching those heights implicitly embedded in GEMS, where human beings are treated as wholes. Instead, the current model sees only a group of organs (each requiring its own "specialist") that are disconnected from each other, not understanding how one individual organ is connected to another as a complex of mutual interdependency. The mutually interdependent complexity of life is where GEMS leads us. It rights the ship and helps us to steer our own course to the land of *kailo* — whole, health, heal, and holiness.

Sacred medicine is a different sort of healing endeavor from conventional medicine. It is based in a spiritually developed holy system, whereas conventional medicine is predicated on a materialistically based anti-spiritual one. The latter focuses on administrating physically manufactured synthetic pharmaceutical agents from outside the individual's person, whereby the physician arrogates power to him/herself as *the* agent of cure. For sacred medicine, the approach is to place the administrator of the process on the individual sufferer as the agent of his/her own healing. The health-care provider recedes into the background, becoming merely the technician providing tools and steps for the proto-healer to use to discover his or her own source of healing. These tools and methods can range from mental healing to natural physical substances like herbs and homeopathic remedies to mental processes like imagery, hypnosis, and meditation.

Sacred medicine is included in the realm of sacred sciences, all centering on you, the individual, as the source and knower of yourself, being born in the image and likeness of God. We have come to Earth as co-creators here to emulate God's work — or not — as we so choose. We are formed symbols of God's presence on Earth, here to carry out the mission of making a divine life for ourselves, others, and the world in general. In doing so from the healing perspective, we are spiritualizing medicine and health care by reversing the conventional paradigm. As a spiritual medicine, GEMS is a natural outgrowth of the practical application of choosing the path of life.

The GEMS model is a two-pronged method of education of self-care and self-education to shift into a spiritually based way of knowing ourselves and our relationship to health needs.

1) A shift away from making the content of your thought process

important and/or relevant — that is to say, speaking about the stories of your personal or interpersonal experiences, almost all of which detail what happened in the past. In other words, the past is better left behind you. Contrary to psychology, your personal and interpersonal history does not impart meaning to life. Neither does its counterpart, speaking about the as yet uncreated future. Talking or thinking about the past or future doesn't provide any greater understanding, wisdom, self-knowledge, or harmony to life. The same goes for any distressing emotions, feelings, or moods. They are always *attached* to stories about the future or the past and the unanswerable "why." To become an open self-organizing system, we abandon our attachment to the stories of our lives that inevitably lead to fixed conclusions, in themselves closed systems subject to entropic breakdown.

2) A shift to new ways of thinking and feeling where we may find connections and relationships. In detaching ourselves from the incessant commentary, interpretation, judgments, opinions, analysis, speculation, editorializing, and psychologizing, we absent ourselves from inessential chatter and instead think spiritually and receive information from invisible reality. This new way of thought process is called intuition.

The accompanying feelings arising with becoming accustomed to this revised thought pattern are harmonious, such as: love, calm, peacefulness, equanimity, faith, hope, and mental states of balance, sobriety, temperateness, and clarity.

This shift leads us to look at life experience from a different frame of reference. Instead of becoming mired in the stories to find answers to our troubles, we turn to discovery of the sources, the birth of those troubles — what I term the "errors of living." A bevy of them will be described in the next chapter. These errors are inculcated in us by the faulty conditioning, miseducation, and misdirection of life's purpose heaped on us throughout our upbringing. In undertaking the practices in the book, we repurpose our life and reverse this error-laden way of living. We then go further to identify the spiritual mistakes that have birthed these errors of living.

Here are two examples of thinking the GEMS way. Both are acute. One is an emotional issue presenting as an acute response to a chronic issue. The other presents as a physical issue, never encountered before. In chronic illness (chronic response to chronic issue), you can easily discern the five dimensions. In acute conditions, we may see only some of them leap to the forefront. Overall, even in acute conditions we can identify almost all the dimensions.

Sheila
Sheila was in despair, crying hysterically, ruining her life, not seeing a hopeful future for her current relationship, which had now reached a crisis point. She had just moved in with her boyfriend in a small town where she felt isolated and was uncomfortable living with someone 24/7. Over the years she had worked assiduously on her spiritual practice, and a once constricted and constrained life had begun to blossom effervescently through this work. Many benefits came to pass socially, emotionally (she overcame a phobia for good), financially, in her place of living, and in her health. Moving in with her boyfriend was the fruit of her spiritual labor.

Yet despite all the blessings, which included a genuine turn toward invisible reality (that has been generally termed God), she "fell" off the spiritual wagon when she realized how hard it was to give up her independent living. The face of adversity is commonly a test of our faith and fortitude. These adversities are tests we need. How we meet them is the key to our personal evolution and spiritual growth. They are a fact of life.

Sheila's temporary fall away from what she had learned and accomplished is not unusual. Her experience is a widely shared one where we forget our spiritual connection and fall prey to old habits and conditioning. These old acts never really die away, but spiritual practice permits us to take charge of them. The adversities or shocks bring them up again. When we are equanimous and balanced, they appear as blips in our consciousness screen, and we shed them like water off a duck's back. Our response to them is a gauge of our progress along the ladder of self-mastery.

The therapeutic basis of GEMS is to reverse our doubt-driven thinking that is the source of future-based scenarios, distressing feelings, and erroneous judgments, choices, and compulsive actions.

We started focusing on Sheila's false emergency state, i.e., her misconception of this "crisis" as a presumed threat to her existence. This included a litany of beliefs and feelings about what the future held for her love relationship and her overall ability to sustain her current lifestyle in a steadfast way. She was especially concerned about losing Ted, the man she had loved over the past ten years. He was dependent on her financially at present, and was embroiled in what appeared to be a frivolous lawsuit lodged against him by a former employee. By her own account, moving in with him had been a difficult adjustment.

The most important factor for the GEMS direction was for her to get out of her "invented realities" about an illusory future. Instead, she was directed to examine the facts that were apparent right now in front of her, that informed her what actions to take in the moment. That's how it works. The facts beget the appropriate reactions.

We based our get-together on looking at three levels to intervene and make necessary corrections: 1) immediate solution-based reme-

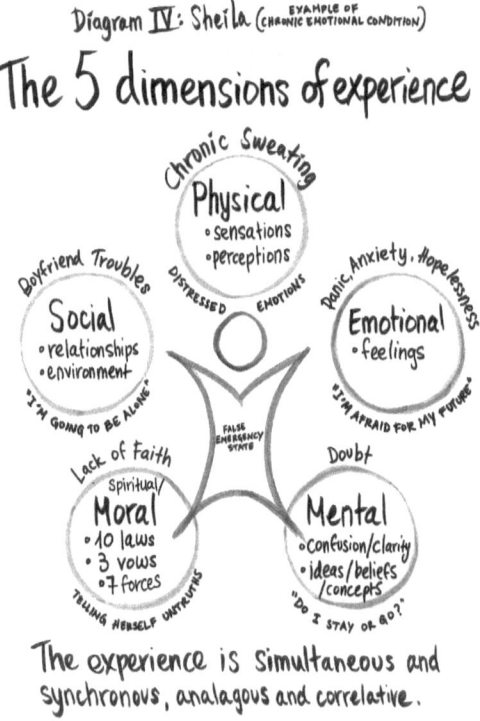

dies, such as mental imagery and other practices contained here; 2) social error(s) of living — these are errors that are universal and apply to all human beings on Earth; 3) spiritual error(s) — these birth the social errors of living and are universal.

Here the remedy was given as two imagery exercises: Tunnel of Love and Crossing the Red Sea, along with a behavioral recommendation to act gratuitously. The first imagery exercise reinforced her hope that her love would endure the changes she was confronting; the second imagery reinforced her faith in taking steps toward personal freedom.

We next examined the facts of the matter: She could not continue to live in this isolated manner away from city life in her own personal space. She decided to move out and not prolong the difficult arrangement she had created "to make him happy." Since his new digs would be far simpler than hers at her new location apart from him, she gave him the furniture he could use from their shared apartment, gratuitously, requiring nothing in return.

We reviewed two main errors of living: mainly the false emergency state and sacrificing herself on the altar of Ted's needs. These errors tie into our moral dimension as well: The illusory thinking about the future and its attendant emotional feelings of despair, hopelessness, anxiety, and worry runs afoul of the spiritual law of not telling the truth, i.e., bearing false witness, including to oneself. Sheila's awareness of what she was doing created an awakening and an accompanying self-composure back to the unity of herself. She remembered the holy, pure nature of her human being. Those disruptive emotions receded. A feeling of hope emerged. Despair lifted. What had seemed impossible suddenly appeared possible.

Paula

Paula was at home. She blacked out momentarily and felt nauseated and threw up. She was scared. What to do? She did mental imagery and the nausea abated. She took her own immediate self-care step, becoming an agent of her own healing, which quieted her fears and worries that she was facing death. She wanted to be "sure nothing was going on." She had an associated headache that her imagery didn't touch. She called an ambulance and went off to the hospital emergency room.

At the hospital an MRI showed what appeared to be a tiny flash of light in her left temporal lobe. She was told she was suffering from a ministroke. All other immediate testing of vital signs and the usual bloodwork were within normal range.

Hearing the "bad news" set off another false emergency state. She countered that she felt well and there was no finding to support the presumptive diagnosis. Again, she became her own authority, her own agent of self-care. Paula felt well. The medical staff encouraged her to stay overnight for observation. She reluctantly accepted. The next morning more tests were done. Nothing abnormal discovered. She was ready to leave when the staff requested she stay another night for more observation and testing. After two days of tests, visits by specialists, observation, vital signs constantly being recorded, and many dollars of accumulated fees, she was told by the main doctor in her "case" that he and the staff were "perplexed" — puzzled that no conclusive evidence could be generated to support the diagnosis, that no signs nor symptoms appeared consonant with the diagnosis. Naturally, not being able to say "I don't know" and living with that ambivalence, they sought to relieve their tension by encouraging her to stay a third day. But she said that was enough and hoped to leave before noon so she wouldn't be charged for an extra day. Days later we spoke. She was feeling fine and had returned to work.

Diagram V: Paula (EXAMPLE OF ACUTE PHYSICAL CONDITION)

The 5 dimensions of experience

- Physical
  - sensations
  - perceptions
  - Blacked out / Fainted
- Social
  - relationships
  - environment
  - earthquake activity
  - Uncongenial Work Environment
  - WHIRLWIND OF ACTIVITY
  - "I NEED TO FIND A WAY OUT"
- Emotional
  - feelings
  - Feeling Pressured
  - "I HAVE TO DO IT ALL"
- Spiritual / Moral
  - 10 laws
  - 3 virtues
  - 7 forces
  - Lack of Faith
  - "TELLING HERSELF UNTRUTHS"
- Mental
  - Confusion / clarity
  - ideas / beliefs / concepts
  - Doubt
  - "DO I STAY OR QUIT"

FALSE EMERGENCY STATE

The experience is simultaneous and synchronous, analagous and correlative.

When we met, she mentioned how hard it was getting back to work after her vacation idyll where she relaxed and shed the tensions of her everyday busy work life. Adapting back to her daily life routine was a chore — so many things and little things to attend to, pressed to complete everything. She really didn't want to go back to work but was not ready to give up this "day job." Paula remarked that she felt like going "on strike against myself," by not resuming her job. She knew her life had taken on a "whirlwind" course in the past days. She also knew she was out of balance, moving too fast, taking on too much.

Together, we took up the error of living in creating a false standard that everything had to be done now…or else. This error is reflective of the moral spiritual one of bearing false witness to herself.

We investigated further the whirlwind, flash of light, ministroke, blackout, headache, nausea, vomiting, all of which subsided rapidly. I alerted her to the relationship between her wanting to go on "strike" against herself and the occurrence of a "stroke." For GEMS understanding, the connection was made between going on strike and having a stroke. Her body is reflecting her mental wish to stay away from going back to her routine life. She now saw the need to take some extra days off to adapt and prepare herself to return to work.

In addition, I was taken by her term "whirlwind," and that she had suffered concussions to that area seven years earlier. When many people call me with acute symptomatology to various parts of the body — and knowing that at least 80 percent of patient visits for symptoms have no discovered organic pathology, plus nothing immediately discernible in the routine day to account for the symptom — I look elsewhere.

I start with climatic disturbances: volcanic eruptions, earthquakes, tornadoes, hurricanes, tropical storms, monsoons, cyclones, El Niño, sun storms, meteor showers, eclipses, full moon, barometric changes indicating rainstorms, space launches, atomic explosions. With these occurrences, many people feel wiped out, enervated, unexplainably tired for no accountable reason or they experience symptoms in areas of vulnerability physically, mentally, and/or emotionally that no remedy seems to help. The answer to these disturbances is to *rest*! — for "this too shall pass." No need to worry. It's happening and is not harmful to us overall. I have found how often I have been correct in this assessment and how comforting and reassuring to the sufferer when I can alleviate their anxiety, fear, and worry.

In Paula's situation, I discovered that North Korea had set off an underground nuclear bomb at the time of her symptoms "explosion" that was also accompanied by a 5.3 earthquake.

Living on this singular organism called Planet Earth, we are all subject to vibratory alterations and turbulence no matter where in the world it is happening. Our relationship to nature and to the cosmos is a unitary one. We all participate together at each moment. As nature and the cosmos go, so we all go, and vice versa. All of it has been created by God. Distance does not determine our response. The more sensitive we become intuitively, mentally, and consciously, the more acutely aware we become attuned. The 80 percent are responding but have not been taught about the climatic, cosmic, and human-made disturbances.

My teacher Colette studied for many years at Sorbonne University in Paris. In the course of her studies in a number of subjects, including psychology and sociology, she took classes in the effects of the near and far influences on our overall health. Near and far constituted climatic (near) and cosmic (far).

In 1980 I suffered from acute right lower-quadrant pain lasting some days. I visited an MD, who examined me and determined he felt a mass there. He recommended I see a surgeon for further evaluation. The surgeon examined me, found nothing on the order of a mass, and agreed with me to keep an eye on the condition. If it got worse, it might warrant a surgical look.

The pain persisted. The next day I received a call from Jerusalem. It was Colette's first cousin Renée, who was visiting and had an apartment directly across the street from Colette. She told me there was extremely heavy volcanic activity going on at Mount St. Helens in the U.S. Pacific Northwest, and that I was responding to it. I checked it out and discovered this to be true. The eruptions were subsiding and so did the abdominal pain. Within the next two days, no pain, "fit as a fiddle."

Paula's doing quite nicely so far. She used the shock experience to take stock of her life, to reconsider what was of true value for her life. Out of the self-contemplation, she chose to fulfill unfinished business. She had originally wanted to be an actress and chose New York City to get into show business. She felt daunted trying to break in and left this pursuit and now, after 25 years, decided to write a one-woman show and become the performer she had always wanted to be. This ministroke galvanized her intention to take active steps to learn this craft while still earning a living at her regular job. On follow-up one year later, there has been no recurrence of the original condition.

Paula is functioning at a high level in her work and in her spiritual life practices. Recently she experienced the unity of all things, and the "moment" preexisting the creation of all form and with it, knowing God and the "truth" of immortality in our spiritual work together.

Amidst the endless strife seeming to beset us on Earth, ending in death and dying for each of us, there is an alternate path hidden from our notice called the "Path of Life," encompassing within it order, bliss, eternal life. I aim to impart this path, to plant a new seed in the garden of human awareness that is the force of salvation for all of us and for our planet. It is a gift awaiting our reception. It's there for the taking, and *We Are Not Meant to Die* offers a way for us to be recipients. The GEMS class is now in session.

We Are Not *Meant* to Die

SECTION II

The Death Plan: How Death Works

"In embracing a spiritual direction, we become acutely aware of the need to live a simple and pure life. We are to be kind to ourselves as we are all prone to errors and mistakes. The beauty of those errors is that they serve as the "hidden teachers" (my phrase) to remind us to make the corrections to keep our lives uncontaminated, unpolluted, cleansed, bringing goodness, truth, love, peace, and harmony to ourselves and others."

CHAPTER VII

Theater of Life

*"All the world's a stage,
And all the men and women merely players."*
— WILLIAM SHAKESPEARE, *AS YOU LIKE IT*, II:7

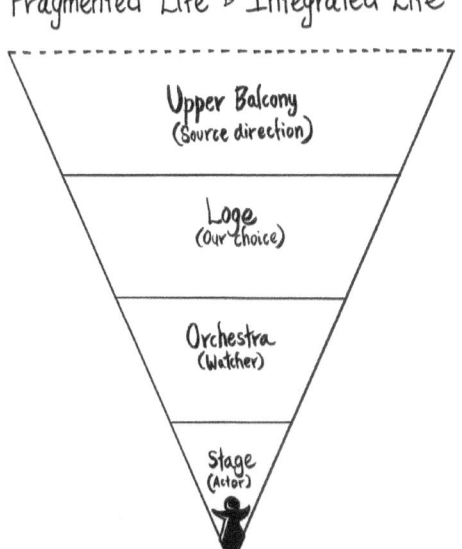

The Theater of Life

THE WORLD WE INHABIT IS A THEATER OF LIFE. In leading a spiritual life, we want to use the dramas of our daily-life situations to prod us "to remember" — to awaken, to recall our wholeness and divine connections as well as to act — "to go and do."

Our Theater of Life (See Diagram I) is a stage with three tiers – an orchestra, loge, and upper balcony. On the stage is the actor/us performing — thinking, feeling, and behaving in the world. In the orchestra is the audience/us observing the actor/us. Above the orchestra in the second tier is the loge, occupied at first by forces that disturb and disrupt who we create through feelings of anxiety, worry, or fear. We call these disrupters *false selves,* inner terrorists, or inner parasites that enslave or drain our life energy. It is here the social errors of living are birthed that interfere in our growth and personal evolution. Our job is to dislodge these saboteurs and the errors they perpetrate so we may become free. The choice is ours — live with terrorists or replace them with allies, helpers, and guardian angels.

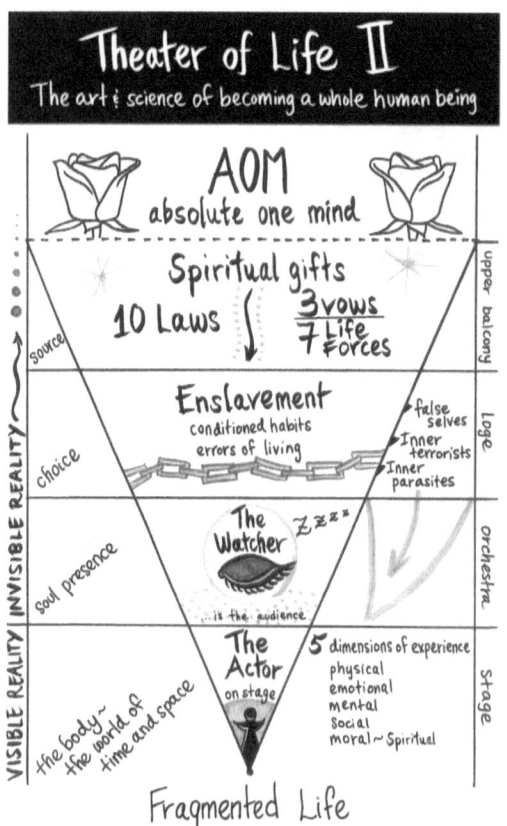

In the top tier, the upper balcony, resides a reflection of Spirit in the "form" of gifts of life that are bestowed on us to become whole, free, and healed and to shed our enslavement. The theater has no roof, but it is a direct opening to the heavens. The high balcony is where we are shown the possibility of how to reach our Source, the Light of God, to become one with the Absolute One Mind. That's what is awaiting us.

Looking in more detail at this Theater of Life (See Diagram II), we see the drama unfolding as a fragmented and conflicted life.

The Stage
As actors, our very being weaves together five threads — physical, emotional, mental, social, moral — and as actors, we find ourselves to be sufferers. It is the way of life on Earth.

The Orchestra
In the orchestra we find the audience or "watcher" asleep. The watcher is our True Self or Soul presence, who has been distracted, hypnotized, or lulled to sleep by what's going on in the loge.

The Loge
The lower balcony is occupied by a rogue band of inner terrorists (i.e., false selves) that are carousing there, unregulated, wild, undisciplined, texting, talking, preoccupied with past stories or future worries. They are disruptive, creating disturbances in the orchestra, distracting the audience (i.e., the watcher) from paying attention to the play and the actors. In turn, the actors are influenced by the inattention and seeing those terrorists hurling banana peels and tomatoes into the orchestra and booing, catcalling the actors. The actors can't remember their lines, and the connection between actor and watcher is broken. Put another way, the audience/soul is separated from the actor/body, who in turn is now at the mercy of the inner terrorists.

Those inner terrorists are busy doing what they do best: enslaving us. They create errors of living and veils of obscurity that block our awareness and attention from the spiritual gifts in the high balcony.

Errors are imbalances, tipping the scales, so to speak, created by unchecked, unregulated desires attached to false beliefs. We are prone to creating imbalances and complications. These all abound out of unmet desires orbiting around a central nucleus. This nucleus is called the *False Emergency State*. All maladies stem from this experience of false emergencies, which account for roughly 99.9 percent of all emergencies faced by us in life. A false emergency is any life situation we encounter that we misperceive or misconceive as some form of threat. The threat can be external or internal. These false emergencies abound in our day-to-day doings. The emergency state induces biological and physiological breakdowns, ultimately leading to death. I became wise to this monumental (for me) understanding through the teachings of Dr. Robert Rhondell Gibson.

There are three major seed sources of all our errors that I call AIDs: Attachment, Insufficiency, and Doubt that lead to our slavery. These seeds, along with their derivatives, account for all false emergencies that in turn become the source for all physical, emotional, mental, social, moral disturbances, the "lot of suffering."

Here is the list of the major errors that literally take the life out of us: greed, grudges, guilt, self-deprecation, shame, fantasies, distressing emotions, false beliefs, suggestions, projecting into the future or dwelling in the personal past, wanting to change what is to what ought to be, expectations, and standards. All are predicated on those three basic seed functions.

Why these errors occur takes us to the Upper Balcony of Spiritual Gifts and the Absolute One Mind from which everything is birthed.

The Upper Balcony — Spiritual Gifts
Looking above the loge we find the Upper Balcony. Here resides the spiritual Gifts supplied by Invisible Reality to energize and sustain us with the fuel for life.

The Gifts include Ten Laws (commandments) and the Three Virtues derived from them: obedience, poverty, and chastity. Springing from this source are also the Rainbow of Seven Divine Forces converted into energies serving to direct our lives. They are: Love, Faith, Hope,

Will, Intuition, Imagination, and Light. Taken together, they teach us the practices directed toward wholeness, healing, health, and holiness. These are called the practices of detachment from attachments to the man-made world replaced by a loving attachment to the Invisible Reality. The Ten Laws provide the spiritual truths that govern our life on Earth, to live a balanced, contented, and harmonious existence. They are translated to us as actions, to be fulfilled in the moment, either physically or mentally as the Ten Commandments. The Three Virtues derived from the Ten Laws succinctly address our attitudes to adopt in our thinking, feeling, and instinctual/behavioral life. The Rainbow of Seven Divine Forces are showered on us continuously. They form the bridge between ourselves and God so we may fulfill the sacred contract (known as the covenant) to "love God with all our hearts, soul, and might" (Deut. 6:5).

Love, faith, imagination, and intuition are practices that quash the inner terrorists. Hope and light propel us forward in our desire for the ongoing continuation of life to reverse the apocalyptic messages that bombard us daily of the end of the world. As we practice these unconditional ways of being with our neighbors, we attune ourselves to higher levels of spirit.

Likewise, as we quiet the inner terrorists by correcting our social errors of living, by engaging in the practices of reversing, we find that the seven forces are more readily available to us.

The rub concerning these spiritual gifts is that they can be misused, perverted to become "weapons" used to dominate and enslave others. In fact, all the errors of living can be traced back to the nonadherence to the spiritual gifts. When we are inattentive or misuse or purposefully disregard the gifts, we birth the errors of living that in turn birth our daily problems. The excesses of the Seven Divine Forces beget errors; for instance, smothering love, blind faith, willfulness, hopelessness — all create trouble. Fantasy can be mistaken for creative imagination, the sun's light misconstrued for God's light, and intuition misperceived as counterintuitive. Calling into play the opposites of the Three Virtues brings destructive behavior: greed in lieu of restraint (poverty); addiction in lieu of sobriety (chastity); murder; tyrannical or dictatorial behavior in lieu of humility (obedience). Not following the Ten Laws can spell ruination for individual and communal lives, including war and the heinous destruction it brings.

Everything starts from the top down in spiritual life, just as it does in our everyday work and family life. For example, in sports teams, the worse the ownership, the worse the general managers, coaches, and team members. When heads of companies — CEOs — malfunction, the factory and workplace often go down the tubes. Strong leaders make for strong families, corporations, and organizations. In spiritual groups, strong leaders bring cohesion and a sense of mutual purpose, respect, and friendship to those communities. In the East, Zen rōshis, Tibetan lamas, and Indian gurus enjoy that position. In the West, God takes the reins as overall supreme leader. When the leader's emissaries here on Earth misuse their sacred position, harmony disappears and disharmony ensues within the group, a rupture that is difficult, if not impossible, to repair.

In embracing a spiritual direction, we become acutely aware of the need to live a simple and pure life. We are to be kind to ourselves as we are all prone to errors and mistakes. The beauty of those errors is that they serve as the "hidden teachers" (my phrase) to remind us to make the corrections to keep our lives uncontaminated, unpolluted, cleansed, bringing goodness, truth, love, peace, and harmony to ourselves and others. We recognize we are all brothers and sisters, the many in the One, as the ancient Roman mystic Plotinus framed it nearly 2,000 years ago.

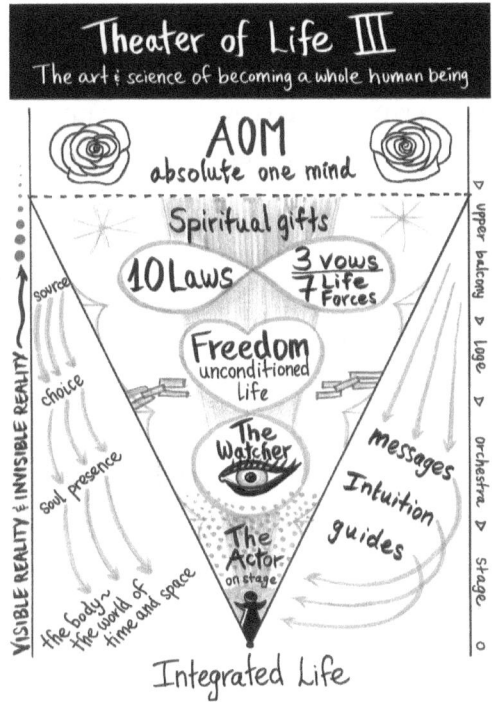

The Absolute One Mind

The Absolute One Mind is the ALL *that* is and the ALL *there* is. It is sometimes referred to as God, cosmic consciousness, universal, invisible, or vertical reality, or the "that without end." Though not quantifiable, it is the ultimate concrete reality of existence of which we are its abstraction! Abstract usually means to take away from — thus we are all abstractions from the "ALL there is."

The Integrated Life

Here in the Theater of Life III (see Diagram III), we are awakening, actively searching for integrated wholeness or *kailo*. No longer are we at odds with ourselves, fragmented, or asleep. No longer are we exclusively focused on solving the current set of problems we face. Instead, we go beyond problem-solving (which we definitely do not neglect) to a higher level of understanding and knowing. We go from problem-solving to self-knowing, and then to a higher level of self-knowing, understanding, and wisdom to accomplish more profound integration, which is a portal to the unity of our oneness, reuniting body and soul, and reuniting our selves then with One — that's integration!

For example, if faced with ill health, we stop focusing on the diagnostic names of diseases to search for the presumed causes of them. Causes, in this context, are seeking to find something or someone else to blame. We habitually lay blame. It makes us feel good to release like that. But here we are not interested in blaming or naming that supposed culprit (bipolarity or cancer, for example). Instead, we begin to look into ourselves to discover the errors we have wittingly or unwittingly committed that have taken a toll on us in these five dimensions of living comprising our human experience, which feed into the false states of emergency.

Your awakened "watcher" (in the audience) becomes the active guardian of yourself, the actor. The watcher, now sentry on duty 24/7, reports to our higher Source of Wisdom all that transpires in your theater of life stemming from the injurious effects of the false selves/terrorists. In turn our Higher Source of Wisdom sends information to the actor on how to proceed to take health-giving actions that curb the false emergency states. The information comes to us inwardly as perceived messages of the Seven Forces, Ten Laws, and Three Virtues as flashes of knowing, feeling, and acting. Once we curb the false emergency state, we are able to discern the correct actions to take to repair ourselves in our fivefold realm of beingness.

In reaching an integrated life, our job is to clear the way to climb the ladder of self-mastery to reach that Edenic existence we yearn for. We make sure to not put anything in between ourselves and the Light of the One. In so doing, we clear away the errors of living and repair the discontinuity between ourselves as actor and as audience/watcher. We fuse those two energies to regain our wholeness, remembering ourselves and restoring the memory lapses we've created by allowing the inner terrorists to hold sway over us. Bit by bit, the hooligans are pushed out of the loge and replaced by helpers and guardians who relay and amplify these heavenly messages.

Each correction we make reinforces our primal memory of our heavenly Father and Mother. When we remember our Origin, we are given a "strong hand and outstretched arm" (Exod. 6:6) to take us out of the bondage of enslaved mentality, enslaved emotion, and enduring attachment that hold us in captivity that leads to decay and death.

As the actor in this drama of life — and death — we also pay attention to our tapestry, the fabric of life encircling us as our bodysoul, to make sure it remains intact, that we repair any threads out of order, sew up any tears, iron out any wrinkles. We know this cloth is out of order when we experience disturbances or imbalances along the lines of one or more of these five threads. We do know that wherever there is a thread out of alignment, the other four are involved. They all reflect or mirror each other. We can be certain that this is the truth of the matter. They cannot be divorced from each other. Now that we understand the framework of our Theater of Life, we'll take a look at the errors of living in more depth, first exploring the physiology of death.

CHAPTER VIII

The Physiology of Death: The False Emergency State

IN TRUTH, ALL THE ERRORS OF LIVING CONTRIBUTE to enslavement and loss of freedom, embodied by the physiology of death. These errors lead to a chronic condition that besets us called the *false emergency state*, the core of the errors of living.

Let's start with a definition. What is a false emergency? It is a lived experience in which we falsely believe we are facing a threat to our existence. The threat can be blatant, it can be subtle. It can be here this minute, it can be looming on the horizon. It doesn't matter. Whenever we sense or feel a distressing experience as a threat to our well-being, almost invariably we are facing a false emergency.

Here are two simple examples. You are running to reach a bus before it closes its doors. Thoughts are racing through your mind. "I can't miss the bus. I'll miss my appointment. I'll be in such trouble." This is felt in your body as an emergency.

Another example. A glass falls from your hand, and as it drops to

The Physiology of Death: The False Emergency State

the floor, you feel a sense of threat and blame yourself, for you are not the kind of person to whom such clumsy and inept things happen. Your image of self is chipped — not much, of course, and maybe not for long, but still momentarily chipped. And for those moments, it's an emergency.

We viscerally respond — a shock response. And then we create a story, a misconception on top of our misperception. "Oh, it's a threat to me. It's going to hurt me. I could step on the broken glass." We tell ourselves stories about what is going to happen. It's future talk, and we are in fabrication land, Illusionville. And we pile story upon story about the awful things that are going to happen to us in the future. You can see that the false emergency state is a projection into a time, place, and circumstance that simply does not exist. You become untethered to the present, to truth, and allow your fear-laden fabrications to take you wherever they go.

A more precise understanding of emergency experience is to put it in the context of stress and distress. When external shocks or stresses show up, they are most often received as an emergency, some sort of threat. We respond to the stressor with either equanimity or distress. The latter response is called a false emergency state. When the response is one of equanimity, equilibrium, balance, stability, or sobriety, there is no false emergency or distress state registered.

In the distress state, our physiology and biology begin a process of being worn down. Over time the repeated false emergency response wears out our physio-biological systems to the point of decay, decomposition, and ultimately death.

False Emergencies vs. True Emergencies

As experiences, all emergencies are real. But not all are true.

The fact is, most of the so-called emergencies that any of us experience — 99.5 percent, minimally — are false emergencies. It is very rare to be involved in a true emergency situation. The model for a true emergency is when someone presses a gun to your head and threatens to blow out your brains. This can be considered a true emergency because your life appears to be genuinely at stake. As you may see, it is almost unheard of for there to be a true emergency in one's life, in the sense that one's life is at stake at that moment.

Even so, I think I can fairly claim that a large percentage of you now reading this book have had at least one experience that you perceived or defined as an emergency stressor, at least one, between the time you got up in the morning and the time you sat down to read the book. But was it a true or a false emergency? And, more importantly, why does it matter?

Here's why. If it's a false emergency, then, of course, we are telling ourselves an untruth. We are fabricating to ourselves that some disturbance constituted a true threat to our life existence, or at least a threat disturbing our nondisturbed state, comfort, pleasure. But so what? So what if some of us view much of our lives as one emergency after another? Here's what. Here we come to the heart of the matter.

The Physiology of Emergencies: The Physiology of Death
In all emergencies, false or true, we go through the same normal physiological reaction called the fight-or-flight-or-freeze response.[28]

---

[28] This acute stress response was first described by Walter Bradford Cannon and later by Hans Selye. In recent years, the theory, now deemed Polyvagal Theory by Stephen Porgess, PhD, has been expanded from fight-or-flight to include a third response called the "Freeze" response. If neither of the former strategies is available to us, we immobilize in an attempt to survive. The goal of all three strategies is to survive the emergency until we can return from an emergency to a state of rest, social engagement, openness, and groundedness in the present. Further models have expanded this theory even further to include a fourth response strategy called "Fawn." Within the context of the discussion about escaping false emergency states, the response strategy chosen is not relevant, and our focus is on intentionally navigating normal stressors we encounter in modern daily life, recognizing that they are not true emergencies.

The Physiology of Death: The False Emergency State

When we perceive a threat to our lives — an emergency — we can fight the person or the event that is the source of the emergency, we can flee from it and run away, go unconscious, or lapse into shock and immobility, as in the "freeze" response. But with either "fight or flight" or "freeze," our body gears up neurologically, hormonally, and muscularly in the same way to prepare us for any of the three responses. The thyroid puts out thyroid hormone, the pituitary puts out the pituitary hormones. The pancreas puts out insulin, the liver puts out glycogen. Adrenaline comes out of the adrenal glands, including the component of noradrenaline, the most dangerous component of adrenal activity. Steroids come from the adrenal cortex, especially cortisol. Lactic acid is coming from the muscles that have tightened up, creating a neuromuscular tensing.

You get the picture, even if you don't know the exact purpose of each of these elements. Basically, the body makes you ready to do something.

Now, if you are facing a true emergency, whether you respond with fight, flight, or freeze, you deal with the emergency, and your energies are released. Even in the case of a freeze response during a true emergency, your body goes through a sympathetic action/readiness state to release energy before being able to return to a parasympathetic resting state. This is what is important: Your energies are released. But of course this cannot happen with a false emergency, for the obvious reason that there is no emergency to deal with, so there is no real outlet for them. For example, you are sitting in the middle of your living room waiting for that "important" call that doesn't come. Becoming a virtual pharmacy, your body fills with the chemicals you are producing, because the body believes you when you signal you are facing an emergency. The body cannot distinguish between a true emergency

---

See Stephen Porges's 2009 article in the Cleveland Clinical Journal of Medicine (doi: 10.3949/ccjm.76.s2.17) for more information.

and a false emergency. That's *your* job, and every time you say "Emergency! Emergency!" when there is none, your body still goes through the virtually instantaneous process of preparing to fight or flee — and you have no one to fight, not even a windmill, and nowhere to run. But you are ready to go! Your body is humming, your eyes are bugged open — all because you saw on television that your stocks lost a lot of money or because you received a phone call telling you that the person who hired you at work has just been fired and you may lose your job; or because someone received a promotion and you didn't; or because of a thousand other reasons, **not one of which is a true threat to your life's existence at this moment.**

Here's where we come to the damaging physical effects of conjuring up a false emergency. Since the chemical materials in our body cannot be released, they break down and become metabolic toxic elements, waste products in the system. Loaded up with these poisonous products that have to be discharged, we begin to feel uneasy, jittery, on edge, maybe anxious. There is a natural movement in us to seek balance, and our bodies want to help us discharge these products, calling on one or another cellular response to get rid of them. There are many possibilities. We can experience this response as nausea, vomiting, diarrhea, frequent urination, pain, soreness, sweating, or many other kinds of what are in reality *cleansing responses.*

In conventional medical circles, I should note, these kinds of responses are viewed as dangerous symptoms of bodily disorder. This is a faulty designation. The responses are ways that the body is cleansing itself of its self-created poisons in its natural movement toward balance.

Fine, you might think. But watch what happens. The body is using its natural sanitation system to clean out the debris that the poisons are creating — the urinary system, the intestinal system, the lymphatic system, and so on. When this is happening, we often feel that something is wrong — that the diarrhea is "not good," the pain is not good,

The Physiology of Death: The False Emergency State

the repeated urination is not good. We react with dismay. We apply our emergency way of thinking, and all at once we have another emergency. The feeling that something is not good intensifies. The sense of emergency heightens. The cellular system keeps trying to do its job. The process is like an unending loop, and over time it happens enough to create a chronic condition.

In this process, the cellular organ systems begin to age. They get tired, start to break down, and function less adequately. What takes place in these systems is what we call decay: The cells lose their structure, they become malformed, the whole cellular configuration changes.

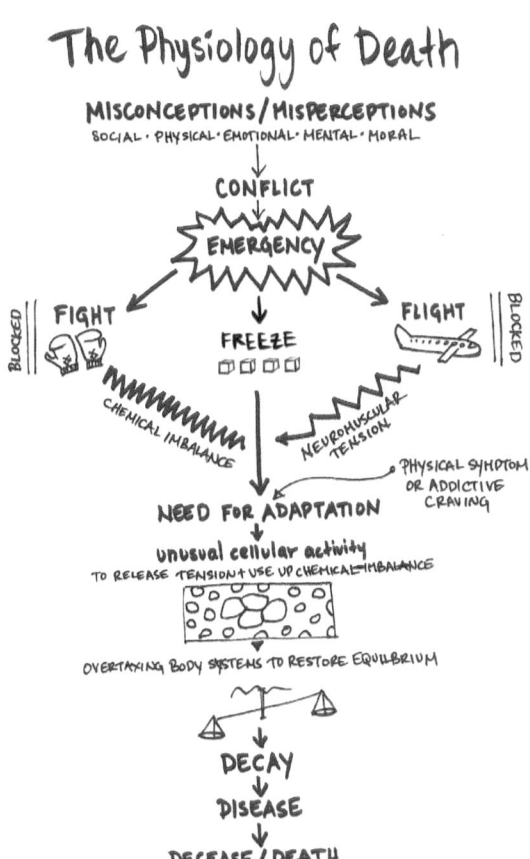

Here, too, conventional medicine offers a faulty designation. What we see as the breaking down of the cellular system, the decay of the cellular system, conventional medicine describes as one or another "disease." I think we can see in this atomization of a broad cellular phenomenon one reason why some so-called diseases have proven so resistant to treatment with atomized Western medicine... a misapprehension of the situation as it actually exists.

Now, the process I have outlined for you, of false emergency building on false emergency and the cellular cleansing system being in constant motion to clear the debris created by the body's inability to fight or flee, ultimately spirals down into the physiology of death. What I have outlined is the body wearing out because we invent dangers and threats of false emergencies and the body reacts accordingly.

Going deeper: What has generated in us the false emergency state?

The answer has two parts. One comes to us from outside, commonly where we have been conditioned and educated to consider as emergencies situations imposed on us by time. This conditioned time-determined state is a very common source of "emergencies." We feel that in getting something done, we must meet a time standard or limit that has been imposed on us — and when we don't, it's an emergency!

We live in the present but are pushing ourselves into and worrying about the future. We *must* get it done, we are *supposed* to get it done, if we don't get it done, then this "bad" thing will happen. We can also see that as long as we are thinking this way, about warding off an emergency that will surely come if we don't finish this or that by a certain fixed time, we are already living in an emergency state, wearing ourselves down.

But from a more general point of view, the second aspect of the false emergency state is what we impose on ourselves by our misconceptions and misperceptions, incubated by our education and institutions. These are covered in the next section.

Who of us has not suffered from self-created emergencies? Don't berate yourself. We all create inside-generated emergencies. How we handle this state is the key to whether we enter into the physiology of life or death.

How to know you are in an emergency state.

You know because you *observe* your feeling state and your thinking. You feel distressed, and your thinking is about the past or the future.

The Physiology of Death: The False Emergency State

You observe ways in which you are feeling a sense of imbalance and unevenness in yourself.

It's a matter of being willing to look at yourself, to become vigilant, a self-observer, to take stock of how you are feeling physically, what your emotional state is, what your mental state is, whether your grammar puts you in the future. For all intents and purposes, everything is a created or false emergency until proven otherwise. There is nothing but false emergency states all day long with all of these projections going on in every single one.

A true emergency has an action in the moment connected with it. A friend of mine lived in Israel for a while, and she was there when fighting was going on and people were shooting at her. She told me that when the bullets come, you duck. That's a stimulus response — you duck. You take the action, you don't make up stories about it.

You may notice numerous instances where there is no distressing feeling with a true emergency state. One often feels a state of dynamic balance, a state of neutralization — of just being — as if all conflicts and difficulties have evaporated. It is a feeling of honing in and focusing in the moment, nothing more. There is no elaboration, there is no story, and a certain sense of peace comes from that. One acts according to being in the moment fortified by the truth of the matter. A man stuck a gun into the abdomen of a friend. "Your money or I'll kill you!" was the demand. My friend, maintaining his composure and balance, broke out in laughter. The man ran away. Was that a true emergency? Certainly, from all appearances it was.

In contrast, in a false emergency, we are being driven by a story — an if-then story. For example, *if* I don't find a new job, *then* my family will starve. No! If we need to support our family, we create the *intention* to support our family. No concern about controlling the outcome of that action. The rest of it is stories, opinions, rationalizations. The fact that we feel "driven" is a sign that we are living a false emergency that we have created. Based on an untruth, it is bound to lead to greater difficulties powered by doubt for getting that job. The universe will come in and help us if we are in truth. But when we are "driven" by our invented stories, we fill the space with our clutter, and the universe has no room to make itself felt.

If a response is geared to the moment, as it is in a true emergency, then all the feelings that pour out in response to a false emergency — anxiety, worry, fear, panic, guilt — are cut from the moment. We extract ourselves from the web of linear time. We are dealing in no-time: no past, no future. We are only of the instant. And in this sense, when there is no past and no future, only what is, there is no emergency. Another example of a chronic false emergency state is PTSD. This is evident in war veterans who display imbalanced thinking, feeling, and behavior connected with this syndrome.

Did you know that during the Holocaust, the Hasidim danced into the oven and sang as they were herded into the gas chamber? Was that a true emergency? Not for them, in the sense that they treated it as what it was. No stories. Simply facing the moment and finding the transcendent third point between fight or flight in praying and singing to God.

Donald, a strong, robust 78-year-old man with all his marbles, was diagnosed two years ago with cancer that affected his liver, duodenum, pancreas, maybe spleen, aorta, hepatic vein — all happening after "losing" his wife to Alzheimer's. "She was my friend, wife, sister, mother, and daughter."

I explained to him the consistent correlation between suffering a loss and the onset of cancer. I also related to him the correspondence between the various organs where lesions were found and their emotional equivalents: liver reflects anger; pancreas reflects bitterness; spleen reflects humorless/seriousness; duodenum reflects indigestible

The Physiology of Death: The False Emergency State

situation; aorta reflects the flow of life; hepatic vein reflects feelings of stagnation. He commented that he was engaged and full of hate toward his wife for "failing" him (liver); found the new shift in his life indigestible and nauseating (duodenum); lost the humor in his life (spleen); saw his life ebbing away (aorta); life became bitter, no more sweetness (pancreas). All of these feelings were pouring out of him, corroborating each and every analogy to these organs. He was glad to vent them at this point and said that he felt calmer than he had in a very long time, and that all the muscles in his back suddenly became relaxed. He said he was always the little boy in their 45-year marriage. She was his protector and sheltered him from life. Donald finally had to grow up over these two years and take over all the responsibilities of their home life as an adult.

Yes, he felt guilty about wanting her out of his sight, having to sit there 24/7, watching her decline in front of him and feeling the "burden" of the continuous care she required. He recognized the emotional turbulence in the recent past and came to an acceptance of the situation as it is and the need for her care in a facility better equipped to handle the situation. I explained the conflict between his wanting to change what is to what he felt it ought to be. After all, wanting to change the present *is* into what it *ought to be* — the future — is a central source of all social disturbance existing between us.

We came to a central explanation of the creation of this decaying process called "cancer," based in the false emergency state, always products of misconceptions and/or misperceptions tied to projections into the future, again a projection into what isn't, what is uncreated.

Parsing out the false emergency state, we see three layers operating here: (1) I'm dependent on my wife to take care of me, which she no longer can. (2) Now the tables are turned; now I have to take care of her — I am resentful, tired, and in chronic distress. These two chronic emergency states are reflected in the decay of the body called "cancer."

(3) With the cancer, there is a new emergency called "I'm going to die." Embedded is a belief that "I can't adapt to what is in front of me . . . it seems impossible to cope, and I would rather die."

There is an irony in the development of bodily decay like this. It is true about all illness and symptomatology: There is an upside and a downside. In this case the "cancer" cure as an awakener allows Donald to grow up and discover a real possibility and potential to become a mature, genuine, authentic, autonomous human being, no longer a child — even at that age. Here a golden opportunity presented itself. The imbalance is not an enemy, more a friend. His wife could no longer sustain the dependencies they created. She lost strength, and simply, to his mind, she bailed out, leaving him in an existential moment: to follow her or choose his own life. Cancer represents the call to death yet gives one at the same instant a call to life.

He started off our meeting by stating that he was feeling hopeful *for* his future, not an illusory or delusional belief of hope *about* his future. He wasn't merely wishing for a continuance of life but experiencing a genuine inner light that is hope for continued life and wanting to do something to fulfill that hope.

As we uncovered all of this in 45 minutes, I concluded our session by giving him an imagery exercise for healing cancer called "The Tornado" and prescribed the rhythm of its use. His response to all we went through in less than an hour was "The muscles of my face have relaxed. I'm sitting up straight and my eyes are wide open." We finished where we started: with a feeling of hope and of eyes wide open about looking forward to life.

He continued life for another three years, keeping the cancer at bay and his hopes up, as he had first experienced three years earlier at our first and only meeting.

The Physiology of Death: The False Emergency State

> IMAGERY EXERCISE

THE TORNADO: FOR CANCER HEALING

Sit up straight in a chair with uncrossed arms and legs. Close your eyes. Breathe out long, slow exhalations through your mouth, each followed by a brief or normal inhalation through the nose. Do this three times. Imagine a dark funnel tornado cloud in the distance. Hear the whistling of the wind getting stronger and stronger as the tornado approaches you, until finally it spirals through you, carrying away all tumor and tumor cells out of your body. Breathe out one time, and hear the rush of torrential rain. See it swirling through your body, cleaning out any remaining debris of cancer cells and tumor that may be remaining, carrying them out of your body. Breathe out one time, and hear the chirping of birds, signaling the end of the storm. Everything is peaceful and quiet. The sun is shining brightly above, sending its rays of health-giving sunlight to you, permeating and penetrating into your body, filling you with its health-giving and strengthening light; know that it prevents the growth of any more of those dark abnormal cells. Be aware that healing is taking place. Breathe out and open your eyes. Do it each morning in the early morning, late afternoon, and before bed for some seconds regularly for 21 days.

Dis-Emergency State: Stopping False Emergencies

Can the habitual initiation of this process be stopped? Can we stop reacting to distress or disturbance or a thwarted activity — being stuck in a traffic jam, for example — as if it were some sort of threat when it is entirely self-invented? You will not be surprised that I believe we can. What's more, I believe when we do so, we can reverse the physiology of death so that it becomes the physiology of life, restorative and regenerative.

Let's go back to the question we asked originally. What is the difference between a false emergency and a true emergency? An emergency, we saw, is a perceived or conceived threat — to some degree — to our life existence. We took as a model of a true emergency someone holding a gun to our head. The question we have to ask our self when thinking we are facing an emergency is simple: Is what is happening to me a true or a false emergency? You have to be honest with yourself, you have to be frank. Look at the situation and ask: Is this a true threat? Is there a gun to my head or is my life at stake? If there is no gun, you answer your question honestly and frankly that the situation in this moment is a false emergency. I emphasize being honest and frank, because it is not so easy at first to see that what we almost instinctively react to as an emergency is in fact a fiction we have created. It is fake news!

Once you see this, how do you acknowledge it? You say to yourself that you are creating a false emergency. You use your own name and say, "So-and-so is creating a false emergency." You say that there is an untruth here, there is no emergency, that the emotional state connected with a false emergency, like anxiety, fear, worry, etc., has no value, and that you are fabricating a story about your life's existence at this moment. Or you simply say, "fake news," or "propaganda," or "inner terrorist," or whatever may come to you.

When you do this, the emergency state stops, and what happens after that is a natural unfoldment showing you how the universe is coming to help you directly in a life-affirming way. It often happens instantaneously. There is no chemical imbalance. There is no neuromuscular tension. There are no uneasy feelings. There is no unusual cellular response that needs to take care of an imbalanced metabolic state. Finally, there is no decay — and, I maintain, no movement toward death. It follows all of a piece. Again, we are creating order out of disorder.

By simply asking whether or not a situation is a true emergency, we have the capacity to stop our own false emergencies. As you do

The Physiology of Death: The False Emergency State

this, you begin to find life energy opening up in another way, because you have participated in stopping the physiological aging process and called in the life force.

Seeing Your Emergencies and Finding Faith
I want to explain another approach in the effort to stop creating emergencies, one that enables us to *see* what the particular emergency you are in looks like.

Francine came to me quite concerned about her financial life. She was not earning enough to take care of her rent, and she was also falling into some tax difficulty. She was worried that a tax penalty would be placed on her. She told me she saw herself becoming destitute, a bag lady out on the street, with no one to take care of her. This image of herself as a destitute bag lady became the image of her false emergency situation. As we shall come to see, our beliefs are associated with images, and it is clear that the belief of this woman was also equal to a false emergency.

To relieve her sense of distress, I instructed her to reverse her image. I asked her to close her eyes and see herself as someone who is enriched and that money is coming to her, flying through the windows on wings, and that she is receiving the sustenance she needs. The immediate result was feeling more grounded, stronger, better able to examine her situation without the created shadow of being a bag lady. What is inside is outside. The lesson is clear. You take your situation, see what it looks like, and then turn the image into its opposite: You create a new belief. In the case of this woman, the belief was: I am able to gain the income I need.

Now comes the startling part.

"Out of the blue" — her phrase — she received a $3,500 check from the federal government because she had *overpaid* on her taxes the year before. What's more, in another few days, a $2,000 check came to her because she had a refund due to her from the state. So, in a period of days, she received $5,500. How do we understand her phrase "out of the blue"? This phrase, in my view, means from the Invisible Reality. She changed her beliefs. She withdrew from the false emergency state that she had created. She understood its falsity. Shifting her beliefs by changing the image, the universe suddenly came to her aid. That's the way spiritual life operates. You have no idea how it's going to transpire. It's not important; you don't have to know. You cooperate with the invisible world, and it cooperates with you. It gives you what you need.

The beauty of the emergency state is that it gives you an opportunity to find your faith. Faith means, among other things, your relationship to the Invisible Reality. It also means making up your mind to step in a direction not knowing where you will end up or what the outcome will be. Just step into a relational experience with the invisible world. All we know is that we have faith and trust that we are connected to a source that is there for us, to inform us and sustain us and support us. The universe has given us emergency states to test this.

When we begin looking at our emergency states, asking if they are true or false, we begin to take it upon ourselves to live. We find that 99-plus percent of our perceived emergencies have emerged out of misperceptions and misconceptions about a threat to our existence. As we stop relating and responding to them, we begin to turn around a situation simply by recognizing that it is not a true emergency. The accompanying emotions of anxiety, worry, fear, panic, guilt, etc., etc., have no value. They are just fuel for the engine of the concocted false emergency state. We have discharged the false emergency state by simply taking charge of our inner state of experience.

Changing Your Life
Now that we have made an opening, we've allowed the universe to come to serve us. Remember Francine, who reversed her fear that she

The Physiology of Death: The False Emergency State

would become a bag lady? She decluttered her space of stories and commentaries. In this new inner space of freedom, she collaborated with the universe, which came to her aid.

Our job is to make room for the universe to help, and it's giving us the opportunity to do this in this beautiful way of constantly throwing emergencies in our face. Once you know that misperceptions and misconceptions are lurking when an emergency comes, you can ask yourself, "What does the misperception/misconception that is generating this look like? What image do I see?" Once you see the image of the false emergency, you can turn it around and convert it, reverse it to its other side, to the beneficial image we have charge of, thereby making a new space in our lives.

To recap, the *Dis*-Emergency State takes you away from the misconceptions and misperceptions that are deenergizing your life through the depleting physiological processes that accompany an emergency state. The basic point to remember is that your life changes when you deflect these false emergency states.

Now, I am not establishing an ideal here — that we *must* deflect every false emergency state. We all fall into these states, and we may not always be alert enough to see it or may not want to deal with it. We have free will. We are in charge. We can choose to deal with a situation as an emergency state and experience it as such. Or we can choose to step back and observe it, and respond to it as a false emergency that we have created.

But the more we deflect false emergencies — the more we use the *dis*-emergency state process — the more often we will see that doing so opens up our life.

Here is a personal example that happened to me recently. I was going to a concert, and I had a number of tickets for succeeding days. On the way, I saw that the organization that mailed me the tickets sent me only one for a concert that was scheduled for the following week. I had already made arrangements with a childhood friend to go with me to this concert, but I now saw I had only one ticket. In a sense, this was an emergency, or I could have treated it as such, with all the facets of the fight-or-flight response pumping away in me. Well, you know, I've been doing this long enough that I didn't think about an emergency for an instant. Instead, I went up to the box office when I arrived and outlined the situation.

I explained that I had paid for several pairs of tickets — and I was able to demonstrate that they were paid for — but I had received only one ticket for the concert next week. The man in the box office said, "No problem. I'll print you out a ticket that you can use next week." He then made sure that the ticket was for a seat next to mine. And that was that. Except that he said, "I hope you enjoy the concert tonight, and I look forward to you enjoying the concert next week."

This is what happens constantly when we don't automatically treat a situation as an emergency. The distressing feelings don't build up as we stop ruminating about how terrible the ticket company was and that they didn't do the right thing and send enough tickets, how incompetent they were, and on and on it goes, finding a bottomless well of reasons to blame and complain and feel we must stick up for our rights and fight back. To the making of complaints and the finding of faults, there is no end, because we are being asked by the inner terrorists to behave that way. To generate a gale-force storm of an emergency, we are going to lose life force.

When you respond to a situation as an emergency, there is nothing to be concerned about. Be aware that it has happened and know that you responded to the situation as though it were a true emergency. That's enough for you to know at that point. Not to worry. It's going to happen again, and keep happening until, sooner or later, you want to inquire into the sources of the emergency, and then you begin to master the process. Then, down the road, you get to a point in your life where you are not ruled by false emergency responses. Is that a life you want for yourself? I think so, because when you come into a position absent of false emergency responses, you are moving in a direction in which life takes on a different color. You move through life now with a certain ease, dynamic balance, and a sense of contentment, peace, and happiness. Who doesn't want that?

PRACTICE

To start reversing this error, we observe, step back, and ask ourselves, "Is this a true or a false emergency? Is my life hanging in the balance right now? Is my life at stake right now?" Once you begin asking questions along these lines, you have a leg up on what is happening, because now you are starting to take charge of yourself and the fears instead of the fears taking charge of you. I can't emphasize too strongly how important this is, not just for you in the moment but also for the possibilities in your life.

The Genesis of the False Emergency State
False emergency states are generated by us from early life onwards; first from biological, instinctual needs to be met, then social, moral ones.

As mentioned in the preface, the existential question of life and death is upon us soon after birth ("To be, or not to be, that is the question," *Hamlet* 3:1). Right then some sort of emergency state is felt around the threat of death when with our first breath of life we cry out. Next, as we go through the developmental phases of life, new, more acute emergency feelings ensue. These phases are marked by conditioning culminating in a series of implanted seeds in the form of beliefs in our awareness through social miseducation I term AIDs = Attachments, Insufficiency, Doubt. Here we are misled to depend almost entirely on the world around us for our rewards, pleasure, comfort, and protection. These beliefs seem natural enough for young children to absorb till they become completed beings by age seven, in coordination with the losing of baby teeth and the greater development of the neural networks of the brain. I mean by completed in that their major belief systems are in place and ready to look outside the family hearth for a larger social network (such as educational, political, and religious systems) where additional false beliefs in the form of man-made standards will be incorporated. Here, acute false emergency states begin circulating in connection to the dependent connections to both family and social institutions that promise help for continued survival.

When we become adults, a new set of false emergency states are afoot based on the socially created false beliefs we all face. These errors of living are more established patterns of thinking, feeling, and behavior. We turn next to explore these errors.

CHAPTER IX

The Social Errors of Living: The Death Plan

I. AIDs

NOW THAT WE'VE GOT A HANDLE on the emergency state and its genesis, let's look at the errors in detail.

Whenever we suffer any sort of malady (maladaptation or uneasiness), we know immediately there are errors of living perpetrated by those saboteurs called "inner terrorists." These errors are hidden teachers of life, prompting and pointing us toward making corrections. But how can we easily recognize them?

As the watcher, guardian, and keeper of ourselves, here's what to look out for and how it got to be that way. We started with recognizing the three glaring little unhealthy seeds from which the weeds take root and sprout: (1) We think, feel, act as though we are insufficient; (2) attachments; and (3) doubts. These all eventually lead to slavery, and together they form the AIDs trio.

We Are Not *Meant* to Die

(1) Insufficiency is the mistaken belief that we are not whole and are incomplete. We misperceive and misconceive that we must add more to ourselves and do all that is possible to prevent being subtracted from, as though we can "really" be added to or subtracted from by the man-made world of false standards and ideals. Poppycock!

Eve faced this when the seed of doubt was planted in her ear by the serpent that she was insufficient. Feelings of shame and guilt are the consequences of believing we are not already the perfection of God's creation. Shame is the social experience of feeling exposed in the eyes of others for some thoughts, feelings, or actions we try to hide just as Adam and Eve tried to hide their nakedness from God. Guilt deals with perceived or misperceived acts against conscience for which we feel in debt to others or ourselves. The feelings of shame or guilt are unwarranted, arising from an awareness of errors that is then followed by critical or blameworthy judgments about ourselves (or others). In either case, we can discharge these feelings by acting to correct, compensate, or confess to relieve them and let them go! If we don't make the necessary corrections, we remain fearful of exposure, become unbalanced, compound the trouble, and make more complications as we wear ourselves out in constant states of emergency.

(2) Attachment is the sibling of insufficient/not enough. We look everywhere and cling onto practically everything — thoughts, fantasies, words of advice, goods, others' assets, money, power, status, and worship of celebrities. Through those myriad dependencies, we bow down before them, give away our power, and become slaves in one way or another. Our vital life force is sapped and weakened so as to age and die. It's a parasitic life

out there and in here. We prey upon ourselves (the medical community calls it "autoimmunity") and are preyed upon, all in the desire to become more and to protect ourselves from becoming and feeling less.

(3) Doubt is a major player and instigator here. It is the voice stilling and muting the voices of faith and trust in ourselves and in the divine. Doubt is the experience of being pulled between two contrary or opposing tendencies in ourselves. Doubt leads us into a paralysis of action, blockage of energies, and physical maladies. Afraid to let go or relinquish the familiar in favor of something new or unknown, we stay stuck. The indecision, the inability to choose and decide, inhibits the movement of life energies. It could be said that all physical maladies are the expression of the body in doubt! It is a relative of insufficiency and attachment. We attach to the status quo; we feel insufficient to make a choice, doubting our capabilities, doubting ourselves. We fear if we make the "wrong" choice, we will be "subtracted from and made less." We forget that we are complete in ourselves and have all the answers within. Instead, we turn from one outside authority to another, which only adds to our inner confusion. In fact, from our earliest educational system, we are taught to doubt ourselves if we do not fit into the norms and standards imposed on us by outside authorities.

Medicine and psychology firmly focused on "what's wrong with you" (i.e., insufficient in you) encourage you to doubt your physical, emotional, and mental stability. This of course leads to an immediate state of emergency, as a threat to our existence is implied. Labeled with a medical diagnosis, we now become identified and attached to the diagnosis and the pathology rather than to making the necessary corrections in the five realms of our existence to mend the tear in our fabric of life. When AIDs is functioning within us, it culminates invariably in slavery, an excessive bowing down and dependency on the powers of the human world. We mistakenly believe our survival is dependent on the outside world.

All three seeds are the sources of the disturbances we face as the basic thematic structures governing our lives on Earth.

II. Weeds
The offshoots of these AIDs seeds are the many weeds of our garden of life that, if left unchecked, become our Death Plan. These weeds reflect our personal development and our relationship to the larger social culture around us. The inner terrorists propagate these errors of living. Here's a developmental snapshot of how we unfold these errors from core beliefs established in the first seven years of life.

As infants and toddlers we are subjected to two repetitive beliefs patterned by interactions between the young child and its caretakers. The little infant lets adults know that it is distressed or unhappy, primarily through crying as a form of expressing pain. The associated belief is "Unhappiness is pain." Crying also makes it known s/he is hungry and wants the pleasure of being fed. In this way the infant says, *"I want what I want when I want it!"* The caretakers immediately hop to it to satisfy the infant's demands by bringing something of pleasure to the child. Pleasure becomes connected to happiness. As the infant grows into toddlerhood, crying turns into whining and complaining; standing up for its rights eventually leads to blaming others when unhappy. As the caretakers don't approve of and resist this intimidating ploy, the child shifts gears to appease, please, and accommodate the caretakers' demands. This interaction becomes the beginning of the false social errors process. As adolescence merges into adulthood, the

The Social Errors of Living: The Death Plan

final common pathway of those two earliest primal beliefs becomes: (1) "unhappiness is pain"; "happiness is pleasure" —> **The purpose of living is to become nondisturbed, seek pleasure and comfort, and avoid pain** —> "pain bad!"; (2) "I want what I want when I want it" becomes the greed factor of wanting more, better, or different. Of course, when we don't get our way, are frustrated, or are pushed out of our comfort zone, this ignites an emergency state reflected in all five dimensions of living on our stage of life. With this background we can examine ten basic errors in living in more detail. You may discover more errors of living as you move along the path.

The diagram enumerates the three seminal seeds that give rise to the ten major weeds that are the genesis of the physiology of death.

Social errors of living that drive the false emergency state

Although there are so many disparate parts to keep track of, they are actually all pieces in a mosaic, all connected to each other and all derivations of the big three. In turn those three all serve to redirect us from our purpose of being here. Following them turns us away from our connection to our soul nature and spirit in favor of an excessive interest in material life. At first it might seem overwhelming to keep track of all the saboteurs operating in and around us. To help familiarize yourself with how each error operates in daily life, I've included a brief practice for each error. Focus on only one error per week, in any order you like. With vigilance and practice, it will all come into organization, order, and a new way of life.

Error #1: Being open to suggestion
Suggestions are ideas about what someone *should* do or how someone *should* behave. Most of what we say, hear, or read are suggestions. We are all subject to suggestions all the time, from within or from outside of us. Suggestion is the basis of hypnosis, and we are constantly exposed to these hypnotic-like suggestions every day. This hypnotic effect is a device to make us want more or feel threatened that we are insufficient or have less. Hypnotic suggestions are a powerful way that we stay attached. Being open to attachment and caught by doubt, we become 100 percent *open* to suggestion nearly 100 percent of the time. Now we become somnambulistic, walking around in a post-hypnotic waking and walking sleep, doing as we are told in a compliant way, never questioning the legitimacy of the suggestion.

There are two types of suggestions: placebos and nocebos, those that please (Latin *placer*) us and those that harm us (Latin *nocere*), respectively. Nocebos stimulate anxiety, worry, and fear, even dread. There are three components I have discovered comprising the function of placebo: (1) It gives a feeling of pleasure: placebo's meaning is to please; (2) it offers a sense of hope for the future; (3) it provides a new belief, which in turn stimulates a renewed sense of faith. Placebo, then, addresses our senses, feelings, and thoughts (belief) in one unitary experience. Imagery is a powerful form of placebo. The image, of course, holds the seed of conception in the womb of consciousness, where it gestates and is finally birthed. The image provides a perceptual reality of the conception, making it much easier to hold onto, while amplifying hope and faith. Imagery is a mental placebo, realizing its fulfillment in how balanced we become, signified by a sense of well-being, feeling happy, veering toward a simple life, and forgoing the world of "I must be missing something, so I gotta have it at any cost" — one belief that creates havoc eventually in the time-space world in which we live.

Nocebos, on the other hand, tend to bring us down, dampen will, and deplete faith and hope. They are negating beliefs focusing on what we can't do, what is not possible for us, and what gloom and doom await us, and overall they are nihilistic and negativistic. They are common statements we hear all around us every day. They are the destructive images portrayed in violent movies, violent video games, violent TV serials. Their aim is to render us impotent and powerless. Eventually, they numb our senses and put us into some form of sleep state where we can easily be manipulated and enslaved.

As a clinician and teacher, I hear story after story about things said to people that create harm. These suggestions, such as "you have three months to live," "your condition is incurable," or "there is nothing that can be done for it" are typical nocebos in the medical field. Generally, they are projections into the future. William, who came to see me with metastatic prostate cancer, was told exactly that. He came with an associated PSA blood test of 24 and urinary frequency and urgency. We had two sessions of imagery, the second at his demand four weeks after the first, where he experienced the end of his urinary problems, restoration of sleep, and an increase of well-being and strength. About six weeks after the second meeting, he had radiographic and PSA tests done: prostate normal, metastasis gone, PSA 0.4. He died 11 years later of a heart attack.

In relationships, nocebos include "you'll never get married," "you're a good-for-nothing," "why can't you be pleasant?" Personal self-talk nocebos include "I'll never get a job," "I'm not pretty/handsome enough," etc.

Just listen to yourself and others, and you will find much chatter is in the form of suggestions. These suggestions — both placebos and nocebos — are seeds that are planted in our field of consciousness. We often accept suggestions that fit our preconceived worldview about life. When we are "awake" to suggestions, we can ask ourselves, "Are these suggestions true or not?"

Here are some ways to know: Is there credible evidence to support it? Are there facts verifying and validating the suggestion(s)? Are the statements crafted in the future or past tense? If so, not true. This brings us to (2) future or past talk.

In William's case above, he had credible evidence that something was out of balance, from his objective experience and the objective test results, both of which constitute the facts of the matter. However, the doctors' assessment that he had three months to live was *not* true; the only truth was that their past interventions of hormone therapy had not worked.

William rejected the nocebo about the absolute statement the doctor made, based in the medical orthodoxy of their preconceived idea that if their way didn't work, nothing could work. Rejecting the made-up stories about future events, he began to look for other possibilities, and my book, *Healing Visualizations*, came to his attention. Mental imagery is a powerful form of placebo. In providing hope, displacing the nocebo of "no-hope," it plants a new seed in the field of consciousness of a blueprint of healing that your "mindbody" can follow. It is an autosuggestion given to you from Invisible Reality to actively use for yourself. It neutralizes the many nocebos you accept from the world, allowing your life-affirming beliefs to take root.

Here is another example of a nocebo developed in early childhood that I call "limiting beliefs," as they can shape and define and limit our freedom.

Thomas, a middle-aged man, suffered throughout his life from being an outcast from his family. He understood this situation to have been a boon to the evolution of his life, but still fretted over not being included in his family of origin's life. His memories of family life were of finding himself alone in various locations. Although he was popular outside the family orbit, he was not accorded the same "honor" in his own family but instead was rejected and often disparaged. Regardless of this early treatment, he married successfully to a woman he met in college, living in a solid union, fathering two children, and creating a thriving business, becoming a man of means. However, he could not put to rest the absence of an early family life, even though his current life had been so fulfilling.

Explaining the matter in terms of beliefs he held about his family, he suddenly realized a core belief imparted to him by his mother (who died at 45 of a physical illness) that life is a tragedy and things end tragically. This nuclear belief has been his creation since early life and has organized his life's view in spite of all the "goodness" happening to him. Consequently, his feelings of happiness are always tinged with feelings of sadness. It was a revelation to him to realize how blessed he was to have been "thrown out" of the family constellation so early in life. He did not succumb altogether to that morbid conditioning. He had escaped.

Now the need arose to reverse the limiting conception. I ask him to *see* what tragedy looks like. He sees himself bent over, holding his head in his hands, crying, looking sad, tears streaming down his face. I ask him to reverse that image. He experiences the tears becoming tears of purification. He loses his form and sees a smile happening. He has the sense of standing erect now and senses the hands of God as light coming down, taking hold of his hands and lifting him up. I ask about the feeling and sensation. He says his chest opens and he feels his heart open. He describes the change as "love." I prescribe he do this exercise every day for 21 days, knowing the new belief, of feeling of love, replaces the old belief. He can call on this new image anytime he recognizes himself lapsing into the tragic mode. Note, he does not need to see the sad image again, just recognize the feeling and reverse it. At the end of his experience, he sees the sun come up, everything around him becoming bright. A new day has dawned in his life, literally.

Another example: Barbara called in a panic. She was at her house upstate, gardening at a frenzied pace, and an avalanche of red welts had appeared all over her body, accompanied by an occipital headache. She went to a local MD. He immediately ordered oral steroids to quell the inflammatory response. Unfortunately, he jumped to a conclusion that her weeks-old headache required a CAT scan to rule out a possible brain tumor. That's all she had to hear, and there came the phone call several days later, feeling out of sorts on the prednisone, mentally flaky, knowing she would not take a CT scan.

"After all," I rebuked her, "you decided to call that MD first rather than call the MD [me] who took you through a life-and-death crisis over two decades ago." She appreciated the chiding, realizing she had made a mess and now had to pay the price for the nocebo that he had planted regarding a possible brain tumor. She calmed down and composed herself, and together we investigated the false emergency state that reflected itself in the physical welts and the headache she was experiencing.

She explained that she had plans to complete several paintings in anticipation of an art exhibit the following summer. Her flower garden had to look just so in order to capture its beauty on canvas; hence the self-imposed demand to plant, plant, plant.

She conceded that she just wanted a quick fix — a strong cortisol cream that would allow her to continue to work in the garden. She knew the garden environment, filled with bugs, was toxic to her health, yet she did not want to take the necessary step that was staring her in the face: to stop gardening and return to the "healthy" city environment. She was attached to the future — to the exhibit a year out — all the while making up a story that she could not paint without the outdoor flowers in place.

We discussed how emergency states stem from "*wanting to change what is to what ought to be*" and are violations of the *2nd and 9th Commandments*. The 2nd Commandment speaks of the error of constructing mental idols (i.e., she "must" complete the paintings for the exhibition). The 9th Commandment speaks of not telling the truth. She lacked *faith* that the invisible universe would supply another avenue for her to complete her paintings or that something new would emerge from *sacrificing* her *attachment* to her future vision.

Looking at her core belief, she confessed that she found herself over-striving in her creative life, wanting to paint her best for a community of artists she loves. One of the most important lessons my teacher Colette taught me was "too much is too much." It is important that we know our own limits and remain sober/balanced. Striving can be a form of greed, in our wanting more, better, and different — and wanting it all now!

Barbara's mental emotional turmoil was reflected in a more weakened immune system, making her more susceptible to infectious bites or allergies from those predatory insects that can sense a weakened prey and attack. Insects bite many people, but not everyone contracts an infectious ailment, poisonous response, or rash, unless they are in some sort of weakened state as just described. As for her headache? I asked her if she was stooped over and bobbing her head up and down while she planted. She answered yes and understood the source of the headache as a repetitive syndrome of overworking the muscles of her neck. Too much is too much! Looking beyond the physical to the entire breadth of Barbara's existence revealed many facets to this seemingly simple environmental reaction to bug bites.

With this new understanding of the source of the emergency state, Barbara made appropriate corrections: She let go of her expectations of how things ought to be, let go of over-striving, and engaged in mental imagery to cleanse herself of the welts. At her last follow-up, she was feeling fine, the rash all but gone. No medication needed. No unnecessary testing required. She sobered up emotionally and mentally, and came back into balance.

PRACTICE

For the next week, watch the suggestions that come your way from others and within yourself. Are they solicited or unsolicited? Are they placebos or nocebos? Helpful or unhelpful? Future-based or present-based? Jot down any observations that are new to you.

Error #2: Future and Past Talk
Of course there is a future. Living here in this world of linear time, there is consciousness of a possible next moment. But that next moment or future moment is not a thing, not a material *something* as we are miseducated into believing it to be. It is in fact a potential or possibility that can be fulfilled. It is a construct, manufactured or reified into an object when mistakenly viewed as a factual thing that can be put under one's control as we tend to do with objects or things we own. However, this nonexistent or no-thing is not possible to own, control, dominate, run, or otherwise take charge of. Thus, thinking into the future or emoting into the future is to think and feel about what isn't! About nothing! To do so is to engage in an illusion or mirage that reflects itself physiologically in a depletion of life force. At the same time it splits us in two — the being right here and the being right there mucking around in the field of illusion. We *all* do it. It is a natural effect of early conditioning, but it is not *normal*. It is normal to be whole and unified, not split in two. The extreme degree of that split is schizophrenia. Schizophrenics are not different from us in kind, like an extraterrestrial or subhuman

android, but are only different in degree. They, like us, are all part of the same human brotherhood.

To wake up, we start listening to our grammar — literally. Are we speaking in the future or the past tense? You'll notice most talk is about the future — that uncreated realm of potential.

The past is a canceled check, the future a post-dated one of oaths, pledges, promises, vows. They exist in a la-la land of fantasy and tombstones. The personal past is over, ended, dead, buried, finished, finite, done, no longer exists. The check has been cashed. We've spent it. It is no longer here except in feelings of regret, guilt, recrimination, fond memories, should, could, oughts, and the like. Similarly, the future is based on what isn't: speculation, conjecture, if-thens, supposeds, hypotheticals, projected fantasies forward, conclusions, presumptions, going to, I will, imperative have-tos, musts, and the like. No evidence here in support of such future talk. It is treating the uncreated as though it is a fact right here and now in front of your face, a living reality in the present moment. Yet nearly every conversation we hold or overhear is about what is coming to be: predictions, outcomes, results, consequences, or what was, and it amounts to unsubstantiated heresy and rumor, and "self-gossip." We seem to be content living mentally in a never-never land of illusion, mirages, or fantasy, past or future reveries, delusion.

I mention delusion, a psychotic form of thinking denoted by holding fixed beliefs contrary to the evidence of any reality in opposition to it. We all hold pockets of such thinking but are able to function well otherwise, but we will eventually be tripped up by it. For instance, a man or woman who holds onto a relationship despite clear evidence the partner no longer (or never did) love them. By being afraid to part from this damaging belief, a huge toll is taken on us physically, emotionally, mentally, and socially, not to mention morally. *The latter is denoted by lying to oneself about the truth of the matter, violating the*

Ninth spiritual law of "tell the truth" (don't bear false witness). I suspect almost everyone reading these words knows clearly what I'm talking about. It really is a movement toward health that we understand the toll taken on us when we live in the grip of illusory time — personal past, personal future.

Distressing Emotions
The importance of future and past talk is underscored by the emotions invariably accompanying these errors. Notable among them are those attached to thinking in the future, or "futurizing", (e.g. anxiety, hysteria, fear, worry, anger, panic) and those attached to thinking in the past, or "pasturizing", (e.g. guilt; shame; depression and its variants of pouting, sulking, sadness, melancholy, blues, funk, etc.; regret; recrimination; sour grapes).

Regret
Regret is a form of "could have, should have, would have." Henry, a man in his early 40s, suffered from a decaying process (a better term than "cancer") of his lungs. We worked together with imagery and he healed. End of story? Not yet. Ten years later a recurrence took place with a lesion in the spinal column. Now he was prepared to explore the source of his illness. Interesting revelations emerged when we excavated deeper into his life story, a phrase I call "health-care archaeology."

Henry revealed that he was overcome by regret triggered by the impending marriage of his son, whom he felt he had "abandoned" after his divorce when the child was young. He regretted not being there "enough" (a standard) and the supposed damage that it might have brought to the young boy. This boy had grown into a fine man functioning quite well in his life and career, emotionally, mentally, and physically. He had established a loving relationship with his fiancée. Meanwhile, Henry continued to hold onto this delusional belief with its attendant detrimental feelings, despite evidence presented to him to the contrary. Although the young man did not easily accept Henry's recent choice in his own second marriage, he had since come to appreciate his stepmom.

The regret, lingering in the shadows of the years, became exacerbated by a sudden discontinuity, a shock of sorts. Henry had established a strong connection to a cousin's little boy, with whom he spent time every weekday for over a year. However, suddenly the relationship was interrupted when the cousin and his wife decided to send the little boy — aged five now — to nursery school, drastically reducing his contact with him. It seemed, in his mind, that he was getting "punished" in return for the "crime" he had committed against his son. He was feeling inconsolably sad, distressed emotionally, and mentally at a "perceived" loss as he continued to have less frequent, periodic contact. In spite of the minimized contact, he was conditioned to respond to the separation, partial as it was, in the same way as the original circumstance after his divorce a decade and a half earlier. Wouldn't you know it? That's when the cancer happened again, this time showing up in the spine as well (our pillar of strength). Did he feel like dying over the "crime" he had originally "committed" and now reawakened full force? He said so.

Let's look at the nuances of the errors of living embedded in Henry's recurrence of illness. First, he is caught in despair at his lack of contact with his nephew — wanting to turn *what is into what ought to be*. Likewise he has an ideal of how his relationship with his son *should* be now — different from what it is. He is also filled with regret at what ought to have been in the past. He holds an *accounts payable* that he feels he can never pay off because he has a "standard" of what "enough" should be, and of course it can never be fulfilled, as the son is now fully grown. Living in regret, with his hurt and pains, he is making up stories of how the past — something long dead and gone, but not altogether buried — should have been. He is making up stories about how the present should be and the future will be without the love of this nephew or his son's affection. All these stories are untruths, disguised falsehoods, and a bearing of false witness — the 9th Commandment.

After all this was explained to him, he felt much better. He felt relieved at unloading a fictitious debt that he truthfully never owed. He also received imagery for removing regret along with imagery for reversing guilt.

IMAGERY EXERCISE

PILLAR OF SALT: FOR REMOVING REGRET

Sit up in a chair with uncrossed arms and legs. Close your eyes. Breathe out and in three times slowly. See yourself like Lot's wife, who cried salty tears of regret at the loss of what she had to leave behind. These tears cover your entire body, turning you into a pillar of salt, sclerosing you by making you hard and dry.

Breathe out one time. Have with you a fireman's hose, spraying that immobile pillar with a powerful stream of warm to hot blue water coming out in a reverse (counterclockwise) spiral, melting the salt, bringing you back to life here in the present moment. How do you feel? What do you physically sense? Know regret is buried in the past.

Breathe out one time and open your eyes. Do this each morning upon awakening, near sundown, and before bed for a number of seconds for 21 days.

Expectations — Future Talk
One ubiquitous feature of future talk is expectations. We all do it as a natural way of desiring, looking for something to be given us to satisfy our wishes. As an example, we are miseducated to expect perfection to come from our social relationships. Everything depends on what is

The Social Errors of Living: The Death Plan

given to us from elsewhere. Again, we find ourselves contending with attachments creating pain.

Most often, expectations go unmet, unfulfilled, thwarted, frustrated, or whatever. When that happens, an excitatory spark is set off through the five dimensions of living: We feel disappointed and hurt. Simultaneously we seek to blame someone or something else or oneself for the failure. We are always ready to blame and complain. That's what the inner terrorists have us do. Along with blaming come disturbing or distressing feelings — anger, anxiety, fear, guilt, shame, worry, the whole bevy or even singularly. Within one or two hours we experience a physical symptom and/or an additive craving — the latter serving to mollify those painful feelings.

When this scenario is repeated consistently, as has to happen, because we are expecting constantly, the chain reaction is set in motion instantaneously, culminating in chronic illness and/or addiction. Opioid addiction and chronic illness with physical pain are prime examples of the link between the two.

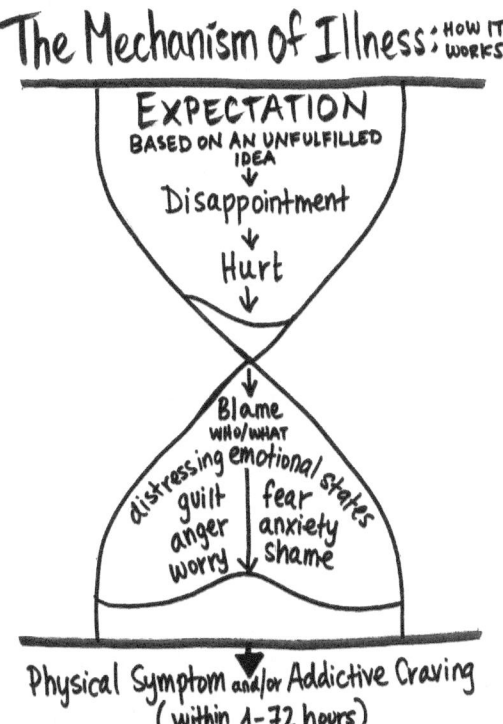

One remedy is to stop expecting, as doing so is a function of future talk. Expecting is looking for a result. Either use your will to restrain expectation or continue expecting — but step away from requiring a result. It's okay. You just expect for its own sake.

- 155 -

It seems unnatural not to expect, but the negative health effects far outweigh the arguments for the need for expectations.

Another effective remedy to reverse the chain of expectation: Start from the effect — such as illness, addiction, or any suffering — and work backwards to the distressing emotional state(s) to blame, to hurt, to disappointment, and back to the expectation. Tell your inner source of wisdom this is future talk, a lie about nothing tangible, it has no relevance and is essentially an untruth. Doing so, you detach from another piece of future talk. Here you may ask what this expectation looks like. If an image comes, then proceed to get rid of it, burning it, drowning or submerging it in water, burying it in the earth, or casting it away on the wings of the winds.

This genesis of the development of illness and its repair was first established by Robert Rhondell Gibson,[29] and for me has borne fruit: It provides a clear explanation of how illness arises from unmet expectations and how it may be reversed.

Rose, a consultant who worked from home, required focus. She expected her children to be quiet so she could concentrate. When they made noise and interrupted her flow of thought, she was disappointed they couldn't obey her. She blamed them, was angry, and developed a pain in her neck, a vulnerable area where she had previously recovered from a whiplash injury. She did say at the time of the current neck pain that when the children made noise they were "pains in the neck."

Not only did Rose demonstrate the movement from expectation to physical symptom but she also demonstrated the connection between a physical symptom and vernacular language, a connection easily established when addressing any symptom. The body speaks in its own language that can be translated analogously into vernacular or common parlance language.

---

[29] Robert Rhondell Gibson, *Science of Man*.
Available at http://www.harmonyworkshop.org/som-english-audio-1-30/lesson-1

The Social Errors of Living: The Death Plan

We approached the neck in two ways: reversing the flow described above and making the connection between the physical disturbance and its social counterpart in her relationship to her children and to another relationship who may be a "pain in the neck." Here the scope of understanding is deepened and enlarged. Awareness is broadened. The picture becomes whole = healed, and health ensues. Rose experienced the benefits of this process.

All distressing emotions supply the fuel, the charge to the engine of past or future talk, giving them an intensity to make us believe that the thoughts and the attendant feelings have credibility and meaning. Not so! As they are expressed, our body simultaneously responds to the turned-on switch of false emergency, leading to the breakdown depicted in the earlier diagram of the Mechanism of Illness.

On the other hand, we can be thankful for these emotions. They bridge the mental to the physical, and thus they alert us that we are out of balance, heading toward instability, reminding us to compose ourselves and bring ourselves back to balance. Rather than their being enemies needing to be numbed and deadened by Big Pharma, they can be accorded their due, giving us pause to become awake and alert to actively bring ourselves back to our unitary self rather than allowing us to be torn apart. With this new understanding in hand, we begin to realize that these demonlike feelings are actually friends — teachers here to alert us to our false emergency state. While future talk can give momentary pleasure, such as looking forward to an event, most often it eventually turns into an emergency state.

Sidney, a high-powered businessman, is on the go 24/7, under pressure to produce, as a promotion possibility is looming. He wanted my services for a physical condition called "hyperhidrosis," the fancy, mysterious medical term for excessive sweating. He gave me the usual story of people who come to me as a "last resort," having by his own account "tried everything and everywhere." Except he hadn't tried this: imagery, techniques of will, remembering, self-methods, spiritual education.

We took a survey of his life situation. How was he functioning physically, emotionally, mentally, socially/relationally, morally (spiritual life or interests)? What *we* discovered was how gripped he was in the endless pressure of the next day: goals to accomplish, deals to complete, money to make. He was without doubt successful at all the above, but at a cost of excessive sweating and accompanying insomnia. Up a good deal of the night. Sweating through many shirts.

I gave him two remedies — will and imagery. After a brief spiritual education about future talk and its destructive impact, I had him watch/observe its illusory nature in his day-to-day work — conversations with others, his inner conversations — and recognize all those untruths. He was willing to try this for a period of three weeks without fail and to *stop* himself mentally from doing so once he discerned the truth of what I was telling him. On his own recognizance, he found out the merits of this *new* education. To aid him along I asked him, as he was paying attention to future talk, to become aware of the accompanying distressing emotion of anxiety. At that moment, he is to imagine a large, bright-red octagonal STOP sign with the word *STOP* in the center, flashing a few times, knowing that he is coming back to the moment.

After taking up this mental exercise of will, he became aware of decreasing anxiety, found himself more relaxed at work and more comfortable in his time at home with his wife, sleeping better, and enjoying an abatement of the "hyperhidrosis." In addition to this combo remedy of image and will, I explained to him that sweating is a function of the parasympathetic nervous system, the quieting system of the body. The excess sweating was the body's way of cleansing out the toxins created in his body by the constant false emergency state he was generating, highlighted by incessant future talk. The sweating was actually there to protect him, it was not an enemy come to undo him! After putting two and two together, the insomnia faded, and the excess defensive expression of sweating disappeared.

He was forever grateful to me, but in truth, I was forever grateful to him for having the courage to try a new way that was foreign to his life's pattern. I may get the credit for introducing him to a new possibility for life (the stop sign can be used for anything in life), but he gets the credit for taking the risk to change his frame of reference about life.

PRACTICE

For one week, observe when you or others lapse into future or past talk. What are the attendant emotions? Jot down any observations.

Error #3: Five Dual False Beliefs

These next errors emerge early in life. These five dual false belief systems form the core beliefs of our adult life to dominate the landscape of our social lives. These are:

(a) a need to be important to avoid inferiority
(b) a need to be accepted to avoid rejection
(c) a need to gain attention to avoid neglect
(d) a need to gain approval to avoid disapproval
(e) and the fifth that incorporates the other four, the overarching one — experienced early in life — a need to get to a non-disturbed state to gain pleasure and comfort and avoid pain.

These five mass-conscious false beliefs are part of the entropic function of life. They are instinctual, emotional, and intellectively inculcated in us early on. While the need to get to a non-disturbed state to avoid pain and gain pleasure has a biological protective basis (i.e., a child cries when hungry, we reflexively move away from fire to avoid injury/pain), these instinctual responses morph from a protective biological impulse into a socially regulated habit, where we require something from the outside world to protect us. We lose our self-agency and turn it over to the man-made world to define happiness and comfort for us. We attach ourselves to the false five beliefs, making ourselves dependent on the forces in this world to give us the rewards and safety we seek. In essence, these beliefs are the natural mental children of feeling insufficient.

Here is a typical example of how one error flows into another and how they reflect in our physical, social, moral, mental, and emotional spheres of existence.

Diana is with her husband and two children at the in-laws' home in the country. He is convivial with his family, chatting, drinking, laughing. She is not brought into the circle (she didn't insist on being brought in) and is left alone on the lawn. Her two young children are being enjoyed rapturously by the grandparents. Sitting by herself she finds herself "drowning in a sea of emotions." A mixture of sadness, weeping, anger, and frustration swirls. She feels rejected, neglected, and unimportant. She has the urge to get into the car and go home, leave him there, perhaps taking the kids or not. She is torn between staying or leaving — fighting or fleeing, especially the latter. Eventually she sits there frozen, stuck in indecision. Does she yell at him there in front of his folks, or just leave? She projects a variety of outcomes that could transpire, depending on her action, but has now been frozen by indecision. Physically her "stomach is tied up in knots."

We see here in a common social experience how physical, emotional, mental, social, and moral factors all interplay. In addition they are reflecting spiritual errors of living: She is expecting him to be sensitive to her needs (he had recently done so, responding to her speaking up about the significant strain in their relationship); she feels disappointed and hurt when the leopard's spots haven't changed, blames him, finds herself "drowning in a sea of emotions," and suffers the physical analogy to her confusion with knots in her stomach. She wants acceptance, attention, to feel important, and have pleasure in the outing. She wants to avoid neglect, rejection, feeling unimportant, and most importantly, pain (on all the levels cited). All of these desires add up to inducing her self-imposed imprisonment, depending on the other for her worth, value, meaning, and happiness.

Then there is the emerging false emergency state, a common denominator of all disturbance: powered by misconceptions and/or misperceptions created mentally about something that does not exist — the future. She is making up all sorts of stories about what results her action to leave would incur, basing her inaction on an illusory/delusional idea about what isn't, what is uncreated, therefore about nothing. She cannot bring herself to face a different sort of adaptation than the one her intelligence has become used to. The refusal to act is a function of doubt, another common denominator of all disturbances intertwined with misconceptions and misperceptions.

Persistent, self-imposed false emergency states coupled with persistent, self-imposed doubts, coupled with self-imposed false beliefs about needing approval, importance, acceptance, and attention, all in the service of having to gain pleasure and avoid pain, — all of this creates a chain draining the life out of us. What comes after that is the inevitable "clarion call"[30] not to extend life but to go in the other direction toward ending life.

The final touch on this exposition about her is the moral element. All the thoughts and feelings tsunami-ing through her on the lawn

---

[30] I am indebted to my mother of blessed memory, Celia, from whom I first heard this phrase in regard to being summoned to death.

were about false thoughts and ideas, untruths, falsehoods, unintentional lies. In other words, not telling the truth, or the ninth spiritual law — bearing false witness, an overarching common source of all disturbances. But telling the truth, acting in truth with herself, without story-making, rationalizations, and other sundry interferences, she began a new chapter of life. She started being truthful to herself, recognized the story-making about the significance of not being included by the in-laws, and watched her expectations within the marriage. These adaptions in their many forms are called upon us to make throughout life. Currently, Diana is enjoying a stable, happy, married life.

PRACTICE

For one week observe when you feel disturbed because you don't get your way or are pushed out of your comfort zone. Observe how you handle the disturbance: Do you stick up for your rights and complain? Do you sulk? Acquiesce? Do you slip into a false emergency state? Do you have physical symptoms or addictive cravings? The following week, observe where you seek approval or attention, feel inferior or rejected, or complain.

Error #4: Institutional and Cross-Cultural Standards and Ideals
The monolithic organizations, conglomerates, and corporations that dot the Earth wield their power to enslave us to their standards and ideals. These groups include organized religious institutions, government and political parties, the military-industrial complex, big business, natural sciences, and the conventional medical arts. Standard education, the media, and advertising all reinforce these mostly unreachable and unattainable standards.

And how do institutions exert their power? By cleverly conditioning us to these millennia-old, *man-made*, unholy, nonspiritual standards.

The Social Errors of Living: The Death Plan

While standards are fine for measuring objects and building machines within the man-made world, they have no place in the world of human becoming. We are more than things. No two humans are alike, so there can be no set standards.

These standards are always dually conceived: right-wrong, good-bad, rich-poor, pretty-ugly, in-group-out-group, normal-abnormal, real-unreal. These standards are all relative ideals set up as absolute ones of perfection to make us believe that when they are achieved, we will reach the happiness and bliss we yearn for to make us whole and complete. Believing in them, we remain enslaved, trying to reach the promised land of reward, pleasure, pain-avoidance. Since we are asleep to this trick, we don't realize, in our mesmerized state, that the effort involved to gain the carrot at the end of the stick depletes our life force, enervates, and disintegrates us. At the end, the severance pay is suffering and the final severance is . . . death.

Each institutional group focuses mainly on one ideal standard. Big business has its singular ideal of maximizing profits. The conventional medical model is premised on a standard of normal where it (not us) defines what is normal and what is abnormal health. Religious institutions, self-designated representatives of the divine, become arbiters of what is right and wrong, what is good and bad. The natural sciences, including psychology, define what is real and what is unreal, conflating material objective reality with the only reality. These groups mutually fortify one another, such as politics and the military-industrial complex, which together determine the *in* group, the people in power, and the *out* group, those on the outside, without power. The world of advertising is designed to reinforce the other institutional standards. By constant repetitive suggestions, it reminds us of the need to be physically beautiful, ultraclean, completely healthy, well-to-do, powerful, and comfortable. At the same time, advertising sends endless nocebos that dangerous maladies are around the corner if we don't monitor our health incessantly. You can verify this yourself by noting the percentage of advertisements for cell phones, cars, cleaning products, fast foods, clothes and makeup, pharmaceutical tests and drugs, and entertainment.

From early on, our educational system is designed to inculcate cultural and global mass conscious belief systems and to ready each of us to participate in these various societal "games." But these "games" disempower and weaken us through the never-ending comparisons and competition of self against others or some ideal. It is easy to understand how the institutions help to perpetuate the five core false basic urges covered in Error #3.

Collectively, these institutions are entwined authoritarian systems that dominate our individual lives. By contrast, in spiritual life we seek to make ourselves servants only to the One, our source of Origin, not to become subservient to institutions, tyrants, and dictators or to their false belief systems about the purpose of living.

Along with the institutional standards come their partners, our personal man-made ideals and standards and our quest for self-improvement, all of which are to be reached IN THE FUTURE. There is always more to get to reach that perfection, since we are told we are imperfect, insufficient beings to begin with.

Self-Improvement Game

Much of our life is dominated by constant suggestions to improve ourselves. Many women spend years of effort and money to lose those unsightly "five pounds." Men judge themselves and their status by their bank account. Even spiritual seekers berate themselves for not practicing enough or failing at (the game of) enlightenment. We each construct personal ideals and standards to be reached, goals to be met, and in not achieving them, we feel deflated and defeated, blaming ourselves.

The Social Errors of Living: The Death Plan

PRACTICE

For one week, become aware of how the institutional standards operate in your life. Note when you get down on yourself because you goofed or are imperfect (i.e., abnormal, not rich enough, not attractive enough, not in the right group, not good enough).

I can feel amused at all this nonsense since I've been there, done that, but still have to be attentive and awake to the banana peel someone threw before me that I didn't see and can slip on, though now I have the means to recover quickly.

Error #5: Changing What Is into What Ought to Be
Nowhere do the "weeds" of standards, ideals, and the self-improvement find a more fertile garden to grow in than in the social relationships of marriage, friends intimate and platonic, and casual and professional acquaintances. Here the crucial destructive worm (destructive belief) emerges from the weeds when we "want to change *what is* into *what ought to be.*" This belief is the pivot point of all the conflict, struggle, and resistance that disrupt and rupture relationships. Here the three essential AIDs seeds coalesce nicely. For example, in a relationship the other person isn't fulfilling my image and/or demands. I need him/her to be "more and better" (i.e., self-improvement). Further, I'm attached to this need for "perfection" (standard) in the other guy/gal. In fact, I know exactly how the other person needs to change — and if he/she just took my advice, there would be no difficulties. In addition, this urge to have him/her change reflects my doubt about my satisfaction in this relationship. Ironically, what we weren't expecting from this "labor of love" was enslavement. Now that we are unhappy with the way things are, we become dependent on the partner's change to make us happy, to get to a non-disturbed pleasure state, and to avoid the pain

and disappointment of the unfulfillment we are now experiencing.

So how do we want others or ourselves to change? We want them to fit into the institutional standards — be pretty, handsome, sexy, thin, healthy, smart, rich, powerful, etc. Or we want them to change to be "good" and "sensitive" partners, compassionate, or just have the ability to "read my mind." Likewise, we ourselves want to "self-improve" and be different, sexier, smarter, richer, thinner, healthier, cooler, etc.

In sum, we keep expecting the other to change instead of recognizing the truth of the matter and accepting that they are what they are and do what they do. This is natural for them. Only from the vantage point of acceptance can you make a clear and sober choice to stay or leave the relationship.

Valerie, a young woman in her mid-30s, just couldn't establish a longstanding relationship with a man and had remained unmarried until we met. She was on the verge of desperation about her prospects. Through our work together she succeeded in meeting a man who appeared to return her affections, and they hit it off.

They planned to get married after a short engagement of a number of months. During this time she complained to me that she didn't like the shape of his nose and wanted him to have an operation to change it. He was reluctant at first to do so. She showed me his photo and described what the nose change would presumably look like. She asked me my impression (I do incorporate the practice of facial morphology [face-reading] into my work).

I said the change might result in a change in his personality that could be difficult for her. I asked her why disturb a working relationship when her dream of marriage was to be realized. Valerie was dead set on going ahead with her demand. He finally acceded.

After the operation his personality did change, and he drifted from a placid, mellow guy to an angry, physically abusive one who hit her several times. When this happened, she broke off the relationship.

The Social Errors of Living: The Death Plan

I offer this vignette as a stark example of what can happen when we want to change what is to what ought to be. Valerie had an image, an ideal, and a need for self-improvement, all to be satisfied by her fiancé. She needed him to satisfy her needs, instead of her facing the truth in herself that this matter of his looks could not be accepted. To do so she would have to either accept him as is and grow up, learn to live with it, or look elsewhere, learning to face her future talk: "There will never be anyone else. I'm too old. I have never had success in the past, so I'm bound not to have success in the future." These are common comments with regard to social relationships. You may notice how they are future- or past-based. They are to be discarded as untruths. Therefore, there is no value hanging onto them. Bury them somewhere. Anywhere imagined will do.

PRACTICE

For a week, watch how you want the other to change to satisfy your own needs, i.e., the image you have to be fulfilled, the standard you are holding to be met, the other's self-improvement that has to be accomplished, the ideals that have to be lived up to.

Error #6: Dominate Others/Subjugate Self
To get to the non-disturbed state, our inner terrorists have developed two major tactics of deployment — to get the outside world to give them what they are seeking: They threaten and intimidate, or they seduce and flatter. The threateners and intimidators blame, complain, stand up for "rights," and want "the other" to accommodate the blamer's needs. The seducers and flatterers please, appease, and follow the authorities, whom they presume know more about them than they know about themselves. Lastly, they want to be different to get rewards. Both groups depend on the outside world for fulfilling their aims. As

parasites, they are wholly dependent and at the same time voracious predators. Note that we don't have any rights in regards to our relationship to the world. Instead, we have privileges. The latter are given to us or taken from us by someone or something outside ourselves. For example: There is no right to citizenship or to vote. The only rights we have are inner rights — the rights to change beliefs, to love, to image.

Though we all contain characteristics of both blamers and pleasers, most of us lean to one mode of behaving more strongly. Stop and consider which parasitic group inhabits you: the intimidators or the flatterers? These two camps of social engagement have two strong correlating emotional states: anger and guilt.

PRACTICE

For a week, notice how often you and those around you blame, complain, appease, please, and submit to authority.

Error #7: Accounts Receivable and Payable

Feelings of anger and guilt long held onto give way to errors called "accounts receivable" and "accounts payable," respectively. These accounts are held in big, oversize ledger books and bank vaults in consciousness. Accounts receivable means "you owe me" for some mis- or ill-conceived or supposed unjust transgression(s) that we hold over the other. Accounts receivable can be used as emotional blackmail or hurled as weapons of chronic blame or complaint by our inner terrorists against others to cow them into answering their demands. Typical terrorist talk includes: "They are making me miserable"; "They are making me angry, sad, fearful"; "They are responsible for the mess we're in." Funny thing about these "you owe me"s — they can never be paid off unless some event or situation occurs that prods us to close the ledger book. That can happen through forgiveness of the endlessly imposed debt or through some shift in the course of life. I know a gentleman who had a falling out with his younger brother. They didn't speak — literally — for 35 years. He held this account receivable against the younger sibling for an indefinable transgression. At the 35-year juncture, the younger one was made a judge in a state Supreme Court. The older man, becoming aware of this honor bestowed, picked up the phone to call and congratulate him, reconnected with him, repairing the discontinuity that had occurred 35 years earlier.

Regarding accounts payable, we "lay a guilt trip" on ourselves feeling we owe a debt to another. These supposed debts are usually made-up stories in our own mind. We believe these fictitious IOUs, or even actual ones, incurred at some point in the past, can never be paid off. No matter how hard we try, the ledger book remains open.

Guilt means to be in debt. If you have a debt in truth, pay it. Like a financial debt, pay it off as you are able. If it is not a genuine debt, drop it at once. Don't let the inner terrorists get the upper hand. Guilt feelings are unwarranted and unnecessary punishments for these "supposed" crimes or transgressions. These payable feelings are prompted by those inner terrorists.

Anger is at the base of all accounts receivable. Anger is a real feeling but most often unjustified. Irritation, annoyance, anger, and rage all proceed from a childish response to feeling frustrated, slighted, insulted, disparaged, or discarded. Our vanity has been pierced, and we act in anger to defend and prop it up. This anger violates at least three of the Ten Laws: idolatry — 2nd Law; murder — 6th Law; and envy/jealousy — 10th Law. Likewise, revenge, a form of anger, violates the 3rd Commandment of taking God's name in vain. After all, God clearly states "Vengeance is mine" (Deut. 32:35) and not for humans to reckon.

In either case, we have a responsibility to ourselves not to be hoodwinked by those inner terrorists for accounts on either side of the ledger. We can never become free, autonomous beings as long as we blame others or ourselves.

IMAGERY EXERCISE

FOREST OF FORGIVENESS: TO FORGIVE OTHERS

Sit up and close your eyes. Breathe out and in three times. See yourself walking on a country road. You are dressed in white. Walking along, you come to a forest. Approaching the first line of trees surrounding the forest, you see the people who have caused you much pain, hurt, and grief in your life emerging one by one from behind the trees.

Breathe out. Identify each of these people and have them approach you one by one. Tell each one what pain they have given you and ask them why. Hear their answer, and forgive each one and send them on their way behind you.

Breathe out. Taking a light with you, enter the forest, walking till you find a clearing. Stand in the center of the clearing. See the sun's rays beaming down, enveloping and penetrating you, cleaning and giving strength to you. As you leave the forest to return to your chair, be aware of the fragrance of the flowers and sound of the birds chirping. Breath out and open your eyes. Do this twice per day in the early morning and at sundown for some seconds each time, for 21 days.

Note: The people you encounter may change as you do the exercise. Anger is intimately connected to blaming another for your difficulties and/or their lacks. Here, you forgive them for being "imperfect beings."

PRACTICE

Make a list of all the accounts receivable you hold against others. Now make a list of accounts payable — who have you wronged? Confess to yourself the errors you have made and forgive yourself, asking your higher source of wisdom or God to forgive you as well.

Error #8: The Five Dark Currents of Will, Greed, and Vanity
Longing for a "nondisturbed" state, to have pleasure and avoid pain, leads us to use our will on a destructive course called the Five Dark Currents of Will: to take, keep, hold onto, and advance at the expense of others, and lastly, the desire to be great. The last, of course, refers to vanity. All of them add up to the *greed factor*, simply defined as wanting more, better, and different, an endless urge for the next big thing or the next largest bank account. To be caught in the grip of greed satisfies the demands of the god Mammon, the god of wealth, avarice, greed, and evil. Mammon is an idolatrous deity whom we are suckered into worshiping. I would recommend seeing the film *The Treasure of the Sierra Madre*, with Humphrey Bogart. It's hard to think of a clearer depiction of the consequences of such worship. Perhaps the fairy tale of the Midas Touch might rival it. Nevertheless, the promise is the reward waiting for us at the end of this journey through more, attachment, arduous effort, offering no happy ending, just suffering, misery, and decay in becoming a glutton of greed. Ordinary social mores place a primary value on attachments to the five dark currents. These five dark currents to possess what is not ours actually restrict our freedom because they reinforce our dependencies with decreasing self-empowerment. (See Dark and Light Currents of Will chart. See page 207)

Vanity and Pride: The Desire to Be Great
"Vanity, vanity, all is vanity," said the preacher in Ecclesiastes. Vanity is a false image we create about ourselves to make us appear perfect. We venerate our self as a god. At its extreme, we want to be worshiped and have others do our bidding and serve us. We exert our power to control others, to dominate and subjugate them, so we may feel we are the

most important. Examples abound in dictators, rock stars, celebrities, and athletes, but traces of vanity can be found in us all. Vanity's partner in this cosmic crime is pride, the defender of that false image. Pride makes us feel gratified and satisfied that what we are doing is honorable. Vanity is the fundamental moral error of human existence in the Western wisdom tradition. It stems from the seed source of feeling insufficient, as our greatest vanity is wanting to be God — omniscient and powerful.

I knew a man who was obviously vain, handsome as the day is long, the girls drooling all over him. He spent his days at the gym, extolling and pampering his body. He found a trophy wife — a woman loving and adoring by nature, as beautiful inside as outside. Needless to say, this unfortunate man was not able to consider others, as they were merely shadows there to serve him. He would pay no attention to her, leaving her feeling desperate for loving companionship and meaningful sexual intimacy. She became love-starved, malnourished physically, and suicidal while he masturbated away, naturally pleasing himself. Can we detect here the relationship of the physical, emotional, mental, and social parts of her life, not to neglect the moral? When asked why she didn't leave him, she replied, "I love him." Love him at the risk of your own life? Sacrificing yourself on the altar of his imbalances? An error of the second cosmic law — idolatry. Eventually she accepted his limitations, stayed in the marriage, and created her own independent life, rich in what she came to discover in herself, finding talents and qualities she didn't know existed. In accepting his limitations, she stopped making up stories of how he should be, took a leadership role in their relationship (rather than trophy wife), and sought her own inner development. He then began following her initiative and strength.

The Social Errors of Living: The Death Plan

PRACTICE

For the week, watch and observe when the urge for wanting more, better, or different arises.

Error #9: Enslavement
Choosing life means in one respect choosing freedom. Choosing death is to choose enslavement, the natural opposite choice to freedom. There are a number of such enslaved positions we can easily observe in ourselves and others. Let's look at several of them I have seen stand out in long experience as a clinician, healer, and teacher.

There are some generated at first internally and some created from our social relationships. The former result in erroneous thought patterns that enslave us mentally. One such common pattern is that "what was will be." If it happened, then it's bound to happen again. What happened in the past is bound to happen again in the future. By this inductive error of thinking, we can see there are no options, the past determining the future unerringly. But, indeed we have options moment by moment. At any moment we can change those seemingly hard and fast beliefs to create change in our situation.

Enslavements = Idolatries

1. *Enslaved thinking* = what was will be; what was then is now
2. *Determined* = by what another says, does, thinks, or feels
3. *Importance* = making someone or something more important than you
4. *Sacrificing Self* = on altar of another's imbalanced or dysfunctional needs
5. *Defending* = justifying, explaining, defending yourself to another
6. *Rejection* = believing others are more important than you
7. *Expectation* = expecting the external world to give us what we need

It's time to stop being grounded and to fly!

Another internal enslavement takes place when we find our mood determined by what someone else says, does, thinks, or feels, singly or in combination. Here we give away our freedom, cede our power to someone else, and find our self at the behest of another. Think of a holiday dinner where one person's bad mood casts a pall on the entire celebration.

A third type is a behavioral sort. Here we make someone, or something, more important than we are as we are now dependent on the other. This is a form of idolatry, violating the second spiritual law not to erect nor bow down before idols — including, of course, other human beings.

Out of this mistaken conception, we characteristically become anxious and weak. Another socially based enslavement rears up when we find ourselves mistakenly becoming subservient to the imbalances, instability, irrationality, and derangements of others. We sacrifice ourselves on the altar of the needs of another individual, group, institution, or principle. The slave world demands such sacrifice, but we are never to sacrifice ourselves if in doing so we bring injury or harm to ourselves. For example, a son or daughter sacrificing his/her life to the needs of a dysfunctional mother.

Here are two examples from my practice:

An "emergency" call from Wendy. She was up all night with nausea, constant diarrhea, and abdominal pain. "What's the false emergency?" I inquired after explaining to her that the symptoms were actually a cleansing response to the toxins created by the false emergency generated by some misconception and/or misperception going on. She replied that before calling me she had made her own effort to figure out what the false idea might be. She found that a great break came to her in a pointed way two weeks before when she was offered a job that gave her and the family much needed financial relief for a considerable number of months. Wendy found herself at that moment anxious and full of doubt. The latter got thrown up (vomited) into the mix when she weighed taking the offer against the burden — gladly taken — of ferrying her three children to interviews for choral solos. Carting them around and other side tasks were a financial burden that neither she nor her husband could afford at this time. They had some credit card debt hanging over them as well. Doubt tears us in two, as we all have known. She was torn between taking the offer and denying the children the opportunities offered to them.

Of course, there was no true emergency here. No one's life was in the balance, although by false emergency standards it might appear to be so. In the false emergency state, she took the if-then approach and destructiveness that phrase brings: "*If* I don't take them, *then* there won't be any further opportunities for these evidently talented children who had been praised and appraised before as talented." I explained to her the presence of the false emergency, which she was aware of through her studies but had forgotten. I then reminded her of the spiritually incumbent need for us to be prudent. She was further reminded of the ancient maxim of Rabbi Hillel 2,000 years or so ago: "If I am not for me, who will be for me?" Once in order, through attention to be good, kind, loving, respectful, honest, and caring for oneself, then the second part of the maxim follows: "If I am only for myself, then what am I?" The third part: "If not now, when?" She took it to heart, and we took up the lesson not to lie down and sacrifice herself on the altar of another's needs so as to bring harm, injury, or expense to her. The intestinal symptoms reflected her trouble digesting this conflict and the error of becoming a slave to her ideas around what her children needed. With that I recommended Kaopectate for diarrhea and gave her the Swallowing the Rainbow imagery exercise to relieve the nausea.

We Are Not *Meant* to Die

IMAGERY EXERCISE

SWALLOW THE RAINBOW: FOR NAUSEA

Close your eyes and breathe out and in three times slowly. See yourself swallowing a rainbow moving as a spiral gently through your digestive tract in a clockwise manner, the muscles of the intestinal walls moving gently in the same direction as the rainbow, sensing the nausea ceasing. The rainbow moves throughout the entire intestinal tract, taking away the toxins and bringing them out through the anal opening as black or gray strands getting buried deep in the earth. Know your digestive tube is normalizing. Breathe out and open your eyes.

Do again as needed until the tract becomes normalized.

I was speaking on the phone to Alice, an older woman, about her chronic conflictual relationship with her husband. She said that recently her thoughts turned toward considering death. She reasoned that at this time of her life, it was natural to be thinking about the end of life. I offered that thoughts can be about life rather than death. I mentioned that King Solomon offered an antidote to death in his comment in the Song of Songs that love is strong as death. I referred to the statement in Deuteronomy about the option of choosing life and... At that moment her husband came unannounced into the room. She asked me to hold on and returned two or three minutes later. She apologized for going away, saying the husband asked her to get his wallet. She accommodated him at the expense of missing out on further comments about a subject that has now become vitally important to her. I asked her if he was disabled, couldn't retrieve the wallet himself, and was it an emergency that she "steal" time from herself? She responded that he was perfectly able to get the wallet himself, and the situation did not constitute a true emergency.

This interruption set the stage for an opportunity to provide a round of spiritual education. It is precisely in the everyday, ordinary life situations that we find the turning point to take another step in our personal, spiritual evolution on the path to life. The circumstance surrounding the interruption becomes the hologram for understanding a habitual, conditioned way of living in the manner of a slave from early on in life.

She agreed that his demand for the wallet elicited a false emergency state powered by anxiety. The content associated with the anxiety was of the "if-then" variety: "If I don't respond to his directive, then he will be angry at me." It did occur to her to tell him at first that he should fetch it himself and in addition that she was on a telephone call. However, she didn't. Note that it was an unnecessary addendum to even mention she was on "a call" to justify why she didn't hark to his immediate demand. Firstly, he noticed her on the phone. Secondly, having to defend, justify, or explain your position to another human is a major form of enslavement, in which we commit an error with regard to the 2nd Commandment not to erect or bow down before idols.

When we feel compelled to justify ourselves, we are in essence bowing down to another, making this person the authority over us. The only authority over us is Invisible Reality — God. Underlying these errors of idolatry is the belief that if we act autonomously, we will be rejected by the other. We can only feel rejected if we make the other more important than ourselves. When we truly act for ourselves, we act in a balanced manner that often has the effect of bringing others into balance.

As long as Alice commits to an enslaved way of living, she can see no way out of her husband's imposed "me real, you shadow" game. And is it no wonder that our conversation began with her musing about death?

The final type of enslavement actually incorporates an inner emotional and mental error with a social one. Overall, we are miseducated to expect — a feature of future talk itself. This error is to expect perfection to come from our social relationships. Everything depends on what is given to me from elsewhere. It is felt particularly strongly, as mentioned above, when we seek to change what it is to what it ought to be. To repeat: All of those dependencies coalesce in the absolute false belief around which our human world revolves: The purpose of living is to get to that promised non-disturbed state and avoid that dreaded pain.

PRACTICE

For one week, watch when you get caught by one or another of these seven major idolatrous behaviors.

IMAGERY EXERCISE

ALTAR OF IDOLATRY: FOR COMING OUT OF ENSLAVEMENT

Close your eyes and breathe out and in three times slowly. See yourself bound up on the altar of your own enslavement, allowing yourself to be sacrificed.

Breathe out. Have with you *whatever you need* to remove the restraints.

Breathe out. Stand up, stand erect, and see yourself walking to a new future bathed in light.

Discover what's awaiting you there. Breathe out and open your eyes.

Do this exercise every morning for seven days upon awakening.

The Social Errors of Living: The Death Plan

Error #10 — "But Seriously"

The last great social error is seriousness. In the words of my teacher Colette, "Seriousness is the gravest error that exists for an individual." When I thought about it, I became increasingly aware of how pervasive this quality is in our lives. It literally rains down on us constantly. We are flooded by serious news broadcasts, serious personal situations, and serious feelings about events taking place in the family, in the neighborhood, in the community, nationally, globally. It is a chronic condition of medical and psychological diagnoses that are delivered in serious tones. Seriousness is the chronic, ceaseless bombardment connected directly to the emergency state. It is a deflated, down, even depressed mood and state of emergency, the latter being the anxiety, worry, fear-laden side. Taken together, seriousness and false emergency are the bipolar analogy to bipolar mental disturbance. This counterpart team prods us with future talk — what's ahead — and past talk, or what's behind. Seriousness has us constantly looking at what was as it invades our present calm and serenity. It is a perfect example of how the concern about the past vaults ahead into the future, giving us cause and pause to concern ourselves with future consequences that are always attached to the seriousness of how we live that serious moment.

One other area that relates to seriousness as a kind of sibling is poor self-image. In the competitive dog-eat-dog world, we are commonly pressured to compare ourselves to others in so many ways. Certainly, the fashion industry, which we take seriously, is always setting trends that you must adhere to if you want to be in fashion, to have the correct self-image to present to the world, to be in the in-crowd.

All of the man-made standards are touted by the authorities as the means of our self-preservation. The authorities require that we be serious and have the "correct" self-image. Many people give serious attention to and ascribe much meaning to achieving the perfect image. It's not surprising how many fall short of accomplishing such a spurious standard, because it's not meant to be fulfilled. What's meant is for us to waste our energy scurrying hither and thither in a serious state of mind, maybe beating ourselves up for failing to have the proper self-image.

I know of one antidote that cancels out seriousness and poor self-image: *humor!* We can stop taking ourselves seriously and find ways to laugh at ourselves, at the goings-on in the world, at the farce played out by those authorities who claim to stand up and speak for us. In the ancient wisdom, such merchants of fame and seriousness were called "black magicians." Today they still exist prominently among us all over the world.

In general, attitudes of seriousness make us feel weak and without hope. Humor and laughter, on the other hand, make us feel stronger and hopeful. That is why comedy and comedians are important vital factors for health in our lives. Robin Williams, after giving a performance in Germany, was interviewed by *Der Spiegel,* the most prominent German newspaper. The reporter asked him why Germans are serious so much and don't have the humor and comedic talent that exists in America. Williams responded: "Because you killed all the funny people."

It is of interest to note a comment Woody Allen made to me about 65 years ago, that "manslaughter" is "man's laughter." It is a shorthand way of understanding the vast, socially destructive implications of seriousness, not only in personal terms where we see how serious one becomes when incurring any sort of physical malady, but in the larger context of war. Here seriousness and strife are constantly conveyed on TV through endless scenes of killing, murder, carnage — manslaughter — keeping seriousness center stage, preoccupying our thoughts on a day-to-day basis with how unsafe we are. In the wake of the destruction, man's laughter is an imperative for health and healing.[31] To laugh

---

[31] In 1990, Norman Cousins, the editor of *Saturday Review of Literature,* wrote

The Social Errors of Living: The Death Plan

is a holy act. To laugh at someone's disability is a cruel act. To laugh with someone and to make someone laugh are acts of love.

I was in conversation with Darlene: Her demeanor was very serious; she was talking about eye cataracts. Her elderly mother was found to have one on a recent exam. She did research on cataracts and discovered a lot. She said that if she had recognized some earlier sign of her mom's complaint about the eye, she would have taken her for an eye exam. She blamed herself for not realizing it then.

I intervened here. Her seriousness gave way to her emphasis on the past, on self-blame: "If I had only understood then." She was focusing on "how stupid of me," the NO of life, instead of the YES of life here in the present. Together we came to an understanding and knowing that what had passed was finished, dead, buried, ended, gone. The present yes was given short shrift, trivialized in favor of what was, which was no longer accessible. The present wasn't neglected but it was overridden by the unimportant, meaningless concern.

The spiritual point here is subtle but no less significant. Seriousness brings a sense of gloom. The practice is to say YES to life. The choice is always there: YES or NO. Almost everyone's preference is for NO, as the trend of general education since infancy is to elect NO.

Plain and simply said, the Life Path hasn't been taught. The Life Path is the spiritual one. It's a new education. The example of Darlene portrays that choice in the subtle way just cited. She got all out of joint ruminating on what was "wrong" with her. It was all the more intense since it had to do with her mother, whom she was "diligent" in caring for. She was pointed to what was "right," what she accomplished in learning about cataracts that could now be put to use for her mom sans

---

Anatomy of an Illness, his groundbreaking book on combating and curing cancer through humor. The book was published by W. W. Norton (New York).

the seriousness but with firm action. The YES of now as meaningful replaced the NO of meaningless and uselessness of personal past critical judgment.

PRACTICE

For a week, laugh, smile, and greet everyone with a cheerful face. Notice when you are unable to. What is the error you are falling into?

SECTION III

The Life Plan:
Laws of Detachment and
Practices of Ectropy

We Are Not *Meant* to Die

"Synchronicity is another form of watching that increases
our field of awareness and gives us a deeper
understanding of chance, coincidence,
and the simultaneity of thought and events."

CHAPTER X

Developing Spiritual Awareness

The Heartbeat of GEMS

WE HAVE ARRIVED AT THE HEART OF THE BOOK — the foundational principles and the practices to detach from our conditioned life and make a turn toward Spirit. This is what makes GEMS work. Here we find our antidote to our errors of living that quell the inner terrorists and cultivate the spiritual gifts within ourselves. We adopt new attitudes and practices: We relegate logically based mechanical thinking to its proper place and elevate analogic/intuitive thinking as a primary mode of thought in our socially based world. We reorient ourselves to new values, discarding our pursuit of quantity and the control of the future to embrace the moment. Pursuing this path grants us freedom from the constraints of authority-dominated life, where an authority presumes to know more about us than we do. Not so here: We are educating ourselves to know that we know more about ourselves than anyone else, or what we thought we knew. We turn to the invisible world, to our inner self, to make our own self-discoveries to become free, whole, healthy, and holy — "*kailo.*" Here we have the possibility to heal, to become unified with ourselves and our Source. All the practices described here are aimed toward our becoming our own authority, self-knowing, self-sufficient, self-empowered, and responsible — summed up as a mature, flexible adult. Out of this self-knowing, change occurs naturally. We don't need to chase it or strive after it.

Each of these varied practices is an unconditioned approach to life: to replace doubt by faith, the primacy of logic by direct intuition, anger and hate by love; to turn personal willfulness into moral action; to reverse pipe dreams, fantasies, and mental mirages, turning them into creative imagination; to emerge from the fear of darkness into the radiance of light.

When I had my turning point in 1974 with Colette, described in the Introduction, I actually enrolled in a school where she was the headmistress — a school of spiritual education much like that spoken of in the Book of Kings called Sons of the Prophets. Here she became my teacher. Now I am enrolling you in this school of spiritual education to go to a higher level of education beyond the formal one received in the ordinary course of life. Here you are intended to graduate with a degree — called DSM, Doctor of Spiritual Medicine, or, if you will, Doctor of Self-Mastery. The process has actually begun by introducing you to the errors of living.

When I took up my studies with Colette, I found myself naturally taking on another way of life. I began to see life through a different lens, repurposed and more conflict-free. I not only followed her teaching and prescriptive practices but also experienced a new relationship alongside hers – one with the Invisible Reality, an alliance with that Reality I called God.

To enter the school, you need to have some sense of an Invisible Reality beyond a mere materialistic worldview. One student called my work "secularized faith," as it spoke to his yearning for a relationship with the divine without the dogma or man-made standards of organized religion.

For many, reestablishing a love relationship with the vertical is the starting point; for others detaching from the false selves is the initial quest toward freedom. Some gravitate to mental imagery as a central practice, others to the development of will through observation and stopping exercises. All act to remember ourselves in a new way. As to change, we don't set out to "improve" ourselves; rather, we come to a place of self-knowing. Inner "change" then happens naturally, as I just mentioned. This in turn is reflected in our outer experience of circumstances and relationships. It doesn't really matter where we start, because we all are climbing the ladder of self-mastery.

The material world is a world of ceaseless change. What is immutable is our relationship to the vertical. When we experience this, we learn to feel comfortable in the sea of change of our daily life.

Now we can get started on our exploration where life begins and never ends. We are about to discover those practices for bringing life to create endless life. Get set to become the captain of your ship. Here are some major ports of call:

- The Alliance: A Love Relationship with God
- Will: The Force of Life
- Remembering: Restoring Ourselves to Wholeness
- Watching: Observing the Inner Terrorists
- Reversing: The Way to Self-Organization and Eternal Life

The Alliance: Creating a Love Relationship with God

So what is the Alliance? About 4,000 years ago, monotheistic spirituality was born in the momentous meeting between the human father, Abraham, and the intangible father, God. God offers Abraham the "sun, moon, and stars," everything the human heart could desire in exchange for Abraham's swearing an oath of allegiance to the supreme One Mind, to enter into a sacred contractual relationship swearing to live and abide by God's laws and ways.

God asks Abraham to forsake the murderous ways of the idolatrous people and tribes around him that engaged in human sacrifice of men, women, and children to propitiate their gods and be granted bounty in their crops, rains, goods, progeny, and victories in war. God's deal is a 180-degree turnabout from the other tribes' contracts with their gods; he asks Abraham to curb murderous impulses. The penultimate expression of this contract is the gift of the Ten Laws of balance and salvation for us and the planet given at Mount Sinai, known as the Ten Commandments.

As Abraham's progeny, we too are asked to reaffirm this pact of life; to turn away from our own errors of living — our attempts to appease our modern false gods to control the "future crops."

In return for fulfilling the terms of the agreement, Abraham is promised that his people will become as numerous as the stars in heaven and the sand of the sea. How could Abraham, in this unimaginable encounter, experiencing awe, bliss, and "supernatural" illumination," answer anything but yes? And so, monotheism was born. And so, all of us wanting to follow this glorious path to become spiritual beings of light ask ourselves, deal or no deal? If the answer is yes — proceed.

If the answer is no, you can still benefit from these practices and find renewed health, more harmonious relationships, and less distress. As you explore the inner realms of existence through mental imagery, quell the inner terrorists through the Ten Laws, and think intuitively, you climb your ladder of self-mastery. On its rungs, like Jacob, you may encounter an angel or two. To help you up this climb, there are three seminal principles and practices to remind us how to "think vertically": Remembering, Watching, and Reversing. We use our will to direct our attention to them.

Will: The Force of Life

Will as the spark of life is a necessary precondition or component of any activity, be it mental or physical, inner or outer. Will acts as the steering wheel in our ship of life. It comes to us as a Divine Force that we choose to use as we wish. We may use our will in a new way, to choose a new direction in life, to make a turn to spiritual life, to forge an alliance with Invisible Reality, and to align our will with Divine Will. In the next chapter, we shall explore this use of will in depth as one of the seven Divine Forces.

Remembering: Restoring Ourselves to Wholeness

The "trick" to keep track of the moment and not lapse into the web of linear time — or the future and past — revolves around the practice of remembering. The term "remember" has a special currency, as it involves both a physical and a mental attribute. To remember on the physical level means to restore the body to wholeness. To remember here entails re = again and member = body parts; specifically those body parts, namely legs, arms, and penis, called members. Remembering refers then to attaching one or more of these members to the torso proper. To remember mentally is defined as bringing back to mind or recalling, recollecting to memory, what has been or may have been forgotten. It is to become mindful, to be or become attentive to the practice of life and longevity developed here.

Remembering, as a holy act of living, is deeply bound to memory. There are four types of memory:
1. Factual
2. Logical
3. Moral
4. Vertical

Factual memory consists of those mountains of facts we retain that form the focal point of early education. Logical memory is how we are taught later on in childhood to make sense of these facts. These might be seen as how we are taught to function adequately on the everyday level, the horizontal.

Moral memory connects us with the vertical reality and reinforces our connection to divinity. Vertical memory is what we learn to make sense out of this attachment to this invisible realm. It provides an option to repurpose our life and supplies a change of reference of how we see ourselves, the world, and our self in the world.

The first two memories gradually erode with age and manifest with the development of organic brain disorders like Alzheimer's syndrome. As we mature, moral and vertical memory, which never erode, replace the other two — that is, if you have sought to take some sort of turn toward Spirit. If not, existence becomes quite narrowed, as we witness to the extreme in organic brain difficulties.

All of the practices hinge on the function of remembering: to do the practice; to stay *in* the moment; to bring oneself back to unity from the dismembered state of being that characterizes most of our existence in this time-space world. What is actually going on regarding our living in this everyday world? It can be schematically diagrammed this way:

FORGETTING ⟵⟶ REMEMBERING

SLEEP ⟵⟶ AWAKENING

DEATH ⟵⟶ BIRTHING (LIVING, LOVING)

Our primary step here is to turn forgetting to remembering. The constant hypnosis we are subjected to each day through the media and advertising plus our habitual inner personal suggestions and beliefs make us forget ourselves. Then we are influenced to give ourselves over to the sway of others, their demands and standards.

The importance of remembering comes to us from the ancient wisdom of the West. The ancient writings are as relevant today as they were then. They are treasure troves of knowledge, understanding, and methods to help us maintain unity, integrity, balance, and above all, life. The ancient stream of spiritual guidelines were written and preserved for eternity. We are graced to be able to draw upon them. A particular one I have in mind comes from the Pharaonic Egyptian tradition.

A Story of Love, Remembrance, Resurrection
The legend derived from the Pharaonic wisdom of Osiris and Isis speaks volumes in how its impact and influence spread to the culture of ancient Greece and the formation of Christianity, influencing also, in some measure, the development of Hebraic spirituality.

Osiris was the Egyptian god of the netherworld, that which existed between this world and the world beyond life to that of eternity. When a person died, Osiris weighed his or her heart against a feather. If the heart outweighed the feather, that soul would have to return here to live through this sort of life again. If the feather outweighed the heart, the soul was freed to set off to the realm of eternity. His wife was Isis, the goddess of wisdom, and no mortal man could know her mystery. Osiris's brother was Seth, the god of disorder, violence, and storms. Seth was jealous of Osiris and his greater status. One day he murdered Osiris, placed his body in a coffin, and sailed it down the Nile, where it floated into the Mediterranean Sea, landing on the shores of Lebanon. Isis got wind of what happened, turned herself into a swallow, and flew from Egypt across the Mediterranean to Lebanon. She alit by the coffin, becoming Isis once again, and opened the coffin to find the dead Osiris. She bent over and kissed him on the lips, and he came back to life, and both returned to Egypt as the restored couple. On the shores of Lebanon grew the now renowned Cedars of Lebanon.

Here we have the story of love and how it brought the dead one back to life — resurrection. The story continues:

Seth discovers Osiris is now alive. He seeks out his brother and murders him again. This time he dismembers him into 14 pieces and buries the parts in different locations of Egypt. Again, Isis finds out and sets off to collect the dismembered parts. She re-membered him back together physically and mentally (through imaging him as whole). He returns to life again, this time resurrected through remembering, the first time resurrected through love. Isis holds the key to love, wholeness, health, healing, holiness, and resurrection, while Osiris holds the key to eternal life.

Many mythological tales are really archetypal messages about how we can live our time here on Earth. The archetype is a model that demonstrates what quality is available to us to fulfill here on Earth in our time. The story of Isis and Osiris represents the possibility of defeating death when we engage in acts of remembering ourselves. As remembering grows, we awaken, becoming increasingly attuned to Spirit, where we find our freedom. Eventually the contribution of re-membering and awakening leads to coming back to life, a rebirth, itself a mini resurrection, a continuous choosing of life onward to eternal life that includes a synthesis of body, soul, Spirit.

In contrast, the usual state of affairs is represented on the other side of the trichotomy. Forgetting is a general state of being. We see its effects certainly in older people suffering from the avoidable maladies of old age — Alzheimer's, organic brain disorder, arteriosclerotic degeneration. Here, memory has diminished markedly and existence becomes narrowed to a bare shell. I say avoidable maladies, because in practicing remembering, you are taking steps to prevent these situations. Forgetting leads naturally to, and is the younger brother of, sleeping, which in turn is the younger sibling of death.

Developing Spiritual Awareness

Remembering God is paramount. We want to love God with heart, might, and soul. We want to be in the Alliance. Remember to have Invisible Reality in your thoughts. The practice ground for this love is to love your neighbor as yourself. This love is one of putting yourself in the shoes of the other to understand the other. With this understanding comes the recognition of what he/she is about, the realness of who he/she is. We understand their struggles are no different from ours. Knowing this allows us to accept the other's foibles, liabilities, limits, and all. And with acceptance comes the possibility for forgiveness; with that forgiveness comes the ability to love, to become loving. At the same moment we know that everyone has a redeeming feature and everyone has consequences for their actions. There are karmic debts to take care of and the scales of justice must be balanced. Loving your neighbors doesn't relieve them from having accountability for the errors they've committed.

We often buy into false beliefs such as "People know what's right but do the wrong thing anyway." In fact, the truth is they are what they are and do what they do. They need to be seen in the proper light, not through rose-colored glasses, otherwise we are trying to make what is into what ought to be. Take the enabling spouse who unfortunately promotes the alcoholism of their mate. This spouse has fallen asleep and needs to be awakened. You see, we really can't afford to forget and fall asleep.

I know how hard it is to stay awake and to keep remembering. After all, we have a tough time facing our own limitations and accepting ourselves to end up loving ourselves just as we love God and our neighbors. Actually coming to love ourselves (not the pseudo love of vanity) will feed the other two loves. And this self-love comes through accepting ourselves for strengths and weaknesses, limitations and talents.

The task before us is to remember and reverse. When you fall asleep and forget, or when you forget and you suddenly remember you forgot, do not get down on, criticize, or judge yourself. Simply use this painful experience as the prompt to make the necessary correction through one of the techniques you find in these pages.

It looks like a new relationship is forming, one between remembering, becoming whole/unified/one, and life. This understanding is fortified by variant terms connected to remembering: recollect, recall, remind. To collect is to bring together. Recollect is to do this again: collect ourselves once more after living a dismembered, scattered life. The call is to hear a summons to live. Recall is to hear that call again, that original call from our divine nature to come back to ourselves. Mind is that channel of communication between invisible and visible reality. Remind is to alert us to be mindful of that link existing between the two realms. The act of remembering (and the awakening to life it brings) exerts that call, bringing us back to life from the brink of death. This is a resurrective act enacted while we are in life. It is the appetizer of the banquet we are invited to, called immortality = im = without, mortality = death.

The premier memory exercise I've found is simply to constantly keep in mind — remind ourselves — the Ten Commandments, love of God, to be harmless and considerate (these two are part of loving one's neighbor), and to share your wisdom with others, when asked.

What puts a strain on memory is loss. In research done on centenarians about the ability to sustain longevity, one common thread stood out: the ability to bear loss. Loss is significant in the response of depression. In this mood state, memory becomes diminished (and can often be mistaken for organic brain deterioration). Loss and depression can also be a major factor in dying: the inability to rebound from the loss of loved ones. Memory loss, loss of loved ones, depression, and organic brain breakdown seem related. Remembering our spiritual connections acts as immunity against these erosive forces, a prevention of aging and a pathway to longevity and unending life.

Developing Spiritual Awareness

When the people of the Earth become attuned to their spiritual calling and, in the Western tradition, remember God, *then* God remembers us in a two-step process: resurrection and eternal life.

Resurrection reflects the mutual process of our remembering God and God's remembering us. Without the latter there is no defeat of death. But defeat of death will take place, for God loves us and will never desert us, no matter how long it takes. Once all are called to return to life, the mission of this Earth will be fulfilled.

What we remember mentally is most significant, because it is a key to unending life as well as its forerunner, longevity. As noted above, the practice of the Ten Commandments is a constant act of remembering: remembering God and the Alliance. Remembering also plays a fundamental role in all the methods and techniques outlined in this book.

God said to choose life or death. Each act of remembering is a device for life. Every time you remember to carry out a spiritual act or practice, there is a concomitant uplifting response physiologically! You have chosen life! What more could be asked of us than to remember? What could be a more difficult task to ask of us? We develop habits early on that follow us through life. Habits work by having us forget so we come to respond robotically, mechanically. On the other hand, we can work against mechanical behavior by remembering, practicing faith, and accepting change. Most people are afraid of change to some degree, even to the point of dread. Unfortunately, this resistance is so strong that it often takes a war to affect some shift (namely, a great breakdown [entropy] followed by a greater buildup and organization [ectropy]). In my lifetime I have noticed great changes in the movement of our society and many social shifts that ensued. World War II ushered in TV and many home conveniences like air-conditioning, washing machines, and jet travel. The Korean War opened up the technological revolution and the beginning of the computer age. Also, *Brown v. the Board of Education* marked the beginning of the civil rights movement. Vietnam opened the door to the East: meditation, healthy food, health-care techniques like acupuncture. The Gulf War, Iraq, and Afghanistan thrust the Arab world onto the world stage. What that will bring is yet to be determined. There is certainly a palpable shift in health-care awareness and the breakdown of institutions that have held sway for millennia.

We don't need war and the sacrifice of so many young men and women who are viewed by the power brokers on all sides as nothing more than anonymous shadows doomed to die or be maimed physically and/or emotionally. Remembering creates an antidote to all this violence. Fifty times in the Bible we find the most oft-quoted comment to *remember* the widows and orphans in their need.

Watching: Observing the Inner Terrorists

The purpose of watching is dedicated to our coming to know ourselves so we can take steps to reunite ourselves. In spiritual terms, suffering is synonymous with becoming dismembered. A disunity has occurred between the two fundamental natures of self: material and soul, form and formless. Our quest is to put ourselves back together (as described in the Egyptian legend of Osiris and Isis).

In the theater of life, these two natures are both you the audience member, or soul/watcher, sitting in the orchestra and you the actor, material body, on stage carrying out your way in the actional world. The two are in a mutual, entwined relationship until the intruders, the inner terrorists, enter the field and act to bring divisiveness between the two. These interlopers exert their power of hypnosis to put the soul nature to sleep and/or entice the material side to come under its sway. Whichever takes place, the net result is a severing of this union.

The watcher or observer is an inner information network. It's a *function*, not a thing like a physical object. Rather, it's an internal function within us that observes us participating in our inner stream of conscious thought and outer interpersonal behavioral world. Unlike mental imagery, another information network between the worlds, the watcher is passive — an observer. The watcher sits in the audience of the Theater of Life to observe and report back to the Higher Source of Wisdom. Much of the time it is asleep, crowded out by the false terrorists in the loge who have taken over the theater, directing the actors in a pulp-fiction play.

Spiritual life is the process of awakening the watcher through an act of will. As the watcher awakens, we act to curb the false selves by telling Higher Wisdom the truth as the observable facts of the matter at hand. As the false selves are quieted, the emanations from the Seven Divine Forces stream down from above, bringing us information in the form of intuition (unconditional thought), mental imagery (unconditional language), love (unconditional feeling), and faith (unconditional action).

As we start cleaning out the mistakes of living, we pave the way for reuniting the two natures to become one again. The disunited, dismembered self becomes one unified Self. This movement toward Self is where health, healing, wholeness, and holiness take place, where death is disappearing. A normal occurrence is our opening up directly to the messages coming to us from our Universal Source in the form of intuitive knowledge, clarity of vision, foresight, moderation, and balance.

Discernment: An Active Form of Watching
To discern is to distinguish between things, to make distinctions, to recognize and detect mentally, to separate and sift. The definitions can go on even further. Discernment is an act of perception or conception, externally or internally. Why is this practice important to us? The answer: because we need to be able to detect what is true and false, facts from various forms of fiction (opinions, conclusions, assumptions, and

the like), accuracy from misperception.

Let me give some examples. We are always called on to discern whether we are attending to what is true — the idea expressed *in the present*, or what is stated in the future or the past — false, untrue. This premise is central to the whole possibility of longevity and immortality. Why? Because our connection with time or timelessness has a direct influence on our biological/physiological system. Each time we advance into the future or regress into the past, the biological system takes a hit. As you may be realizing, we *are* a biomental, mindbody, essence-existence, invisible-visible unity.

Everything that is true comes to us as a direct perception and conception with no distortions added by embellishments, unnecessary descriptors (as most are), stories, opinions, or explanations usually considered as fact. The straight perception/conception in front of us at this moment is called a *phenomenon*, something that shows or appears, an observable fact coming to awareness. Perceptions are gleaned through the senses as direct apprehension, without the mediation or interference of interpretative thought. These perceptions occur when the senses are turned toward the everyday world or are turned inward to apprehend dreams or discover our inner information network called image. Sometimes we can perceive other inner image phenomena that are real but *not* based in truth, such as hallucinations.

Inner conceptions bearing the stamp of holiness are flashes of insight, intuitive thoughts, sudden "aha" understanding, and the ability to discern inner qualities and relationships called "wisdom." When conceptions occur, something is birthed in the inner forum of consciousness, either as an idea or image, gestating, about to burst forth. We become pregnant, as it were. It happens personally, irrespective of the world around us. Can these perceptions and conceptions be untruthful? Definitely. Misperceptions and misconceptions are facts of life. A story from India highlights this point:

Developing Spiritual Awareness

Two men are walking through the jungle. Suddenly one man recoils in fear. The other asks what's wrong. The first man says there is a snake (cobra) on the ground in front of them. The second man looks at what is pointed at, walks over to it, picks it up, shows it to the second man, and says, "See, this is a rope. You misperceived it as a snake."

The first man projected his own personal fear onto the situation and jumped (literally and figuratively) to a faulty conclusion. He stepped outside the Alliance at that moment and created a false emergency state, responding as though there truly was an emergency. This action then set off a host of physiological and biological reactions, throwing his system into imbalance and necessitating inner activity to recover after recognizing the untruth of his conception/perception. Furthermore, an energy depletion took place. He went the Death Path: depletion, leading eventually to decay, ultimately to demise. The other friend was sober, chaste, thoughtful, calm, temperate, and moderate, not extreme. He kept his wits about him and acted appropriately. He didn't disperse his life force and was able to show his fearful friend the error of physical, emotional, and mental jumping. He discerned. He saw what IS and was immediately in receipt of an appropriate action to take: making a contribution to his friend, being considerate and harmless. He was a lifesaver, showing his friend how to become his own savior.

Synchronicity: A Law of Unity

Synchronicity is another form of watching that increases our field of awareness and gives us a deeper understanding of chance, coincidence, and the simultaneity of thought and events. I call it the law of unity: two events occurring at different intervals, or at simultaneous moments, that are experienced as uncannily connected though not by ordinary logic in a linear cause-and-effect manner. We feel surprise and perceive right away that these two events are related to each other. Here are some examples to demonstrate, *not* to convince:

In the late afternoon I arrived to find my daughter at home. She was dressed rather elegantly in a long, tapered outfit of black and white garments meaningfully arranged one around the other. On seeing this, I exclaimed, "How beautiful! You look like a penguin." She responded, "It's funny you said that. I went to see a movement therapist this morning [dressed in an exercise outfit], and she asked me to do an exercise she called the penguin!" Being alert to the simultaneity of relational thinking, that is the law of unity in which two things come together as one in a unity of experience, shows the underlying origins of life upon which our ordinary life of time-space reality rests. I became aware of the two events becoming one and felt a moment of joyful exuberance. The outer world awareness reinforces what I'm coming to realize through the rejoicing in my inner awareness. Just that noticing is enough. There is no need to find, nor attribute any further meaning to the event. Only to say "thank you" above for showing it to me.

One more: I'm in conversation with a friend by phone. During the course of speaking, I quote Lao Tzu from a book I was reading. It had to do with what can be named is *not* the Tao. We go on talking about that and other things. I did not tell her the title of the book, or the author. Almost ten to 15 minutes later, she uttered an unusual word not part of her daily vocabulary, using a word I hadn't heard within our frequent contact over a three-year period. She exclaimed she is having an "ultra" feeling (meaning high) about something. The book I had quoted was called *Ultra Solutions*.

Quite commonly, as I sit and write, whether it be a book or blog articles, I usually have the radio on to music with some interspersed announcements. The announcer says a certain word at the exact moment I am writing that word! I certainly notice the simultaneity and enjoy the moment of astonishment.

The law of unity touches on coincidence and chance. For spiritual life nothing is left to chance, nor is there "coincidence," as generally understood in common parlance.

Coincidence is directly associated with chance in the broad material scientific community. There coincidence and chance mean something just happens at a given moment for which there is no rational or natural scientific explanation because such happenings defy the law of cause and effect underlying the way experience is understood. Once some event is perceived to lie outside the realm of cause leading to effect, essentially what we call "acausal," it bears no further investigation, is not really subject to natural scientific investigation, and becomes summarily dismissed.

However, the true meaning of coincidence is a foundational point of spiritual science. It means: two things *happening together*, simultaneously, at one with each other. Coincidence = co + incidence. An incidence/happening occurring "co" = together as one. This spiritual experience of perceiving or receiving oneness cannot be in the purview of natural science. Nothing blameworthy, no criticism there. Simultaneity — or its more common usage, synchronicity — is not a premise that informs natural science: biology, chemistry, physics, quantitative mathematics, medicine, psychology, or any other field of inquiry that bases itself on the linear deterministic idea that one thing determines or causes what comes next.

Given this dedication to this one-purpose, materially influenced understanding of experience, it is not surprising that a spiritually directed, acausal, no-time-bound phenomenon is excluded from the scope of the material sciences.

Nevertheless, these phenomena are happening constantly, acknowledged and recognized by most everyone, everywhere. Synchronicity is a law of spiritual science whose domain is wholeness, unity, oneness, in contradistinction to the laws of material science cited above.

It is coincidence, synchronicity, simultaneity, the law of union that guides the development of the spiritually based GEMS.

I could go on with many other examples I've encountered. It happens consistently, as I see life now through a different lens than previously. It is a matter of making oneself acquainted with this phenomenon that often appears before us. What we need to embrace is a new view of coincidence, chance, and the simultaneity of events to realize there is an existence beyond time and space that is truly astonishing, where linear time dissolves into no-time, causality into acausality, disorganization becomes organized, disorder disappears into order, and duality becomes unity.

Reversing: The Way to Self-Organization and Eternal Life

I once asked Colette how she would sum up the entirety of her work. She was someone given to very pithy statements: short, piercing, and informative, telling statements that got to the heart of the matter quickly. This was someone who had been engaged in spiritual healing work since she was six years old. Her answer to me was "reversing." She wouldn't go any further to define what she meant by her terms. I had to make my own investigations about it, of course, which is the way we always worked.

We start off with the definition of "reversing" as turning "back." In a global sense, we turn back to the vertical reality to God, to Source. Reversing, detaching, returning, and renouncing are synonymous terms. The Master of Christianity said to his disciples: "You must renounce to be my students. You have to renounce all" (Luke 14:33). As we are not becoming monks, what does "renounce" mean in our life? It means to begin to detach from the morass of the man-made world. On a personal level, we ask ourselves to reverse the faulty belief systems that are rooted in attachment, insufficiency, and doubt. These in turn give rise to our errors of living, our pain and suffering, the "diseases," and our belief in our "inevitable death." To reverse is to come into balance. Only by reversing, or going in the opposite direction, can we attain balance. Balance is deeply connected to coming into order. All the practices outlined in this book are *actions* of reversing — in the mental, moral, social, emotional, and physical sphere — to shift from entropy to ectropy. Mental imagery is a type of reversing showing us possibilities if we look down an alternate and opposite path. Each of the Ten Commandments asks that we reverse our habits to come into balance, inwardly and communally.

Ten major practices of reversing are described in this book. These are in addition to actively calling and cultivating the Seven Divine Forces in your life. For me, the Ten Laws and, by extension, the Three Virtues have been central in my own spiritual unfoldment. As you engage in this work you may discover other reversing practices or you may be familiar with them from your spiritual quest, religious tradition, or mentors. Prayer asks us to reverse our habit of addressing our false selves and instead choose to speak to the One Mind. Stopping Exercises put a momentary wedge between our habitual stimulus response arc and an action that permits us to change direction. The "grammar of self" reverses our relationship to the troubles that our language gets us into. Imagery reverses our habit of thought as we turn to the imaginal (no-time zone) for answers rather than the habitual realm of logical thought. All spiritual practices take us out of attachment to linear time. We reverse our habitual stance toward wanting to move into the future rather than focus in the here and now. In the yes/no process, to be discussed, we reverse our habit of wanting our cake and eating it too — wanting perfection and certainty of outcomes. We also choose to eliminate doubt through faith-based action. In sum, we repurpose our habits through feelings and behavior to take a Life Path and return home.

CHAPTER XI

The Seven Divine Forces

- Will: Engine of Change, Creative Force, Life Force
- Love: Unconditional Feeling
- Faith: Unconditional Action
- Intuition: Unconditional Thought
- Imagination: Unconditional Language
- Hope: Perpetuation of Life
- Light: Driving Away the Darkness

As you recall from the Theatre of Life III Diagram (Integrated Life), there are Seven Divine Forces, gifts showered from the universe on us.

The Seven Forces nourish us and propel us to live freely. These forces act upon us as they simultaneously act through us. We engage with them as living, dynamic practices and attitudes toward life and to sustain life.

The first force is will. I call it "the birthing center of all life." Without it, nothing can proceed. The next four — love, faith, imagination, and intuition — I call the "Four Freedoms." Each is unconditional and independent of anything in the material world. The last two forces, hope and light, along with will, are inherent components of being that come into life with us and act as accelerants, propellants, or fuel igniting the other four.

Let's expand our understanding of these forces in greater depth.

Will: Engine of Change, Creative Force, Life Force

Will is the spark of life. That spark lights the fire of faith to move rather than remain static or become paralyzed by doubt. It is the life force impulse that enables us to make choices and take action. We each have a will and it is reflected in the choices we make each day, all day, when we arise, get up, dress, go to work, or engage in a spiritual practice. When we give our will a direction, we have an intention or aim. When we manifest our will through intention, we initiate the process of making visible what is invisible — we manifest and create. When we choose to watch, it is a function of our will as well. Will + direction = intention. Intention is an aim without consideration of a fixed goal or outcome.

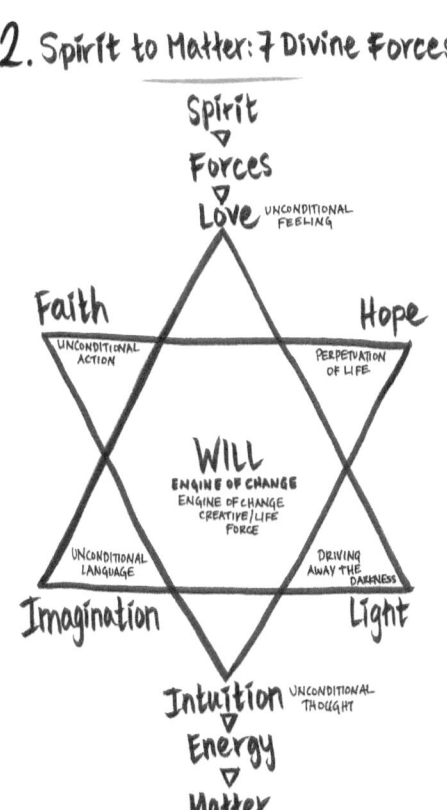

The intention is to will

or not to will, "that is the question." It is an act of faith, leaving the outcome in the hidden hands of God, who is in charge of the product. Each practice associated with spiritual education is will-based, in the sense of intention. It is neither willfulness nor even willpower. We do have to be willing to follow such a path. Will here is intimately tied to choice, always about choice. Want to find God? Want to find wealth? Want to develop the highest form of spiritual attainment in Western spiritual life — intuition? Want to become mindful passively as in Eastern meditational experience or mindful actively as in Western spiritual imaginal practice? It all depends on the choice of the use of will.

Will is the divine force that provides us with the possibility of true freedom. It is the will to live that keeps us going. It is this same sort of will that is used to die when individuals find the world is "too much with us." Free will — and choice — is a gift from God blanketing the Earth, giving Life to life. In using our will, we emulate the Great Will that directed the creation of this world. So it is given to us to give direction to this force, individually and in larger measure, such as the will of the people. This will is precious, and if we don't use it, we lose it and become somnolent, helpless, vulnerable.

In the exhortation of that monumental statement in Deuteronomy to "Choose life!" to choose is an act of will. We then take action, based on choice. That action is again an act of will to move. That action is called "decision." Decision means to act from. Mentally we make a choice in the moment and physically we take action to fulfill it. The choosing is paramount, not the choice. There is no right or wrong, good or bad choice. To know right or wrong, good or bad is virtually an impossibility, a burden heaped upon us by an authoritarian system. Buying into that impossibility makes it necessary to call upon authoritarian representatives to answer those future-based questions for us. Playing that game takes away our responsibility for taking immediate action as long as we insist on linking decision-taking with future possibilities rather than seeing it as a continued action of will to fulfill a choice.

The impulses of will are of five distinct kinds, first introduced in the Errors of Living. They can be classified as five *dark* currents (flows) or five *light* currents. From them we will derive a number of offshoots that have profound bearing on the type of life we are destined to lead.

The Five Dark Currents are: (1) to take, (2) to keep, (3) to hold onto at the expense of others, (4) to advance at the expense of others, and (5) the desire to be great (vanity). These dark currents follow the "laws of the jungle," survival of the fittest. These impulses pertain to our everyday living and become the basis of what we accept from our earliest conditioning to the various jobs we hold.

The everyday world operates according to the Five Dark Currents of Will — at home, in the neighborhood, the community, nationally, and worldwide. Our choices and free will allow us to temper and modulate them. We can reverse them to their opposites, the Five Light Currents: (1) to give, (2) to share, (3) to renounce, (4) to mentor or teach others, and (5) to become humble. We have the opportunity at each moment to take charge of them, to create an action to exemplify and concretize the reversed use of will while adapting a spiritual approach to life. This is where the technique of stopping comes in, found in Chapter XII. To stop means to curtail our impulsive activity, consciously. Stopping practices reverses our habitual way of thinking, feeling, and acting.

Do we direct our will to detach from hankering after material things, inner fantasies, beliefs, conclusionary thinking, goals, future thinking? Or do we misuse this precious life force to become a slave to the Five Dark Currents of Will that stoke the fire of greed?

Our heart and brain are acting together to bring a change in the direction of the will from its habitual way. The direction of the light currents provides an incredible access to a spiritual practice. Living out light currents gives us a direct connection to the light of Spirit, and that's a great beginning of turning to a new life. These Light Currents of Will provide the matrix for living in a socially shared collaborative world where love, cooperation, and altruism replace hate, anger, and greed.

Love: Unconditional Feeling

> Love God with all your hearts, soul, might. (Deut. 6:5)
> Love your neighbor as yourself. (Lev. 19:18)

In creating us, God bestowed on us unconditional love. Unconditional means no strings, conditions, contingencies, or dependencies. The act of creation via God's own contraction from all there is was an act of love.[32] Love equaled withdrawal! Now, we are left with a paradox. We think of love as merging, an attachment *extremis*. It is! And it is also the reverse! We detach, create a space — a space of freedom. This allows others to be who they are without being judged, accepted for who they are without conditions or standards to be met, without hav-

---

[32] In the Jewish spiritual tradition, an explanation of creation is given so: God covered everywhere and was everything. In an act of unimaginable love, God contracted to create a space so the created world could come into existence. This contraction is called *tzimtzum*.

ing to satisfy our needs. This love differs from the other five habitual forms based on satisfying mutual needs. These are: parent to child (pia), lover to lover (erotic), friend to friend (philo), teacher to student (the academic sense), and pastor to flock (theological). Instead it is a spiritual love of merging and detaching at the same time. It is one where I understand you by placing myself in your shoes so that I may love my neighbor as myself.

What has just been described here is unconditional love: The love King Solomon called "as strong as death." This is a healing power of the universe that comes to restore us to wholeness and unity. This is also the unprecedented sixth relationship formed between human beings that permits healing changes and forward movement in life (agape).

What becomes of this love that has no limits and is producing endless energy of ectropy to our physiology? It becomes attached vertically toward loving God, amping up the Alliance to a fever pitch. We yoke (yoga) ourselves to God as free beings willingly wanting to obey, listen to, and become messengers for the Eternal. I say as free beings, not as slaves, since God will not hear of us being slaves under any circumstances. We bring a healing power to this earth, eventually creating what began in Genesis in Eden and will end in Eden; to restore Eden here on earth as God originally created it. That's why we are here . . . to bring God's love and law from His celestial realm back to this creation for all of us to share in the bounty and bliss awaiting us.

Love is an energy that maintains order and balance in our system. If nothing else, love has a curative quality on the horizontal everyday level, regardless of whether or not we want to turn our love to the vertical spiritual level. In this regard, love seems to maintain and extend longevity. Longevity is the extension, prolongation, and elongation of time-bound life. This is a worthwhile pursuit, giving us more time — paradoxically — to turn our attention to pursuing immortality or the conquering of time . . . to live in no-time and detachedly to things, be they objects, persons, beliefs, distressing feelings, and so on. Love is the bridge between the two realms, taking us from time to no-time, from longevity (where death is inevitable) to immortality (where life is inevitable). Hence, King Solomon's statement in Ecclesiastes that "love is strong as death." It provides a means for living in time-space in a vertical way simultaneously, moment to moment to moment.

When asked about her understanding of love, Colette answered, "It just IS." This spiritual love is unconditional; it has no standards, ideals, contingencies, or strings, no set conditions attached to it. I experienced this kind of love from my teacher of blessed memory, Colette. In that regard, when Moses encountered God at the burning bush and asked Him who the speaker of the messages given to him was, God answered, "I AM THAT I AM." Put another way, "I AM THAT IS, I IS THE IS — and by extension — I AM LOVE." Later on, Christianity undertook to state it as "God is love."

To love God is to form an alliance where life is *lived* in the present, not something to be done at a future time. And like intuition, faith, and imagination, love is rooted in the present. When we harp on the past and the future, we dance with death; *the movement of time from past to future equals entropy* (second law of thermodynamics). As has been emphasized throughout this writing, entropy = death. No linear time = no entropy = no death. We are asked to love the One who gives unconditional love, who is permanent, never changing, never veering from the ISness of this instant, and is always there. God asks of us to ally ourselves with such a Oneness. To be connected to the IS, we are asked not to wander away from this relationship I call the Alliance. Why would we want to? When we wander away, especially to the future or past, we not only leave the Alliance, we also find ourselves suffering some sort of pain, cutting across the five dimensions of experience. Wandering away is *always* accompanied by distressing feelings: anxiety, fear, worry, anger about the illusion called future, or depression, guilt, regret, sadness, and shame about the illusion called past. When pain arrives, love departs. Energy becomes absorbed in dealing with the disturbances, so love plus the Alliance are forgotten. We also forget to follow the Ten Cosmic Laws, our protectors against the malevolent forces of life on Earth.

Stepping away from the Alliance will never give us a chance to be able to explore this ineffability, the purpose for being born onto Earth, to evolve into conscious oneness with Spirit. This marriage, our coming together with the Alliance, takes place on this morally created ground called Earth, blessed by Divinity, who called it "good." The Alliance existing in no-time is holy, the giving of eternal life.

We maintain the Alliance by remembering it, sustaining its memory through actions and practices, which we are soon to examine. Faith and trust set the stage by conceiving and accepting the belief that the universe gives us all we need, sustains and supports us, and is ever-present to help and share with us all of ITS life-giving essence.

Only individually and collectively can we maintain the connection. The universe isn't going anywhere while we stray, but we are always welcomed back with love, like prodigal children finally returning home.

Here are some imagery exercises on love.

IMAGERY EXERCISES

LOVE
(Colette)

Close your eyes. Breathe out and in three times slowly. Imagine entering your heart. Sense here that your love has no limits.

Breathe out one time. See and recognize the unknown sage dwelling there. What does the sage tell you? Give thanks.

Breathe out one time. Leave the heart. Breathe out and open your eyes.

ROAD OF LOVE[33]

Close your eyes. Breathe out and in three times slowly. See, sense, feel, know, and live that the Ones who walk the Road of Love never walk the Road Alone. Breathe out and open your eyes.

ABOUT LOVE
(Colette)

Close your eyes. Breathe out one time slowly. See and feel how love is a *unique* state of consciousness in importance and quality.

Breathe out one time. See and live the transcendent possibilities of love. Breathe out and open your eyes.

MISTAKE IN LOVE/MISTAKEN LOVE
(Colette)

Close your eyes. Breathe out one time slowly. See and know what happens if we are not ready for love.

Breathe out one time. Live and know that love is sometimes lovesickness, obsessive, blind.

Breathe out one time. Live, feel, and know what it is to be loved in this obsessive way. Breathe out one time. See and feel that love may be mistaken as self-pity or pitiless.

Breathe out one time. Live and know what is possessiveness, blindness, jealousy, being mad about.

---

[33] Adapted from *The Way of the Jewish Mystic,* Perle Besserman [Ed.], Boston: Shambala Pocket Classics, 1994.

Breathe out one time. Live and know how this love is precluding, even extinguishing love.

Breathe out and open your eyes.

DEVELOPING ENNOBLING[34] LOVE IN OUR RELATIONSHIPS
(Colette)

Close your eyes. Breathe out and in three times slowly. Live and know if it is possible to create a fresh, intellectual, reasonable climate in which to approach ennobling love.

Breathe out one time. See how ennobling love is an orientation, attitude, approach in front of the loving being.

Breathe out one time. See and know how this ennobling love is deeper and more enduring than the moment-to-moment change of emotions and feelings.

Breathe out one time. See how this feeling is a disposition to experience the loved being as an embodiment of your deep personal values that are is a real and potential source of joy.

Breathe out one time. See how the need to value may be at the origin of love.

Breathe out one time. See why we need to find in the world things we need to care about, to be inspired by, to love.

Breathe out and open your eyes.

---

[34] To ennoble is to elevate.

VISIBILITY AND ENNOBLING LOVE
(Colette)

Close your eyes. Breathe out one time slowly. See how ennobling love is making us *visible* by *discovering ourselves* through the responsiveness of the other.

Breathe out. See and know how a sustained experience of *visibility* is stimulating the process of *self-discovery* and *expanded awareness* of self. See how this brings us to another dimension of awareness and perception.

Breathe out. Feel and know how the more aware we are of accepting what we are, the more transparent we are, the more loving we become.

Breathe out and open your eyes.

FRUSTRATED LOVE
(Colette)

Close your eyes. Breathe out and in three times slowly. Imagine that you are failing in love or in your capacity to love.

Breathe out one time. Feel and know that being unaware may kill the ability to love, that ignorance may kill it, that blindness may kill it.

Breathe out one time. See and know how rigid *life attitudes* are changing our *potential* of love, our *expression* of love.

Breathe out one time. See and feel how our *potential of love* is changed in individual variables such as *rhythm, energy, intensity*.

Breathe out one time. Feel and see how to change our attitude to love in front of 1) communication, 2) nurturance, 3) sexuality, 4) marriage, 5) divorce, 6) jealousy, 7) children, 8) admiration, 9) courage, 10) anxiety, 11) happiness, 12) personal transformation. (Breathe out one time slowly between each.)

Breathe out one time. Now feel and know how ennobling *love* is: It is a great challenge, a great adventure.

Breathe out and open your eyes.

Faith: Unconditional Action

Faith is an action taken without having to have knowledge or consideration of an outcome or result of that step. Its purpose is that of knowing oneself to be acting without becoming dependent on some second thing that would seemingly provide certainty and safety in the fulfillment of that action: "I act in faith when I take off for second base. Don't know if I'll be safe or not. Not thinking about that. Just running. Trusting my body to guide me to that destination. There is only faith in myself."

Doubt, the seed source of all mental disturbances, has a natural antidote in faith and its partner, trust. Doubt, besides its destructive function, has also been, and is, the father of the natural sciences. It is doubt, the father of these sciences, that spurs inquiry into seeking deeper understanding of the perceptual material world around us. Ironically, faith is the mother of these sciences. No materialist scientist would become one if he or she didn't have faith in this model. Without it no natural/material/physical scientist would engage in scientific inquiry, believing it to yield answers to life. Believing is the verb form of faith.

In contrast to the "objective" sciences are the revelatory, spiritual sciences that are based in faith. Faith itself is a unitary experience that has no opposite in doubt. Doubt forces you to look to the future to resolve the doubt. Faith has us act and choose in the immediacy of what we face here and now. Faith is an exploration of phenomena not based on outcomes, results, end points, and conclusions. Since conclusionary thinking is not part of spiritual thought, doubt doesn't enter the picture.

Here is an example of this understanding: Jean was a successful businesswoman who decided to explore life in a spiritual direction. Beside her ongoing and meaningful high-powered business life, she also belonged to a group of adventurous seekers who were intent on expanding their collective consciousness. Along the way she was involved in a difficult personal relationship and had two children.

She began to experience great pressure as she had to coordinate business, parenthood, and the spiritual direction of the group that was in some measure at odds with her other directions. As the anxiety mounted about handling all of this (she had not yet committed to marriage and was raising the children herself), she was aware of one phrase that kept pursuing her as a kind of mantra: "I *must* get out," over and over.

When we are in conflict, meaning being pulled in two directions simultaneously, to stay or go, we generally conceive of a third way out to relieve the pressure from both sources, and that is by far the most common path taken. That is, we become ill so as to find some respite from the tension, or to give in to the tension, where we opt out of responsibility for a time and "legitimately" gain sympathy and understanding.

Our work was to focus Jean on the fourth way: *to choose* any of those three *musts* one at a time, to take a step to do so without thinking about any future consideration, as that would take care of itself in her favor as long as she faced the pain and forged her way through it.

When we first met, she had taken the third way: She went to the bathroom late in the evening, felt faint and dizzy, and suddenly fell in a heap to the floor, suffering a mild concussion and injuring her neck by a whiplash effect, displacing cervical vertebrae. The injury necessitated some remedial intervention, but the real work lay ahead of her. She came to recognize the connection between the heavy weight of those three pressures bearing down on her and physically succumbing to them via the fall. She couldn't bear the weight. However, the incident allowed Jean to take another kind of look at her life. That was where the shock allowed us to look at the fourth way, the *need to take action and get out!*

She chose first to leave the group — one she now found flawed and could no longer abide after over a decade. After taking this step, she felt immediately relieved, and real healing was starting. Next, she left her job. It was easier than she thought. Her boss was really supportive about this move, although she would be missed. Finally, she chose to move to a smaller city that was more suitable for her needs, more welcoming. In doing so she left the man behind while taking her children with her. He was left to his own devices and the choice to stay or come as he wished, and she knew that what he chose would have nothing to do with her. She was not feeling dependent on what he was to do. By removing the weights, healing proceeded quite rapidly. Balance was restored. She became an independent consultant, got her children well placed, and found another group of like-minded people to connect with. Her "friend" decided to leave his job and join her, and they subsequently married.

Jean faced the truth of her life, took action — a step of faith — and wisely chose to free herself from unnecessary burdens. She did what was necessary to liberate herself and bring more Life to her life.

Faith has many facets. Technically it is the passive side of unconditional action, while trust is its active component. Breathing is the physiological analogy to faith. I know that I am given continued life through breath. The way to Source continues to make itself present through breathing. God breathed into the inert substance (Adam) to give it life, thus creating the first man. He did so, I believe, because He had faith in creating humanity. Many spiritual practices include some element of breathing.

Faith represents the certainty of experience, certainty in the existence of Invisible Reality, certainty in the ongoing existence of life, no matter — at this point — whether the physical body ceases to exist.

When Moses led the Israelite nation out of the land of bondage, Nachson first walked into the Red Sea. He knew that freedom lay beyond this body of water. His impulse to get to that freedom — both inner and outer — impelled him to enter the sea *before* it parted. He walked a number of steps till the water was beginning to fill his nostrils. His next step would submerge him under water, presumably to drown. At that moment the sea parted. The hidden, imperceptible divine hand parted the sea into two walls of still waves, permitting the group to pass through. Did his act of faith have a part to play in that "impossible" event? A mutual process between Nachson and God? I say yes. We ask and we are answered.

Faith is *unconditional* action, the result of making up our mind and choosing this force attaching us to the Alliance. Faith is the force allowing us to believe in ourselves, imploring us to become our own authority, to become spiritual beings who can exert an influence on this time-space reality to help restore us to the garden of Paradise. Faith directs us to engage ourselves in such practices as described herein without concern for the end product.

Faith doesn't know anything about time or entropy or doubt. It has no ties or attachments in our time-space world. Faith has no relevance in the everyday, materialistic, logically based mechanical/technological, horizontal world. Instead, we aim faith vertically, attaching to the Alliance. Thus, faith serves the Alliance. As it is clearly attached to the Alliance, we become like Adam and Eve in the Garden. We regain

Edenic consciousness. Of course, we have free will, and through our mis-education, we can deceive ourselves and misplace our faith in our conditional world, placing it in others who exist in the same dimension as we do. Misplaced faith in others often leads to idolatry — a seed of the errors of living. Our media is constantly full of stories about frauds committed financially, religiously, and politically by those to whom we extended our faith. In this regard, it is not accurate to say, for instance, "I have faith that my business venture will succeed." What is accurate here is "I have faith in God that He will show me the way to have my business succeed." Or "I'm learning to play tennis. I have a good instructor. I have faith in him to teach me how to play this sport." Rather "I'm learning to play. I have a good instructor. I have faith in the One that I will be given the means to learn how to play this game." Faith/trust cannot be associated with the linear time-space world only. Its abode is our relationship with Spirit.

On the other hand, doubt is connected with the everyday world where logic and reason prevail as primary building blocks in time-space. As such, doubt has no direct (or indirect) association with the unconditioned, nonlogical, intuition-based world of nonlinear time, nondimensional space.

The two domains are categorically separate. Logic and the rule of reason dictate how the time-space world operates. There is no place for faith here, nor should there be. Conversely, the spiritual world operates according to the conditions of intuition, faith, love, and imagination. There are no "rules" here, for no limits can be placed on what can happen here. All is happening in no-time and infinite space. There can be no place for doubt here, as doubt always asserts and imposes rules and limits on the flow of energy. It acts as a dam on the movement, stifling its flow and imposing time-bound restrictions in life.

So, when books and other publications question the existence of God or the legitimacy of spiritual life, they themselves are illegitimate commentaries. It is a form of adultery, or mixing, for the certainty of faith cannot be called into question by nonspiritual, rationalistic means. It is like comparing oranges to the ocean — that's how far apart the two realms are. The only pertinent question that grows out of making the clear distinctions elucidated and maintaining the purity of Spirit vs. materialism is "Does God exist? Yes or no?" Either answer is correct, depending on the direction of truth you are coming from. If, for you, God exists, that's your truth. If, for you, God doesn't exist, that's your truth. Everything you want to state, agree, debate, and convince others or impose on them comes from falsehoods: stories, conjectures, surmises, conclusions, and any of the other distorting comments you might feel compelled to announce. What is left for you is to experiment with a course in spirituality, such as is presented in these pages.

We can misplace our faith in our spiritual teachers, both in the East and the West. Rather, place your trust in the teachings, not on a fallible human being. A person of my acquaintance found his teacher having sex in the sacred sanctuary of the tradition that the teacher advocated. The master espoused celibacy in the teaching. My acquaintance was shocked by the discovery. He previously found his guru drunk on a number of occasions and having a fond taste for steak (although professing the benefits of vegetarianism). All of it was overlooked (perhaps by some form of teaching, as many teachers and gurus rationalize it to their students) until the sexual episode. My friend summarily abandoned the guru but did not abandon the teaching. Good for him and others I have known who have been able to make the distinction between the "game" (the teaching) and the "operator" (the teacher) of the game. As D. H. Lawrence, in *Studies in Classic American Literature* (1923), said, "Never trust the artist. Trust the tale."

There is an ancient statement about faith described in the book of Deuteronomy: "Thy life shall hang before thee; thou shalt fear day and night; thou shalt have no assurance of thy life" (Deut. 28:66). These words echo here what God said to Adam and Even upon their eviction from the Garden of Eden. These words mean to say that we (all of us Adam and Eve thrust out of Paradise), you and me, shall live a life of perpetual doubt having eaten, and continuing to do so, from the tree of doubt, itself equivalent to the tree of knowledge, itself equivalent to the tree of death (don't eat from it, lest you die).

Our faith in the power of intangibility, invisibility, uncertainty, nonattachment is what keeps us in the flow of the stream of life. It is the singular remedy against doubt, itself the obstacle to flow, movement, action, becoming, creating, LIFE.

While doubt curbs movement, impedes flow, and is a given for our lives, the beauty of God's love and mercy is that we are born with the capacity to redeem ourselves and reverse this imposed punishment for ever doubting God. Our love for One and faith in God's forgiveness, mercy, and compassion dispel doubt.

Practicing Faith
The practice of faith quells fear. With respect to mental imagery, an interesting point was made by Emile Coué, a French writer back in 1922, in his book *Self-Mastery Through Conscious Auto-Suggestion*. He pointed to the example of a tightrope walker. When the latter begins to step on the high wire, he, at first, *sees* himself at the other side, safely on the opposite perch. This is a perfect example of how imagery can instill faith in oneself to undertake a dangerous task. In everyday life, there are numerous situations testing our faith, particularly when we have been conditioned to be afraid in so many ways. I would recommend when you are afraid and want to counteract it, you spontaneously discover an image of faith or trust and experience that, including the feeling. As you do this repetitively, you are replacing the old habit with a new one little by little. As another possibility, you can see the image of fear and correct it, change it, reverse it, thereby taking charge of it.

Whenever you become afraid, immediately see and feel and perhaps sense physically the now corrected image.

One tip about fear and all other distressing feelings. The general tendency is to fight them. You know the government is always declaring a war on drugs, smoking, guns, and so forth. What happens as a result of these wars is an increase in usage of the very thing being warred against. Every "war" like this paradoxically increases the strength and resolve of the opponent. The spiritual point here is the acceptance of everything as legitimate and genuine. Without prejudice and bias, everything is possible. The first order of business, then, is to give credence to whatever is disturbing and accept it, then something meaningful can be done, instead of creating and enhancing conflicts by stubbornly opposing them in some moralizing, often hypocritical way as bad and in need of being destroyed. With regard to distressing feelings, we are not judgmental about them and don't exhaust and waste our energy fighting them, dissipating our life force as a result. Rather, we accept them, conserving our energy, and then seek to make the necessary corrections as mentioned above.

Prayer is a potent form of faith practice. When we pray, an offering is made to the Invisible Reality, to our Source. The power of prayer has been amply demonstrated in Dr. Larry Dossey's groundbreaking book *Healing Words: The Power of Prayer and the Practice of Medicine* (1993). In it he garnered information from around the world on prayer, practice, and the results of such practices. We have a prayer group in New York where we use imagery as the focus of prayer. As a group, we image the person being healed by a shared image at certain times of the day. I do know of other prayer groups in New York and elsewhere (Rosicrucians in California) doing their own type of practice, such as group mantra chanting. In prayer we put our faith and trust where it needs to be rather than extending it to other fellow humans who so often disappoint us, sometimes in ways that are devastating. King

David said, "Don't put your stock in the princes of this world." We know quite well what has happened on several occasions when people put stock in the stock market and Bernie Madoff. Faith-based people, interestingly enough, are not dismayed when prayers are not answered. They understand that when some prayers are not, that's what is meant to be. Nonetheless, their faith is not shaken. By my personal experience, I can say prayers are often answered, and when they are not, that is also an answer.

Taking the vow of poverty and its allied practice of sacrifice is another form of faith practice. Here we curb the Dark Currents of Will, not sure what lies in store for us in doing so, but realizing there's virtue in giving rather than taking, giving away, and sharing rather than keeping. These acts of sacrifice give us an unrivaled feeling of accomplishment: Being harmless, being considerate, and making a contribution can fill us with what can only be called a feeling of faith.

Perhaps the easiest way, and the starting point for many, to develop faith is the "yes-no" practice where we practice making up our minds without knowing the end point. This practice is covered in chapter XII.

While writing this section, I am reminded of a story told to me by Colette. When she was four years old, she was with her father (an MD) in his office in Algiers. In came a Sufi teacher — his patient. He pulled Colette aside and told her to meet him by the river at dawn. The next morning at dawn, she clambered out of her window adjacent to the garden, rushed to the river, and met up with the master. Without a word, he picked her up and threw her into the swirling currents of the river. She cried out that she couldn't swim. The Sufi responded, "Either you swim or you sink and die." She swam. The test of faith and trust came to her rather precipitously, as a lesson that sustained her throughout her life, especially when she organized the North African resistance against the Nazis during World War II, where they succeeded in defeating those forces of evil and driving them out of North Africa.

She certainly had trust in the Sufi master — enough that she would go out and meet him in the early morning. Her faith bespoke the certainty she experienced in herself. Her bravery then came to the fore again in her early 20s when confronted by the Nazis. The future mission of her life was betokened in that event at four years old. In spiritual wisdom there is "future karma": An early event foretells future life direction.

Paradoxically, an extreme example — faith also speaks to certainty in delusional people when they are certain about the reality of their beliefs, contrary to any evidence presented to them. In contrast, here I write about certainty in the truth, where truth is experienced as an inner knowing that is verified by outside experimentation that validates this knowledge. Colette's faith in the Sufi sheikh was rewarded by the unshakable faith she had in herself that saw her through the most harrowing of times.

Faith doesn't only go in one direction. Not only do we bear the force of faith and trust given through God, but also faith comes to us through God's faith and trust in us. This has to be the case, because above and below are in reflective relationship with each other. Nowhere is that faith highlighted more than in the story of Job, on whom God is willing to wager the preservation of humanity in a game of cosmic Poker with His "favorite" angel Satan. Satan has no faith in human faith and piety toward Spirit and wagers an "all-in" call on his certainty that Job, the most pious man in the world, would turn his back on God in the wake of inconceivable calamity hurled toward him — the loss of health, wealth, and family. But Job's faith in God never falters. God calls Satan on his bet. Eventually Satan loses, is tossed from the heavenly realm, and takes up residence on a planet called Earth. Here, he is forever dedicated to winning his bet, using death as his final card to ultimately win the bet. God refuses to lose. He never forgets us. We forget Him, and Satan stops by to claim another impious soul. God is relentless in providing more souls on Earth to claim the final pot.

The Seven Divine Forces

In fact, we are sent here to reclaim the sore-loser Satan and turn him back to find his place again in the heavenly court. As we remember the Lord, so does the Lord remember us, and we live and thwart Satan's intention. There will come a time when Satan will mend his ways and finally acknowledge the supremacy of God's love and faith in us.

One thing to note here: Satan never wants to interfere with our freedom. He is not here to invade and take us over, only to provide the tests of our faith, love, trust, and attachment to the Source. We are tested, but we always maintain freedom and choice.

Another piece to faith/trust is us. We can cultivate faith in ourselves. Without it, we become vulnerable, physically weak, and susceptible to becoming enslaved to this error-filled reality and to those black magicians who are forever presuming to stand in our stead, speak on our behalf, and promise to see to our freedom. They are easy to spot. They usually have a personal agenda and spearhead some institution promising a new day, freedom, golden parachute, peace, economic Shangri-La, and all other sorts of empty nonsense that no human being can possibly bring.

On the other hand come the white magicians who seek to wake us up to our own strength, power, competencies, self-authority, enhanced physical life, and self-awareness without a personal agenda, teaching us to speak and stand up for ourselves. They bear the seeds of liberation and freedom, ready to plant them in the field of our consciousness to awaken us. Colette was such a person for me. The way of Spirit can be practiced in the course of everyday, ordinary life conflicts and circumstances. To do so is the thrust of the spiritual teaching I do. It provides a new education of spiritual principles and practices not found elsewhere. Take the case of Emily:

She lives in a rented house. The dishwasher and washing machine go on the blink. She needs them repaired. The landlord sends repair people (needlessly) when new appliances are needed. She is charged for repair visits and a new appliance, the latter installed without consultation or consent. She is angry at the landlord and wants to fight this injustice. Her husband is also distressed about the situation. However, he lends no active support, leaving her to handle it alone. Referencing back from this immediate conflict to her legal case against an institution for whom she worked, she found herself unsupported by colleagues, who bailed on her under threats and intimidation for their jobs from that self-same institution. A pattern emerges over a lifetime of circumstances where she seeks support but finds none — neither from her immediate family or otherwise. The theme she presents is experiencing a lack of support — a ubiquitous experience of life for many.

Together, Emily and I look at the call to her from our universal support system to become self-supporting by seeking answers from within and to gather the strength of faith, to become self-dependent and self-reliant. By turning inward she gains access to her inner or higher source of wisdom to ask for guidance from a higher reality rather than depending on the outer world — humans, who have enough trouble handling their own lives, never mind hers. The experts she habitually turns to could not know more about her than she knows about herself.

As she became more aware, she recalled an early memory of growing up in a family environment that was frankly unsupportive of her. A concurrent belief emerged that she would not find support for her endeavors in life. This belief accompanied her into most situations, which manifested in nonsupport. Once realized, she changed the belief to its opposite, seeing herself supported. Then, gathering herself with more unaccustomed aplomb and composure than she had known throughout her life, she faced the landlord with a sense of inner strength to reaffirm what she knew to be the truth of what she rightfully owed. The upshot: She paid $100 for each appliance. One was repaired adequately, the other was replaced with a brand-new model. Having faith in herself and the divine, she has since settled her legal case successfully and purchased a new home.

Here are imagery exercises to develop faith.

IMAGERY EXERCISES

EXODUS: CROSSING THE RED SEA

Close your eyes and breathe out and in three times slowly. Experience the awesomeness: midnight, thunder, lightning, great waves. Venus is close to the moon, exerting great gravitational tidal force. Pharaoh's soldiers are behind you in pursuit, coming to kill you. How do you feel? The sea hasn't parted yet till you start to pass. Not knowing if you will drown or not, you step in and start to cross, knowing freedom awaits you on the other side.

Breathe out. Now what happens? What do you do, and what is your feeling? Breathe out and open your eyes.

THE ARK OF SAFETY

Close your eyes and breathe out three times slowly. The great flood is coming of emotions, mental turmoil, and social confusion.

Breathe out one time. Build your own ark like that of Noah — no motor, no sails, no wheels, and no rudder — to take you across the raging sea to a new land of safety. Know that this ark is guided by God's hands. How is the journey? Do you get to the new land? What do you discover in the new land? Breathe out and open your eyes.

We Are Not *Meant* to Die

THE SINAI DESERT
(Colette)

Close your eyes. Breathe out and in three times slowly. Imagine you are in the desert for 40 years. See Moses, Miriam (his sister), and Aaron (his brother) taking care of you.

Breathe out one time. See the "Seven Clouds of Glory of God" coming and protecting you in all directions: up, down, North, South, East, West, and directly surrounding you. The front cloud is killing the snakes in front of you that pose a danger.

Breathe out one time. Now sense the different fragrances and taste the manna from heaven. Keep the feeling. Use the wellspring that is there to wash out and purify yourself. Drink from this well and know God is with you to the last day as on the first day.

Breathe out one time. See and feel that you are saved by reason of your confession of error after your doubt has driven you to construct the idol of the golden calf.

Breathe out one time. Know that you are forgiven for your errors of living as you attempt to repair them.

Breathe out one time. Feel an inner surge of the presence of Spirit's breath called faith. Know by your use of will you are connecting with what seems impossible and making it possible.

Breathe out one time. Feel an inner healing force. Breathe out and open your eyes.

Intuition: Unconditional Thought

The intuitive mind is a sacred gift and the rational mind is a faithful servant. We have created a society that honors the servant and has forgotten the [sacred] gift.
—Albert Einstein

The Seven Divine Forces

When I succeed in actively keeping my intellect from forming all kinds of conclusionary thoughts and actively restrain my desires to get something, an inner space is created. This space allows for a stream of communication to enter awareness, free of any associations, attachments, or conditioning. It is pure, unadulterated thought, received through the bodily channels of gut, heart, or neuro-optical (light). This is called "intuition."

What is the intuitive mind? Intuition, or unconditional intelligence, is the communication network between ourselves and the unending world of Invisible Reality; it is the culmination of detachment, because there's nothing material in the way, nothing to attach to, as it is happening in the no-time zone. Intuitive reception prompts clarity of action, activity rendered in the service of self and others.

Intuition is a way of receiving information as a revelation from our highest subjective source, in connection with our Divine Source. It is the preeminent way to receive prophetic or higher-worldly knowledge. Given that we are made in the image and likeness of God, we are already subscribers on the inter-celestial network, born with an innate link connected to a cosmic network. In this tradition, to become intuitive is the highest spiritual level we can attain.

Intuition calls upon a directed use of will that puts us squarely in touch with our Invisible Reality while casting aside the incessant noise of the world around us. Here, three major practices of will are required for the development of intuition — one physical, called *disinterested instinct*, and one mental, called *detached intellect*, and one emotional, called *balanced feeling*.[35] (1) Physically we stop the habit of fulfilling our urges to acquire based on curbing the Five Dark Currents of Will; (2) mentally we stop creating fixed thoughts, or conclusions, about a

---

[35] The terms "detached intellect" and "disinterested instinct" were first coined by the 20th-century French philosopher Henri Bergson.

nonexistent future; (3) emotionally, we are not taken over by distressing feelings. In short, we curb our distressing emotions and tendency to think into the future and our greed factor to create a space of freedom for receiving the intuitive messages of truth. You may realize now how false emergency states impede intuition. Let's take a closer look at these three components of intuition.

Balanced feeling means there are no charges to them, be they on one side elation, joyful excitement, any sort of high, or on the other side, anger, fear, worry, or any other sort of distressing feeling. In other words, we are not to have an investment in some outcome connected with intuition practice. We are creating an open space of freedom to receive messages of truth, intuitions, coming to us from the universe of truth, Invisible Reality. Unbalanced feelings create doubt and a pre-existing bias, either for or against what we want to know. In that case, the space is closed and clarity obscured.

Instincts are our sensory, biological impulses and urges, such as breathing, hunger, sex, aggression. In a disordered world dominated by the disordering law of survival of the fittest, our natural instincts, much like our attached intellect, want to fulfill themselves by attaching to the objects of their desire with their concomitant energy released. Although we appear incapable of curbing and taking charge of these biological instincts, quite the opposite is true. By an act of will, they can be contained — we can withdraw from their urge to take hold of or capture its object. In other words, like intellect, they can be detached, withdrawn to create a space of freedom for something new to take place. Such a practice is known in the East in a group practice called tantra or seminal retention. Here, couples have sexual interplay, copulating to the point of consummation. At that juncture, the emissions are stopped by an act of will and the secretions are brought back into the body. By not discharging the energy, it is turned back as a life energy conserved for the self.

The Seven Divine Forces

For *detached intellect,* we refuse to jump beyond seeing the relationship between facts or things rather than draw conclusions about the facts or things. We look at or evaluate the perceptions in front of us, accepting their presence without having to be judgmental, form a conclusion, or fashion a story to account for them. In other words, we need not "run with it" or project constantly into the future or past, usually with "if-then" thinking.

We have been trained to use our intellect to look for outcomes, end points, or conclusions. By its very nature, this type of thinking puts a *stop* to any investigation of and acquisition of further knowledge. The knowledge valve is shut, and with it the flow and movement of the stream of life stops. When movement stops, so the movement of life stops.

Intuition embraces another spiritual practice: the vow of poverty, whose opposite is greed. By divesting ourselves of an excess of thought, we become quiet as the chatter of life recedes. Ironically, impoverishment of this sort leaves us richer in the inner world. The rewards are countless and of lasting benefit. Eventually we may come to feel and know what we are told is unthinkable by organized religion and the normative scientific and educational communities — we may come to know God as a lived experience, understandable, perhaps unspeakable to others, but a truth for us that we never need to question.

The practices described above lead to making space — mentally, emotionally, and physically — as we divest. Through divestment, awareness is expanded, attention is deepened, and an awakening happens. The astonishing thing about the process is that there is no cost required, either materially or energetically. In fact, instead of an energy outlay occurring with attachment to thought, emotional lability, and instinctual fulfillment, the exact opposite takes place: Energy is conserved and turned back to us, ever increasing and supplementing our life force. Likewise, in material terms we are able to conserve funds and perhaps unnecessary labor that is an inherent part of attachment to mental and material things.

In the West as well as in the Near East, the highest states of spiritual quest, culminating in union with the Absolute One Mind, are attained through intuition. All the practices here could be considered practices to open the intuitional door to freedom.

Here is an imagery exercise to help this process along.

IMAGERY EXERCISE

THE LAKE OF INNER KNOWING: TO DEVELOP INTUITION

Close your eyes and breathe out and in three times slowly. Imagine peering, with focus, without distraction, into a gigantic dark lake of silent knowing. Keep for yourself what you discover in that instant. Breathe out and open your eyes.

Practice this exercise for a few seconds, three times a day, early in the morning, at twilight, and before bed, every day for three months. Afterwards, use it whenever you wish or to answer a question you may have.

Imagination: Unconditional Language

So far I have interwoven a number of threads into the fabric of the development of an unconditional Life: love, faith/trust, and intuition. Now it's time to take up the fourth major unconditional state called imagination — the divine language. When I voluntarily turn my senses inward to discover the inner repository of knowing, I have embarked on the active experience of imagination. Imagination is a multidimensional term encompassing at once: a real level of existence — as real as waking life; an inner sense (analogous to our five outward senses); a light illuminating this inner realm of existence; and a therapeutic method to access this inner world of truth — known mostly to the public at large as mental imagery (or a more commonly used, less accurate term: visualization).

The image is a divine, creative language of communication served to us here in the visible time-space world from the Invisible Reality in a form we can learn to comprehend. These images are sent through a channel from there to here called "mind." The scope of this language is limitless. Images are stored for us to discover in "storehouse consciousness," a term coined by Prof. Toshiro Izutsu, a scholar of Islamic mysticism.[36] They are the shared social language of the world, a *universal* language, quite in contrast to the plethora of discursive languages pervading the world and made reference to in the Bible as the Tower of Babel (Gen. 2:11). These images circumvent ordinary language of linear time. Imagery is a language of no-time and of no conditions (associations, attachments, logical connections) such as those that exist with discursive, spoken language. Imagery is a language bridging two worlds. As such it is naturally revelatory, much as the picture language of ancient Egypt called hieroglyphics — glyph = image, hiero = higher — referred to in the esoteric wisdom of the Pharaonic dynasties. These inner hieroglyphics are a language that can be read and learned. They are the bearers of knowledge of ourselves both in relation to our connection to this time-space world and to the divine world. We are the bearers of the divine wisdom, standing as messengers between the two worlds, whose mission is to lead the human world out of the darkness into which it has descended and into the light.

Images are unconditional phenomena, discovered internally, unalloyed by the external language of words that defines human communication. They have the capacity to show us new ways of behavior

---

[36] Toshiro Izutsu, "Between Image and No-Image," in *On Images: Far Eastern Ways of Thinking*, Eranos Lectures Series #7 (Dallas: Spring Publications, 1988).

untainted by habit. They show us new possibilities for us to fulfill. They help us shape relationships in a new way and give us a clear perception of reality.

A distinguishing feature of the spontaneous imagery experience drawn from the never-ending well of imagination is the image appearing and meeting the imager. The imager is looking into the universe and the universe is looking at us. The imager has not brought his/her own prejudices or preconceived ideas to the process; rather, the image brings itself to the imager, who receives it. As such, the images are not scripted in advance, nor are they "visualizations" constructed or engineered out of the imager's personal inclinations, prejudices, and habitual conditioning. The images are freely met and can be and are called "unconditional." They are untarnished, uncontaminated, received in an unhabitual state, unafraid and unresisted.

As inner space "astronauts," we explore the inner forum of consciousness, making discoveries. We ascend and descend to the heights and depths of consciousness. We explore not geography but geo-cosmology, as these dimensions are not comparable to our waking-life dimensions of quantitative space. The beauty of such a process is that we are able to bring back what has been learned there and use this information to guide us in everyday life. It can be understood as dreaming while awake. We do have an inherent understanding of this natural and true language of the mind that enables us to understand ourselves more deeply.

Actually, almost everyone has had the experience of this imagery phenomenon through the night dream, the vestibule to the main room of imagination. The dream, like all other imaginal events, is revelatory, giving us an immense amount of information about our lives.[37] Imagery is also a major technique of healing that employs your mental

---

[37] See my book *Waking Dream Therapy* available at www.Acmipress.org

life to create changes in your physiology, biology, emotional, mental, social, and creative life.

As the image experience happens in no-time, naturally there is no aging. Aging is a function of linear time with all its decaying processes. It never hurts to continually remember what I have discovered as a truism for me: "No linear time and no entropy equals life" and its corollary, "Linear time equals death." Thus, imagery has the power to play a significant role in longevity in our physical life and in immortality for our spiritual life. Imagery process is analogous to the *disinterested intellect* and *detached instinct* described above for intuition. It is detached language. Wow, we have just overcome the Tower of Babel! Now, we are all able to share in one language. What a peaceful idea. Ah, that's just what the dream is. It represents the themes we *all* go through in this human existence.

Yes, we each have different fingerprints, so we each live out these themes through the unfolding of our individual life experiences. However singular our unfoldment, one person's dream is everybody's dream! One person's image is everybody's image! We all are the image held in the Absolute One Mind. We are all one!

Introduction to Mental Imagery
Analogous to taking medicine for ailments, imagery is dosed as well, generally taken three times per day for several to many seconds each time. Colette always emphasized the *brevity* of time to allot to the process. The main point is to make the time *short*! All that is needed is a small shock, a spark — to ignite the inherent healing forces with which we are born. In regard to the foregoing, I term short mental imagery exercises the "homeopathy of the mind." By invoking "homeopathy," I allude to the most ancient health intervention ever recorded. Its main characteristics are twofold: 1) a micro input/dose for a macro output; 2) like cures like. For example, we give a poison to cure a poison. Many

homeopathic remedies have trace elements of arsenic. A negative plus a negative creates a positive!

In modern times the conventional medical system is becoming attuned to the homeopathic way by introducing its term "micro dosing" for the application of medication. It's a much needed "big" step in the possible evolution of what's called "allopathic" or conventional medicine.

I use short imagery exercises as solutions for everyday topical therapy for our problems. Exercises are short: Most exercises take only a number of seconds! Even the mental relaxation to take on the imagery requires only a few seconds of specialized breathing; long, slow exhalations, each one followed by a brief or short/normal inhalation once, twice, or three times. That's it. Here the parasympathetic nervous — quieting — system is activated, while the sympathetic — excitatory — system is quieted to become relaxed, to make connection to imagery experience. Prolonged relaxation breathing tends to stop movement. In our proactive method, we like to keep movement moving. Hence, short relaxation breathing.

To sum up: These Four Freedoms are all unconditional, inherently not requiring anything else to authenticate or validate their existence or truth. Through these four forces, we maintain our life here in a healthy, holy way, seeking to preserve not only our self, but also the world around us, by establishing and keeping our alliance to the vertical world. We shall see how the remaining two forces, hope and light, act to propel the other four freedoms.

Hope: Perpetuation of Life

Hope is an inner light, giving us the impetus to go on living. It is the eternal prayer offered for the perpetual creation and continuation of life. Hope is the inner impulse that urges a woman to become pregnant and give birth. It is the source of respiration, that very energy of life.

The Seven Divine Forces

In the Western tradition, the rainbow was gifted to the world after the flood as God's message of hope. The rainbow is the life of color, the color of life. These colors appearing in that beautiful arc always enliven us, giving us a lift, motivating us, spurring us to keep our spirits up. No wonder it is the symbol of hope, never to give up. There is always another day, another hour, another minute, another second. There is always life.

Hope is the inward expression of the rainbow. It is the inner light auguring a new beginning, a new discovery for/of self, a bright new day, a light at the end of the tunnel. This light of hope can be experienced in a number of ways: "Aha!" "Yes!" or a sigh of relief, flash of happiness, to name a few. Most of us have had contact or awareness of this feeling at some time in life.

There are other ways the inner light can be observed. Imaginal experience is one such example. Imagination is an inner light cast into the darkness of inner subjective reality to pierce that unknown and startle that reality to reveal the knowledge it holds in "storehouse consciousness." That's just what happened when the Divine uttered "Let there be light." It might be said that we are the birthed product of God's hope and imagination. That was God's way. God hoped for humanity, hope that we would return home to the house of our Source. We are not hopeless in God's "eyes."

Hope is that inner light that never dies in the heart of humanity. The great work of Stephen King in his book and later screen adaptation *The Shawshank Redemption* portrayed this never-ending aspiration cloaked in love that spurred the hero into a never-ending belief turned into an experience of the hope for liberation and freedom (as a Scorpio, I loved the posters).

When the inner light of hope is extinguished, we feel, sense physically, and see no hope. We feel hopeless. There is also "false hope," lulled into an illusion about future prospects that don't materialize, where these unrealistic hopes are dashed. There are expectations that are not fulfilled, as most expectations are not. For the former hopeless state, one believes there is no future possible. For the latter "false hope," one believes there is also no future other than a contrived one. Unconditional hope has no connections except the life of the planet continuing, future generations existing, and ourselves carrying on the light of life. Without this latter light of hope never-ending, a woman would never contemplate, no less go through, the exquisite "trial," labor, and pain of pregnancy and childbirth. The child becomes the physical expression of that hope.

Here is an imagery exercise to help us make contact with the force of hope.

IMAGERY EXERCISE

THE RAINBOW BRIDGE OF HOPE

Close your eyes. Breathe out three times slowly.

Imagine crossing a rainbow bridge. Climb by any means you need through each section of color, one at a time. At each color, become that color. What feelings and sensations do you experience? What aspect of your soul, your invisible nature, does each color give you? Breathe out one time between the colors. When reaching through the final color, find yourself at the end of the rainbow full of hope, seen now as your own inner rainbow.

Breathe out and discover there what awaits you for your new future. Breathe out and open your eyes.

Light: Driving Away the Darkness

Light is an attribute of God, the Absolute One Mind, making its presence known in a personal relationship, as an eternal beacon for us to follow on our journey on Earth. It encompasses the other six forces.

The Seven Divine Forces

It is the highest-octane fuel we know. We have the choice to partake of this light and become beings of light or turn away from that light and live in darkness, despair, discord, and suffering, ultimately dying. The imagination is an inner form of light that can lead you back to our source of light and life.

Into the pitch-black of all there is, a voice from no particularly placed location boomed out, "Let there be light." This supernal light became divided into day from the dark called night. Following this trail of eternal supernal light down to the next level of light come the light reflectors, called stars, that draw down the energy from all the other galaxies. The sun, a giant star, beams its life-giving energy to support life on this planet, taking on the task of supporting the growth of vegetation that actually preexisted before the advent of the sun. And then there is the moon, a reflection of the sun on its surface, whose body of light is responsible for the movement of water on Earth, like the tides of the oceans, and that helps to birth those life-giving plants called herbs that have to be harvested under moonlight. Then there is the reflection of Northern Lights and the green light that surrounds the Earth as a protective shield of ozone. There is, too, the natural light of fire, with its constructive and destructive sides, given as a gift to us for constructive and destructive purposes. Finally, we have artificial light, provided by those geniuses of the 19th century Nikolai Tesla and Thomas Edison.

Now we turn our attention to the light of beings, human, angels, and other beings of the air: archangels, archai (called principalities), powers, virtues, dominions, thrones, cherubim, seraphim, all the way back again to the Absolute One Mind where we started.[38]

We are born as beings of light, although the vagaries, slings and

---

[38] The western spiritual tradition posits nine angelic hierarchies between humankind and the Divine. Angels act as messengers, protectors, and agents of the Divine.

arrows of outrageous fortune, and the suffering that comes with life here have made us forget our light, which has now been enveloped by darkness, of suffering, turmoil, and much pain. In darkness, the space of entropy, there is no growth, only decay. We can reverse this condition by becoming again the spiritual being of light we once were; born again — resurrected — like newborn babes. This divine life force of light is always present, and the GEMS practice and its way of life permits us to turn the switch back on.

Here are some imagery exercises to experience and recapture that Divine source within us.

IMAGERY EXERCISES

LIGHT OF THE HEART/LIGHT OF THE BRAIN

Close your eyes. Breathe out and in three times slowly. Imagine a river of blue-golden light streaming from your heart to your brain. The stream returns from the brain to the heart, creating a circuit of this light. What is your experience? How are your heart and brain interacting?

Now, imagine a river of blue-golden light streaming from your brain to your heart. The stream returns from your heart to your brain, creating a circuit of this light. What is your experience? How are your brain and heart interacting? Breathe out and open your eyes.

COME TO YOUR LIGHT

Close your eyes. Breathe out and in three times slowly. Physically sense and see that you are a crystal crossed by light. See your form, the rays that are coming to you and the rays that are going out from you. As a crystal, hear the different sounds when different rays are touching you. Breathe out and open your eyes.

CRYSTAL VASE

Close your eyes. Breathe out and in three times slowly. See that you are a crystal vase full of blue light. Feel this blue light deeply.

Breathe out one time. Now, send this visible light to your family, friends, country, and world. Breathe out and open your eyes.

LIGHT — GLORY
(from Proverbs 3:35 and Isaiah)

Close your eyes. Breathe out and in three times slowly. Know that the wise shall inherit glory.

Breathe out one time. See and feel glory coming nearer and nearer till a reflection of the glory is touching you.

Breathe out one time. Physically sense this light:

1) surrounding you. Breathe out one time.
2) permeating you. Breathe out one time.
3) penetrating you. Breathe out one time.

Physically sense your becoming a spiritual body of light. Breathe out and open your eyes.

CHAPTER XII

Reversing: Practices of Detachment

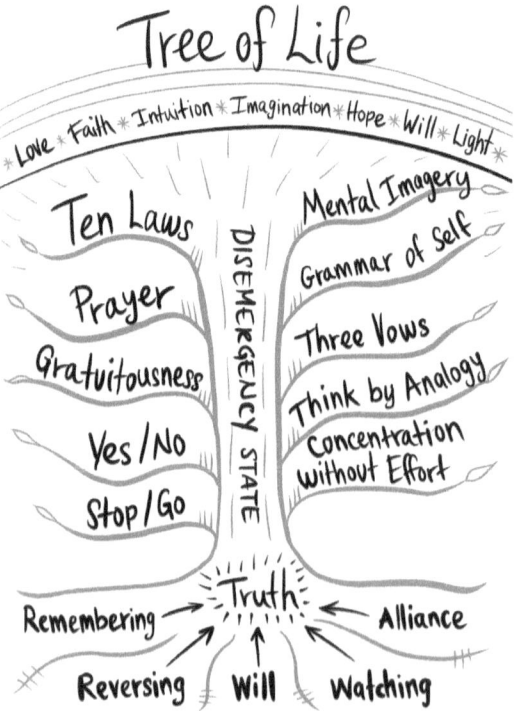

THE FOLLOWING 11 MAJOR PRACTICES in our plan for life are not only designed to awaken us to living in a new direction promoting life, they also have effects on rejuvenating our biological and physiological life forces. They are all aligning us with the vertical, permanent reality of the never-ending forces of

Reversing: Practices of Detachment

life, pouring its energy constantly into us.

Start with any practice. Remember, you are going through a transformation, remembering to think vertically, turning awareness, via sensations and feeling, inward and upward. Turning means reversing, separating from the usual, habitual, or familiar. Little by little we go. Be careful not to overreach. Step by step, rung by rung is the way you climb the ladder of Self-mastery to become the king or queen of yourself. As you move along, you may discover more practices.

We practice faith by engaging in these techniques and methods of GEMS and observing what happens. You begin with one day of testing one technique or practice. When you become aware of any change, go to two days, three, four, five, six, one week, two, three, until experiencing an inkling of the presence of the Present. It is helpful to keep a record in a small notebook or cell phone, simple little jottings, noting what has occurred.

- Dis-Emergency State: Conserving life force (covered earlier)
- The Ten Commandments: The Gift of the Laws of Love and Community
- The Three Virtues: Overcoming the Laws of the Jungle
- Concentration Without Effort: Living without Goals; Living the Moment
- Thinking by Analogy: Thinking in a New Way
- Mental Imagery: A New Way of Self-Healing
- Prayer: Conversing with God
- The Yes or No Phenomenon: Resolving Doubt
- Grammar of Self: Reversing the Trap of Linear Time
- Stopping Exercises: Visa to Freedom
- Gratuitousness: Emulating God

The Ten Commandments:
The Gift of the Laws of Love and Community

The Ten Cosmic Laws are the Western spiritual blueprint for living harmoniously with one another and with the Divine. Laws mean in perpetuity, while commandments mean calls to action to be carried out. Collectively these laws curb our destructive impulses, maintain order and restraint, and forge bonds among large numbers of people. The first five define our relationship to Divinity. The second five define the sacred contract we have with each other to carry out the greatest gift bestowed on us: life! Taken together, they are the practices of TRUTH.

Hitler was quoted by the eminent literary critic Prof. Francis George Steiner as saying, "The Jews invented conscience. How unfortunate."[39] Conscience has a number of meanings. It restrains our destructive actions toward self and others as well as providing direction for choices and decisions that are beneficial solutions that serve truth. In both senses Hitler knew full well what he was doing was devoid of conscience — "the faculty of recognizing the distinction between right

---

[39] D.J.R. Bruckner. "Talk with George Steiner." *New York Times,* May 2, 1982. https://www.nytimes.com/1982/05/02/books/talk-with-george-steiner.html (accessed 9/29/2018).

Reversing: Practices of Detachment

and wrong in regard to one's conduct" (*Am Heritage Dictionary*).

Right does not mean what one believes is right for him- or herself. This "right" serves as a rationalization for many tyrants, dictators, sociopathic con artists, psychopathic murderers (like Hitler), swindlers, and some corporate CEOs, as examples. Rather, there is an overarching "right" law or conscience superseding our personal authorship, making our personal laws superfluous.

These laws are the laws of conscience. They serve to help us develop a feeling for the other's suffering, no matter what form that suffering takes. Experiencing those feelings permits us to assist, help, and otherwise share with others.

When we pay attention and follow these laws, we transform our lives and those around us to create an expansion and deepening of consciousness. In other words, we heighten our awareness and wakefulness. The more attentive we become, the higher our vibration and overall physical status become. To awaken is to become a being of light no longer trapped in the darkness of the forces and clutches of death.

Attention to the laws permits a practice of consciousness in the waking field of everyday life. The beauty in this is the development of moral conscience and transcendent consciousness at the same time.

 This is the monotheistic spiritual way: There is no spiritual attainment without social cohesion. The Ten Laws are the Ten Laws. You can't concentrate just on the second five without the first five, and vice versa. You'll notice that in every Hebraic depiction of the Ten, they always look thus: a complementary pair joined at the hip.

The Ten Laws were the priceless gift bestowed by God at Mount Sinai on the just illuminated group of more than 600,000. That these two events coincided is obviously not by chance. They are intimately related. How so?

The first step is the illuminative experience brought by God — like the illuminative experience I became when I first met Colette that fateful Thursday afternoon over 40 years ago.

Well, if the group was illuminated, why did they need the gift of the Ten Laws? Illumination was the *necessary* spiritual experience but not the *sufficient* one for continuing the enduring spiritual path. For if that realization is not continuously tuned, polished, and shaped, the light will eventually dim and likely burn out. Many of us have revelatory experiences, a sudden "hit" or light. Then that's where those laws come in. They provide the essential practices for keeping the light glowing, the light of unending life given us, not to be extinguished. God's promise to Abraham in Genesis about endless life was reiterated in Exodus when God says as much: "If you give ear to My statutes and obey My commandments I PROMISE: I will not inflict on you the diseases I am about to on the Egyptians for *I am the healer*!" [The Egyptians here stand for those followers of hedonistic tendencies who are attached to sensory pleasure and material greed.]

After my illuminative experience of May 1974, I realized the need to "polish the diamond." Here, then, is the polish for your diamond. The label reads "The Ten Laws or Commandments." The Commandments — or the "Demandments," as I call them — mean a call to action, an inner demand in the moment to carry out those holy laws in our direct encounter with others in our socially shared world. In addition, I have broadened the scope of their activity by also deeming them the "Ten Laws of Collaboration."

The laws were designed to reinforce what has been asked of us: to show our love and to become vehicles of love; to love God with all your hearts, soul, might (Deut. 6:5); and love your neighbor as yourself (Lev. 19:18 and Mark 12:31). As we shall see in due course, a third love also comes into play: Love yourself as a servant of Invisible Reality.

As noted above, the first five reflect our collaborative relationship to God; the second five, our collaborative relationship to each other.

For them I have taken yet another liberty: As they are framed in terms of "do's" and "don'ts," I have placed alongside each a "remember" as the opposite of "don't." We apparently have an easier time dealing with "yes" than "no," as recent scientific brain research studies have shown.

The Ten Laws:
Do's and Don'ts

1) Don't put any god before God —> Remember to keep the path clear between you and Source.
2) Don't erect idols or make graven images —> Remember to stand erect as your own authority and independently think into the present.
3) Don't take God's name in vain —> Remember to praise and give credit to God. Remember to speak kindly without unholy language (cursing).
4) Remember and observe the Sabbath.
5) Honor father and mother —> (above and below) to live a long life.
6) Don't murder —> Remember to preserve life.
7) Don't commit adultery —> Remember to follow a path of purity without contaminating or polluting.
8) Don't steal —> Remember to be honest.
9) Don't bear false witness —> Remember to tell the truth.
10) Don't covet —> Remember to preserve the other's freedom.

I asked Colette and my friend Sybil about their understanding of the Ten Commandments and the multitude of troubles that arise from deviating from these laws. I asked Colette naturally as my teacher, and

Sybil as my friend, who was the most gifted psychic I knew and the most knowledgeable person about spiritual traditions I knew aside from Colette.

Colette responded that the violation of the First Law — putting something between you and God — sets in motion the dark current of will that is the desire to be great, or usurping the knowledge and power of God, the rest of the following nine, like dominos falling, would result. From One came Two — making graven images and idolatry in general, either bowing down before one or erecting yourself as one (vanity, megalomania); to Three — taking God's name in vain, the presence of Invisible Reality disappearing from consciousness; to Four — forgetting altogether about remembering or observing the Sabbath, as we see happening in America where there is no Sabbath, just the business idol bowed down to 24/7; to Five — not knowing, but rather denigrating our earthly Mother and Father; to Six — murder: no respect for our Source, no respect for human life; to Seven, adultery, losing a sense and understanding of leading a pure life; to Eight, stealing; Nine, lying, rumor, gossip, slander, libel; to Ten — coveting, envy, jealousy, greed, avarice, claiming and possessing for ourselves what is not ours. Without adhering to the First, there is no chance for a lawful society to emerge. All bets are off. Every man and woman for themselves. The laws of the jungle prevail.

Sybil said everything begins with violating the Tenth: claiming, possessing, envy: the seed of war, jealousy: the seed of murder, greed, avarice, all set in motion by the forces and Dark Currents of Will = to take, keep, hold onto, and advance at the expense of others. Once the dark currents are activated, the rest of the nine follow: lying, cheating, stealing, adultery (mixing or impure living and behavior), murder, defaming of parents, no Sabbath, taking God's name in vain (there is no God), idolatry (in all its "glory"), putting you or someone/something else between you and God.

Reversing: Practices of Detachment

They were both right. Colette took her cue from the Bible, which emphasizes the dangers inherent in violation of the first law: to wit, usurping the knowledge and power of God, inherent in the myth of Eden of the serpent's proposition to Eve.[40] Sybil started with the materialists' fallacy of living, emphasizing the greed factor: wanting more, better, and different, the impulse to war, murder, violence, and mayhem, stemming from and as an outgrowth of going afoul of the Tenth Law.

Each of us observing our daily situation and/or behavior can begin by categorizing which direction we are coming from. This will make it easier to correct the commandment or commandments we've broken and to use that knowledge as the prompt to make the necessary corrections and compensations to bring ourselves into alignment along the five dimensions of human experience. Maybe then we can become more sensible about social, economic, and environmental justice issues facing us today.

The overall practice of the Ten Laws involves the interplay and expression of three functions, all cooperating at once in an environment of expanded consciousness and focused attention. These three functions are mental, emotional, and behavioral. The mental part is to give thought to these commandments. Have them in mind. Put attention and awareness on them and their existence in our lives. As in everyday legal matters, ignorance is no excuse. We are watching, observing, taking notes, paying attention, and becoming aware of their presence in our daily lives. We amplify our endorsement of them through feelings they engender. These feelings are indicated by feeling considerate of others; wanting to help, give, share, teach; sacrificing for ourselves and for others; being careful we don't unnecessarily harm or

---

[40] Myths are the spiritual foundation legends lived out as historical truths: The first 11 chapters of Genesis are the legends/myths that are unfolded historically thereafter, beginning with Chapter 12.

injure ourselves in the process. How we think and feel is reflected in our actions. If we are considerate, harmless, and make a contribution, then we are acting in good conscience and are mature human beings. Developing conscience of thought, feeling, and action reflects itself in increased awareness, focused attention, and expanded consciousness. Putting them all together, we have before us a premier practice of the sacred operative in everyday life. The moral reality, the pure reality of life, has come to clean up the messes we have made, cleansing us in the process. Coming clean makes us a receptacle for the light of grace to enter us, reigniting our alliance with divine reality and self-organizing, endless life.

How do we integrate this practice into our lives? How do we become active watchers? For some, a particular commandment may jump out at you. Commit yourself to observing how it plays out in your life for three weeks to start with, to get used to this practice. After three weeks of observing, note how you feel and how life is going. Are there changes you are aware of? For others, look at your current life challenges and see what commandment you or another who is impacting you are breaking. Often a pattern of one or two will emerge. If so, choose those to focus on for a time. Others may resonate with Colette or Sybil's focus and concentrate on keeping God at the forefront or watching the impulse to covet. Yet another way is to review your day before going to sleep and identify areas of difficulties and what commandments you struggled with. You can correct the incident with imagery or make a physical correction the next day, but even just mentally noting it, with repeated awareness, will bring a change in your thoughts, feelings, and behavior. Vigilance is the key. Fact is, doing so doesn't make us weary. The more we observe, the stronger we become. Our physiology is reflecting life force.

Finally, don't fall into the blame game. Becoming a watcher of the commandments is not an excuse to tyrannize others with your opinions and judgments about their shortcomings. In general, tend to yourself, unless their actions are impacting you — then speak up! Likewise, this practice is not about guilt, supposed accounts payable. Quite the opposite: As you practice, you will come to love yourself and others more, and close the ledger book on accounts payable and accounts receivable.

The Laws

First Law: Keep God Center Stage
The first states not to put anything or anyone between you and God. When one doesn't have the sense of Divine existence, or reality, or any variant of this sense, there occurs the singular fundamental error in human existence: vanity — making or believing oneself to be a god, trying to usurp the knowledge and power of God. Vanity is the creation of a false image of oneself so as to avoid feeling inferior. Vanity seeks to have others serve it. Its opposite is humility, becoming the servant of and in the service of Invisible Reality.

To reinforce humility, we practice the Law of Detachment. With vanity, in contrast, we are enmeshed in the Law of Attachment and the struggle for existence. If I am attached to being important — the source of vanity — I must maintain this position, usually at your expense. The struggle for survival of the fittest fits in perfectly here. I am the great one, and you must bow down to me and serve me. I am "real," and you are a shadow whose survival depends on my largesse — or lack thereof. As a shadow without an individual identity, you are virtually anonymous and can easily be replaced by an equally anonymous shadow whose main — if not sole — job is to serve me. My false belief is "The more power to control I believe I have, the more am I a god, the more immune am I."

Second Law: Idolatry —> Be Your Own Authority
At this juncture, the Second Law comes into play. Remember to stand erect, refuse to bow down before any other human or external authority, make no one an idol for worship and don't make yourself into an idol to be worshiped. Essentially, put *nothing* between you and One. Keep the path clear.

Idolatry is the most pervasive and destructive practice that a person or community can undertake. It comes in many packages, is oftentimes subtle, and then again not so subtle in making its appearance. The sum and substance of this law — not to make anyone nor anything that is tangible an object of worship — is to keep us free from enslavement. Forming a personal relationship — what I call a "holy attachment" — Invisible Reality promises freedom, while worship and erecting of the visible objects (people, things) promises enslavement. It is clear that becoming enslaved creates weakness, illness, and eventually decay and death. In the social relational sense, which is the focus of our living experience on Earth, we commonly find ourselves responding to what others may say, do, think, or feel. In other words, our mood and other responses are dictated by them. To the extent that this happens, we have allowed ourselves to become slaves. As a slave, we fall prey to the other's will, surrender our power and become subjugated. The consequences speak for themselves as we create our own private gulag of captivity.

Other relevant variants of this idolatry phenomenon include: making the other(s) more important than we are, again a form of idolatry, or bowing down; defending, justifying, explaining our self defensively to another human; believing that those who fob themselves off as authorities know more about you than you know about yourself; enabling and/or justifying the deviant behavior of another; allowing our self to become a shadow in the dyadic relationship to support the formula laid down by the other, "me real, you shadow or nonentity, or anonymous"; depending on the other to make you happy. Lying down on the altar of another's dysfunction, imbalances, deranged behavior — that is, sacrificing our self this way, becoming injured and harmed in the process. On and on this list may grow. However, these are the salient features I've endeavored to make clear.

We have just looked at some outer forms of idolatry. Now's the time to look at inner forms. What goes on in our inner life to create idolatry? What comes first to my mind is thinking *into* linear time, already described as the future or personal past. It is worth repeating: Future is uncreated; it hasn't happened. It is about what isn't at the expense of thinking about what is; what isn't is only a possibility or probability at best, yet it becomes the major investment of our thinking. It is a place where we want to control, be the master of (uh-oh, remember the First Law), be in charge of. We concoct stories about it, around it, wanting to be able to predict it, fix the results, know the outcome, and be in charge of the consequences of our decisions and actions. Of course we end up with lies, convincing ourselves that we can master an illusion. Instead we discover that we are burdening ourselves with falsehoods and untruths that are weighing us down, eventually making us sick.

In Western spiritual terms, the source of this overriding characteristic dominating the lives of practically all people all over the world is the urge to usurp the knowledge and power of God, of that who or which is in charge of the future and brooks no trespass in that realm. This spiritual point is disregarded by the vast majority of people, and the result has a direct adverse influence on our health. It is a violation of the First and Second Laws.

Combining the insights from Colette and Sybil, the First and Second Laws and Tenth Commandments lay the ground for understanding all the order and disorder in our lives. Idolatry of the Second Law deals not only with erecting idols externally but also internally, mentally in thought, as a deeper understanding of the part of that commandment that speaks of creating graven images.

External graven images are easier to identify and include our attachments to money and any of the "ten thousand" physical objects, including addictive substances, that we can attach to. In the extreme, we actually bow down to them and become their servants.

The clearest example in the ancient Israelite world was the creation of the statue of a foreign god called Baal, commissioned by the then-queen Jezebel, to whom children were sacrificed. A human example occurs in the book of Esther, where the populace is asked to bow down before the newly appointed "secretary of state" called Haman. The Hebrew, Mordecai, refuses. From that act unfolds the story of Purim, when Haman hatches the plot to exterminate all the Hebrews from the kingdom of Persia (Iran).

The mental counterparts of idolatry, the basis of the Second Law's counterpoint, are those very fixed mental images of unwavering thought, including misconceptions, opinions, and conclusions — in short, fixed containers and certainties of this and that. These mental idols are *fixed* images we erect inwardly that have limits and boundaries that preclude openness to so many possibilities of life. Such mental thoughts are indeed mental objects analogous to physical ones. The significance of mental idolatry, as exists with all physical objects to which we enslave ourselves, is the entropy or decay inherent in everything that has limits and boundaries. All closed systems, be they physically attached to or created by us in the inner forum of consciousness, are subject to decomposition, decay, and eventual demise.

An example is the general misunderstanding pervading psychology, medicine, and natural science that what happened in the past creates what becomes the future; what we will become is determined by what we came from before. It presupposes an opinion that something that happened in the past shall create what will happen again. Fundamentally, a speculation like this is a variant of the basic material position of cause and effect, the effect being dependent on a preceding thing, or object, as its source. Reliance on the presence of another has enormous implications for our freedom or enslavement. Dependency, an extreme form of idolatry, becomes the seed for enslavement, by making someone or something more important than we are, a process that can't be emphasized enough.

Every issue of life turns on the proposition of freedom and enslavement, the former taking the road of life, the latter the road to death. We need to recognize the constancy of these roads presenting themselves to us. Recalling Deuteronomy 30:15,19, at every moment the universe sets before us two options, and then instructs us to *choose*. Either choice is legitimate and genuine as long as we are mature, accept the consequences of either, move on from there, and realize the main point is *choosing* either life or death. This is a spiritual point that's not so easily understood in everyday life. My purpose here is to alert you to become consciously aware of that point. Do we choose the spiritual path or the material one, freedom or enslavement, ectropy or entropy, life or death? The choice of idolatry, for instance, is a choice for death.

It is clearly understandable that without this education we could not know or conceive that suffering may stop, and that the path of life, the "Way," as is said in Taoism, brings Life to life. We begin now to get a clearer picture of the value of taking the life road, showing us the way to end suffering, which means putting an end to idolatry in ourselves.

Third Law: God's Name in Vain —> Appreciate the Invisible Reality
The Third Law, not to take God's name in vain, gives us pause to think deeply about its meaning and application to our daily life, as all of the Ten Calls to Action are designed to do. We contemplate it more because it is not as clear-cut to understand as the other nine.

At first, we can look at three instances to which "in vain" may apply and reflects on our daily experience: substitution and blasphemy and apostasy.

Let's take a look:

As for substitution, what comes up for us to observe are those religious pundits of all stripes who want to stand as intermediaries between us and the Source. (Recall Law One: put *nothing* between you and God!). They try to tell us what God wants of us. In contrast, a teacher of Spirit has not the faintest desire to tell you what is wanted of you by God; instead, it is known and understood that you have to find that for yourself. We seek to tie ourselves to Spirit. That is the true definition of religion! And finding it out for yourself is a distinct and definite possibility. Refuse to let yourself fall into the trap of allowing any prelate to presume to tell you what God wants of you. To do so is for them to invade your domain of freedom, and by unwittingly participating in this error, you risk having freedom co-opted. It's understandable that we do so because the solo march into freedom seems scary, as we all have been conditioned to be afraid of freedom and hypnotized by this endless conditioning that enslavement is preferable. It seems preferable to be dependent on others who promise comfort to us by supporting our major false belief system governing our lives.

Depending on others for our well-being without attending to it through our own inner resources is to turn our backs on our alliance to the Source, substituting human intervention at first, based on the assumption that they know more about us than we know about ourselves — a faulty misconception if ever there was one. We don't negate human influence, which can be prudent, such as finding a trustworthy mentor or teacher. We can assess their genuineness if they teach us at first to turn to our inherent inner resources to discover our health and to know ourselves. Here I am not speaking of certain circumstances that may demand immediate physical intervention — for example, needing oxygen in acute congestive heart failure, or an operation to repair a bone fracture where the bone has pierced the skin and is sticking out. But in the general run of things, turning to inner resources is *not* to be neglected. For acute conditions like those mentioned above, it is a good idea to pray for divine help to assist in the human efforts to effect the cure. Even in those cases where we call on others, we need to be mindful that we owe our return to order and balance to God, who clearly states in the book of Exodus 15:26 that the One is the ultimate healer:

> And He said: "If thou wilt diligently hearken to the voice of the Lord thy God, and wilt do that which is right in His eyes, and wilt give ear to His commandments, and keep all His statutes, I will put none of the diseases upon thee, which I have put upon the Egyptians; for I am the Lord that healeth thee."

No humans can either cure or heal you. They are the agents, not the ones ultimately doing the job. I think we may be getting the hang of how such substituting turns us away from our alliance to the Source. Someone taking credit for that cure or healing is dismissing God and taking God's name in vain.

Before going on to blasphemy and apostasy, we might look at the genesis of this commandment. Its origin actually appears in the book of Genesis in the discussion of the Tower of Babel alluded to earlier. This event takes place within the first 11 chapters of Genesis that together present the spiritual foundation of the Western monotheistic tradition. With the advent of Abraham in the 12th chapter, we begin the historical unfoldment of this path.

The stories in these 11 chapters speak to the obstacles that prevail on Earth in our time-space world that we must overcome to advance our present and communal evolution. They tell us not only what the obstacles are but also about what this tradition of Spirit offers us to repair and reverse them, especially the ones we create.

The builders of the Tower wanted — and still want — to take charge of heaven and earth, to have the Tower reach into the heavens and supplant the force of Spirit that descends from above into our sphere of life. This is probably the first written account of usurping God's position, clearly taking Its name in vain.

Building the Tower refers to the edifice of vanity — the false image we create for ourselves in the world — by indulging in the fundamental moral error of wanting to usurp the knowledge and power of God. The ramifications of doing so are legion. It contributes centrally to all the mayhem and marauding plaguing the world for now, past, and evermore unless something is done within ourselves to renounce this tendency. Making oneself into a god creates an insatiable thirst for power, the kind that gives one pleasure by creating suffering and enslavement of others to do our bidding as they surrender their freedom to us.

In our current era, natural science too has overstepped its boundaries. While it may have value in mechanical life, it cannot hold the existential answer(s) about truth, reality, life, and death. It has clearly built a Tower of Babel, making it clear that God is a fiction while claiming to be the authority over those three areas just mentioned. We are asked to bow down at the feet of science, a field of inquiry based on prediction, on knowledge, and on control of an illusory future. It is a tower of specious premises based on cause-and-effect thinking (conclusionary thinking) and chance, both idolatrous forms of thinking. In addition, both freeze God out of the loop. Both deny the reality of a nonmaterial consciousness, the intercession of the Divine, our ability to encounter the Divine, and our free will and choice.

By now I've actually touched on blasphemy and apostasy. Blasphemy is a denunciation of God — see atheism — while apostasy is a renunciation of God. One form of apostasy is to thank God when things appear to go favorably in life and to blame God when things go unfavorably. This is an instance of selective responsibility: When it's going well, I'm proud of my own achievement(s) and may even forget to thank God. When it's not going so well, it's God's fault, God's responsibility, or there is no God — play the blame game against God and duck out on our personal responsibility.

Carrying out the Third Law requires us to become aware of when and how we are making the error, and to know when and how we are being duped by others who want us to collaborate in their folly. Remember, there is no such thing as chance. To insist on chance is to deny God, known in this case as Divine Providence. In this regard, spiritual practice and adherence to principles of Spirit are experiments for us to discover their veracity and validity. To make experiments that deny God continues the habit inculcated in Eve by the serpent who induced her to turn away from the one true voice and replace revelations from the Source with experimentation from the tree of death.

We see the first three commandments breached with the first bite of the apple of the Tree of Knowledge: putting someone/thing between us and God; making oneself into an idol by usurping God's knowledge and power; and taking God's name in vain, to replace it with choosing from the Tree of Knowledge of Good and Evil (death).

Raising our own image while diminishing God's, presuming ourselves to be *the* creators or manifesters of things, is an example of blasphemy. Giving credit to the Source counteracts the tendency. All too often I have heard MDs, other clinicians, and healers claim credit for their efforts when sufferers recover. Not to give credit where credit is due, claiming it for ourselves, not only violates the Third Law, of dismissing the One who is the ultimate healer, but defies the Tenth Law of coveting by claiming what doesn't belong to us; the Ninth of bearing false witness, by lying; the Eighth by stealing, by taking the credit away from Source; the Sixth by murder, by murdering the name, obliterating it, effectively destroying Its identity and soul for us; and the Second, idolatry, by seeking to elevate one's name, reputation, and status undeservedly at the expense of another.

The errors just cited are committed either unwittingly, without a desire to injure or harm others, or intentionally, with the desire to harm. The last is called an iniquity and has the most disastrous consequences. All of them can be repaired through the Light Currents of Will that offer compensation and correction. All in all, we are almost always given a second chance to correct. We certainly don't want these errors to pile up to the point where we become incapacitated through illness or disability, or loss of mental acuity and awareness to act. These infirmities, by the way, are to be considered a natural consequence of behaving outside the Ten Laws and a loving heart. Recall in Exodus 15:26 where God clearly states that we don't become ill if we obey the spiritual laws and statutes; rather, we are given a second chance to escape death.

One primary purpose of this book is to provide the means to use the second chance either in the life before us now or after death by life restored as the second birth called resurrection. Our rebirth can take place now or then. The groundwork is now supplied by biological science establishing a lengthening of days so we can have more years of time to accomplish and fulfill the gift handed us in this era. We are not to degrade nor denigrate this gift. We are an elected generation of people on Earth to make this shift. We have been selected to preserve the Earth, become One with God, and bring love, light, law, hope, faith, and truth here.

We can only speculate why this is the case, but it is unimportant to do so. However, we are noticing drastic things happening to the planet, some of a seeming magnitude never witnessed before, leaving us with a sense of urgency to right the ark that is perilously floating, dragging us all down to the murky depths of disappearance. Is this a redux of Noah's Ark? Perhaps so. (As Woody Allen stated once, "God says to Noah build an ark, lay out for the lumber, I'll pay you back later.") We are asked to do our part in this Alliance. Don't betray the gift now being bestowed on us. Let's reverse and renounce the apostatic condition blanketing the world at present and turn back to our Source from whom all gifts come, including the greatest of all — immortal life, the love that trumps death.

Fourth Law: Sabbath Practice —> Reversing, Resting, and Reconnecting

The Sabbath is the only event in the Bible consecrated as holy by God as an emphatic stamp on the importance of this day. It is another instance of Reversing and Stopping, for in observing and remembering on this day, we reverse the habits of the week and stop habitual activities of the week. The day is devoted to communion with God; building a supplementary soul, one of energy that helps sustain us through the succeeding week; becoming aware of no time as a prelude to the Great Sabbath of the Earth described later in its own chapter. It is a day of feasting and conversation about holy matters not ordinarily part of our daily social intercourse. Called a 'Day of Delight' (Isaiah 58:13), it is a day of celebration and of "not doing."

The whole of the Sabbath is a practice in and of itself, in whatever way we might turn attention to Spirit. To my mind, it is a practice of no death by turning away from the grip of time and turning toward and communing with that which exists in no-time, where immortality lives. No-time/space = no death! The Sabbath observance foreshadows the end of linear time, which foreshadows the end of death. What I propose by carrying out the techniques and methods described in these pages is concerned with bringing Sabbath no-time/space practice into the week, suffusing the daily life with timeless and spaceless experience to be incorporated in whatever we are doing, relating, and thinking. Eventually our life becomes Sabbath-oriented, changing our outlook, behavior, and conscience to provide a new foundation of living while still pursuing life's activities, but in a new way. This practice adds a necessary dimension to the biological discoveries, itself providing a new opportunity for biological longevity and soul-directed immortality. They each complement the other, the sacred giving meaning of spiritual value to our biological existence, where soul and body are reunited.

Since creation ceased on the seventh day when God rested, so we too don't start anything new on that day. The day of rest is a necessary must in our lives. Today in the United States there is no true Sabbath. Activity goes on at a frenetic pace 24/7 in the desperate search for pleasure and comfort to satisfy the urge for material gain. The incessant, nonstop style of life contributes mightily to the morbidity (sickness) rates, leading eventually to destabilizing and disabling chronic illness.

There are many paths to develop our Sabbath practice to separate us from the habitual. Here are some examples to get us started and reverse our daily life routine:

- Prepare a pre-Sabbath meal with family or friends each week to share on the Sabbath.
- Avoid speaking about business and finance.
- Let go of the "have to dos"
- Experiment with not spending money or shopping on the Sabbath.
- Slow down & Smell the Roses! Engage in activities that center and quiet us: contemplation, mental imagery, meditation, yoga, breathing exercises, walking in nature, reading and discussing sacred texts.
- If possible, walk or bicycle rather than drive a car.
- If you are a workaholic, don't work on the Sabbath — take a day off!

Reversing: Practices of Detachment

- Close the computer for the day.
- Don't check your cell phone for updates, emails, or texts. Start with a few hours, and build up your mental muscle!
- Engage in a ritual or mental exercise to start and end your Sabbath practice, marking this day as separate from the mundane.
- Commune: Go to a house of worship; pray with a community.
- Celebrate & Connect: with ourselves, loved ones, nature, and the Divine.

The purpose of these activities is not to cut us off from social life but to cut off the noise of habitual daily life, to begin to listen to our inner voice, and to stop the clock of time.

IMAGERY EXERCISE

A SABBATH EXERCISE:
THE CESSATION OF TIME
To be done on the eve of your Sabbath.

Close your eyes and breathe out and in three times slowly. Imagine, as the sun sets and night falls, the Sabbath dawns for us.

Breathe out one time. Imagine now the Light of Sabbath giving us a taste of the coming world, the world to come. Sit quietly in the conquering wonder of silence separating us from habitual daily activity, seeing happy people walking noiselessly about.

Breathe out one time. Sense and feel the beatific blissfulness of this new heavenly City of Peace. Breathe out and open your eyes.

Fifth Law: Honor Mother and Father —> Honor the One Who Chose to Give Birth to You

Honor father and mother brings to light two essential features right away: 1) They are to be respected for giving birth to us, bestowing on us the gift of life; 2) they are the conduit through which the Source of the Origin makes its presence felt on Earth. The parents are the pivot point between the four preceding commandments defining our relationship to God and the succeeding five defining our relationship to one another. The previous four are "asocial," meaning that carrying them out is singularly between you and Invisible Reality. It is an internal matter based on our conscience and commitment to a personal, individual connection. As it is an intrapersonal matter, we have choices to make and decisions to take as to whether to carry them out or not for our own sake. Even so, action taken in this way does reflect on our social connectedness with others. Saddam Hussein, the tyrant of Iraq, in violation of the 1st Commandment, held himself to be a god, and like all other murderous tyrants, long did the populace pay a heavy price for that megalomania.

With regard to the second five of the commandments, they are overtly expressed in our actions toward others, and as such they are directly interpersonal, socially based, and have palpable, direct social consequences. Murder, mixing, stealing, lying, avarice, and greed are in our faces all the time.

What helps us to maintain these laws is the fifth one of honoring — not loving — mother and father. The focus is squarely on honor, not love. They may be loved or not, but "honoring" mom and pop is to respect them. However, we need be careful *not* to honor their behavior should it be deviant, aberrant, abusive physically or mentally, or otherwise destructive. Obviously, distinctions need to be drawn between their being — mom or pop — and their behavior. Describing a destructive piece of behavior is not them. By making this distinction, we don't condemn their souls. We realize everyone, including parents, has errors they must take care of. We are not responsible *for* our parents (or for others as well). Each individual has responsibility for his- or herself. No one can take on the karma or the way another person chooses in life. We have enough to do to take care of our responsibilities, but we don't neglect others in need. We have responsibility *to* them to educate, share, help, and care for them, as well as to ourselves.

The important spiritual point of the Fifth Law is that if we can't or don't honor our progenitors here, we shall not be able to honor our Progenitor above. When we stop honoring that which is above and that relationship disappears, the misery and suffering in the world is our lot, the life impulse is forsaken, and the death impulse takes over to consume our life. Then there is no sacred Alliance and our way is lost. The fruits of understanding mom and dad rather than condemning them, together with honoring their being simply by the fact they took the decision to bring us onto Earth, is a blessing beyond compare that promises us many fruits in return. This truth is verified by the end statement of the 5th Commandment after "honor your father and mother" thus, so you may *live long* (Ex. 20:12).

Applied to our life, when things are going seemingly adversely, don't lapse into the inner-terrorist-created blame game of taking the parents to task for what they supposedly did or didn't do for us that ends in taking responsibility off ourselves for self-examination of our errors now. We don't want to lapse into that anti-spiritual psychologism of cause and effect or to buy into the materialistic belief pervading all the natural sciences that experiences, materializations, end points of any sort create what I believe now or have determined what I am now. *Then* does not create *now*! The stories associated with them have no bearing on what is now in front of us. Such an assertion has never been proven to be the case. Pare away the stories simply by noting to yourself that they are merely stories, not facts, not true. Yes, something may have occurred between you and mom and/or dad, but the story built around that is nothing but . . . story. The beliefs mom and dad inculcated and the other forms of patterning that took place become what's meaningful in our life. The patterning, not the stories or drama built around such conditioning, is valuable to examine, as it is subject to change. The rest may be the good stuff of literature and the analysis applied to it that makes for a nice, heady, fun course in college.

Finally, if we approach the law correctly, mom and dad are not burdens; rather, they are benefactors to us.

Sixth Law: Don't Murder —> Preserve Life
A maxim attributable to the Eastern spiritual tradition is that "When the tiger comes to kill you, you must kill it."[41] This maxim actually reverberates throughout all traditions. What I have noticed and has caught my attention throughout my life, is the equating of killing with murder, as though they were synonymous with each other. I don't know the source of this ellipsis. It's certainly not in the sixth of the Ten Commandments, which says, "Don't murder," *not* "Don't kill." It is helpful to discern between the two.

When a man puts a gun into a two-year-old's mouth and pulls the trigger, he murdered that tot. He didn't *kill* the child, as the TV and newspaper stories reported. When a suburban doctor's family is brutally murdered in Connecticut (mother and two daughters), the police didn't apprehend the killers, they apprehended the *murderers*. When a policeman is assaulted by a man wielding a gun aimed at him, the policeman succeeds in killing him, not murdering him.

Murdering is done with intent and premeditation, even in the heat of the moment, as commonly happens during an argument. In that highly escalated condition where the act seems to be impulse-driven, the perpetrator has "murder in his/her heart," as the saying goes.

The drunk driver who mows down the pedestrian and flees the scene has murder in his heart, even if it's considered an accident.

---
[41] His Divine Grace A. C. Bhaktivedanta Swami Prabhupada, Lecture BG 02.02, London, August 3, 1993. https://vanisource.org/wiki/730803_-_LectureBG_02.02_-_London (accessed 9/292018).

Reversing: Practices of Detachment

Adults don't kill children, they murder them.

Killing is an act of protection meant toward oneself or toward a group. It is an act of self-defense, a recourse necessary when no other seems apparent. Murder is an act of self-offense. These distinctions are really not murky and are distinctly discernible. Even if some persons are in an altercation and put in a position of sustaining harm, and they strike back to defend themselves, it is killing, as, for example, in many battered-women cases.

These differences have judicial relevance. The designations mean a lot for sentencing and to the families of the victims. The pain of murder to the surviving loved ones can never reach closure, no matter the penalty imposed.

This brings me to the imposition of the death penalty. Capital punishment throughout the course of history has never been viewed as a deterrent to further murder in society or as a means of bringing closure to the aggrieved family or society. Rather, it has been viewed as an apt punishment to fit the crime. It was only in the 20th century that the mixing (aka, adultery) of psychology into the field of law distorted the punishment value of capital punishment by offering the dark, unprovable assertion that capital punishment does not deter future murder. That claim is a case of future talk of what is supposed to happen that makes an adulterous, oil-and-water connection between punishment and deterrence.

Tragedy such as murder was met in biblical laws by identifying 80 different ways capital punishment could be implemented. That's far more than we have in modern times. Yet, ironically, it was unheard of for someone to be executed because of the stringent rules applied to testimony of witnesses, some of whom for specific reasons of character were excluded. But, make no mistake, murder was considered the most grievous act a person could commit. To actively extinguish another's life, premeditatively, goes against the wisdom of "be fruitful and multiply"; "I set before you this day *life* and death. *Choose life* . . ." We are always asked to choose life, not murder life.

The reasoning behind this punishment — if the act of murder could be proven — lies in a twofold understanding: (1) Many acts of murder are mass murder. Murdering a young man, woman, or child has destroyed a wealth of progeny, a lineage of that family, a severing of "be fruitful and multiply." To murder one is to murder a multitude at the same time. Thus the Talmudic sages said, "Whoever destroys a life, it is considered as if he destroyed an entire world. And whoever saves a life, it is considered as if he saved an entire world." This is how we understand that the grief of the living relations is incalculable and may never be healed. Yet murderers not relieved of their lives may generate progeny, as many do. Unfortunately, the scales of divine justice come into balance only in the long run, repairing this earthly miscarriage of justice. (2) In terms of looking at an understanding of reincarnation: The one who inflicts cutting off ongoing tradition (life) by murder can get to feel the pain and torture thus inflicted. By doing so, such experience can help that person reverse these murderous tendencies in the next incarnation, establishing a different relationship to life, one more productive and contributory, one of conscience.

A third item may be noted here. A serial or child murderer who escapes the death penalty is housed in prison where the cost of keeping him can be anywhere from $40,000 to $80,000 a year. Such money could actually be well spent on the victim's family, who may have lost their financial support through the loss of the breadwinner and come to suffer incredible hardship and privation, not to mention the emotional and mental devastation incurred. To date we have not seen any real accommodations and heartfelt feelings materially expressed toward the aggrieved victims. Such is the persuasion of a social system that is more concerned with the "rights" of the incarcerated than with the calamities suffered by the families and their "rights." It is a curious turn

Reversing: Practices of Detachment

of so-called justice where the victim's families in effect are punished long after the crime has taken place, while the offender is extended a much more compassion-filled life.

By the way, the above is not an endorsement of the abuse of power and justice rampant in the current penal system that protects the wealthy and incarcerates and executes the innocent, the disadvantaged, and the disabled.

The most ubiquitous crime in recorded and prerecorded history begins in the West with Cain and Abel: Brother against brother still rages today in all-out fury throughout the world. A turn in civilization occurred when Abraham discovered through his conversations with God a new direction of life that sought to stem the bloodletting and murder of adults and children rampant in 750 or so tribes surrounding him in the ancient Middle East.

To exemplify this turn, and to concretize it, circumcision was created as a symbol of excising the murderous impulse from men's consciousness. It was to mark a redirection in the use of power to trample over people's lives. It also was used as a symbolic way of excising lust from the heart, an organ we can't really perform this operation on. The heart is not only the seat of love, it is also the seat of lust. Lust can have dangerous repercussions if left unchecked. This is why it is stated "Love God with all your heart...," the *all* heart being the seat of love and lust. Both need to turn to loving God.

Suicide is problematical. Generally speaking, this act is considered a homicide against self, with many reverberations taking place in the families and other loved ones who have been intimately connected with him/her. Often family members are so affected that they become ill, or end up killing themselves. In this instance, the initial suicide person unwittingly may have contributed to committing "homicide" from beyond the grave. One difficulty I have observed personally has been that situation where the person who is in the most dire pain at their perceived end of life, where they are unable any further to combat the grip of death and have resigned themselves to leave, seek to put themselves out of their misery and pain. One can only extend appreciation for the choice without being judgmental.

From the point of view of Spirit, there are other forms of murder, aside from the physical, that are tantamount to murder, essentially co-equal. In those instances, it is a sign that if you are the "victim" of that murder, some action needs to be taken immediately to stop being the victim. I shall enumerate three primary ones I know of:

1) **Humiliating someone in public.** Opening a person to public degradation and derision is an act aimed at destroying his or her soul. Children are particularly vulnerable. I was humiliated in front of the classroom in fourth grade by my teacher, twice: once criticizing my appearance/dress and once poking me in the chest vigorously for making noise in class. And then there was my eighth-grade teacher, who took pains to exclaim to me, in front of the class, that I was a Nothing and would "amount to nothing in life." Nowadays, if I were a Zen practitioner, I would take that as a compliment. In those instances, I had little recourse to remove myself from them in the context of being a student at that elementary school (I did not tell my parents or seek to have disciplinary action brought against them). Ordinarily, when you are the butt of this humiliation, your action is to cower or turn away from that person, to have nothing to do with him/her ever again, or to reverse course and attack that individual by physically or verbally lashing back to make everyone aware of what he/she had done (Remember! When the tiger comes . . .). As you might glean here, by the act of humiliating and shaming, there are other commandments involved — the Ninth comes to mind: bearing false witness seems

the most prominent. If you can, fight back. Try to recover from the blow. Tell everyone you know what has happened, who was the thief: no confidentiality here. Aid in your own recovery. Find and summon support.

2) **Depression**. Depression reflects the feeling of anger or homicidal rage turned against oneself. Depression is self-murder, culminating perhaps in suicide. Common mood states such as moroseness, sulkiness, pouting, blues, funks, gloominess, solemness, somberness, and seriousness... are all on a continuum toward actual depression and are forms of partial suicide. It requires depressed ones to take active steps, or have taken for them, to overcome the malady. Don't let a depressed person continue to feel sorry for themselves, rather give them an active, non-injurious outlet for their anger (sweeping the floor, cleaning the house), any active use of the musculature will do. Also, a punching bag does wonders.

3) **Having your work stolen** or simply not being given credit for your work. There might be, for the latter, no intention to steal; nevertheless, one who doesn't give credit for your creation violates the 6th Commandment. Here your name is destroyed, your soul murdered, and you become deflated, daunted, and defeated. Many times my work was stolen, including the idea for a book. And in postgraduate training school, I suffered the opposite, when I was falsely accused of plagiarizing, stealing from someone else, and that accusation was brought before a committee in public.

By not giving credit, we can also see how other commandments are involved: Eighth, stealing; Ninth, bearing false witness; Tenth, coveting, claiming something as one's own. I have also seen where others have had their work stolen and have not been able to recover, even developing cancer and dying. Others have sued in court and been successful. Like being humiliated and shamed, don't take it lying down. People who have violated the Sixth Law have no privilege of confidentiality.

All of the above goes to say: Be aware of the errors we are doing to others and stop them. Like all the laws, they are to be carried out. It remains for us to be vigilant in maintaining law and order ourselves.

Let me end this section with a note on the relationship between saving the world and murder:

The Jewish holiday of Purim captures man's genocidal impulse that has pervaded our world for millennia. In the Western sacred tradition, it is said that in every generation there arises a villain whose aim is to eliminate an ethnic group considered a danger to the larger social order in power.

The story of Purim takes place in the Persian kingdom ruled by King Xerxes. His top advisor, Haman, is infuriated when a certain Jew, Mordechai, refuses to "bow down" to him in a public procession. In retaliation, Haman procures a royal edict to exterminate all the Jews throughout the empire as "these people" have different customs and may be a danger to the country, and even potential traitors.

Unbeknownst to Xerxes, his new queen — Esther — is Jewish and the niece of the very man Haman seeks to annihilate, Mordechai. Esther keeps her identity secret from the king, who has selected her from many virgins in a beauty contest. As it turns out, Mordechai had previously alerted Esther to a secret assassination plot against Xerxes. Esther relates the information to Xerxes, who then apprehends the traitors. He asks Esther how she came by this knowledge. She states, "in the name of Mordechai I have this knowledge." That is, she gives credit

to her source and does not claim the credit for herself! This pivotal attribution fulfills four of the Ten Cosmic Laws that sustain the world:
- Honesty, i.e., not stealing (Eighth Law);
- Truth, i.e., not bearing false witness (Ninth Law);
- Preserving freedom of others, i.e., not coveting or possessing for yourself what doesn't belong to you (Tenth Law); and
- Preserving life, i.e., don't murder physically or psychically by destroying another's name, for example by taking away what she or he has created or achieved (Sixth Law).

The simple act of giving credit to another sets in motion the possibility of redemption and salvation for the world. In our "worldly," everyday affairs we give credit to others, and in the larger scope of life, we give credit to our Source that sustains life and order in the universe. If we don't give credit to the Invisible Reality, we are doomed to "bow down" and serve the Hamans of the world, inadvertently participating in our own enslavement and destruction.

For me, there are two central points to saving our world:
1. Giving credit to our Source;
2. Choosing life over death.

Both these points are encapsulated in a verse from the Song of Songs: "Love is as strong as death" (8:6). This statement even encompasses all ten of the commandments, for when we love others and God, we do not murder, steal, cheat, bow down before other people or idols, but rather we preserve freedom and truth. For the Ten Commandments and Love are two sides of the same coin.

Seventh Law: Adultery, Don't Mix, Don't Serve Two Masters —> Live a Pure Life

The word "adulterate" means to mix. To mix is to weaken. When we mix, we contaminate, pollute, and poison the original substance. Contamination results in a decaying process ultimately destroying the system into which the impurity is introduced, be it carnal, psychic, spiritual, or material. One of the preponderant difficulties I have met in my practice of spiritual therapeutic education over four decades is the question of mixing that comes up so readily for everyone. The temptations are enormous. In spiritual life, people flit from one spiritual philosophy to another, mixing and matching, without remaining pure to one path and following it to its depth.

Spiritual practice requires discipline. To be disciplined means to become a disciple, just as you do in any other field of endeavor you want to master. We take on mentors, become apprentices or dedicated students, and discipline ourselves to take on the required practice of the way we have elected to pursue. Yes, we have chosen to wear a hair shirt, another meaning of discipline, meaning we voluntarily act to embark on a path fraught with irritation, frustration, pain, hardship, and disappointment; but it's also endowed with pleasure, gratification, competence, facility, and adeptness. We become adepts, devotees of a special way. On the way, we endure our created errors of living that are part of the process of learning to live a spiritual life. No pain, no gain!

Whether we have been aware of it or not, this process we sought was done in a pure way. We took one way and followed its precepts to the depths, breadths, and heights of what it had to offer. This practice of purity is exactly what the Seventh Law — the law of adultery — is about. We want to live purely in all the five different dimensions of life to avoid contaminating, polluting, and poisoning ourselves and our relationships.

The Torah gives a succinct comment in Lev. 19:19 about the Seventh Law: Don't put two different seeds in the same field; don't put an ox and an ass on the same plough; don't mix milk with meat; don't wear linen and wool together. The first two apply to many areas of life — trying to live by two philosophies at the same time, such as materialism and spirituality, aptly termed "spiritual materialism."[42] The mixing of milk and meat alludes to dietary and nutritional concerns. Linen and wool alludes to the social mixing of the historical stratification of classes, each with distinct educational standards, social mores, and values, particularly with respect to distinct attitudes of men and women toward each other that prevail in different socioeconomic levels. Endless troubles and inevitable clashes across economic, educational, political, and religious backgrounds create intense, volatile friction, anxiety, and not infrequently, violence. I have seen this phenomenon on numerous occasions in my clinical practice, particularly in marriage. Sorry to say it is more factual than fancy, although saying it openly may rub some the wrong way. Being open to this point and examining such relationships/marriages may reveal the difficulties inherent in this mixing. Can this conflict be remedied by education? Yes, if efforts are made.

The main point of mixing is that of contamination. Polluting an otherwise pure function can cause incredible devastation and destruction. Consider the environmental nuclear devastation that occurred in 2011 in Fukushima, Japan, and in the 1986 Chernobyl, Ukraine, meltdown that have polluted our air and water worldwide and have led to innumerable deaths. Nuclear fission is a form of mixing in itself, whereby we mix or split a heavy atomic nucleus (uranium) with neutrons that releases energy and radioactive particles.

For the inward effects of mixing, we are concerned with five streams of life expression. What are some of the inward contaminants and pollutants that affect these streams? We begin with the mental stream and perhaps the biggest contaminate of all — doubt.

Here we have the seed source, mentally speaking, of all the diffi-

---

[42] See the book *Cutting Through Spiritual Materialism*, by Chöygam Trungpa (Boulder: Shambala Books), 1973.

culties in the world. It engenders a myriad of difficulties, paralyzing our progress individually and collectively. It stifles action and snuffs intuition. It pollutes the mental stream by introducing secondary thoughts impeding the flow of mental life. We stop short or are cut short when that second thought appears. We enter into the mental conflict of yes *and* no in its many forms. Yes and no equals indecision accompanied by anxiety. "Yes" doesn't remain pure but is interfered with by "no" cutting off the clear path created by "yes," and vice versa. Now the friction happens, like rubbing two sticks together, creating sparks. We have created a combustible energy produced by friction. In frictional energy — electrical, steam, nuclear, etc. — something lives while something else has to die in the process. In physiological terms, as our body responds to doubt, some cells live (are fired up), while others die. Eventually, the latter wins out.

Looking in more depth into contamination and pollution, consider the moral stream. For this stream, consider cursing. Curse words exude hate and are said as efforts to defile those toward whom the expletives are aimed. To defile is to render impure. Hurling a curse, or curse words, at someone tries to make the other impure, thereby weaker and submissive. Our ancient spiritual teachers simply stated that what comes out of us can defile us more than what we take in. What we ingest, indeed, may defile and sicken us, but what comes out is worse. Cursing is an unholy language. Its intent is to injure when aimed at another.

What about the other pollutants? For the emotions, I would include every distressing emotion. Why? Because every one of them is attached to some mental thought, idea, belief, or concept that is conceived in either the future or the past, the lands of untruth and falsehood. Put it this way, attachment to future and past runs counter to the Ninth Law to tell the truth. Once we wander away from observing truth for ourselves, we have slipped away from holiness into unholiness.

Reversing: Practices of Detachment

The power of these distressing emotions — anxiety, depression, guilt, regret, anger, fear, worry, and shame are among the most prominent — creates an illusory bridge between now and then (future or past), making it appear that then is now. They are contaminants diverting our pure flow of thoughts connected to each other. No way, Jose. This is a mirage. Now and then are not inherently attached. About the present we have a lot to say. About the future we have nothing to say, nor do we need to. The past, well, that's a story that has seen its day, is a canceled check, and needs no further attention from us. These emotional states draw down our life forces, wearing out our hormonal and immune systems.

The social contaminants are well known to everyone. Without them we could not have primetime TV, or much TV at all. They form the substance of almost every dramatic situation in these stories. There is some shadow of a third party hanging over the relationship, a dark cloud that may descend to bring a disruption and eventual breaking of the two, usually with a good deal of pain and suffering, onset of disease, suicide, murder, and long, agonizing misery for the immediate family, including extended members as well. On closer inspection of these programs, we can spot the disturbance. It is the behavior repudiated by the Tenth Law — coveting by claiming and possessing what doesn't belong to us. Lust, avarice, greed, envy, and jealousy are the prime ingredients in adultery stew.

Immersed as I have been in the human condition for the bulk of my life, as a healer, educator, and observer of human experience, I return to the three conditions that are determinants for social disturbances and conflict, especially between couples. These are: (1) religious differences, which don't create much turbulence until a child comes into the picture and the parents are faced with how to rear the offspring; (2) socioeconomic status; and (3) ideological differences. Such differences, I have found, usually sabotage the couple's ability to build bridges to each other. The difference could be as "seemingly" trivial as each wanting the bedroom painted a different color. Or they could involve political differences — he's a Republican, she's a Democrat. Or spiritual differences — she takes the direction of Zen Buddhism, he wants to embrace Sufism.

Finally, physical mixing is pretty clear cut. Food combining as to what goes together and what doesn't has become of greater awareness in the public consciousness. Food purity is being incorporated more actively in many people's lives. Movies like *Supersize Me* and the greater awareness now of the obesity scourge and the connection between diet and the occurrence of physical maladies highlight the dangers of mixing. Kosher food laws prescribed in the wisdom literature are an example of an attempt to mitigate the possible harmful consequences of such mixing.

I go so far as to question the mixing of different modalities of health-care interventions. To be a purist, we might be careful not to mix pharmaceutical products with natural ones like herbs, or to mix chemotherapy with homeopathy. This teaching has a good deal of meaning to me. I take it to heart and seek to follow the prescriptions rendered by ancient spiritual doctors of health and holiness.

Why do we want to mix? There is always one answer: errors of living that lead to the social errors of living. Here are some of them again: the Five Dark Currents of Will; mistaking happiness as pleasure; believing that unhappiness is pain. All these errors may be huddled under the umbrella of greed, defined as wanting more, better, and different. As noted earlier, there is a connection between the Seventh Law of adultery and the Tenth Law of coveting, crossing boundaries to intrude on the freedom of others.

Eighth Law: Don't Steal —> Be Honest
This law speaks for itself. There are many ways stealing makes itself

apparent. Generally speaking, stealing creates harm to the victim and gives an advantage to the perp. Most of these offenses are crimes against people or things belonging to people. In certain instances, stealing can serve as a benefit to a deserving person or group, such as a spy on "our side" stealing info on a planned attack or the building of a new weapon for use against us. Excepting these more unusual occurrences, clearly stealing is injurious and inflicts great pain as well.

There are subtle forms of stealing that go on in the ordinary course of human relationships. They go unnoticed or don't seem to be harmful when they happen. Someone goes ahead of you on line at the movies or in the supermarket. We let it go if we assess it doesn't make any difference to us. Or my friend said she'd meet me at the theater at 7 p.m. She didn't arrive until 8 p.m. Sixty minutes were "stolen" from me, as I hurried to the theater to make sure I got there on time. Things happen, though. It may not be a purposeful act. I could choose to enter the theater and leave the ticket at the box office. No need to feel irked, offended, or robbed. Take the action you need, and everything will turn out okay. Plagiarism of intellectual properties is yet another form of theft. It is a somewhat frequent occurrence in the arts and sciences, where writings and research results are stolen and ideas "lifted" without attribution.

I think in these small examples we can also see the influence of violating other laws, particularly the Ninth and Tenth: bearing false witness and coveting, respectively. After all, why would I steal something from you unless I was claiming and possessing something for myself not belonging to me or feeling envy that you have something I don't have that I want (Tenth Law). Or, I make you a promise that is not kept. Promises, pledges, vows, and oaths not kept are all part of bearing false witness (Ninth Law).

As was mentioned earlier and is well worth repeating, not giving credit to the source of your "inspiration" violates not only the Eighth

Law but also the Ninth, Tenth, and the Sixth (preserve life/don't murder). In those instances of stealing, irreparable damage to the victim's life can often be the result. Those of you who have had this happen know full well the pain and suffering inflicted by this act of stealing.

There are so many ways stealing rears its ugly destructive head. Margo is a 55 -year-old who has worked for an insurance company for 30 years. One day she is notified that her services are terminated and that she has all of a half-hour to clear out her desk. Within the next week, her boss calls his private clients to smear this woman's reputation and inveigle these clients to give over their accounts to him instead of remaining with Margo, who is moving on to another company. Margo is slandered (false witness) and can be deprived of income. To top it all off, she receives a letter from her former employer saying that she has violated confidentiality by seeking to take her own clients (all of whom she has procured on her own) to her new firm. She is accused of stealing! Sounds like a familiar theme. Something like this may have happened to you, or you have heard many times over in many scenarios akin to this one.

Ponzi schemers (e.g., Bernard Madoff), con artists all over the place, bank robbers galore, and people in high places up to skullduggery. Extortion, blackmail, and kidnapping all over Central and South America. And there is identity theft wreaking havoc in our financial lives. Not to mention those celebrity gurus who arrogate to themselves the place of God as authorities about this and that.

Then there are those who are stealing our climate, animals, and flora. And of course there are those substances that steal our souls: heroin, cocaine, crack, alcohol. Woody Allen's epigraph at the beginning of his film *Take the Money and Run* is "Crime lives," and so it is the case. All of it done in the name of and service to Mammon, to whom we bow down in an unholy alliance.

Reversing: Practices of Detachment

The wonder of it is that with all the criminality, the world is able to remain cohesive. For me, that we are able to carry on and make progress in the wake of all the unholiness surrounding us is proof of God's love for us and forgiveness for scarring Its countenance, deforming the "face hovering over the deep." I refer again to the statement in Genesis that we are born in the image of God, in the likeness of the All. Image means becoming the immortal seed that we have the possibility to become; likeness means born with the moral purity that is our endowment. The former stares us in the face, announcing we are born to be immortal. The latter reveals how by emulating God we may live a pure life that leads us to eternal life in this body. When we choose to live an impure life (always subject to correction and repair), we scar and mar the beauty that surrounds us, that God gifted us.

I'm not sorry to be so passionate about this matter of stealing. Like anyone else, I've stolen at some point in my life and have been stolen from. The scales of justice, in the cosmic sense, are always coming into balance. The justice meter never fails.

Again, we get a clear sense, if not picture, of how those laws interweave with each other. Trip over one, and suddenly we find a number of commandments become involved.

Ninth Law: Don't Bear False Witness —> Tell the Truth
The Ninth Law, bearing false witness, has obvious consequences for us. Many people have been wrongly accused, imprisoned, and put to death based on lies and false testimony. Reputations have been ruined through rumor and gossip. In my clinical experience, I see many people with dire physical ailments that reflect the breakdown of their existence as recipients of lies. Unable to move past the mental, emotional, and physical pain, they wear themselves out and die.

To not bear false witness means to speak truthfully. This law covers a wide swath of thought and speech. In its simplest form it includes rumor, gossip, saying something that is true but shouldn't be said, saying something *not* true that shouldn't be said, not saying something that should be said, slander, and libel. Distortion of a fact is a form of false witness or lying as well (currently known as "fake news").

I remember as a kid in school the teachers remonstrated to us that we shouldn't "tattle" or squeal on our fellow students, or by extension, on the teachers. There is something to be said for that if you live in KGB Russia or in Nazi Germany. But when your fellow employees, students, or teachers blow the whistle on criminal activities, or your local mafioso is stealing money by extortion from your uncle's company, or when you are aware of the incompetence of your fellow doctor colleague and you inform/tattle, that's *not* gossip. Actually, you are saying something true that should be said and is salutary.

More broadly, it includes: fobbing off opinions and explanations as facts (as happens frequently in the doctor-patient relationship), rationalizations, conclusionary thoughts about what will happen, as well as all other forms of future talk: predictions, outcomes, results, consequences, goals, what could, should, would be, must have to, if-then constructs, doubt, indecision, could have, should have, ought to have, ought to, try, going to, "I will" vows, pledges, oaths, promises, hypotheses, and assumptions. Anything that brings us into a closed system of conclusions.

Harking back to my oft-repeated example: An MD says to the patient, "You are incurable," or some variant. By stating this, the doctor has violated four holy laws. They are:

- Law Two = refrain from creating a fixed image, a conclusionary statement, or graven image etched mentally;
- Law Three = speaking in an unholy manner, stating as though God that there is no hope. This serves to weaken the patient even more, who becomes deflated upon hearing these words;
- Law Nine = saying something untrue that shouldn't be said,

claiming the doctor knows the future;
- Law One = there is no God but God. To state that one knows the future, presuming to be God.

An appropriate statement by the MD is like this: "In my estimation, given the limits of what I know through my medical knowledge, your condition defies cure by our means. Perhaps there are other methods to reverse this condition. I know of none personally to recommend. But, that doesn't mean something else may not exist." Or, say nothing!

Let's look at doubt and indecision as they relate to this commandment. One of the main mental acts that breed false witness is doubt and its offshoot, indecision, where we refuse to act. *Doubt is the seed source on the mental level of all of our troubles.*[43] It is essentially an act of mental self-murder (6th Commandment), a mental act of lying to life. Doubt paralyzes action and incurs and breeds anxiety, fear, and worry; slowly but surely, we murder ourselves through these partial acts of suicide. Doubt makes us want to be certain about the future to seemingly ensure safety for our actions. It is making us want to know and control the future. This concern, which can never work, drags us into the murky realm of untruth and illusion. This future talking is by its very nature untrue and a form of "bearing false witness."

As for secrets, there are also circumstances determining whether to keep them or not. Generally, secrets have more to do with saying something true that shouldn't be said. If you're keeping secret something that you feel guilty or ashamed about or that you fear can bring reprisals to you or others that may harm, it may be better left unsaid, as we shall see below.

---

[43] Sorry for the repetitions of certain features within the commandments appearing in this chapter. Pedagogically, such repetitions are useful to imprint certain truths (to be corroborated through your experience) and displace what are currently held false beliefs or destructive habits.

Another variant we all engage in frequently is giving unsolicited, unbidden, uncalled-for, unasked-for suggestions or advice (for example, each August we are repeatedly given the health warning "you'd better get your flu shot because an epidemic is expected later this year" or "bird flu is coming." These unsolicited negative suggestions or nocebos can diminish our will to live and even kill us!) (Julia Indichova's book *Inconceivable*[44] tells of her journey to motherhood following a nocebo of being told it was "impossible" for her to conceive.") Perhaps the most common act of bearing false witness is the endless thinking and speaking poorly of ourselves (poor self-image, low self-worth), denigrating ourselves, comparing ourselves to another, telling ourselves that what happened in the past is bound to happen again or that my past experience determines what I will become in the future, and our own expectations and anticipations as part of future talk.

Of course we cannot forget the myriad of other false beliefs we buy into or have bought into as part of generally held beliefs (in addition to our personal ones), perjury, propaganda, lying, story-making, delusional thoughts, i.e., those fixed ones that are held onto despite all evidence to the contrary shown to the person or community. "There are weapons of mass destruction in Iraq" is an example of such a delusional statement. Another example from the political arena: John F. Kennedy's eloquent falsehood that inadvertently hoodwinked the populace during the Vietnam War: "Ask not what your country can do for you, but what you can do for your country." This asked people to sacrifice their lives on the altar of the self-serving needs of an institution, in this case, the military-industrial complex. A collaborative approach would have been to ask "What can we do for each other?"

On the eve of Yom Kippur, the Jewish holiday of the Day of Atone-

---

[44] Indichova, *Inconceivable* (Adell Press, 1998). In her book she references her work with me and the imagery she employed to change her hormonal level to normal, allowing for conception. She also did yoga and changed to a healthy diet.

ment, the heavenly court descends to meet the earthly court and the Book of Life is opened so that we each can be inscribed for another year of earthly life. The opening prayer chanted by the community forswears all oaths, pledges, vows, and promises made in the preceding year and the year to come. Many of the prayers that follow concern acknowledging, atoning, and doing penance for the countless varieties of bearing false witness. Our atonement is only complete when we ask forgiveness of those whom we have harmed and give charity to those in need, beginning with those most close to home, as the ancient saying goes: "Charity begins at home." Making these corrections is a cleansing, and cleansing oneself is a step toward longevity, not to mention immortality. The prayers during the service constantly praise God for bringing the dead back to life via resurrection. By analogy, bringing us back to life from the brink of death. God, Truth, Resurrection make a great trinity for life.

Finally, with regard to truth-telling and the Ninth Law, there are two instances when we can lie (and keep secrets):

1) To save a life. For example, a Jew walking down the streets in Berlin in 1937 is approached by a Nazi who asks him, "Are you a Jew?" His answer, "No."

2) To keep peace in the family. I knew a family where the matriarch developed cancer but wasn't told. All the family members kept the secret. After ten years of relatively good health and disease-free living, a family member let slip to her, in a casual conversation one day, that she had cancer. She died of cancer within a month of the discovery of that piece of truth. Sometimes it's important to keep our own counsel. To speak inadvisably can be quite disruptive and invasive of the freedom of another (Tenth Law) and perhaps prompt dire consequences.

On the other hand, some family secrets must be shared. For example, you are aware of molestation around you, supported by evidence, or have been molested. For spiritual sake, report this behavior to someone.

It is possible, on self-examination, that the majority of what comes out of our mouths is false witness talk, so it is no surprise that the sages of all traditions generally adopted an attitude of silence. Silence is very golden!

If secrets or errors are grabbing at you, then the following imagery exercise may help:

IMAGERY EXERCISE

CONFESSING THE TRUTH

Close your eyes. Breathe out and in three times slowly. Confess five errors in your life you have been aware of.

Afterwards, breathe out one long slow exhalation and ask God (if not available to you, then your inner source of wisdom) to forgive you until you are satisfied within yourself that you have completed the job. Know this to be true *without a doubt*. Do every morning and upon going to sleep for seven days.

Tenth Law: Don't Covet —> Respect and Preserve the Freedom of Others

Coveting means to want to claim and possess for oneself what doesn't belong to us. There are eight dimensions comprising this subject:

1) Envy
2) Jealousy
3) Competition
4) Comparing
5) Claiming for oneself what doesn't belong to oneself

Reversing: Practices of Detachment

6) Possessing for oneself what doesn't belong to oneself
7) Avarice
8) Greed

Two of the dimensions to specifically consider here are jealousy and envy:

Jealousy means "I want *who* you have." It always refers to a three-party or triangular social situation. To want who you have is the seed source for murder. To have that third party that I crave and so desire, I shall resort to anything to get him or her. The ultimate act to accomplish this is to murder the party who stands in the way. (Adultery, too, is about three-party situations and murderous impulses.)

Envy, on the other hand, is a two-party circumstance. It means "I want *what* you have." Individually it can be as mundane as, for example, envying the other's watch or car. On a larger scale, it could include wanting the oil you have that I need for my automobiles and to support that industry so vital to our economy. Shakespeare's *Othello* and the biblical story of Cain and Abel illustrate jealousy and its destructive consequences. As for envy, it is the seed source of wars.

Both states reflect the coveting impulse, the destructive use of power moved by uncurbed, instinctual desire that arises in life. Criminal organizations are institutionalized forms of the coveting impulse brought to an unharnessed degree.

So why do we covet? Let's return to the story of the Garden of Eden.

When Eve turned her gaze away from the Divine One and the vertical Alliance, her horizontal gaze rested on the Tree of Death. She saw there the fruits of temptation and was struck with the immediate misconception and misperception that she was missing something (the "I" of insufficiency in the AIDs trio). There was a presumed lack! This was the spiritual error *de tutti* errors. Divinity spoke to the couple saying they lacked for nothing. In Eden there was/is eternal life: bliss, happiness, peace, neither disease nor suffering. All the "comforts of home" were supplied. Then came the test to see how faithful they would be to God in return for this bounty. As soon as Eve listened to the serpent's voice (Adam was asleep in the corner under a nice shade tree), she exercised the first instance of free will and choice. Though these two features were not required in Edenic living, the potential was instilled in her, lent to her, as it is to all of us by God. Even there in Eden, God had the couple's freedom in mind because those qualities could be needed to propel them to the next level toward unity and oneness with One.

So, she opted to turn away 180 degrees and here comes civilization. The very first awareness outside of the awareness of divinity was stated in terms of "*not*": "I am missing something," "I'm unhappy and pained," "I gotta have it to become complete." Among other things, the "not" paved the way for the devastating dogma of Sigmund Freud, who reiterated the serpent's suggestion that something is missing by declaring that women suffered from penis envy. Yes, women were supposedly missing something they coveted and were forever consigned to the pain of lack. Have you ever heard of anything so nonsensical?

We lack for nothing! The Tenth Law says don't covet and remember to preserve the other's freedom. Envy, jealousy, avarice, greed, possessing and claiming what is not ours, comparison, and competition are all BEWARE signs of danger. Avarice is an extreme impulse to acquire, hoard, gobble up, and overstep boundaries, while greed represents wanting more, better, and different, with its attendant feeling of discontent, in spite of the blessings already available or apparent in your life. Can we think of a more representative quality than greed to define a primary — if not *the* primary — value system propelling American society? Once we covet, we face the scourge of war, murder, mass murder, genocide, bondage, torture, disorganization of cultures, through inhumanity of humans to humans, humans to animals, and humans to nature. Coveting bears the seed of all these destructive functions.

Expressions of coveting can be quite subtle. Take, for example, comparison. Every time we compare ourselves in any manner to someone else, we are expressing envy. To repeat, envy means "I want what you have." As indicated above, the extreme of this tendency is war, invading someone else's environment to obtain and gain something they have that we want, no matter the cost. More commonly, it crops up in our everyday lives, as in this example: In a group dream class I was conducting, one young man said he dreamt a lot, "almost every night." A young woman across from him exclaimed, "Gee, I hardly dream ever. I wish I could do that." She was comparing her dream life to his and envying/coveting his capacity simply by acknowledging her lack in comparison to his, believing her paucity compared to his was of less value. He was getting more knowledge than she. But why make a statement? None is needed, because it makes entirely no difference in the world whether she had the same quantity of dreams as he did. Only being concerned with lacks led her to compare. These casual phrases crop up reflexively in our daily lives. Let's pay attention to how we compare ourselves to others.

We don't compare unless we have been miseducated to envy. Isn't the social network of the world based on comparisons, being in the in-group rather than the out-group, in the in-group hierarchy of social status or "A-list" where so many of us fiercely compete to be? We are continually led to believe that we are lacking, are less, and need more to compensate, to become complete or whole. It's the way the governing powers maintain a grip on us, enslave us body and soul.

It behooves us to bring these coveting feelings under control, otherwise we cannot find peace and harmony in ourselves. In doing so we prevent ourselves from seeking to enslave others or becoming enslaved to others, common consequences of coveting. It takes an effort of will to detach from these feelings, but the effort is worth it, for to pull back is taking the choice and path of life. To do otherwise is to take the path of death, obviously, as we can see from the havoc wrought by jealousy and envy. Without bringing them under our charge, there can never be health, harmony, peace, and happiness in our lives, personally and on the Earth generally.

Here are some examples of the Tenth Commandment in action:

Thorn in My Side

Debra, a young woman, says the one thing that is a "barrier" troubling her most in life is connected to her relationship to a wealthy sister-in-law who has co-opted the affections of a young grand-nephew, not letting Debra near the young boy for a number of years now, and also "needles" her with provocative statements. This behavior rankles her and disturbs what she considers to be an otherwise harmonious life. She was aware there was jealousy about the relationship. I pointed out how the universe has lovingly given her the painful situation, allowing her at once to see a lifelong reflection of her own jealousy of long years feeling passed over, or cast aside in numerous three-party relationships ("I want who you have"). She agreed. Now this sister-in-law is a blessing giving Debra the opportunity to practice the Tenth Law.

To start this process of change, I ask Debra to detach from the desire "to change what is to what ought to be" and to avoid the pitfalls associated with unmet expectations. She is asked to step away from the sister-in-law who is not only a reflection but also "is what she is" and "does what she does," and has for long before Debra ever met her. Using her will and reason, Debra is to curtail and restrain her reflexive response to change her vain, haughty, and arrogant sister-in-law who contradictorily believes Debra has everything. Really, behind the vain façade lies a feeling of inferiority.

With this sobering explanation, Debra is asked to execute her purpose and will with regard to the little boy whom she loves and does not want to covet. The purpose is her intention toward connecting with him in love. Will is doing what she needs to fulfill that intention. She is asked to act without concern for the outcome and without bringing injury to the other. Working on oneself in this way, inner messages are received as to the correct actions to take.

We work with mental imagery to help birth a new belief and new possibilities. I ask her to see the "barrier" (her word) to her difficulty. She sees the sister-in-law standing between herself and the grand-nephew. I ask her to *reverse* the belief through imagery that she will never get to this boy and will be the odd woman out in this triangle. Imaginally, she sees the sister-in-law removed out of the way, the path clear between her and the boy. She embraces him. She feels lighter. Her mood lifts, and she feels happy. Then I ask her to see this last image: to say the boy's name and to experience any accompanying physical sensations and feelings. This prescription to *see it, say it, sense it, feel it* is to be repeated twice a day, early in the morning and before bed for a few seconds. During the day, she is to practice the same exercise for a few seconds whenever she thinks about or speaks to her sister-in-law. The sister-in-law is no longer an enemy but a blessing, allowing Debra to change a belief and follow the Tenth Law, not to covet. She is learning to love in a new way and stop the self-enslavement she has permitted by being influenced by external circumstances that determine her mood. Finally, she is no longer making her sister-in-law more important than she is, a form of idolatry.

Everything we did gave her the means to become free and find her own way to that freedom. As she reported to me some time later, her relationship to her grand-nephew became close; her sister-in-law became more friendly and open.

Greed Factor Exercise
For 21 days watch the impulse to take or keep (the impulses associated with thieving) as it manifests throughout the day. Remember that greed can manifest on any plane of your experience — physical, emotional, mental, social, or moral. If or when the greed impulse occurs, use it as a reminder to do its opposite impulse: to give and share, to be generous, to be selfless — without regard for the result. On day one, give yourself the intention that you are changing the greed impulse to its opposite, with no regard for the result. You need only do this intention on day one as you start. During the 21-day period, should you forget to watch and give but remember later on that you forgot, do it right then if possible. When you give or share, say to yourself that opposite term, e.g., give, share, and experience that feeling.

At the end of the three-week period, evaluate your situation.

Once you begin this experiment by putting it into action, you are making a new adaptation in and with your intention. Doing so puts you right back into the present moment and out of the future standards of wanting more and better to get to the state of pleasure and comfort and to avoid pain. Greed ain't the way to the blissful state you yearn for.

Charting the Ten Laws in Your Daily Life
I developed a process called Charting the Ten Laws practiced over a period of three months. The following is a doing of this process and its effects by a student and friend, Lisa Broderick:

Dr. Epstein described a chart called "Ten Laws = Love/Life." Each day, at bedtime, you are to take stock of the degree to which you experienced the day as being in concert with the Ten Laws. I decided that this would be fun, and began to plot each day on a chart with X and Y axes. The X axis had on it the days of the month, about 30 in all, in date order. The Y axis showed a scale from 0 to 10, with 0 occurring at the point where the Y axis met the X axis, and 10 being at the top of the vertical line. A

Reversing: Practices of Detachment

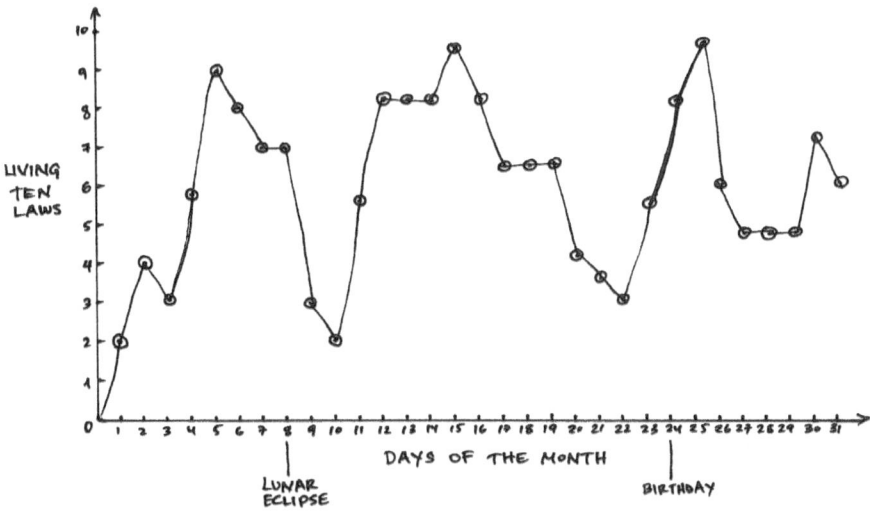

value of "1" would reflect a day where I felt I was not living the Ten Laws, and the value "10" would reflect a day where I felt in concert with the Ten Laws throughout the day. If there was a time of year which for me was notable — such as Mercury in Retrograde — then I delineated that period along the X axis so that I could remember it.

I began plotting each day as small dots, which appeared at points on the chart: one dot for each day, appearing on the page as a value from 1 to 10. When I experienced a day where I felt that it had value to make a notation about why I felt the way I felt, I made it on an adjacent page and included the date. What I soon learned was extraordinary.

Beginning in early May, the dots ranged from a low value of "3" to a high value of "8" and were scattered on the page as if they were not connected. I waited until about the end of the month to review the dots and the notes that were sometimes associated with a particular day. I soon learned that — for me — the low-value days almost always occurred when I felt physical symptoms, such as menses, unusual tiredness, or other feelings of unwellness. Almost never did a day warrant a low value because I felt out of concert for another reason. After completing a month of charting dots, I connected the dots by drawing a flowing line from Day

1 through Day 30 (or 31) to become aware of the flow of life and how our consciousness is awakening.

So I began to address the relationship between physical symptoms and feeling out of connection with the Ten Laws. Each day during which I felt a physical symptom that was unpleasant, I would intentionally increase my awareness to inspect conflicting and unpleasant emotions, disallow myself from spending moments where my mind was busy with thoughts about the future or the past, and live each moment as though it was a beautifully wrapped gift which was mine to open with delight and surprise.

The next month, I experienced the first day where the only value I could ascribe to it was "10." That day, I remember awakening with a feeling of joy and presentness in the moment that never left me — no matter how often I wondered how long it would last. This occurred again a few days later — the feeling of near-perfect synchronicity with the Universe and the Present Moment. Toward the end of that month, I began — much to my astonishment — ascribing the value of "10" to successive days. I remember lying awake at night and reexperiencing the day in my mind — and inadvertently thinking that the number "18" was the value for the day (the chart only goes to 10). And then I laughed that I had just called my day "an 18."[45]

During the course of the next two months, the majority of the days could only be ascribed the value "10." I felt an effortlessness — a "presentness" — which I had never felt before and which I didn't believe was possible for me. At this point, I began to wonder what it is about living the Ten Laws that brings about these feelings?

My answer was contained in the word that repeatedly comes to mind when I think about each day: presentness. If one is present to the moment,

---

[45] Eighteen is LIFE in the sacred numerology of Western spirituality, unknown to Lisa at the time.

there are no errors made that concern thoughts about the future and the past. Should a thought like that occur (they still do, and I'm certain always will), then one inspects it as though it were the offbeat idea of someone else — not this I — nothing much to pay attention to. If one makes an error of being caught by jealousy, vanity, greed, or lies, then one inspects those errors from the distance that seems to come with detaching from that personality called self, which is often prone to making errors. And because one remained present during and after the error, little more than the acknowledgment that an error occurred is ever needed for one to be on one's way.

So for me, the Ten Laws — understood individually as to each of their inner meanings — are a prescription for humans to become present to the moment. To become increasingly free of the errors we make, and to live with effortlessness. Currently, I am completing the month as nearly a "perfect 10." Next month I'll begin a new chart, and another after that. Maybe someday I'll make it all the way to "18."

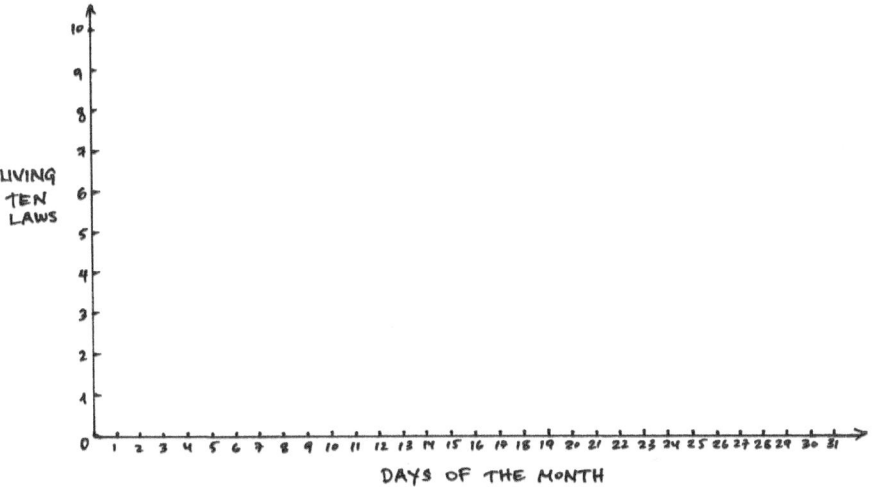

Charting the Ten Laws

Each night before bedtime, take stock — without judgement —of the degree to which you experienced the day as being in concert with the

Ten Laws. To do this, plot a chart with an X and Y axis. Place the days of the month on the X axis (horizontal axis) from 1 to 30 or 31. The Y axis (vertical axis) shows a scale from 0 to 10, with 0 occurring at the point where the Y axis meets the X axis, and 10 being at the top of the vertical line. For example, a value of "1" reflects a day where you felt you were not actively aware of the Ten Laws and a value "10" reflects a day where you felt you were in concert with the Ten Laws throughout the day. If there is a particular time of year that is notable — mercury retrograde, birthdays, anniversary days, full-moon phase, menstrual cycle, etc. — then delineate that period along the X axis to remember it. For each assessment, place a dot. At the end of 30 days, connect the dots to establish a flow chart to show a rhythm to your life. Repeat for two more 30-day cycles to show a larger picture of your inner rhythm.

The Three Virtues: Overcoming the Laws of the Jungle

Renunciation: Learning to Divest Rather than to Invest

Renunciation is a pivot point for embracing the practice of the Three Virtues. (These Virtues are commonly referred to as three Vows.) Renunciation is a self-organizing, life-growing practice. It relates to so many other techniques. For instance, detachment reflects renunciation of attachment. Renunciation also pertains to restraining the impulse to think into the personal future or past ("grammar of self" practice), or curbing the impulse to acquire needlessly and heedlessly. Unconditional love requires renouncing any love necessitating strings or conditions. When we stop to consider, renunciation encompasses practically every facet of life experience taking us away from the moment, from wandering into untruth, distressing emotion, moral wilderness, social mischief, and everything sabotaging our holiness. Living through renouncing preserves our holiness and life force. It is no wonder the Master of Christianity told his disciples in no uncertain terms to renounce all if they wanted to become his students. The renunciation he was most concerned with is inner attachments. The Three Virtues of obedience, chastity, and poverty to be described now are all renouncing functions, reversing habitual ways we approach life. When we survey the broad expanse that renunciation covers, it seems to simply point to one overall gigantic reversing of life's conditioning and education that has pushed us to attachment. We are back to Buddha applying his simple truth to living as aware, awakened, and unattached beings.

At the heart of the practice of renunciation, we give up our earliest conditioned *errors* of living begun in infancy: happiness is pleasure, unhappiness is pain. It is accompanied by the instinctual urge: I want what I want when I want it. The two together evolve into the false purpose of living to get to a non-disturbed state seeking pleasure and comfort and avoiding pain. Rather, by renouncing voluntarily, we ask our self to voluntarily give up repetitive pleasurable habits or fulfilling habitual desires. To make the sacrifice means to give up something of value for something of a higher value. That higher value is holiness, as the meaning of sacrifice literally means "to make holy." Through the practices of renunciation, we sanctify ourselves to make ourselves holy, cleansed, and pure, which in turn makes us feel worthwhile and self-loving. Regimentation of everyday life engenders boredom and tediousness for which we seek relief through self-indulgent activities to satisfy the senses: drinking, smoking, gambling, computer games, anything to break up the monotony, by depending on incessant outside stimulation, instantly elating and then numbing as we become habituated to it. By sacrificing this way, we would not be giving up much that would turn a profit on eBay.

The Virtues
The Three Virtues are an expression of the renunciative experience and the laws of detachment. They are allied practices to the Ten

Commandments and the Seven Divine Forces. The Three Virtues of obedience, chastity, and poverty are part of every spiritual tradition cast in terms suitable to each of them. They have been given primacy within the Christian tradition, extracted from the Ten Laws. In Chinese Taoist philosophy, they designated three components leading one to immortality: (1) dedication (obedience); (2) morality (chastity); and (3) sacrifice (poverty). These three Taoist components bear a striking resemblance to the Three Virtues as well.

Stepping into spirit requires taking an oath of allegiance to the Alliance — that is, to the ongoing, endless relationship between ourselves and the Absolute One whom we have not yet met face to face, but we know is there without question. The Virtues are our oaths to truth.

I have come across people who claim to be spiritual, who want to be au courant by hanging on the spirituality bandwagon, all the while maintaining a materialist perspective and philosophy of life. The "spiritual materialists," as the late Tibetan Rinpoche Chögyam Trungpa termed such individuals, are easy to identify simply by asking one single question: "Have you taken the Three Virtues that are the necessary first steps for taking on a spiritual life?" The usual response I've gotten is a blank stare and the utterance of the word "Huh?"

Obedience, chastity, and poverty are the practices of restraining our instincts. They separate us from instinctual desires connected with attachment. When attachments become strong, they shift into idolatry. For instance, our instincts attach to phenomena that become objects of worship: We seek power over others instead of obedience to the One. We engage in excesses of drugs, alcohol, and sex instead of chastity; and we operate on principles of greed and avarice instead of poverty.

Early in life, instincts and drives hold sway. After extracting the momentary pleasures they afford and suffering their aftereffects and consequences, we may eventually reach the point of "been there – done that." Value systems seem to magically shift. They actually shift as hormones — the engine of drives and instincts — begin diminishing with age. (Note: This is correlative, not causative.) Then we become better able to take charge and become responsible for the instinctual actions and traits we have adopted.

This shift in value systems begins taking shape between the ages of 38 and 42, when the first significant life change takes place. Whether bidden or unbidden, one's life direction usually veers, like making a sharp 90-degree turn. The second great change occurs between the ages of 49 and 56. Here, the shift is 180 degrees (bidden or unbidden). The ages 37 and 48 are, respectively, preparatory years when we have cleared the decks to permit entry of new shifts.

Spiritual life becomes more prominent in our consciousness after 40. Carl Jung, who was interested in spiritual life, indicated he would not take anyone into treatment under the age of 40. The transition from being driven by the "slave master" of instincts to becoming the driver, and with it practicing the Three Virtues, becomes a viable possibility after 40. People under 38 to 40 are by no means left out: Those who have had some inkling or direct experience of another reality before age 40 have laid the groundwork for what is to come. Certainly, during the Vietnam War era, many young people were exposed to psychedelic experiences during which they met another vision of reality. Many banked the experience for later returns. Others, too unready, too unprepared, lost their way. Many others recoiled from the experience (perhaps in fear), turning away and forcefully rejecting the spiritual possibility to instead become immersed in the "yuppie" generation devoted to pursuing materialistic life without God.

Pure and simple: There is no spiritual, sacred, holy life without taking the initial inward step of accepting the Three Virtues. Taken together, they lead to a life of voluntary simplicity and voluntary suffering. The term "suffering" doesn't mean pursuing pain and deprivation; rather, it means to *bear* and accept a simple life brought on by detachment from an excess of materialism and the goals derived from it. It includes following the Light Currents of Will, giving service, advice, and therapeutic help while living a "green" life awake to the preservation of our environment and sober with regard to our resources. Doing so *guarantees* that what you have yearned for — liberation, freedom, love, and all the rest — comes to you with ease. You'll receive it without exactly understanding how it all comes about. Everything seems to take care of itself as long as you do your part. *That's how it works.* You don't need to "control" anything except the activity of self-discovery that is "totally" under your charge. Of course, please do not believe a word of what you are reading. Yes, at the outset the words may have an impact, but find out if they are true by climbing your ladder of self-mastery to become the king or queen of yourself. You'll know the effects of your experiment(s) by the fruits born from them.

The Three Virtues are the foundational attitudes intimately linked to the Ten Commandments. Each Virtue covers a portion of the laws; the connections seem easily apparent if we think about it. Let's look at them one by one:

Obedience
Obedience strengthens our relationship to the Divine, forging and reinforcing our commitment to the Alliance. To "give ear," "listen," and "obey" are all synonymous with "obedience." To do so denotes a movement or action toward being in relationship to another. With regard to the world of Spirit, it refers to turning our ear(s) toward spiritual reality to hear its messages and pay attention to our place in that spiritual order. We do not arrogate to ourselves a position of deeming to be God, but rather maintain a position of humility in contrast to the mindless obedience paid to cult leaders, authoritarian dictators, and tyrants. We pay homage and bow down before our Divine Master, and to the divinity within ourselves, to the divine Adam and Eve we

once were and are. We forget all this. We dismiss it. We seek to replace this holy possibility by wanting omnipotence and omniscience for ourselves. We refuse to accept this possibility of humility, preferring the role of vanity. "Vanity, vanity, all is vanity," exclaimed King Solomon, "... a striving after folly and wind."

Obedience encompasses faith in following the ten divine cosmic laws. In essence, the person is attuned to, observant of, and sworn to following these laws, while putting faith and trust first and foremost in His hands, not in human beings. Yes, we can have confidence in others' qualities, talents, and presumed expertise, but faith and trust can only be placed in Invisible Reality.

Another component of obedience also recognized by Taoist philosophy is dedication. Dedication brings obedience to the fore. We will persist in this way if we have asked ourselves what is the purpose of living. For most of us it consists of acquisition and worship of things. For the spiritually inclined, it is that of seeking connection to and union with knowing spiritual reality and truth. Just as the pursuit of money drives people in a singular, unswervingly dedicated way, so does obeying (giving ear) to the call of Spirit.

The opposite of obedience is murder and tyranny. The commandments linked to obedience that stand out are the first, second, third, sixth and ninth laws: nothing before God (#1); no setting myself up as an idol (#2), no forsaking and displacing God, thus breaking the holy friendship (#3); preserving life, no murdering, or tyrannizing (#6); no murdering reputations (#9).

Probably the worst tyranny is that which we impose on ourselves every day. Flagellating ourselves, beating ourselves up for not meeting the self-imposed, irrelevant man-made standards we set, or allow us to buy into. Depression is self-flagellation mixed with self-pity; it acts as an internal penitence and pseudo-repentance fashioned out of misplaced feelings of guilt, self-pity, and anger that brings us to heel before our misguided and miseducated demands of our inner terrorists.

As we engage in the vow of holy relationship, day by day we watch the dispirited vain self melt or slip away and be replaced by a sense and feeling of renewal and rejuvenation. This revitalization of our life energy in turn extends our life span.

Here's an imagery exercise for developing spiritual obedience:

IMAGERY EXERCISE

OBEDIENT EARS

Close your eyes. Breathe out and in three times slowly, making the out breath longer and stronger than the in breath. Then see, sense, and feel a dark cloud over your head. *Imaginally,* breathe out (with short in breaths between each) three strong out breaths toward the cloud, blowing it away to the left. Now, look up into the sky to the right and see, sense, and feel light coming into view and replacing the cloud.

Breathe out one time. Imaginally turn your head 90 degrees to the right so your left ear is facing up. See this ear growing toward the heavens, becoming gigantic and listening to the message given to you by the voice of Spirit. At this moment of hearing it, say "Obey" to yourself. Get that feeling that it gives and the accompanying new physical sensation. Say "thank you." See your head come back to its normal position. Breathe out and open your eyes.

Do this exercise each morning on arising for some seconds, for 21 days.

Chastity

Chastity represents faithfulness to the One. It is sobriety, the absence of intoxication, be it to sex, drugs, alcohol, money, emotional outbursts, obsessive thoughts, etc., or any addictive behavior. Chastity implies being measured, balanced in its fourfold dimensionality: proportion, measure, rhythm, and pace, and especially the first two. To be unchaste is to worship something in the place of God. The first cosmic law, we recall, asks us not to put anything between us and God. The intoxicant becomes the object of worship. To be chaste is to be pure, not to mix a second element into our activities. The cosmic law concerned here is the Seventh — adultery, which means to mix, to weaken, to bring a contaminant into our behaviors: chemotherapy and herbs, business and pleasure are but two examples where each should be kept independent of the other.

Chastity also speaks to the Tenth Law in connection with the will to hold on to and advance at the expense of others, the action of the male hunter and the female who lays traps. Chastity ties together the Fifth and Seventh laws as well. Both require faithfulness: faithfulness to purity (Seventh), and faithfulness to father and mother above (Fifth). It also includes being faithful to the One above (First). If we can't be faithful to another human being (the Seventh), how can we be faithful to the One above (the First)?

Morality really defines chastity, which we could say is at the heart of the Ten Laws. Every one of them asks for consistent purity of Spirit. It is easier to answer the calls of temptations that lead away from the call of Spirit. Actually, it seems — erroneously — easier to die than to live. Spirit asks us to reverse conditioning and regimented habits hinged on the early miseducation that places a premium on fulfilling desires no matter the cost. These beliefs center on acquisition and attachment, and they provide the intellective rationale for pursuing an unchaste life. Common assertions like "I want what I want when I want it" and "Happiness is pleasure, unhappiness is pain," we now know, unfold into a death-oriented purpose to get pleasure and comfort and avoid pain. The consequences of the combination of erratic conditioning and faulty habit patterns are entropy, decay, death, and the seemingly irrevocable belief that death is inevitable. But, on the side of the Three

Virtues lies quite the opposite: ectropy, self-organization, life, and the irrevocable belief that life is inevitable. An illustration of following a sacred vow:

Susan — Her Revelation
Susan told me about her son's impending Bar Mitzvah. She spoke of inviting people to whom she had tangential connection from a training school where she learned graphic arts. "Why invite them?" I asked. She said she was inviting her teacher and was "afraid" the other students would not like her if she left them out. These folks had no connection to her son, nor did she have "social connections" with them. Yet she was concerned about the future — "they would not like me." She understood the untruth and unreality of her scenario. The relevant point of this tale is this: her revelation that there was no evidence to support her future talk and that she was making up a story about what isn't, about something invented.

Moreover, her story is a story of humanity making the same error over and over — that of feeling inferior and insufficient while making herself a slave to what others might think of her.

She said that not only was she getting worried about the unnecessary spending incurred by inviting a swarm of unnecessary guests to fulfill her false story, but she was also feeling physically sick, with a general malaise. I introduced her to GEMS: She is feeling physically sick and mentally and emotionally overwrought; she is depleting her life energy and paving the way for disorganization. When she reverses the process, she is rejuvenating life energy.

In this instance, she reconsidered the guest list, limited the profusion of invitations, stopping her made-up story about not being liked, and took a sober, balanced approach to the oncoming events, concurrently giving up the emotional intoxication of being carried away by her scenario.

By taking charge of the drunkenness of excess, both in mental thought and wild spending, she began following the holy vow of chastity — the vow of abstinence, moderation, and restraint. Through this she began to correct the socio-genetic error of drunkenness passed down in her family line, for in fact, she had a family history of addiction to alcohol. This socio-genetic error manifested itself in her as a need for excess even while avoiding a literal addiction to alcohol.

Curing the excesses is understood as bringing moderation to our immoderate behaviors, feelings, and thoughts. To become chaste is to become moderate. The remedy for the excesses of individual and collective actions in modern life is brought to us through moderation and modesty. Know that to be moderate is to be in the middle, that the model for moderation begins with your ability to modify your behavior and characteristics. Modesty is to be moderate and unassuming in self-expression, to be measured.

Here is an exercise for Chastity:

IMAGERY EXERCISES

SEEING STRAIGHT: SOBRIETY

Close your eyes. Breathe out and in three times slowly. Imagine yourself intoxicated or drunk, in a stupor, walking on a dark street, wobbling to and fro, seeing with double vision, and out of balance. Breathe out one time and come into a brightly lit street full of sunshine surrounding, permeating, and penetrating you. You suddenly become upright, walking straight and determined, sober and with clear vision. See clearly where you are going and what is waiting for you on this new road. Remember what you have discovered. Breathe out and open your eyes.

Do this exercise every day, once in the morning and once at sundown, for 21 days.

BECOMING MODERATE

Close your eyes. Breathe out. See yourself becoming moderate by changing a characteristic that needs modification. What is your behavior now? What does it look like? What are you feeling?

Breathe out. Feel and know that modesty is a virtue. How is modesty a virtue for you? See how modesty creates a balance for your life.

Breathe out. See what is moderate for you. Know how being moderate brings to you an inner medicine that makes you healthy and whole.

Breathe out. Be the moderator of your life. What message does this inner moderator have for you?

Breathe out. Find out now how this inner moderator can provide you with your own inner medicine.

Breathe out. Know how the Western form of meditative contemplation brings you to a new *mode* of being that transcends the habitual limitations of your life. What is your experience? Breathe out and open your eyes.

Do this in the morning to start your day for 21 days.

Poverty

Poverty means detachment from material and mental acquisition. The commandment correlated here is the Tenth, coveting — avarice, greed, possessing, and claiming what doesn't belong to you. We have to make room for the sacred to enter. We can't clutter the space we inhabit externally with *excess* goods and internally with *excess* thoughts and feelings, stories, and fantasies. By poverty, we are asked to detach mentally from constructing conclusionary thoughts, future-based thoughts and ideas, and many other extraneous and actually untrue beliefs and conceptions to which we become attached.[46]

Violating poverty goes against the 8th and 10th Commandments in connection with the will to take and to keep — the actions of the thief.

Poverty is defined by sacrifice, following the Five Light Currents of Will and its life-giving impulses.

It is a curious fact that the single most philanthropic group of people is the poor. In spiritual understanding and experience, when we give without the goal of getting, the Universe sees to it that we receive what we need (not want!). That's how it works! In this way we are able to achieve a "happy medium." As we impoverish ourselves to the dark forces of will, so too do we impoverish ourselves to incessant needs: to speak to, comment on, think about what we want to get; to know what the future holds or determine what our future will be; to accumulate mental wealth, analogous to physical wealth. We are literally preoccupied with concentration on acquisition and greediness for things physical and mental.

We hinder ourselves unnecessarily about what is insubstantial, believing we will become immune to death by becoming omnipotent and godlike; find happiness, fame, and contentment by serving the god of wealth and greed.

Personally giving up something of value for something of a higher value can be done as a daily practice, like "sacrificing" cigarettes for health. Here it is understood as an act of detachment. Detachment is not only a practice in itself but a spiritual law.

The practice of poverty: Give up or sacrifice something simple from your everyday, habitual life such as smoking, compulsive activity like checking Facebook or your cell phone, etc. Sacrifice the same item

---

[46] Certainly, keeping the Sabbath (4th commandment), a practice of voluntary simplicity, is an act of decluttering.

for 21 days or a different item each day. Rest for seven days, then repeat if you wish.

Here is an imagery exercise for Poverty:

IMAGERY EXERCISE

OPEN HANDS

Close your eyes. Breathe out long and slow one time. Imagine your arms extended and in front of you with your hands clenched into fists, holding wads of money that's sticking out through the sides of them and through the fingers. Breathe out one time slowly. See, physically sense, and feel yourself opening your fists, releasing the bills, which are then picked up by those who are truly poor and impoverished. With outstretched arms and strong hands, embrace these disadvantaged souls. What is your feeling? What do you know now? Breathe out and open your eyes.

Here is a simplified Three Virtues chart:

VIRTUE	MEANING	AIM	ACTION TO TAKE	RELATES TO COMMANDMENT
Obedience (surrender)	Give ear to the One	Curb murder, tyranny	Open our hearts	1, 2, 3, 6, 9
Chastity (moderation)	Be faithful to the One	Curb debauchery/ addictions/ immoderation	Don't stray/ be pure	1, 5, 7, 10
Poverty (simplicity)	Voluntary simplicity	Curb greed	Open our hands	4, 8, 10

Embracing Life

The practice of Three Virtues, Ten Laws, and Seven Forces forms the Law of Detachment. They are the core of reversing the Death Plan. Dedicating ourselves to *any one* of the many practices in *We Are Not Meant to Die* with purpose can encompass all the others. The holographic principle is at work: The part contains and reflects the whole. It is an interconnected system, analogous to the worldwide web.

Web is an apt term. There is a central hub with many intercalated strands linking each to the other, each reflecting the other. It is a web of immortality and perpetual life, like a net casting itself out into infinity and eternity, with no end in sight. Just as there is no end to the worldwide web, analogously there is no end to life. I don't merely mean perpetuating life through biological heredity, where we die but our lineage continues through our progeny; or through life extension afforded us through modern breakthroughs in biological science available right now only to the wealthy. Rather, I mean perpetual life where no one dies.

The statement "I'm turning my life around" applies nowhere more meaningfully than in our dedication to the life processes presented here. What a blessed opportunity. Vigilance is a key process that helps us do that. The practices given in this book are designed to help you become a watcher, becoming vigilant at recognizing and ridding ourselves of the impediments that block our way. It is worth noting that simply observing their appearance and increasing your awareness of them actually eliminates them. As the inner terrorists can never grow weary of sending reinforcements, so we can never grow weary of eliminating them as they appear. Fact is, doing so never makes us weary. It is the other way around: The more we take them on, the stronger we become. The stronger we become, the more we shall feel and sense this physically. And the longer we exist on Earth, the brighter are our days, the more meaningful life becomes, and the clearer it becomes what our life purpose is. I have found that personally, by following the commandments and the other practices enumerated here. All of these attainments are waiting to be experienced. It actually is impossible for it to be otherwise. After all, taking the path of life can only lead to Life.

Concentration Without Effort: Living Without Goals

In this great principle of spiritual mastery and spiritual health, we are asked to quiet mental life by freeing it from the habitual processes of thought and fantasy. Free it from the enduring passions, obsessions, and conclusionary logical thinking to which our habitual or conditioned thought goes. Effort is another term for attachment. Attachment is always connected to things, be they outer material ones in three-dimensional space or inner material ones like fantasies, thoughts of the past or future, or conclusions of any sort. We generally don't think of mental processes as things, but they are objects nonetheless, analogous to outer objects even though they don't contain volume and mass. I know it may come as a surprise that thoughts can be objects, but they are materialized by us just as we materialize physical objects with our hands. Beliefs, or conceptions and perceptions by the senses, reveal the presence of inner objects to which we can, and generally do, become attached. Even though the inner responses lack volume and mass, they are still subject to entropy, disappearing much faster than we would see in a physical object.

In quiet enjoyment of life, we concentrate maximum attention on a minimum of space or on a single point. All artists are aware of this process, as they become deeply engrossed in their artistic production at hand. "Oh, I'm sorry, I didn't hear you come in" or "I'm sorry, I didn't hear the phone ring when you called." People who experience flow describe it as "a state of effortless concentration so deep that they lose their sense of time, of themselves, of their problems,"[39] and their descriptions of the joy of that state are so compelling that the psychologist Mihaly Csikszentmihalyi (pronounced *six-zhent-mihaly*) called it an "optimal experience."[47]

---

[47] Daniel Kahneman, *Thinking Fast and Slow* (New York: Farrar, Straus and Giroux, 2011): 40–41.

Reversing: Practices of Detachment

Concentration without effort immediately takes us out of the game of attachment. We are able to still our impulses to go further through our intellect and instinct, beyond the moment of perception, thought, feeling, and desire to acquire. We still the allure of psychological reasoning embodied in "why" questions and answers that succeed only in introducing more accrued beliefs and momentary palliatives and Band-Aids to give temporary relief but effect no substantial life change. Psychological insight is *not* the same as change. The latter bespeaks itself through behavioral/mental/emotional/social action and its ensuing adaptation to one's prevailing circumstances.

Max, a middle-aged businessman, turned his interest and dedication to follow a spiritual program of change I offered him. He spent his first year focused intensely on the work given him to start this journey of Spirit. At the end of his new education, he and I took a summer break. During this time, he sought out a new business venture to find land to build a small set of stores. On the land he found there remained one house occupied by a lone 70-year-old woman. While it made logical business sense to purchase the land, he knew that if he bought the land, he "would have to" (his words) evict the woman and raze the house. In a significant shift in consciousness, he declined to buy the property, as he could not bring himself to evict the elderly woman. He curbed his instinctual urge to take. Note that once the instinct is quieted, the head and heart come into order as well. He said that in previous times he would not have hesitated to buy the land and evict the tenant, but now he was seeing the world through a new lens, able to experience a loving response called *agape* — unconditional love or unattached feeling, putting himself in the shoes of the other, able to understand and feel for their situation.

Concurrent with our quieting and calming mental content is a disinterested stilling of the will. Ordinarily we use our will toward attaching to the everyday world either by mental activity of thinking ahead or behind, making up stories, rationalizing, opinionating, trying to figure it out, and the like, or various forms of daydreaming, day reverie, fantasies. All of these forms require intense effort, active effort, concentration *with* effort, accompanied by heightened emotionality and heightened physiological activity such as increased heart rate, pulse, breathing, like a bull snorting and pawing at the ground. The bull is full of enslaving passion, obsession, attachment, like the bull in the bullfighting arena.

Concentration without effort changes the location of action from the brain (organ of discursive, conversational thought) to the rhythmic system, namely the circulatory and respiratory (heart and lungs, respectively). Thought slows down, emotions quiet, instinctual cries are stilled. We become silent; the moment is experienced as active relaxation. Concentration without effort is a phenomenon of detachment and disinterest, where we need not fulfill goals and standards. One where an illusionary thought such as "this is it" is replaced by a zone of revelation. In this zone, we are able to receive messages from the realm of vertical reality, the spiritual world, that inform and direct our lives in an appropriate manner with clarity, discernment, knowing, understanding, and wisdom. We are able, in establishing this zone of freedom, to become our own sage and mage. We free ourselves intellectively, emotionally, instinctually from the traps of enslavement that we have been looking to escape from since the earliest time we can recall.

The will used for its nonhabitual purpose becomes a "purified will." It is answering the call from the vertical, heavenly, spiritual realm as opposed to obeying the Five Dark Currents of Will. This zone of revelation is the zone of intuition. As introduced in the Intuition section, we practice detached intellect, detached instinct, and balanced emotion, progenitors of the timeless experience of concentration without effort.

As we practice keeping the intellect open, we stop our leaping into

Reversing: Practices of Detachment

the past or future so we can create a space in awareness, uncluttered with our opinions, explanations, fantasies, and false beliefs, all of which we take as facts. It bears repeating that we brainwash ourselves daily to believe that the experiences of the past determine what we become, what we believe, and what will happen in the future. We hold onto this enslaved way of thinking, which leaves us with no options, consigned to a false understanding of life. We can't seem to help cluttering the space, thinking our thoughts are more valuable than the revelations awaiting to rain on us from above. We appear to be subject to our own lack of awareness of the value of detached intellect while being influenced by the "talking heads" around us, plying us with their conclusions cloaked as opinions and explanations passed off as facts. Pundits pass off fake news such as "God doesn't exist" (Christopher Hitchens); "no thinking man can believe in God" (Woody Allen, a confirmed atheist, materialist); or Stephen Hawking's nocebo that mankind must abandon Earth or face extinction.

Our method is to conserve our interior resources just as we do in our material everyday life. Desire is aroused by a plenitude of opportunities in daily life. In the GEMS system we don't fight these impulses. Rather, when they arise, we stop them from fulfillment and discharge. A space in our field of consciousness is created. Something new can enter this newly decluttered area. Suddenly we are able to hear a revelatory message alerting us to forging a new knowing, understanding, and wisdom, usually impelling us to take a new action rooted in the immediacy of right now. Energy is returned to us, analogous to the method of tantra.

Our instinctual and intellective lives have now joined together in holding back, stopping the coming to an end of things. Both have ceded their need for attachment to a conscious act of will to detach instead, reversing their direction to serve the Alliance. There is no mystery as to what this act of will entails. It tells us "*Stop*," turn around, and reverse.

Now that we have a handle on detached intellect and instinct, we can peek at the bridge between the two — called images, the emotional component between thinking and sensory desire. The practice of imagery is a major process to withdraw from habitual emotional responses and to etch harmonious feelings. Recall, all distressing feelings are attached to the future, past, or standards we have bought into.

Having now made space through reeducation and retraining of our intellect, instinct, and feeling, we have changed our physiology! We have permitted a movement of energy flowing between our higher source of wisdom, down to us. Messages are passing through this channel of communication received at the somatic switchboard of the gut, heart, and central nervous system,[48] where operators are standing by to relay these bodily responses to us as intuitive impulses conveying wisdom, understanding, and knowing not available to us by logical means. Note I use the term "knowing" rather than "knowledge": Knowing is an ongoing process; knowledge is fixed, a product of logical thinking.

In sum, attaching to things sets in motion the process of entropy. Effort is the act of attaching. Detaching is the act of ectropy, or reversing entropy by stopping effort.

The scope of concentration without effort is broad and deep. It is a reeducation and a new conditioning process, replacing a habitual value system predicated on dependency on the authorities of this material world with a new value system dependent on a spiritual world where we become willing servants.

Changing our value system by reversing direction from attachment

---

[48] The neuro-optical through a flash of light mediated via the pineal gland and subsequently related to other brain centers.

to detachment places us squarely in the Alliance with our spiritual resources. Becoming a willing servant here is met not with dominance, subjugation, or master–slave responses, but rather a loving admiration of the Lover with Its loved one, joining together in love. In most human relationships predicated on dominance and power, the habitual/natural bond is one of "me real — you shadow." The normal love relationship is "me real — you real," where respect and mutual affirmation, admiration, and understanding are the order of the day. This is the relationship, both natural and normal, in the spiritual Alliance. Detaching from instincts (to claim and possess); intellectual pre-occupation with results, outcomes and goals; and distressing feelings creates a humble withdrawal that leaves space within us for *the Universe's light to enter where we can receive its messages clearly and distinctly.*

Withdraw! By reversing our attachments, we reverse entropy and our concern with time. By stopping our interest in knowing the future and rehashing the past, we come to a point of stillness that brings us directly in contact with our intuitive awareness. This reverses entropy, the ongoing movement toward death. *We live!* We are born to discover this possibility for overcoming death, as we are the only living creatures with the capacity for entropy and ectropy as choices in life. The development of intuition is a major step taken on this road less traveled, this narrow path to accomplish the one thing: to evolve our consciousness to join with our Source through this spiritual Alliance while living in a human body that neither decays nor ages. Time is on our side when we become its master rather than it becoming our master.

When we intuit, two things accompany *the act:* a call to immediate action and some sort of feeling of well-being. It would seem normal for this to happen. Since the intuitive experience is not time-bound, we cannot experience distressed feelings, nor can we doubt, as that itself is directly attached to future thinking.

You may notice that taking on a spiritual life direction emphasizes practicing imagery and exercises of will so we don't cross boundaries or go beyond established limits. Such boundaries and limits have been described here in mental and physical contexts. This is the "no trespassing" boundary sign you might want to observe: "Keep off the property of the future and the past." These lands belong to Divinity. For us, future is uncreated, nonexistent, without substance, about what isn't. And since it's about what isn't, it's *about nothing*! Similarly, personal past is over, ended, buried, gone, finished, without life. Limits are placed on thoughts and instincts. We don't need to collect conclusions or things. All they do is clutter our internal and external space.

By contracting, detaching from time and from space, obeying "no trespassing" signs, we succeed emulating what God did — creating a *tzimtzum*, making space for life to exist! Creating space outwardly leads to a life of voluntary simplicity. Where there is space around us, there is more access to light. Light is the creative source, for all things come into being by "Let there be light." Detaching inwardly creates inner space. We make room for inner light that carries with it messages of truth from "intrastellar" [my term] reality, received by our human receiving stations.

The heart is a special organ in this regard. It is the seat of love and lust. Understanding the lustful nature of the heart's desire(s), the prophet Jeremiah called it a "devious organ." Yes, we can be coldhearted, closed off from love, treating others as mere objects of desire that are to be dominated or subjugated, treated callously, without care. Intuition leads the heart into a more loving connection to life, bringing cold-heartedness into order and changing it into warm-heartedness. We take charge of instincts. We become loving. We make love as strong as death!

Reversing: Practices of Detachment

THE MENTAL GYM: WILL AND IMAGERY EXERCISES

*Here are some mental exercises of will to
develop concentration without effort.*

TO LEARN FOCUSED CONCENTRATION
(after G. I. Gurdjieff)

Go to a crowded place like a diner or park. Have on a watch with a second hand. Now, count the movement of the second hand from tick to tick for 60 seconds. At the same time, be aware of what's going on around you in the restaurant or park. If you become absorbed in the doings around you and lose sight of the second hand, to start anew! If you become engrossed in the second hand and lose awareness of the doings around you, start anew! The idea is to <u>accomplish both at the same time</u>. Do this each day for 21 days for five or so minutes, then stop altogether. If you succeed before 21 days, no need to continue. If you need more than 21 days, do as many as you are willing to do to see if it may happen.

TO LEARN CONCENTRATION WITHOUT EFFORT

Go to a park, store in a mall, or a city street. Close your eyes and see what's going to pass before you in one minute from now. See it quickly. Open your eyes. Time it. Keep a record of your "success." Close your eyes. Do this again at two minutes, five minutes, and ten minutes. Do this practice for 21 days. Stop for seven days. Do another two cycles of 21 days on, seven days off if you are not satisfied by the first cycle.

> **Two tips:** a) You can breathe long, slow exhalations three times (out-in, out-in, out-in) to quiet down before starting the exercise; b) To quell doubt, accept that whatever appears before you with eyes closed is accepted *even* if it appears nonsensical (to the logical, concentration-with-effort mind), illogical, or impossible. Go with it. You are developing detached will. In New York City, practicing this technique, peering down into the city street below from my seventh-floor window, I saw a small airplane! I stayed with it. Didn't try to exorcise it from consciousness. Trusted my will. Opened my eyes. Within two minutes on the side street I was looking at, East 89th Street between Park and Madison avenues (not on the broad avenue of Madison itself), along came a flatbed truck on which was perched a small single-engine Cessna airplane! I said, "Thank you, God."

Here are a number of imagery exercises for concentration without effort:

THE TIGHTROPE WALKER
(in part after Emile Coué, the author of the book *Self-Mastery Through Conscious Autosuggestion* [1920]).

Close your eyes. Breathe out and in three times slowly. See yourself as the tightrope walker at the beginning of your walk over a chasm. At first you imagine yourself having arrived at the other side.

Breathe out one time slowly and begin your walk, holding the pole horizontally across you. You walk lightly, carrying your pole lightly, wearing your special lightweight shoes or slippers. Your concentration is squarely on the task at hand. Not for a moment does your thought and attention wander from what is there in front of your nose. Should you lose concentration, you may slip but be able to regain balance or fall off to be caught in a net below so that you don't get hurt. When you reach the other side, breathe out and before opening your eyes, say to yourself, "Concentration without effort." Get the feeling accompanying the image and saying, and any new physical sensation you might feel. Then, breathe out and open your eyes.

Do once each morning for some seconds for 21 days. If you feel inclined, at some point during the 21-day period you can make the crossing without the net — go ahead!

BECOMING ONE WITH YOUR SOUL SELF

Close your eyes and breathe out and in three times slowly. Imagine yourself ascending a hill. Walking down toward you is your double. You embrace and become one. Know that you are becoming one with your soul self and the silence this brings.

Breathe out one time. Now experience that zone of silence where a revelatory spiritual happening takes place. Keep this discovery for yourself.

Breathe out and experience concentration without effort. Feel and know the basic unity of the three worlds of Nature, Human, and Divine.

Breathe out one time and see, know, and feel the analogy of your heart to love and of your breath to freedom. Breathe out and open your eyes.

Do this exercise for 21 days in the morning upon awakening.

STILLNESS OF MIND

Close your eyes. Breathe out and in three times slowly. Then, imagine your entire being becoming like the surface of calm water, reflecting the immense presence of the starry sky and its indescribable harmony.

Breathe out one time. Drink in the silence. Physically sense and feel what happens. Breathe out and open your eyes. Know now what concentration without effort is.

Do this exercise for a few seconds each morning upon awakening and before bed for 21 days.

TO KNOW YOURSELF

Close your eyes. Breathe out and in three times slowly. See, sense, feel, and know yourself becoming your own sage and mage operating with ease, in a state of active relaxation. Be absorbed in this active playfulness. Keep it for yourself. Then, breathe out one time slowly and open your eyes.

Do this exercise each morning for several seconds and anytime during the day or evening when you remember for 21 days.

Concentration, like all the practices recommended, have their reverberations and benefits throughout our whole organism. Naturally we are reducing expenditure of energy, conserving life force, and infusing life force into our bodily system as a consequence. Becoming quiet, calm, and at peace like this creates inner harmony, a coming together as a unitive experience, life-giving, life-preserving, and life-extending.

This simultaneity/coincidence then is a demonstration of the existence of no-time! as opposed to linear time of past —> future that "takes time."

The existence of coincidence, reflected in the law of analogy and analogical thinking, such as imagery, gives us a further understanding of what GEMS has to teach us.

Thinking by Analogy: Intuitional Thinking

As touched on earlier, we increase our intuition by increasing our field of awareness. In observing events in the outer world, we watch the law of unity operating. Taking this a step further, we increase our awareness by thinking by analogy. Here we take notice of the relationship between our outer world and our inner world, between quantity and quality, visibility and invisibility.

Analogy (ana-logic) is an *inner* logic and a potent form of detached intellect. Analogy simply means to see the relationships between two or more things without drawing conclusions. In common parlance and conventional schooling, analogy is presented as: *This is to this as that is to that*, focusing on points of similarity between two ideas or objects. In spiritual thinking, it is worth remembering analogic thinking seeks out *points of similarity* and *points of differences*. Unlike conventional thinking, we do not rely on logic seeking to reach a conclusion, or push into the future and thus concentrate with effort. Rather we look to discover wholeness, inherent in seeing relationships. In contrast, conclusionary thinking is anti-spiritual, by coming to a fixed point of knowledge, a fixed image; an inner process of idol-making. This type of thinking is necessary for navigating correctly in a mechanical way to carry out daily functions, but not useful in our socially, morally based world.

In the GEMS healing work, thinking by analogy keeps the stream of intuition flowing by pointing us away from conclusions of a misplaced cause-to-effect system. It may be well worth noting again that conclusion means the end of something. What does the end of something equal? If we answered "death," we deserve at last a golden heavenly star.

Here's a simple example from everyday life: Think about an analog-face clock with minute, hour, and second hands. At a glance you see the entirety of relationships of reading the time. In contrast, on a digital clock you see only one time, for example, 10:45. But with an analog timepiece, you are stimulated to describe the time as 10:45, a quarter to the hour, 15 of 11, three-quarters of an hour — you see the wholeness of tracking time as you see the entire watch face. Thinking by analogy encompasses a broad range of thinking; some examples follow:

Hold one hand up to the mirror and what do you see reflected back? Your other hand! Each hand shows distinct points of similarity and distinct points of dissimilarity. Combining both together, we see immediately the *wholeness of handedness,* the *quality hidden in the quantity*! (Handedness = quality, hands = quantity.) Carrying this explanation a bit further, we can look at mental imagery the same way. The function of image is to bring together what is seen and not seen at the same moment. Images serve as a mirror into the hidden. What is demonstrated here is the relationship between things seen and hidden simultaneously, the reflections of one thing to another, their mirroring taking place in the moment of the event where wholeness resides.

In the book of Genesis, Adam is described as being in the Garden of Eden, naming the animals. He sees these different physical creatures as expressing the inner quality they are representing outwardly by their physical appearance. For instance, he names courage — lion; gentleness — lamb; peacefulness — dove; industriousness — beaver; ferocity — tiger; slyness — fox; cunning — snake, and so on. He defines the relationship/analogy between a qualitative immeasurable function and its physical form denoted by quantitative measurement. We see here the intimate relationship between the qualitative and quantitative

Reversing: Practices of Detachment

realities — the invisible and visible realities.

There is one more form of analogy to mention, where one physical object stands for another physical object, which we designate as *sign*, not as *symbol*. As an example: pump — heart. The former is an analogy for the heart, and the reverse, where they have points of similarity and points of difference. Same could be said for clock and heart, heart being referred to colloquially as the ticker. Or, pipe and penis, purse and vagina. They can share differences and similarities and can be expanded to reflect emotional, mental, and social relationships. These analogies take on the status of symbols when we see how they point to a *quality*, e.g., rifle < — > penis = masculinity.

Another example in religious ritual can be found with the Passover matzo and the Catholic communion wafer. Both symbols share similarities and differences. Each reflects a relationship to God. The matzah is unleavened bread that the Israelites made in haste as they fled Egypt. In contrast to the matzo, leavened bread reflects material attachment and materialism in general ("bread" = money). Unleavened means detachment from materialism and attachment to Spirit. Eating unleavened matzo is the reminder to keep and affirm that attachment. In Christianity, the thin wafer reflects the body of Christ, which, when consumed, concretizes the conviction, devotion, and communion (co-union, oneness) with God.

As to the differences between the two? They are quite evident simply by looking at them. Their appearance is markedly different, one from the other. Even so, by seeing their differences and their similarities, we have an understanding of the wholeness. Taken together, they reflect the whole of holiness; that is, how the quality and quantity of something can be read together in (w)holiness.

Now let's apply analogic thinking to the GEMS system. The heart — a physical organ — is the physical analogy of love. Who doesn't recognize this fact? Valentine's Day in the U.S., a day dedicated to love, is depicted by hearts; Valentine cards filled with pictures of hearts and sayings of love; Valentine boxes of candy in the shape of hearts sent to loved ones. All of the human body is reflective of emotions that are their analogies.

Perry, a young man, comes to me with a severe digestive disturbance, a lot of burping and stomach acid reflux. He had it for months and was trying many physical remedies that were palliative but not curative. My first question to him was "Who or what are you having trouble stomaching?" He smiled, changing the rather dour countenance he came in with to a smile of recognition and understanding. He said, "My finances! I am overwhelmed by having to handle so many financial matters in my life, day by day, without help. It's gotten to a point where I don't know how I'm going to keep up with my bills. It's getting to me." Here his stomach is reflecting or mirroring the indigestibility of his financial life.

In my practice-based evidentiary healing work, thinking by analogy opens a window into how healing works. It is an *educative* function as opposed to therapy, understood in its conventional sense. Noting there is a direct relationship, a mirroring, or a reflection between emotional, mental, social, and physical disturbances allows me to bring to the sufferer's attention these interrelationships, which in turn fosters a healing response in them. In Perry's situation, somehow becoming aware of the wholeness of the origins of the malady incited change rather immediately. Thus, understanding the relationship between the physically diseased organ and the emotional correlates or analogies precipitates healing.

In my experience, when reflections become apparent, there is regularly a sense of unburdening and a recognition of possibilities of repair/corrections to be made. For, when corrections are made in one area, the repair is mirrored in the others.

In the Theater of Life diagram, the actor/experiencer engages life,

Reversing: Practices of Detachment

at every instance reflecting and feeling the reflection of the simultaneity/synchronicity of those five dimensions of experience in each moment of action. Each moment for us is really a wholeness (*kailo*) of living. Equipped with this understanding, it becomes easier to grasp how GEMS works. Let's see further: One day, when I had a car, I drove to my office. I sought to park the car and tried squeezing in between two cars. It was a tight squeeze, but it happened, even though I lightly tapped the front fender of the car behind me (no dents). The woman in the front car, seeing my efforts, came over to me and apologized for not moving her car. She couldn't, she said, because her "car battery went dead." I said spontaneously, "What about your inner battery?" She was surprised for a moment but quickly answered that indeed her inner battery had gone dead — over the past week she had been suffering from continuous chronic asthmatic symptoms and having a great deal of trouble breathing. She was, in fact, on her way to visit her pulmonary MD to find out what was going on. It happened not by chance that coincidentally — spiritually speaking —I had published two papers on the treatment of asthma through mental imagery. I told her I was also an MD and was glad to share with her my articles that focused on mental imagery. She was open to receiving them. I retrieved the articles from my office, gave them to her, wished her well, and off she went, as AAA arrived at that moment to start her battery (a good sign).

You might now begin to see how it works. I gave her a short course in analogy where the outer car battery is analogous to her inner battery, the outer and inner reflecting each other, simultaneously/coincidentally, bringing them together! This activated her spontaneous response, corroborating the unitive movement. From it came asthma and my having done published research in its treatment leading to the articles, giving her another possibility to deal with her condition. Here the hidden hand of God behind it all was right there, the Universe right there, alongside her — in the wholeness, the instant, the no-time zone. The hidden is always there in every action of our lives, bidden or unbidden, known or unknown. Being in time with it, thinking coincidentally, experiencing synchronistically, feeling at one with yourself, more alert, and awake.

In the process of coming into wholeness, a separation takes place, a detachment from held ideas, beliefs, and familiar habits, because we see the whole of our life for really the first time ever. Whole, heal, unity (*kailo*) erupts into our lives as we become whole.

Another example: Betty came in one day and said she was delayed because the light suddenly went out in her apartment, and she had to find something in the dark before she left. What did I ask her? Yes, you guessed it. I inquired whether she was experiencing a dimming or extinguishing of her own inner light. She responded yes, she was aware of a recent loss of power, feeling generalized weakness and sluggishness. Her thinking was somewhat foggier as well. The "power" in her marriage was waning. No energy was coming her way from her husband, no harmony, just a cacophony of arguments in an atmosphere of coldness. The outer world reflected or mirrored her inner experience of life.

Common mundane occurrences in your lives such as mechanical breakdowns of appliances (external world) can be investigated to see their relationships or analogies to our inner worlds. Thus, when a young woman with chronic digestive troubles reported that her kitchen oven was malfunctioning and unable to heat properly, it came as no surprise. She, too, had trouble with her internal engine of digestion. Moreover, when queried, she responded that nothing in her career life could come to birth — the oven, a slang term for the womb.

As mentioned before, other types of analogic "thinking" are imagery and dreams. These inner languages are complete and whole unto themselves. They are real, like hieroglyphic pictures bearing truth, not "analyzed" with logic and associative thoughts as Freud erred in doing;

not needing other conditions present to give merit, genuineness, or authenticity — independent, free, unconditional!

Images appear to us in their fullness, complete in their appearance, as they are. They are not to be met by commentary, analysis, interpretations, or any other verbal locutions we might want to use. Images exist in one subjective reality, words in quite another. Applying words to them to "make sense" out of them is to use a logical method of thinking to understand a nonlogical, analogical event. It is a mistake to *mix* processes, in the same way that Freud erred irreparably when he sought to make sense of the inner language of dreams and called them a "psychotic phenomenon." No! We don't speak to the images, we let them speak to us.

They are an analogical language. Rather than letting us draw conclusions ("make sense") about them, they show us the relationship, correspondences, reflections, and mirroring of one dimension of thought — images — with other dimensions of thought and knowledge. We learn to *read* them as pointing us to look at relationships between two things where they have points of similarity as well as points of difference. They point to concrete realities. They are never to be mistaken as metaphors, which are understood as not real in and of themselves but merely as conduits pointing us to the "true reality" underlying them, as Freud did in his misunderstanding of the meaning of symbols. That's often the way we read literature, but definitely not the way we read images, not the way hieroglyphic language is to be read.

Thinking by analogy gives us a better understanding of how to see life through a new lens via imagery, dreams, health issues, relationships, and events in everyday life. For the latter, here are some more instances to help reinforce the process we can call "reading the signs."

- Donald lost his wedding ring while doing the laundry. One year later, his wife ran off with another man. Without going into a question of whether he wished to end the marriage, we

immediately knew the marriage was in trouble at the loss of the ring.
- Stewart called his physician with a request for a prescription for Cialis (a sex energy drug) but didn't want to reveal this secret to his wife. A week later, his ring disappeared, indicating to me some sort of trouble in his marriage by withholding the secret.
- Richard, a student, riding in his car, commented to his wife about a cracked rear window covered in cardboard in an adjacent car. He "thinks" to himself "this is a warning — something out of my control." The next day, a violent windstorm cracked the back window of his own car. Note how synchronicities and thinking by analogy meld into intuitive thinking. Time is never the determinant as to the reality of that matter.
- Marlene attended a class of mine at an adult learning center. She followed up by attending the bimonthly salons I held in my home. She said upon entering, "I'm home." I replied, "You told me at the learning center you wanted to study this path, and I'm glad you are happy about it." She said, "No, not only that. I am really at home." She had visited this very apartment many times when her father lived here as its first tenant, I being the second tenant.
- Years ago, a wealthy friend and colleague slowly divested himself of his meaningful "earthly" possessions. A month later, I found him dead of an overdose from sleeping pills. This friend was in psychoanalysis five days a week, without his analyst understanding the depth of my friend's despair or the preparations he was making to leave this earth.
- Rita, a young woman, dreamt of vampires chasing her. She was suffering from digestive disturbances with frequent diarrhea and signs of anemia. I advised her to have a parasite test, in

which parasites were discovered. The vampire drains blood. The parasite is the material form of the dream vampire.

Thinking by analogy is learned by practice. The easiest way to watch it is to reflect on the relationship between social relationships and your physical states, as well as the outer environment and your physical condition(s). Where there is physical strife, there is social strife, and vice versa.

Mental Imagery: A New Way of Self-Healing

Mental imagery is a function of imagination. They are short-active mental exercises. The power of mental imagery is unparalleled and unrivaled in our world. Imagery is a mental process that shows us new ways to approach life and life's problems, establish meaningful relationships, change destructive habits, open up avenues of creative power, and access inner resources of power reserves as a life force for our and others' good. It's a unique process of unconditional language in that it's independent of any external influence or intervention. This means that imagery isn't affected by anything going on outside of us. Imagery happens by going inward. The images directly impact our physical functioning, as we are a biomental unity. This process is naturally healing for us, bringing together the five dimensions of human experience.

How Does Mental Imagery Work

You peer into subjective consciousness to see what's there…inner worlds of consciousness: covert, night consciousness; superconsciousness; storehouse consciousness, other worlds, the cosmos. Everything in consciousness, and beyond consciousness, is available to us through the imagination. It is simply a matter of light. The greater that the light of imagination shines through us, beaming its rays outwardly into the world and inwardly into the inner world, the more we come to know ourselves as truly human beings serving both worlds and God, and in turn being served in this collaborative community of mutual love.

Barry, a young man, comes to me for help and says, "I feel doomed." He is walking around with this belief disturbing his life, an obstacle he creates as a function of his misperceptions and misconceptions about life, feeling daunted by challenges confronting him. At times, all of us do the same thing. The young man lays himself low, then needs to summon his inner strength to overcome the feeling of doom in order to face whatever challenge confronts him. Again, we all go through a similar process, often succeeding in our endeavors. But there is a price to pay, the toll being some depletion of life force and energy.

Are there options? Most certainly yes! Here are two I offered him, both using mental imagery. I explained to him he could not say "doomed" without understanding its opposite feeling, which he could experience as readily as his "doomed" feeling. That's how it is in life experience. It can be no other way. Language is structured along the lines of recognition of opposites. It is always a matter of choice at any instant. Remember, "I set before you [at each instant] life and death. Choose!"

I asked the young man what he saw as the opposite for doom. He saw "blessing." For the young man, then, these were the opposite possibilities: "I set before you blessing and doom. Choose!" Now he was aware of the other choice that had eluded him for a goodly portion of his life. I gave him the opportunity to become aware of another possibility rooted in truth. We all have this possibility; we just don't have the education to know how to increase awareness. Increased awareness brings life! Barry chose "blessing."

Once he chose the opposite, I asked him to close his eyes and see the image of blessing. He responded by seeing himself standing tall with arms inclined forward and up, with his hands open, palms up.

Reversing: Practices of Detachment

I asked him to breathe out and open his eyes. Asked how he felt, he responded, "Elevated and light." The doomed feeling disappeared, the mood brightened. He had given himself a placebo instead of a nocebo. Faith and hope replaced doubt and no-hope.

I continued his education by informing him that whenever he felt doomed, he should immediately close his eyes, see the image of himself standing tall with arms extended forward and up, with hands open and palms up. Then he should say to himself "blessing," feel elevated, and physically sense lightness, and breathe out and open his eyes.

By constant repetition of this practice, he would replace in his life space his habitual feeling response with another. No two contrary habits can occupy the same inner space at the same time. Eventually, by constant repetition one new habit grows and grows and pushes out the old one. Life can now take on a new hue, a different glow and feeling tone. The physiology responds in a like manner.

The other opportunity I offered him was to close his eyes and see the image of doom. He sees himself in a large dome-covered glass enclosure where he feels trapped. I asked him then to *reverse* this image, turn it around. I tell him this is imagination and anything can happen. He can have with him anything he can use to create this reversing. He finds a golden hammer and smashes the glass, which he hears tinkle as it crumbles and falls away. He walks out into a new setting, one of nature, where he can smell the fresh air, hear birds chirping, sense the warmth of the sun, where he feels liberated. The feeling of doom is reversed by feelings of liberation and connection to nature.

I told him to repeat this exercise of reversing each morning and at sundown for the next three weeks to ingrain this possibility of a new life direction as a new way of becoming his mature self. By going, in effect, to his mental gym and creating mental abs, pecs, and lats, he is helping to create a new "spiritual body of light." The dance of doom has been shattered.

He now had two options available to practice: the first one (to change the inner image of himself) to use whenever the feeling of doom arises; the second is to change the image of doom —and to practice twice daily. Using these two exercises, he, as a mental, physical unity, creates new neural and cardiac pathways inside of him, promoting change and a new reality.

Here is a communication he sent to me shortly after our educational encounter: "Thank you for our session last week. It was most enlightening. I love how you've 'secularized faith,' as I'm calling it, and how you got me to essentially take 'snapshots' of pictures in my mind associated with various feeling states and then put all the snapshots together into a movie I can play over and over in my head when I am having negative thoughts and feelings to help me switch back into the positive thoughts and feelings place. It works like a charm, and I have been on a cloud for days!"

This young man came initially suffering from a five-year course of eczema kept under control by a large dose of a drug, cyclosporine. In the communication just cited, he added: "Alas, I had a deadline and an uncomfortable situation at work, and my skin has been worsening somewhat as the deadline this morning approached. I was able to really put the movie to the test and am quite happy with the results at the moment. I am so grateful and looking forward to our ongoing work."

Whatever our career choice or calling, continued repetition and continuous practice is required to hone and perfect that calling. Spiritual life is no different. There is no getting away from this fact. When I had my illuminative experience in 1974 with Colette, it was a *necessary* moment but not a *sufficient* one. The moment of light, becoming a being of light, set my life on a new track without hesitation. But, that moment, taking place as it did, not as an experience of space and time, had to be brought to bear in my daily space–time existence by ongoing application. Otherwise, the immensity of that instant would be lost. It

Reversing: Practices of Detachment

is like taking a talent we have been gifted with, perhaps at birth, and instead of multiplying this gift through work and practice, we bury it under a bushel, where it evaporates or decays. Matthew 5:14–16 states in the Parable of Life:

> You are the light of the world. A city set on a hill cannot be hid. Neither do men light a candle and put it under a bushel basket, but on a lamp stand, and it gives light to all who are in the house. Let your light so shine before others around you, that they may see your good works and give glory [light] to your father in heaven.

This young man has begun to take his life in a new direction. The inescapable suffering he had to deal with served as the motivator, an unusual "midwife," to use his condition as the pivot point of reversing no-health to health, a phenomenon Larry LeShan noted in his book *Cancer as a Turning Point*. We know now that ill health reflects a significant spiritual statement representing a possible, maybe even probable, turn to Spirit encompassing healing, wholeness, holiness, and evolution of consciousness of Self. We come to realize, finally, a purpose of life: to evolve into conscious oneness with Spirit.

This young man had an immediate illuminative experience through the imagery process. There was a sudden shift in consciousness. Next, he learns how to "fix" his life so that he embraces a spiritual value system to bring him even closer to light and hopefully, as he moves ever closer, to that Light that is Spirit...that UNENDING LIFE, the godliness that fills us and by which we fill God simultaneously.

The Epstein Mental Imagery Model — EMIM — is designed in line with the spiritual principle of reversing. This EMIM practice directs you to identify the opposite image and feeling to what troubles you or to correct the troubling image by reversing it. As we have seen in the example of the young man who said he felt doomed, the focus is on quickly changing a disturbing thought, self-proclaimed nocebo, belief, emotion, physical difficulty, or any form of disorder by shifting attention and awareness to a nonhabitual response, bypassing discursive thinking and discussion, turning them around to reveal another dimension of communication. This new form of communication is waiting to be revealed. It is all there for the asking. As both Matthew and Luke mentioned in their gospels, "Ask and it will be given to you"; "Seek and you will find"; "Knock and the door will be opened for you." Asking inwardly is a form of prayer. When our prayer is answered from super-consciousness, we have succeeded in co-creating with God in this mutual participatory act.

Here is another example: Harold, a young man, appears complaining of multiple allergic sensitivities, particularly chemical substances in the environment. The sensitivities began with a respiratory difficulty experienced when he lived in an apartment laden with mold. He finally moved to a new location some distance away, and there he developed chemical and other allergies. I asked him for the opposite of chemical sensitivities. He responded, "Clean air." I asked for the image of "clean air." He immediately said, "I'm at a beach, taking in the pure air there." I suggested that he say to himself "cleansing," and feel it and any physical sensation. I asked him to describe the sensation. He responded that he was feeling light, breathing easier, and sensed his chest opening. This was the homework I assigned him: Each time he felt distressed by a sensitivity response to an environmental trigger, he was to shift to the image of seeing himself at the beach, breathing in the clean salt air. He was to say to himself "cleansing," feel it, and have a physical sensation. This experience may take only a few seconds. It is an example of the homeopathic principle of a micro input for a macro output.

In addition, I invited him to do my original method called One-Minute Life Repair System — a variant of the EMIM — which deals with core beliefs we hold about our lives.[49] Here, I inquired about his belief about overcoming this malady. He said, "I'll not be able to get over it." "What's the opposite belief?" I asked. His opposite belief: "I am getting over it." I requested he <u>see</u> the new belief, physically <u>sense</u> it, and <u>feel</u> it at the same moment of saying it. Attached to this process is a neuromuscular response whereby a thought and a physical response become connected, which demonstrates the intimate connection between mental and physical reflections. This phenomenon is called "kinesiology." When thoughts are pessimistic or offer dim hope of any sort, an outstretched arm held stiff cannot resist a light touch downward on the back of the hand. The arm weakens and is unable to be held up strongly. In contrast, when thoughts are constructive and offer some hope and faith, the arm resists the light touch on the back of the hand and cannot be pushed down, even becoming stronger than before. The arm remaining strong reflects the intention of the new belief to heal.

He went through this One-Minute Life Repair teaching (it takes about one minute to teach/learn it). In reversing the belief, he was again to see, physically sense, and feel it, while the arm was held strongly straight out.

For now, let us be aware of the image as a symbolic/relational/analogical revelatory language accessible to us at a moment's notice, holding, reflecting, and expressing the knowledge of oneself. It's not for nothing that we are created in the *image* of God (Gen 1:26). As this image, reflection, or analogy, we contain all the knowledge of self, but also collectively all the knowledge of the macrocosm and microcosm put together in one neat little package called human being.

Why is imagery valuable? As noted earlier, the image is the language

---

[49] The entire description of this process is to be found in my audio recording set *The Phoenix Process: One Minute a Day to Health, Longevity, and Well-Being*.

of Invisible Reality conveyed to us through that channel of communication called "Mind," making it perceptible to our consciousness in a three-dimensional form having no volume or mass — that is, having no tangibility in a physical sense.

Here are some neurophysiological correlates. A fellow is hooked up to a PET scan, a neurological gadget placed on our skull to monitor the activity of the brain nuclei. When they are activated, they show up on the scan as different colors. He then rides a bike, and the scan records a certain nucleus lighting up. He is then asked to watch another person ride a bike. He does so, and the *same nucleus* lights up! It is explained by the investigator that it is "as though" he was riding the bike he witnessed. (See, for example: http://www.pbs.org/wgbh/nova/body/mirror-neurons.html.)

Thirty athletes are divided into three groups. One group go to the gym and work out on weight machines to increase their hip flexor muscle strength; another group sit at home and imagine they are strengthening their hip flexors on weight machines; a third group does nothing. The hip strength of each group was measured before and after training. Physical strength was increased by 24 percent through mental practice and by 28 percent through physical training, while the third group did not change significantly. The strength gain was greatest among the football players given mental training.[50] We can see the power of mental life approximating here, by percentage, the power of physical life.

One half of a group of young men imagine eating 30 M&Ms and then insert three quarters into the slot of a laundry machine. The other half imagined eating three M&Ms and inserting 30 quarters. Then

---

[50] Erin M. Shackell and Lionel Standing. "Mind Over Matter: Mental Training Increases Physical Strength." *North Am. J. Psychol.* 9 (2007.) See also: DOI: 10.1016/j.neuropsychologia.2003.11.018 and https://www.scientificamerican.com/article/how-to-grow-stronger-without-lifting-weights (accessed August 21, 2018).

everyone was invited to eat their fill from a bowl of M&Ms. Those who imagined eating 30 M&Ms ate about three M&Ms on average while the other group that had only eaten three M&Ms ate about five M&Ms. So while picturing a delicious food—like a juicy steak or an ice cream sundae—generally whets the appetite, it appears that actually imaging yourself eating the entire sundae, spoonful by spoonful, curbs your appetite.[51]

A group of 141 overweight people used mental imagery to lose weight. At the end of six months, they'd lost nine pounds; at the end of one year, they'd lost 14 pounds.[52]

Spiritually speaking, the gentleman in the instance of bike riding was *actually* riding the bike he was looking at. Perception from this perspective of imagery means that at the moment of sensing contact, you are *one* with that which you perceive. Then you separate from the perceived so that you define a separate identity between you and it. When Jack and Jane meet each other, they are immediately one. Then the separation takes place: "Hello, Jane." "Hello, Jack." The man watching a bike rider was one with the fellow riding the bike. The same nucleus was activated in both. It was *not* "as though" he was riding the bike.

In the other instances — the hip-flexor measured men, the M&M eaters, a group who imagines themselves losing weight — we find a scientific corollary in the recent discovery by neuroscientists of so-called mirror neurons.

---

[51] Carey K. Morewedge, Young Eun Huh, and Jachim Vosgerau. "Thought for Food: Imagined Consumption Reduces Actual Consumption." *Science* 330 (6010) (10 Dec 2010), 1530–33. DOI: 10.1126/science.1195701 (accessed August 21, 2018).

[52] Linda Solbrig, B. Whalley, D.J. Kavanagh, J. May, T. Parkin, R. Jones, and J. Andrade. "Functional Imagery Training Versus Motivational Interviewing for Weight Loss: A Randomized Control Trial of Brief Individual Intervention for Overweight and Obesity." *Int'l Journal of Obesity*, 2018. https://www.ncbi.nlm.nih.gov/pubmed/30185920. DOI: 10.1038/s41366-018-0122-1.

When the senses are turned inward, they activate the "mirror neurons" to register what is received. Just like the gentleman watching the bike rider in waking life, so the analogous situation occurs inwardly when action is perceived: *New* neural, vascular (heart), emotional, and thought pathways are opened.

What are mirror neurons? Mirror neurons were first discovered in the 1980s and 1990s at the University of Parma, Italy, by a group of five neuroscientists: G. Rizzolatti, G. Di Pellegrino, L. Fadiga, L. Fogassi, and V. Gallese. They placed electrodes in the premotor ventral cortex of macaque monkeys to study neurons that control hand and mouth actions. They discovered during their investigations that neurons would respond in the same way when the monkey picked up food as when seeing another monkey pick up food. Since then, many reports on the phenomenon have been issued from various centers.[53]

A mirror neuron fires when an individual performs a physical action, performs mental imagery (an internal action), or observes an action performed by another person in everyday waking life. In imaginal thinking we are both the witness and the doer — *observing and acting at the same moment.*

In this imaginal reality, we find the blueprint of our being. It shows us the wholeness we are. When I have a physical cut and look into the reverse Invisible Reality, I see the cut healed and normal. That information is reflected to and by the mirror neurons and relayed to our physical time-space being as an instruction and direction to come back into order and balance. Whatever we perceive, by whatever sense is strongest in us, gives us an instruction to repair, to heal.

---

[53] Rizzolatti G., L. Fadiga, V. Gallese, and L. Fogassi. "Premotor Cortex and the Recognition of Motor Actions." *Brain Res Cogn Brain Res.* 3(2) (March 1996): 131–41. PubMed PMID: 8713554 (accessed August 21, 2018). For a summary of research also see: Lea Winerman, "The Mind's Mirror," APA *Monitor* 36(9)(October 2005): 48. http://www.apa.org/monitor/oct05/mirror.aspx (accessed August 18, 2018).

Reversing: Practices of Detachment

The Invisible Reality is always available to supply us with the necessary means for regeneration, rejuvenation, restoration, resuscitation, and revival. Imagery always reflects wholeness. We enhance the process by sensorially amplifying the experience. Barry, the young man dealing with eczema and feeling doomed, had a firsthand sensory event when he spontaneously smelled, heard, saw, touched, and tasted the image of freedom as himself in a new way, standing tall with arms inclined forward alongside his torso with hands open, palms up. He immersed himself ever more fully into it and became the healer and healee at once. He merged and became healthy. The instruction he gave himself was then accomplished — "became healthy." A new seed was planted in the womb of his consciousness, gestating there as an image, holding it in place. Through tending to this new seed by rhythmical repetitive imaging, a new habit-pattern of change is birthed in him.

What I have discovered through nearly five decades of exploration is that the convergence of the realities of material science and spirituality enables us to understand and realize how imagery *has* to work! It doesn't matter what adverse condition is taking place, the imaginal world always is the way of wholeness — holiness, health, healing, holding the answers to relieving our suffering, and with it our path to unending life.

Through the turn to the Invisible Reality via its language of images, we turn away from this material reality for a moment, attend to another reality through imagery, and come back to everyday life with *a new belief,* a new possibility for living. The image gives form to the belief. A belief is synonymous with conception. Image gives us a greater concrete awareness of what is otherwise experienced as something more abstract. What we conceive we can then perceive, which is then birthed. As we are made in the image and likeness, we emulate God, the Spirit who conceived, perceived, and birthed us. We are co-creators able to carry out what has been done for us. We have been given free will and choice. Our creations can be life-extending or life-ending.

Pamela was a young woman who suffered from herpes genitalis. She had numerous outbreaks, took medication, and was told incorrectly by the gynecologist that her condition was "incurable." She was understandably unhappy about this curveball in her life that has so many unpleasant social implications.

We embarked on a program of imagery practice, which she took to readily. After three weeks of attention to imagery practice three times a day, I recommended she go for a blood test to see if the condition had cleared up. Her previous test had revealed the presence of herpes genitalis. The new test showed the *absence* of genital herpes and the presence of herpes varicella. She reported that she'd had chicken pox as a child (the forerunner of adult shingles/herpes varicella).

Here is a summary of the physician's report verifying this finding.

> Good news — all the recent lab tests that you did were negative. No signs of any STDs and you do have immunity to varicella zoster.
>
> All STD tests are negative. FYI — you cannot see the HIV, hepatitis B or hepatitis C results online. Kaiser doesn't release those for confidentiality reasons. The good news is they were negative also!
>
> I hope you have a nice weekend!

Pamela co-created the healing, becoming at once the healer and healee. This is the power with which we are born and which we are meant to use to heal into LIFE!

Reversing: Practices of Detachment

Prayer: Conversing with God

Prayer is speaking to God or thinking to God. The former is conveyed by words, the latter by image — that is, silent prayer given form. All imagery is a form of prayer. Prayer represents the message delivered from us upward as opposed to the divine language sent from above down to us. Conversations have been recorded in the Western wisdom literature flowing in both directions: of God speaking to Moses, of Moses speaking with God, of visions of the Prophets receiving heavenly inspiration, of Sarah being told by God she would conceive a child, of the Israelites asking for and receiving food from the celestial realm. The stories of these sorts of communication are legion in the ancient writings as well as throughout the centuries into contemporary times by responsible, competent, sober people.

That spirituality and religious feeling and practice play a salutary role in overcoming illness has been highlighted by Jeffrey S. Levin, associate professor of family and community medicine at Eastern Virginia Medical School, who writes as follows:

> Since the 19th century, over 250 published empirical studies have appeared in the epidemiologic and medical literature in which one or more indicators of spirituality or religiousness, variously defined, have been statistically associated in some way with particular health outcomes. Across this literature, studies have appeared which suggest that religion is salutary for cardiovascular disease, hypertension, stroke, nearly every cancer site, colitis and enteritis, numerous health status indicators, and in terms of both morbidity and mortality. Further, this finding seems to hold regardless of how spirituality is defined and measured (beliefs, behaviors, attitudes, experiences, etc.). An especially large subliterature of over two dozen studies demonstrates the health-motive effects of simply attending church or synagogue on a regular basis. Finally, while no one study has conclusively "proven" that a spiritual perspective or

involvement in religion is a universal preventive or curative factor, significant positive health effects of spirituality have appeared in studies of whites, blacks, and Hispanics; in studies of older adults and adolescents; in studies of U.S., European, African, and Asian subjects; in prospective, retrospective, cohort, and case-control studies; in studies of Protestants, Catholics, Jews, Parsis, Buddhists, and Zulus; in studies published in the 1930s and in the 1980s; in studies measuring spirituality as belief in God, religious attendance, Bible reading, frequency of prayer, father's years of Yeshiva, numinous feelings, and history of bewitchment, among many other constructs; and in studies of self-limiting acute conditions, of fatal chronic diseases, and of illnesses with lengthy, brief, or absent latency periods between exposure and diagnosis and mortality. In short, something worthy of serious investigation seems to be consistently manifesting in these studies, and understanding the "what," "how," and "why" of this apparent spiritual factor in health may be critical for reducing suffering and curing the sick.

The "spiritual factor in health" that Dr. Levin mentions is *the* critical factor in all healing. This is an apt place to define the components that make up the spiritual factor and to contrast them with some of the premises underlying medicine, psychology, and science.[54]

In a seminal study by Dr. Larry Dossey, he noted the worldwide experience of prayer for healing.[55]

In a remarkable study on prayer conducted in the late 1980s at San Francisco General Hospital, Dr. Randolph Byrd had a prayer group of the Rosicrucian order working on the opposite side of the city praying

---

[54] Jeffrey S. Levin. "Esoteric vs. Exoteric Explanations for Findings Linking Spirituality and Health." *Advances: The Journal of Mind-Body Health* 9(4) (Fall 1993): 54–56.

[55] Larry Dossey. *Healing Words: The Power of Prayer and the Practice of Medicine* (New York: Harper) 1994).

for 200 cardiac patients who did not know they were prayed for, while another 200 were not prayed for. In all areas of evaluation, the prayer recipients showed greater improvement than the control group, including reduction in medication, shorter hospital stay, and every other assessment value throughout the time prayer was used.[56]

Healing at a distance through imagery can be effective. A woman called to say she was to have a Cesarean section to deliver her breech baby, which the obstetrician could not reverse. Surgery was planned for the following day. I brought a small prayer group together on the night of the call. We did an imagery exercise to turn the baby around while the woman was in the hospital, and we were in my apartment six blocks away. (This exercise is described in my book *Healing Visualizations*). The next day she called me excitedly to tell me the baby had turned and the surgery was canceled.

A group of 16 of us sat in my teacher Colette's garden in Jerusalem. We were shown a picture of an infant who had a supposedly "incurable" liver ailment with which no baby had lived past four months. When the mother originally sought me out, the baby was a newborn. I asked her to assemble a group of friends and relatives to pray using an imagery exercise twice a day at the same time each day, coordinated among them, since a number of them lived in distant locales. She assembled 500 people to do this! When we met in Jerusalem, the baby was about one year old. That morning he was being medically monitored in an MD's office in Brooklyn, New York, as he was on a special diet. At Colette's direction, we prayed together using an imagery exercise she gave. The child's picture was on the ground in the center of where we all sat. Immediately afterward, Colette asked one of the group — who was friendly with the mother and had brought the photo — to call the

---

[56] R. C. Byrd, "Positive Therapeutic Effects of Intercessory Prayer in a Coronary Care Unit Population." *Southern Medical Journal* 81(7) (July 1988): 826–9. doi:10.1097/00007611-198807000-00005.

doctor's office in Brooklyn where the mother was with the baby— 4 p.m. in Jerusalem, 9 a.m. in Brooklyn.

When she returned to the group, she reported the doctor asking, "Has somebody been working on this child [he was told we were planning to do so], because his blood tests are all returned to normal?!"

Time and space do not interfere with the inner process that is prayer. Like telepathy, extrasensory perception, and other similar phenomena, images and inner-generated forces transcend time-space barriers and constraints. Time-space "laws" cannot account for such phenomena. Rupert Sheldrake, an English plant physiologist, conducted an experiment in the late 1970s. He took a sapling from a plant in London and planted it in Hong Kong. He then altered the plant's growth pattern in London. In a week's time, the plant in Hong Kong began growing according to the new pattern implemented in London. He repeated the experience again in London–New York, London–Sydney. Again the same phenomenon took place. Out of these experiments grew a book called *A New Science of Life* (1981)[57] that became a best-seller when the journal *Science* blasted it, saying it should be burned!

Lyall Watson, a high-level biologist, wrote about the monkeys on an island off the coast of Japan who would dig yams out of the ground, brush off the dirt, and eat them.[58] One day a monkey, for some inexplicable reason, took a yam down to the water and washed it before eating it. (Perhaps this happened because of the atomic radiation in the area polluting the earth and the yams of the island. Who knows?) The other monkeys followed suit. One week later, the monkeys of the same species on an island 400 miles away began washing their yams! Events transcending time and space. Same thing with prayer. These are forces

---

[57] Rupert Sheldrake. *A New Science of Life: The Hypothesis of Formative Causation* (Los Angeles: Jeremy P. Tarcher, 1981).

[58] Lyall Watson. *Lifetide: A Biology of the Unconscious* (London: Hodder & Stoughton, 1979).

not understood yet by material science, although scientists in quantum physics and some in biology are attempting to do so.

Sheldrake postulated a "morphogenetic field," an information matrix specific for each species wherein all the knowledge necessary for that species' survival is stored. This information is available to all species members no matter where they live and is gleaned through a transcendent consciousness each species possesses. This is compelling. Why wouldn't a Consciousness that loves us provide means whereby we can communicate with each other worldwide by a force or power requiring no friction to set it in motion, contrary to what is needed in man-made combustible energy? In the former, such power requires nothing to die, whereas in the latter, something must be destroyed for something to live. Celestial power is life *absent* death. Prayer is celestial power.

The Yes or No Phenomenon: Resolving Doubt

To conquer doubt, we focus on the daily business of saying "yes" or "no" to this or that. This is something we all know and do, because we make choices all the time. No, I don't want to see that movie. Yes, I do want to buy that car. No, I cannot support that candidate. Yes, I love you. There is nothing wrong about saying yes *or* no. In fact, saying one or the other is what we need to do.

The trouble comes in when we do not say one or the other but instead say both — yes *and* no — and do not choose but live indecisively, at odds with ourselves. Such wavering between yes and no is a common experience for many of us, and for some of us is a hallmark of how we live, moving indecisively through life without making clearcut choices. What is wrong with yes *and* no? Why do I introduce it in a book that aims at providing tools by which we can extend our health and our lives? I contend that the uncertainty and indecisiveness of yes *and* no brings into our lives a seed source (*doubt*) of all our disturbances — mental, emotional, physical, social, moral. This is a large statement. How is it justified?

The starting point comes from the Sermon on the Mount, when the Master of Christianity is talking about telling the truth and not bearing false witness. He asserts, "Say yes or no, anything more comes from evil" (Matt. 5:37). In the ancient wisdom of the Western spiritual tradition, one meaning of evil is falsehood. So in this assertion, evil means falsehood and, by comparison, good means truth. This assertion is a variation of the earlier statement in the Bible paraphrased here, to set before us life and death, good and evil, choose one or the other (Deut. 30:19). When you put the two statements together, the result goes like this: Saying yes or no means choosing life, anything more comes from evil, which means death.

Now let us look deeply into three terms from the Sermon on the Mount — "yes or no," "anything more," and "evil," for when we do, we find the basis for a bodysoul health-care paradigm that was widely known to the ancients.

The Vertebra of Existence
Physically speaking, the gesture that says yes and the gesture that says no are connected to a cervical vertebra. The physical action of yes is connected with the first cervical vertebra, known as the atlas. So when we nod our head up and down as we say yes, the atlas allows for that movement. As you know from Greek mythology, Atlas was the figure who held up the world on his shoulders. Analogically speaking, then, you could say that we are holding up the world through the nodding of yes.

The physical action of saying no, when you turn your head back and forth from left to right and right to left, is connected to the second cervical vertebra, which is called the axis, and, of course, the axis is what the world spins on. So again, we say that we keep the world spinning when we shake our heads no. We could also say that the vertebra of yes and the vertebra of no represent the macro-existence of this planet — how it is held up and how it spins, or, put another way, that it exists and that it can rotate to continue its existence.

On a down-to-earth, micro-existence physical level, the two vertebrae can also shape and determine our existence and can have a serious effect on our health. For example, when there is a disorder, displacement, or derangement of the vertebrae, the entire spinal column can be thrown out of order, creating all sorts of faulty curvatures and postural disturbances, including chronic back problems. Did you know the latest American Chiropractic Association survey shows that roughly 80 percent of Americans suffer from back problems sometime in their lives? And that 31 million Americans currently suffer from chronic back pain, and it is the leading cause of disability worldwide?[59]

This is only the beginning of the health problems linked to those two vertebrae. One of the many nerves that travel through the cervical vertebrae is the vagus, and when the vertebrae are deranged or out of place, the vagus is impinged on. When this happens, we run a high probability of eye, ear, heart, and lung problems, since branches of the vagus innervate these four areas.

The impingement of vertebral malformations on other nerves passing through the spinal column can have profound effects on the rest of the body. If the musculature and the organ systems don't have the correct distribution and innervation of nerve fibers, these systems begin to break down.

Add to this list of physical concerns the torque produced by spinal-column displacements, resulting in muscle spasm and constrictions of arteries flowing through the muscles, subsequently cutting off

---

[59] American Chiropractic Association. "Back Pain Facts and Statistics." https://www.acatoday.org/Patients/Health-Wellness-Information/Back-Pain-Facts-and-Statistics. Accessed December 10, 2017.

the blood supply to various organs, resulting in organ pathology, in some instances all the way to cancer. When these neck muscles go into spasm, arteries flowing through these muscles become constricted, cutting off blood supply to the eyes and ears.

Undermining Our Vertebrae
Why do your vertebrae go awry to bring about such a raft of problems? In the Western tradition, the answer lies in our disregard of choosing life. According to this tradition, when yes *or* no is replaced by the doubt/indecisiveness of yes *and* no, misalignments abound.

Here is an example from my clinical practice. Carl, a young man in his late 20s, had been courting a young woman near his age. He was unsure whether he wanted to extend the relationship. He certainly found her to have the qualities he'd been searching for. He'd gained and shed many girlfriends previously and was unsure of whether he really ever wanted to marry and settle down. There was a "socio-genetic" error transmitted through his family line where his grandfather and father, along the same family line, married but carried on multiple extramarital relationships. He saw the suffering of his mother, who knew about the affairs and saw fit to complain loudly and often about them, all the while staying in the marriage.

In his own work of self-knowing and life-extending practice, he knew he could not continue to lead his current girlfriend on, as she was definitely in love with him. It would be stealing her time, lying to her, creating a false image of what he was about, violating the Eighth, Ninth, and Second Cosmic Laws, respectively. He was in a yes-*and*-no situation, indecisive, full of doubt. His job was to change yes and no to yes *or* no, for that's the truth. In his anguish about the circumstance, he told me of a sudden pain in his neck that meant he couldn't turn his head and neck to the right and up. I asked him what the pain in his neck was that reflected the yes and no in his life currently. He responded immediately that it was the decision to forsake the relationship although he was well aware of how seemingly "perfect" she was for him.

Returning to the familiar story of Adam and Eve, God tells Eve to listen to His voice alone, the one voice. The serpent appears, bringing a second voice, and whispers in Eve's ear to eat the fruit of the tree of knowledge of good and evil to become as God. God had explicitly warned Adam and Eve against eating the fruit of this tree, lest they die. Now Eve is in a state of anxiety. She heard two voices. Which one does she listen to? The proposition to become as a God is tremendous, but God said to obey only the One voice. She falls into doubt. Adam falls into doubt…and here we are.

This story represents the struggle of all of us as we face our multitude of choices on a day-to-day basis. Many of us are in a constant state of doubt, indecision, ambivalence, afraid to choose, maintaining yes *and* no almost perpetually. Why does yes *and* no have such power to undo us? Try moving your head yes and no at the same time — up and down, and back and forth, right to left, and left to right, at the same time. Notice what happens. You feel confused, disoriented, displaced, unsure. If you continue, you may see that a derangement begins to take place in the vertebral system.

You do not need to move your head yes *and* no physically to bring about confusion and derangement. When you doubt, you are doing the same thing mentally, trying fruitlessly at the same time to use doubt-driven logic to "figure it out." What happens mentally happens in the body, just as what happens in the body happens mentally, and when you are mentally filled with doubt, the vertebrae in the body that let you express yes or no physically are set in motion.

The Effects of Doubt
When doubt persists, the first and second vertebrae begin to move out of place. And when this starts, the rest of the spinal column goes out of place. Osteopaths and chiropractors, whose work centers on the body's structural integrity, maintain that the basis of all physical disturbances is malfunctioning in the spinal column.

As doubt and its created uncertainty continue and expand, we can begin to see a host of emotional and mental reverberations. In the emotional/mental realm, for example, obsessional compulsive activity, phobias, and tics are all examples of the struggle of yes *and* no trying to become yes *or* no.

Mentally, continuation of yes *and* no can eventually become manic-depressive illness because yes *and* no means a condition of constantly going up and down, repeatedly moving from elation to depression and back — up, down, up, down. In medical language, this lability is called "bipolar."

If we extend the condition further, the result is the most severe ambivalence imaginable: schizophrenia, which finds its culmination in catatonia. In the schizophrenic state of catatonia, yes *and* no is brought to its most "exquisite" manifestation — virtually to a standstill — because you don't dare move a muscle. The ambivalence is so severe they are afraid that if they move one muscle, they will break into a million pieces and be annihilated.

Consider the destructive function of "yes *and* no" in medical diagnosis. As my friend and former student Bob Kelly pointed out to me, medical evaluations commonly support yes *and* no. When one is told there is a 10 percent chance of this, 30 percent chance of that, 60 percent chance of that, and so on, a seed of doubt is simply implanted in consciousness, leaving one in a yes *and* no situation. The upside of being saddled with the dilemma is being forced to choose yes *or* no. One falls back on making up one's mind and choosing. Incidentally, making up one's mind and choosing is another definition of faith. Being forced like this — back up against the wall, getting no relief from all the people one asks for advice to help you make the choice; the pressure increases until the mental pain becomes unbearable and yes *or* no can no longer be avoided, leaving some residue or scar of mental pain about whether the "right" choice has been made.

What to do about this unfortunate circumstance? You can begin by asking the physician to put themselves in your place and give you an answer. At the same time, put yourself in their place and find out what they really think about the situation. The answer you need comes immediately.

We see that doubt may lead us along a certain path to certain physical and emotional disturbances and that on the mental level, by choosing the path of doubt, we are reenacting the archetypal story of Eve and Adam, where we eat of that which causes us to die. Once we enter the realm of yes *and* no, the realm of doubt, it stays with us throughout our life from childhood on unless we take charge of it by removing the state of indecision and ambivalence and our unwillingness to take a firm yes *or* no stance about something.

The Whirlpool of Yes *and* No

Earlier in this book came the question Do you want to live forever? Now let's add another choice. Do you want to live forever, yes or no? According to the Sermon on the Mount, once you say one or the other, that's all there is to say, right? "Anything more comes from evil." Once you say yes or no, the question is answered, and nothing more is required of you, except to follow that choice, without wavering, to see where it leads you.

The problem comes in when you go beyond yes or no, as the Sermon on the Mount makes clear, because then you are swearing falsely. You are making rationalizations and fobbing them off as facts: offering opinions, judgments, stories, excuses, interpretations, whatever — all, in this context, falsehoods.

Let's use an everyday example to make the point. Say you are asked, "Do you want to go to a movie tonight?" and you respond by saying, "Well, I can't decide, because I have a test tomorrow [or I have to write a letter, or whatever]; I'd like to go, but maybe I shouldn't." And on and on. But you are not answering the question at hand, which is asking for a yes *or* no. You are answering yes *and* no. You want to go, you don't want to go, yes, no, no, yes. All irrelevant. The question is: What do you want to do right now? Now, the way people express their uncertainty, the reasons they give for explaining why they cannot choose — cannot, that is, answer the question — will differ from person to person. But the common denominator for everyone who chooses uncertainty is yes *and* no. Yes *or* no asks us to go from choice directly to taking action — to *do* or not *do*. Definitive action dispels doubt, honors faith, honors life.

Take a good look at the yes-*and*-no surplus of comments that avoids yes or no and means yes and no. The surplus explains why we can't decide if we do or don't want to go to the movies tonight. It includes the commentaries that you believe have meaning about your situation. It includes the stories you are giving yourself so that you don't choose. You want to please the other person and yourself as well. The dilemma: "*If* I choose one *then* I forgo the other." That is the way it is. It's inescapable, and mature, to accept this truth, but we try otherwise, acting like little children and as childish adults to continue this self-troubling behavior. You are asked to say yes or no, but everything you say is about why you can't say yes or no, why you are uncertain and in doubt, why you are in limbo. In short, these commentaries and stories have no real meaning for choosing the simple yes or no question that you face.

Well, so what if we can't choose and instead give some reasons why? What's the problem with that? What's difficult is that since these stories and commentaries are not tethered to the situation in front of us, they are simply free-floating beliefs, and beliefs like these often lead to the creation of other false beliefs projected into a time, a place, and circumstances that don't exist. By treating the future as fact, we lose all grounding in reality and truth. We go from misjudgment to misjudgment, taking actions *that are not in truth.*

When untruths abound, we become disquieted and upset with ourselves and others. We start to blame others for not helping us fulfill what we are trying to do, or we condemn ourselves. We become judgmental about others or ourselves. If we put ourselves down, we begin to torture ourselves, making us feel unworthy. We distort our self-image, and from there, we create an emergency state that becomes a frequent feature of our lives.

You can see this every day in the 100 million or so people walking around with back problems, hunched over, posturally distorted, having some sort of defect in the spinal column, often taking the shape of a question mark. In their body language, they are speaking of the inability to tell themselves the truth, staying in indecision, in a state of an unanswerable question. Living in indecision is saying "no" to life.

When we do say yes or no, and act in truth, we find not only do we feel unburdened and a sense of relief at that moment but shifts begin to occur in relationships with others, because something uplifting happens when people hear the truth.

Practices to Reverse Doubt

Within the scope of logic, every "yes" can be opposed by a "no." There is practically nothing you can say for which some contrary notion cannot be found. So true is this point that the Austrian mathematician Kurt Gödel gained fame for his formulation, first in the field of mathematical logic, that every major premise of every logically based system contains the seed of its own destruction. Every yes gives rise to no, and vice versa. Thus, the seed of doubt is planted in the yes *and* no. (By the by, yes + no in the mind = no.)

Faith, on the other hand, is rooted in yes *or* no. Choosing one means sacrificing the other. It means detaching. Yes *and* no means attachment, an unwillingness to let go.

One exercise, derived from the gospels of Luke and Matthew, may be among the easiest and simplest spiritual practices I know. The gospels say, "Ask and you'll be answered." Whom do you ask? Appeal inwardly to your all-knowing higher Source of Wisdom. Remember we are made in the image and likeness of the All-Knowing One, thereby born with similar capacities. By analogy, as Above is all-knowing, so we are imbued with that quality. Ask reflectively, not predictively; that is, we don't want to be concerned with future outcomes. By this time we have come to understand we are not in "control" of the future. Leave it to the Omniscient One. Ask something like, "Am I well served by choosing [state the issue]?" Or "Is going in this direction concerning [state the issue] an appropriate strategy for me?" Any such framed self-reflective question will elicit an answer.

Another way of knowing is to close your eyes and breathe out slowly one time and imagine you are Adam or Eve in the Garden. Look around you and see and hear the serpent offering you the opportunity to usurp God's knowledge and power. Say "Nothing doing," turn your back on it, and walk away. As you do, an angel appears to you to tell you yes *or* no regarding the choice at hand.

A third way has to do with a Western practice of meditation. It concerns plunging into thought (this time the question of yes or no) rather than emptying the mental life of thought. This is how it works. Any thought has a beginning, a middle, and a conclusion. For example, "That sweater is red." That is knowledge. Now we *transform that piece of knowledge into more knowing*, such as, "What do I know about the color red?" This mental act opens the door to more investigation. This happens by *going from knowledge to knowing*. Knowledge is fixed; knowing is open, expanding, and deepening.

So, what do I know about choosing (selecting) or decision-taking (taking an action)? Your question doesn't revolve around what the general consensus is, rather, "What do *I myself know* about…?" When the answer is heard internally, a new thought comes, and the question is naturally evoked. Keep going deeper and deeper into the question, and an illuminating understanding and knowing can reveal itself.

The upshot of the inner search is to call upon oneself, to have faith in oneself, to trust oneself about the answers that come. If you don't, doubt will be intensified. However, once you experience self-trust, it builds upon itself. You build self-confidence; develop maturity, self-authority, and independence; and enrich your self-image, and your range of awareness is increased.

Grammar of Self: Reversing the Trap of Linear Time

What's the one course we had the least interest in learning in school? Grammar, of course. It seemed dull, boring, hard to understand, and seemingly unnecessarily complicated. Who knew then how this subject and its connection to the structure of language would be pivotal in helping us maintain the life process? The way we use and understand language and its grammar is reflected in every other dimension of our life process on which this book focuses. Some elements of this section have been covered previously. Here all is brought together to hone in on the specific practices associated with watching language.

The way we construct our conversations, what we verbalize, has reverberations. Just listen to what we and others say. You'll notice how minimally 95 percent of it is about the future or past; most of the other 5 percent contains criticisms or judgments about other people's behavior, way of life, or some other dissatisfaction. By now, you know these evaluations arise from setting standards for ourselves and others, self-authoring them as though they have validity and value. To recap, among these are: right-or-wrong, good-or-bad, normal-or-abnormal, success-or-failure, best-or-worst, on and on. When we reach them, if that ever happens, the usual response is one of immediate but temporary elation — somehow, reaching the pinnacles and goals we sought just didn't quite do it. The happiness we looked for didn't seem to materialize, or if it did, it didn't last as long as we might have liked. We feel envious of others and seek to find something "wrong" with them, hoping this critical judgment will bolster our self-worth. By now you recognize that these comparisons and judgments are violations of the Tenth Law of coveting.

All we need to know for now is that the trap of futurizing and pasturizing — and the associated distressing feelings — brings with it some reflected depletion: in our hormonal and immune systems, in troubling alterations in the vascular system such as hypertension, and in our neuro-muscular tension, creating pains all over the body. And all the while, our telomeres and chromosomes are deteriorating reflectively. What a price to pay just for projecting thoughts somewhere other than what may be called "now," "moment," "here," "instant."

Alicia, a young woman working with me on the grammar of the self, described to me after a month of watching and observing her thoughts and feelings how unburdened she felt. A weight was lifted from her by keeping her thoughts in check and refusing to wander away from the moment. She suddenly became aware that she wasn't feeling worried, a chronic feeling that had compelled her to cloud her judgment and take actions that were not in her interest. She realized and experienced that things naturally take care of themselves. She didn't have to worry about controlling the future — she knew there was a force "out there" who had command of that. She only needed to do her part, and the rest, "thank God," was not in her hands.

Reversing: Practices of Detachment

I was reminded by her experience of what John said in the gospel: "The wind [spirit] blows where it wills and you hear the sound [voice] of it. You do not know whence [from where] it comes, and whither [where] it goes: so it is with everyone who is born of the Spirit" (John 3:8). John put his finger squarely on it. We don't have to be concerned with the past "whence it comes" or the future "whither it goes." Our concern is this instant, right here with the facts in front of our nose. All we need is right here now. And so, Eckhart Tolle titled his best-selling book *The Power of Now*.

There are two other features of the grammar of self that Alicia alluded to and are well worth expanding: feelings and watching.

Feelings play an important role in this grammar. When we project into the future or past, we experience disturbing emotions (feelings) and uncomfortable bodily sensations. These feelings of anxiety, worry, fear, shame, guilt, depression, regret, hate, and legions of others are the fuel for the engine of illusory thought. These feelings form an illusory or mirage-like bridge between now and then (past) or now and yet to be (future), making it appear that these time traps are facts of now. But they are not facts. Then is not now, nor is that this. Yes, the emotion experienced is real, but the thought content to which it is linked is not true. Certainly not to "people born of the Spirit." On the other hand, harmonious feelings like joy, peace, love, contentment, and happiness are invariably connected to truth. These feelings are always of the moment and have the power of everlastingness to them. There is momentary joy and happiness connected to drug usage, for example. However, those states last only as long as the drug does. Likewise, distressing feelings come and go as well. Even if you are anxious or depressed, it will pass, although for some it feels as though it may never let up.

Watching is another thread in the tapestry of life-giving practices. We have already come across the audience as watcher in "The Theater of Life." In Hebrew, the word for watching is *shomer*, which means to watch, guard, keep. By watching, we are guardians or sentries of ourselves, keeping ourselves in check and preventing us from wandering or trespassing into linear time.

Watching is an act of will, a function of ectropy, catching the saboteurs who want to lure us into time. We stand as guardians of ourselves, careful of the obstacles and traps these terrorists set for us. We learn to watch and observe their activity, repelling their assaults and seductions.

How do we effectively watch? By paying attention to grammar. Every comment positioned in the future or past is a sign that the terrorists are at work. Every future or past story is a sign of their handiwork. Future conditional = should, would, could, must, ought to, have to, I will, going to...just some of the utterances making their way into ordinary conversation. Past conditional = should have, could have, ought to have, would have, had to...some locutions falling into the same category. For example, "have to" is a form of concentration with effort, focused in the future. We are bombarded by these humanly contrived standards all the time.

If-Then: This is perhaps the most destructive phrase in the language. We first met it in framing the emergency state and again in nocebos. *If* I do this, *then* this may happen. This conditional phrase is institutionalized in many physical sciences, particularly, in my experience, in medical research. Many studies are based on specious futurizing. Suppositions, speculations, assumptions, conclusionary thinking are all part of this type of thinking. Once you have "this is it" thinking, it closes the door on any further investigation. Thinking analogously or correlatively instead opens a door to continuous investigation, leading to more and more knowing and knowledge.

In our social life, if-then thinking reflects doubt: "If I do this, then that could happen." By now we are becoming aware of the paralyzing effects of doubt, inhibiting action in the moment that supports faith, trust, and confidence. The action of leaping into the moment of uncertainty is faith, not impetuously driven action to relieve tension or to serve some pleasure-driven urge. Act in the moment — including the act of choosing — without future conditions appended.

Colette was always a stickler for precision in language. During my long apprenticeship, her insistence to be precise came through even in her heavily French-accented English. Our use of imprecise language covers a vast area of unseen and unwitting destructive implications that permeate our lives. As you remember from grammar school, prepositions are words that precede a noun or pronoun to show the noun's (or the pronoun's) relationship to another word in the sentence. Let's look at two examples of prepositions to observe in our speech.

For/To: I'm thinking in particular of the word "responsibility" — a word that burdens most all of us. Often, I hear people say, "I'm responsible for so and so.... To which I reply, "Do you have a responsibility *for* or *to* someone?" It makes a heck of a difference. As a human being, I feel responsible *to* my fellow humans to teach what I have learned, especially in the realm of healing and Spirit. What they take away and use to further their lives is their responsibility. Sure, I am glad to clear up possible misconceptions they may have — that is my responsibility *to* them. But I don't have the responsibility *for* them to use or not what they have learned. That is their freedom. I am careful not to tread on their freedom of free will and choice. If I assume responsibility for another, I have crossed a line that may, and often does, violate the Tenth Spiritual Law of coveting: Don't claim and/or possess for yourself what doesn't belong to you. Instead, we are asked as selfless humans to encourage the freedom of others in the course of everyday life experience.

And/Or: This prepositional pair plays a featured role in the function of doubt and faith. "And" is the operative word that defines doubt. It is usually aroused when choices and actions are presented to us. The doubt response to these options brings "and" into the forefront of consciousness. There is this possibility *and* then again there is that possibility. I'm torn between the two, finding myself in indecision, creating scenarios about the two sides — answering both "yes" *and* "no" to the choice at hand. In all spiritual paths the principle is to choose — to turn the "yes *and* no" into "yes *or* no." When we do that, we take a definitive step into the next instant. We call this decisiveness "faith." Otherwise we remain stuck; movement becomes slow, often to the point of paralysis, and action is stalled. Again: yes *and* no, yes *or* no reflect the universal tension between doubt and faith, which lie at the base of the troubles besetting us in life.

Understanding this misleading grammar is emphatically worded to get the point across to wake us up. Futurizing and pasturizing carry within themselves the seeds of false beliefs, distressing emotions, and aberrant anatomical and physiological changes. Of course, much like the health warnings on the sides of cigarette packs, these admonitions may fall on "deaf eyes." Perhaps a softer voice will suffice: "Please remember to live by staying in the gravitational field of God and the alliance of love and life."

All that being said, be on guard against the untruths of future and past talk. "What about planning for the future?" is a commonly asked question. We don't wait for the future to dictate our present. That being the case, let's plan now, this moment, and let this moment birth the future, not the other way around.

Another practice is speaking — or at least thinking — in the present. "I go to the store" rather than "I will go to the store." It may seem limiting at first, but is an interesting exercise to engage in. It keeps you squarely in the moment and is the truth. With respect to how we fall into error, other ways grammar of self can be more or less subtle. They are nevertheless ubiquitous in our thinking. There are three constants of this sort: 1) suggestions, 2) expectations, and 3) comparisons. Though covered under the Errors of Living, I repeat them here again, for spiritual life is about remembering!

Reversing: Practices of Detachment

1) Suggestions are endless. They come from without or from within. They generally come unbidden, unsolicited. They are usually framed in the future tense. Advertising is a major medium for external suggestions. Doubt is a major medium for internal suggestions. In any event, we are 100 percent *subject* to them 100 percent of the time and are *open* to them nearly 100 percent of the time. This last percentage is worth noting: Being open to suggestion is tantamount to being open to hypnosis, for hypnosis is a matter of openness to suggestion. Such openness is to come under the will of another and to be led in this way. This means we are in a walking sleep, a somnambulistic state, zombie-like, coming under the sway of forces other than our own. Suggestions from without have an underlying motive of asserting power to control others, whether intentional or unintentional, and giving in to them puts us in a temporary or permanent captivity. The ones coming from within are even more powerful, as we need to struggle with what's within us day in and day out. Remember, the inner terrorists are constantly seeking control over us. We can't, and are not meant to, avoid them. We are meant to actively recognize them as deceitful intruders. You get to know them quite well, as they are always about time and essentially untrue. Just shake your head "no."

2) Expectations are a form of future talk. Most expectations go unmet, thwarted, frustrated, or otherwise not answered satisfactorily. When this happens, we feel momentarily daunted, disappointed, and hurt, and we begin to blame our self or others and feel distressing emotions. Within one to 72 hours, we experience a physical symptom and/or an addictive craving. This is the genesis of what can turn into a chronic condition. Awareness of this sequence gives us a hint at remedying the sit-

uation. It is a question of reversing the process mentally. Start from the symptom or craving and ask yourself what disturbing emotion is at play. Then, go to what or whom you are blaming. After that, go to the disappointment and hurt. And from there, right back to the expectation. Notice its future or past quality and comment to your inner source of wisdom that [*your name*] is creating a falsehood, an untruth, and that the distressing emotion(s) have no value. When you ask in this way, an answer from within promptly comes to you. Repeat as each suggestion appears. Take notice of how you feel and your physical state of being.

> **A note:** Hope is an expectation. This expectation is of a special sort and not to be confused with expectations as described above. An expectation of hope is the furtherance of life, the continuation of existence into the future. It is not of the same order as the general one of expectation concerned with personal wishes.

3) Comparison(s). Yes, I return to comparison yet again. Watch what comes out of your mouth. Every comparison reflects a belief that we are insufficient and require more, better, and different, that we need to be great and to control others.

Descriptors: We also start paying attention to the adjectival and adverbial descriptions that are quantitative in nature — great, important, significant, immense, very, and really are some examples. The list goes on and on. By using quantifiers, we distort the experience of the moment by adding our own interpretation, which heightens our emotional responses. For example, close your eyes for a moment and experience "I lost a *great* sum of money." How do you feel? Now breathe out once and experience "I lost money."

Some might contend that adjectives and adverbs enrich, define, and describe events more accurately. For me, the opposite is true. They take away from the richness of the experience of events. We lose the immediacy of the direct connection between us and experience. Instead we interject our own interpretation of the experience, which is to disconnect simply because our interpretation is a "distortion" of the moment. It contains a hidden standard, not merely a description. It falls into a connotation rather than a denotation. It is subtle, but as with all practices — experiment. Finally, we start paying attention to possessive pronouns (mine) and possessive determiners (my children, my house, my money, my illness, my troubles, etc.). It is a habit of attachment that we seek to replace with one of detachment.

Is it work in the mental gym to pay attention and become aware like this? You bet. Is it easy or hard to do? Neither, since easy and hard are quantitative descriptors. The work of spiritual longevity...do the work! It is what it is, nothing "more" or "less." Will I be a success or failure at this effort? Neither. No attachment to success or failure, merely attention to and awareness of the process brings you right back into "now."

So you see, the practice of the grammar of self covers the whole gamut of many errors of living:

- Comparing self to others
- Suggestions
- Expectations
- Conditional thinking — should, could, would, ought to
- Dual standards: Good/bad, success/failure, pretty/ugly, strong/weak, in group/out group

- Distressing emotions — rooted in time traps of the future and the past (e.g., anxiety, fear, worry, panic, anger, hate, depression, regret, guilt, shame)
- Descriptive quantifiers (adjectives and adverbs)
- Clarity of thought — if/then, and/or, for/to
- Possessives, pronouns, and determiners

Stopping Exercises: Visa to Freedom

Some of the simplest yet most profound practices for reversing our habits are stopping exercises. Here we place a wedge by an act of will between a stimulus and our response. By doing so, we create a space between the two so that something new can be created. This is analogous to the metaphysical act of creation where God makes a space through a holy act of detachment to permit a creation to enter that space. Reversing the attachment to habitual behaviors creates a new opportunity for change.

Our education and habituation train us to immerse ourselves in an experience where we experience frustration and pain, mental or physical; we want relief from it. Recall that the fundamental purpose of living is to get to a non-disturbed state by seeking pleasure and comfort while avoiding pain. Stopping reflexive activities and placing the will under conscious control is an act of healing. It is a necessary component to train intuition. As explained earlier, to develop intuition, we need to detach from unbalanced, instinctual behaviors, habitual thinking, and unbalanced feelings.

The principle in stopping is to alter momentarily the rhythm of a habitual activity or to delay a particular emotional pattern of reactivity that causes difficulty. Such stopping provides a micro shock to short-circuit the habitual pattern, and it stimulates the body's physiognomy to respond in a new way while waking you up mentally, emotionally, and spiritually. While simple to do, they can be profound with practice.

Reversing: Practices of Detachment

One practice consists of stopping a daily activity done repetitively: clicking on and off a light switch; opening or closing a door that has a doorknob; picking up a phone when it's ringing; stopping before placing a call or writing a text message, checking email, etc.

Set an intention for each stopping exercise. If you wish to stop smoking, you would hesitate for an instant and recall your intention — by saying "no smoking" and/or seeing yourself throw away the cigarette — before you remove the match from the box, or before you strike the match, or as you place the match at the end of the cigarette. The stopping action lasts for only an instant. Whether you complete the action or not is up to you.

In making a telephone call, as you bring your finger to the touchpad, stop this action for just an instant. In that instant, say the intention of the exercise or see an image reflecting your intention. For example, "patience" might be your intention. As you stop for an instant before hitting the touchpad, say "patience" to yourself. You may finish the act of making the call or decide not to. It doesn't matter, as long as the stopping has taken place. With eating, you make a stop as you bring the fork or spoon to your mouth. Whatever follows, accept without judgment.

Certain conditions help the process along: Choose *only one* function to work on at a time. For example, in choosing the light switch, work only on that one for a period of 21 days. Twenty-one days is the time frame for all stopping exercises. Tell yourself on Day One that you are doing the stopping exercise to develop [*you name it*]. This exercise can be used for any condition you choose: physical, addictions, emotions, character traits, anything you wish.

You may like to keep a record of your progress on the Stopping Exercise, jotting down a sentence or two and recording the date. After 21 days, rest for 7 days and then you can turn to a new reversing exercise for another 21 days. And it can go on as far as you want to go.

We Are Not *Meant* to Die

Each action of stopping creates many positive effects: new neural networks develop — a rewiring of the brain — and there is increased vascularization of the heart and changes in physiological functioning throughout the system. We can liken stopping activity to the changes that take place when we go to the physical gym for a workout. In the GEMS unitary system, what is happening in one area — mental — is concomitantly happening physically. At the same time, will is strengthened and awareness is expanded.

Stop and Go: Visa to Freedom

Our last stopping practice is a combined exercise of image and will embodied in two geometric forms: a green circle bearing the words "Go and Do" and a red octagon bearing the word "Stop."

The Talmud advises us to act in the world, and then knowing and understanding will follow. You simply can't figure life out; you must live it. Follow your impulse of faith to go and do. You have a green light to do so. In fact, we are encouraged actively to do so. But you may ask: "What happens about acting impulsively? Isn't there a danger inherent in just doing it? The answer lies in the word "impulsively." There are actually two sorts of impulses at play here: One is the habitual where we act or "act out" an impulse following an urge or overwhelming desire; the other follows the Talmudic injunction cited above. The first is often a compulsive act based on a desire for power (control) or pleasure, to acquire something tangible or gain a competitive advantage. The second impulse does not necessitate acquiring something tangible — no goal or material compensation is required. It is a spiritual impulse, not impulsively driven, but rather rooted in faith. Faith requires no reward in the material sense. It can have a direct relationship to aims

Reversing: Practices of Detachment

(not goals) that are not physically substantive.

Before describing this simple, powerful practice, let's explore the significance of the words and colors. Red and green meet us every day in traffic lights telling us to stop or go/do (cross). No hesitation, doubt, or skepticism here. Neither do we go with blind faith; as the old Sufi (Islamic mystic) put it simply: "Believe in Allah but tie up your camel." Even Nachson, at the Red Sea, didn't rush headlong into the turbulent waters. He reflected on his intention toward freedom and then acted. In the same moment that we have faith in God we have faith and trust in ourselves.

Stop! The red octagon reminds us to stop when the reward-based impulses arise. *Wait a moment!* There, a mental wedge is put between the stimulus and response. The moment of stopping deactivates the impulse. With consistent practice, it can reverse impulsivity.

Red is the color of stopping in everyday life, witnessed by red stop signs and traffic lights everywhere in the habitable world. Red is connected to fire, a natural stop sign. Red, then, means essentially "Do not enter" or "Danger!" Red has the shortest wavelength of all colors. As such, it gets to us more quickly than any other color, which may account for its use in stop signs and red lights. By looking at the red we are able to remember to stop errors of living and the suffering they bring.

Go, do! The green circle reminds us to take action to overcome doubt and inertia. There are a number of other meanings to this pure green color. Most significantly it's a symbol in spiritual lore of the cessation of time. Linear time stops! This green is the center of everything in spiritual terms. It is the predominant color covering the surface of the Earth. It is the primary color of nature. Nature is God's creation, exemplified by the six days described

in Genesis. God's hand is in nature! Green, too, is the center color of the rainbow. It is the fourth color of seven, situated between yellow and blue. The first three (red, orange, yellow) reflect the day colors, the latter three (blue, indigo, violet) the night. On the first day of creation, day was separated from night, the intermediaries being twilight on one side and dawning on the other. When yellow and blue are mixed, green is created. It is, analogously, stationed between day and night. Interestingly, these intermediate times are those connected with prayer, meditation, and imagery practices throughout the world. In Islamic mysticism, green is the color of illumination, the culmination of reaching the Seventh Heaven of the hierarchy of spiritual becoming. As we merge with green, we merge into no-time, becoming one with the hidden One.

Our new motto: REMEMBER, GO, DO! We look at the green card as a call to remember: Go, do! In that moment of freedom, students reported time stopping, feelings of liberation, unity of self, unity of body and soul, oneness with the One, and becoming one with the beauty of nature.

All errors of thinking, feeling, and behaving are subject to corrections by reversing them. The process is activated by will, using one word to do so: STOP!

This game of life is called Red Light/Green Light: STOP! & GO!

Then we move toward freedom, becoming beings of light, moving unerringly to unending life.

How to Use Red and Green Cards

Create a red and green card or download them from www.aimi.us. Type or glue the undersides of the two cards together, then laminate this piece to give it stability. At first, carry the card with you during the day.

By use of will: When you experience distress of any sort, or an unwanted error, take the card out, look at the red Stop sign, then "Stop": Gather yourself by breathing a long, slow exhalation, and reverse the card to the green "Go, Do!" side. The next step will reveal itself to you.

You can practice this technique imaginally as well, without using the physical prompt of the card. Eventually, if you start with the physical prompt, you will internalize it to an imaginal practice.

By the way, if you don't catch yourself in the moment of error and you remember subsequently that you forgot, do the exercise imaginally.

Here, new knowing, new feeling, new behavior, and new view of life may be happening. If so, keep it for yourself! In the green, the world of God and the world of nature become One as you become One. We are led from there to biological longevity, soul immortality, and spiritual eternal life — the true holy trinity of Life!

Gratuitousness: Emulating God

Spiritual practice asks us to pay attention to acting gratuitously, as well as the need to be grateful for the blessings in our lives of every sort, be they pleasurable or painful. In the latter instance, what we experience as a curse or tragedy has a pearl embedded deep within it given to us by Invisible Reality. Gratitude is our mental thanks to God for both; gratuitousness is the physical act of thanks. It is a supreme act of faith and disengagement from attachment.

Gratuitousness is a practice of emulating God. This knowing, understanding, and wisdom was passed on to me through the teaching of Friedrich Weinreb[60] (a relatively unrecognized genius and spiritual sage). The motivation for such a practice comes from the comment in the Book of Genesis 1:26 where it states that we are made in the image of God. Being the case, we are sent to this planet as an attaché

---

[60] Prof. Friedrich Weinreb. *Chance, the Hidden Lord: The Amazing Scroll of Esther* (Devon, England: Maslands, Ltd., 1986).

to represent God's plan (so it was for the patriarchs, matriarchs, and prophets of the ancient days of yore). Each of us is born with this potential to prophesy, meaning to bring this way to oneself and share it with others. Gratuitousness is one such act of emulating God. To say it simply, it is the ongoing practice to give without having to get. There are so many day-to-day opportunities to do so: giving alms to a beggar; buying food for someone in need; holding the elevator door open; helping someone across the street; helping someone burdened with packages, giving donations anonymously, etc.

As you practice, you may see that the canopy of gratuitousness envelops unconditional love, hope (where we seek to perpetuate life), and will. The Light Currents of Will open our thought processes to the freedom of thinking intuitively and thinking in the no-time zone called imagination. In sum: Gratuitousness is a practice of truth, since combining all the properties enumerated above leads one to TRUTH, which is given us by God.

CHAPTER XIII

Health-Care Reform — Health-Care Reformers

*"There are more things in heaven and earth,
Horatio, than are dreamt of in your philosophy"*
—HAMLET 1:5

NOW THAT THE PIECES ARE IN PLACE and healing, health, wholeness, and holiness are becoming restored, real health-care reform can be envisioned. By re-forming, we take the first step toward becoming a personal health-care reformer. Reform means to form ourselves anew, to come back to the correctness of being made in the image (form) and likeness (virtue) of God, the form that has always been intended for us to become.

GEMS is the model for re-forming ourselves. Without taking the reins of our own well-being, we are always left to depend on outer authorities to whom we give away our power. The spiritual, holy beings we truly are means that we cannot lower ourselves to bow before *any* other human, no matter what position that person may hold.

As we are coming to learn, holiness cannot be separated from health. In other words, reform means to take shape once again, oppose loss of shape (death), move life onward. Come into order, help others to come into order. Become a participant in health-care reform and become a health-care reformer for yourself and others.

There is no true health-care reform without Spirit, sacredness, and holiness. All of the messengers of hope and healing have come from the direction of Spirit, the sacred and holy. Without Spirit in our lives, there is no proper health care.

A friend suffered an apparent heart seizure. He was rushed to the hospital, where the MDs attending him saw his laboratory reports and surmised that he was good as dead. Given the myriad number of emergency room patients requiring attention in the very early-morning hours, they rationalized they couldn't advocate spending energy trying to save him. Suddenly, for reasons they could not reckon, they decided to give it a try. After working feverishly on him, he came to; he came back to life. He said that in his nonconscious state he was aware of saying to God, "If it's my time to go, please take me. If I'm meant to live, please give that to me." Meanwhile, a group of people, a loose affiliation of friends who were notified of what had befallen him, spent hours praying for him as the doctors in the ER were attending to him.

Did their prayers have a role to play? No question about it, in my mind. Did it affect his conversation with God? I think so.

I mentioned the effects of prayer on healing when I wrote earlier about Drs. Jeffrey Levin and Larry Dossey as well as the experiment at San Francisco General Hospital with the Rosicrucians.

Timothy, a middle-aged man, received a heart transplant. Post-operatively he developed an infection in his leg from a skin graft used in the operation. He was operated on then to clean out the infection. In the course of this procedure, a nerve in his leg was severed. He developed atrophy of the muscles in that lower extremity as a consequence of the dead nerve. Electromyographical (EMG) studies verified these findings. He was scheduled for amputation of the leg. My student Beth Defuria asked me for an imagery exercise for him. I gave her one I devised to repair the nerve. She went to the hospital on Easter Sunday and did the exercise with him. His nerves were innervated with energy. In addition, he created his own exercise entitled "From Soul to Sole," alluding to the link between his heart and the soles of his feet, sending life force to his leg. He took on the imagery treatment and grafted his own discovered additional imagery onto it. Within a week, his nerve and muscles had healed, registered physically by his electromyographic response, and he walked out of the hospital under his own steam at the end of that week.

The amazed and astounded doctors "took him off the table" for amputation.[61] Shortly thereafter, the hospital celebrated a gala honoring this man's miraculous cure. Fifteen hundred people attended the black-tie affair.

Another example: Jacob came from a long distance to see Colette. He brought his quadriplegic son, Noah, who was wheelchair-bound. Jacob was a medical doctor. Noah was a young man in his 20s who, with his father, had visited as many as 11 doctors over the eight years of his paralysis, wanting to find a cure for him. Jacob heard about Colette and sought her out as a last resort when nothing else had worked.

They came into her garden onto her small patio. Noah sat diagonally across from her. She spoke with him for about 30 minutes and turned to Jacob and asked him to return with Noah the next morning. They returned, and again Noah sat diagonally across from Colette in his wheelchair. She looked directly into his expectant and yet frightened eyes, tinged with sadness, and said to him in a strong, firm, commanding voice without a jot of faltering, "Get out of that chair and come to me." At that moment Noah arose from the wheelchair and walked directly to her, free of the paralysis. Jacob never returned or

---

[61] Gerald Epstein, interview by Penny Price, *The Healing Field: Exploring Energy & Consciousness*, DVD (Beyond Words Publishing, 2017).

contacted Colette again. The earthquake of this healing overturned in one instant Jacob's conventional medical worldview, where he'd been holding on to fixed beliefs of what could be possible only through the interventions of modern medicine. That, I reasoned, was why Jacob could not face this possibility and its implications for his cherished beliefs in the power of modern medicine.

For GEMS, anything is possible. The "imaginable" can become possible. Understanding the relationship of the five dimensions of wholeness as well as including mental imagery (as done in conventional medical treatment of cancer in Brazil), the role of placebo and the social errors of living open new possibilities of healing beyond the current materialistic model of medicine. Likewise, we can no longer write off nonconventional healings to "coincidence" or trivialize as "anecdotal" evidence.

A young woman who'd had cancer of the ovaries 11 years earlier appeared as a guest on *Geraldo,* a national TV show, on the same episode as I. At this point she was active, productive, and leading a full and rich life. She noted to the host that her abdomen was riddled with tumors but that there was no evidence of active cancer. When asked what she did to regain her health, she spoke of doing imagery, practicing yoga, eating a balanced diet, lovingly [my sense] raising a family, and conducting her career as a schoolteacher. She added that she went once a year to her physician for an evaluation of her physical condition. She said the condition remained stable with her body riddled with tumors. The host, eyes open quite wide by this time, seemingly discombobulated, exclaimed, "But the cancer is still there!"

At this juncture she took the opportunity to say she had a message for everyone in the audience and out there in TV land — that she was healed emotionally and spiritually; *that the presence or absence of the physical doesn't define healing!* Further, she was certain the physical condition she once suffered would never kill her. Her annual visit to the doctor was to establish whether any changes were taking place that she might need to take care of.

Note that from our point of view, she did not accept the standard medical nocebo belief declared as conclusionary thoughts that "the disease would eventually kill her" or "cancer kills *if* not eradicated to the last cell" or "cancer will keep spreading unabated unless radically treated."

Three years later, I was invited to be a presenter at an "alternative healing" conference. Standing in a hallway at the conference center talking to a group of colleagues, I was tapped on the shoulder. I turned around, and there stood the young woman. She said hello. She had been invited there as a presenter as well. She remembered me from the TV show. I was glad, excited to see her, to see how she was. Her answer: "Fourteen years." She went on to say she was in great shape. Her abdomen was still riddled with tumors, she was still seeing her MD once a year, and life was wonderful.

With the endless aid and support of the Universe, we are destined to become our own health-care providers and reformers. Our role in fulfilling that destiny is to educate ourselves as to what and how to heal and then teach others what we have learned. If we are unable to create such healing, or at least cure on our own, we always have the fallback of calling on external resources, be they conventional or natural medicine ones. There is value in undergoing some medical procedures, such as surgery, or using technical instruments to revive us or keep the heart beating in acute situations. But wariness is necessary when modern medicine seeks to co-opt the entire field of healthcare and make itself and its practitioners into arbiters of what is normal and proper for our health care (there's no overarching model of normal or health in modern medicine).

My premise here is that you are the final arbiter of what's normal and healthy for you. No one can know more about you than you can know about you. There is no human authority who can claim such hegemony. To allow that to be the case is to become a slave. Health care is about becoming liberated and free, and preserving such freedom. Many "incurables" who have passed through my doors and those of other healers I know have been brought back to life from the consignment heap of "incurable." When and if you hear that word laid on you, use it as the occasion to become a fighter for your life, a health-care reformer. Bless the person who said it to you because he or she unwittingly gave you the motivation to live. By the way, "incurable" is a fixed mental image, a conclusion, violating the 2nd Commandment about making mental graven images.

The story of the prophet Daniel clearly depicts what we can become when following the 2nd Commandment of not bowing to an outside authority. He stayed true to the Alliance, having faith in himself and in Invisible Reality that enabled him to overcome death. Neither the destructive fire of a furnace nor a den of lions — the most powerful predators — could destroy this remarkable life force.

All the men and women who have made a difference in the recorded history of the world and whose names have lived on throughout the ages have really been reformers. As communities, societies, republics, and even civilizations eventually break down and entropy sets in, along come "elected" beings who have been chosen to serve the human race by igniting the spark of re-formation to reverse entropy and deliver a wake-up call with universal significance. These messages have a therapeutic element in common: "Become your own re-former, and here's how you can do it." A number of us pay heed to the call, remember, and awaken; others pay attention and act with prudence, temperance, and sobriety for themselves while sharing the message with others.

The movement toward holiness is at the base of these communications, no matter where they originate.

Health-Care Reform — Health-Care Reformers

This sacred model of health and healing begins with the motto "Go to yourself" (Genesis 12:1). Start with what's been given to you as part of your birthright. There is always something that can be done for oneself, by oneself. Now that the life-extension era is dawning, we have more time given to us to work on ourselves and to become self-practitioners of LIFE — <u>L</u>ongevity <u>I</u>mmortality <u>F</u>reedom <u>E</u>ctropy — and by doing so serve the Alliance, which God/Consciousness has wanted us to do all along. This gift has not been given us to waste! It hasn't been given to us by chance — as a random, haphazard event. It's been given to us so we can become the loving and morally lawful beings God intended for us to become here on Earth.

We Are Not *Meant* to Die

SECTION IV

Future Vision: From Here to Eternity

We Are Not *Meant* to Die

"The way to transcend Life over death is both an individual and communal affair. It is something to be accomplished on both levels and is the possibility, nay, mission of the whole of humanity."

CHAPTER XIV

Becoming an Imaginaut: Imagery for Discovering Eternal Life

"Thy dead shall live; my dead bodies shall arise — Awake and sing, ye that dwell in the dust — for Thy dew is as the dew of light, and the earth shall bring to life the shades."
—Isaiah 26:18, JPS

PRACTICING GEMS, EXTENDING OUR LIVES and readying ourselves for deepening our engagement with spiritual reality, we are becoming practitioners of LIFE: Longevity, Immortality, Freedom, and Ectropy. Here follows a program of imagery exercises to advance this purpose.

Imagery is the language of LIFE, keeping us refreshed, rejuvenated, reinvigorated, and resilient. As a holy language, imagery holds the power to affect and effect healing on many levels of life: physical, emotional, mental, social. It also is a way toward spiritual union with our Source. Like outer space with its planetary orbs and interstellar phenomena, this intra-stellar space is a universe of inner galactic reality readily available for inner exploration.

We have to become the imaginaut (my term), our own Captain Kirk and Mr. Spock going where others have never gone before. Of course, we can find the first written description of this inner journey by reading the first 28 lines of the book of Ezekiel in the Bible (Ezek. 1:1–28).

This powerful tool of imagery and imagination is inborn in us and is activated by a mere flip of the will switch, as we close our eyes to turn our senses inward, with the intention of making discoveries by going where we had not dared to before.

Four Levels of Imagery

In keeping with the theme of *We Are Not Meant to Die,* I've included here special imagery exercises reflecting the spiritual movement from everyday life experience to eternal life. Do these exercises in order. Each day a new exercise is done twice a day, each morning upon awakening and in the evening toward sunset. These exercises are divided into four groupings:

    1) Preparation
    2) Ascension
    3) Resurrection
    4) Eternal Life

List of Imagery Exercises with Attribution

Preparatory Exercises

    The Guest House (GE, adapted from Rumi, trans. Coleman Barks)
    The Color of Your Life (Sara Esterabadeyan)
    Tree of Life – I (GE)
    Tree of Life – II (Colette)
    Tree of Life – III (Colette)
    Return to the Alliance
    Putting Self Together (Colette)

Becoming an Imaginaut: Imagery for Discovering Eternal Life

Becoming a Technician of the Sacred (Susanne Greason, based on John Blofeld, Colette, and Valentin Tomberg)
Burying the Past (Colette)
Untying Knots of Life (Colette)
Agony and the Ecstasy (Colette)
Life and Light (*Encyclopedia of Mental Imagery*)
The Weaver: The Power of Life (Colette)
Light Illuminating Your Road (Colette)
The Foam and the Sea (*Encyclopedia of Mental Imagery*)
Moderation (Colette)
Repentance: Reversing Errors of the Past (*Encyclopedia of Mental Imagery*)
Cleansing Your Soul: The Light-Bearing Soul (*Encyclopedia of Mental Imagery*)

Ascension Exercises
Rainbow Staircase (Sara Esterabadeyan)
Ascending to Your Higher Form of Wisdom (GE, after Henri Corbin)
Ascending Seven Steps of the Heart (GE, after Henri Corbin)
Light of God (GE, after Henri Corbin)
Suprasensory Reality (GE, after Henri Corbin)
The Train of Life (GE)
Returning to the Source (Daniel Singer)
Celebrating the Beloved (Daniel Singer, adapted from the Sabbath prayer L'cha Dodi)
Piloting Your Ship of No Time (GE)
Descent into the Self: The Bottomless Abyss (Colette, after Teilhard de Chardin)
Power of Light (GE, after Henri Corbin)
Prophetic Imagination: The Great Chain of Being (GE)

The Origin of Creation (GE)
The Black Light of Holiness: Die before You Die (GE, after Henri Corbin)
The Gift from God (Colette)
Illumination: Flight of One to the One (GE, after Plotinus)

Resurrection Exercises
Seventh Cervical Vertebrae (Colette/GE)
Round Mirror (GE, adapted from Colette)
Resurrective Process: The Turning Point from Death to Life (GE)
The Blossoming Heart (Sara Esterabadeyan)
From Seed to Tree (Colette)
Overcoming Death (Colette)
Defeating Death (Colette, after Gabriel García Márquez)
Isis and Osiris (GE)
Life Overcoming Death (Phyllis Kahaney)
Re-Birth: A Second Chance (GE)
Trumpet of Resurrection (GE)

Eternal Life Exercises
From Past to Eternity: Finding the Moment (Colette)
Your House of Being (GE, after Guru Nanak)
No Separation (GE, after Colette)
Unbounded (GE after Colette)
Eternity (Colette, after Giordano Bruno)
Anti-Aging (Colette)
Long Life (GE, adapted from the Bible)
Becoming the Wavicle (Dr. Peter Goertz)
Angel of Eternal Life: To Repair the Telomeres (GE)
The Pineal Gland: The Flow of Energy for Living Harmoniously Within Yourself (GE)

Becoming an Imaginaut: Imagery for Discovering Eternal Life

Time Flies/Flying from Time (GE/Colette)
Midnight Sun (GE)
Eternal Life: Drinking the Cup of Heaven (GE)
Bliss (GE)

PREPARATORY EXERCISES

THE GUEST HOUSE

Close your eyes and breathe out and in three times slowly. Know and experience that this being human is a guest house. Every morning a new arrival.

Breathe out one time — a joy.

Breathe out one time — a depression.

Breathe out one time — a meanness.

Breathe out one time — some momentary awareness comes as an unexpected visitor.

Breathe out one time. See yourself welcoming and entertaining them all, even if they're a crowd of sorrows who violently sweep your house empty of its furniture. Still, treat these guests honorably. They may be clearing you out for some new delight.

Breathe out one time. Imagine the dark thought, the shame, the malice. See and meet them at the door laughing and invite them in. Be grateful for whoever comes. Know each has been sent as a guide from beyond. Breathe out and open your eyes.

THE COLOR OF YOUR LIFE

Close your eyes and breathe out and in three times slowly, counting back from three to one, each out breath being a new number.

Sense and see each number, feeling the number 1 as bright and tall. Step inside the 1, acknowledging you are at one with yourself. See and feel the flow of life within you and around you. Sense and see what you need to draw harmony and well-being into your life coming to you as colors from above.

Capture these divine qualities and notice the color that attracts you the most. Allow it to fill you up and let it reveal the attribute it stands for. Know that this particular quality is guiding you through the lessons and challenges of the day.

Breathe out and in three times slowly, making the exhalations long and slow. See and feel your right hand elongating, becoming luminous and translucent. With your hand of light, reach out for the Heights and capture the image, color, or quality that is most important to you now. Bring it into your personal sphere and let it envelop you in its brilliance. Realize how self-awareness enables you to be new forever. Breathe out and open your eyes.

TREE OF LIFE – I

Close your eyes and breathe out and in three times slowly. Imagine yourself in a beautiful garden that appears paradisiacal. There you see the Tree of Life, the tree that *is* fruit, and the Tree of Death, the tree that makes and bears fruit.[62]

Breathe out. At first, become the tree that makes and bears fruit. What is your experience?

Breathe out. Now become the tree that together *is* fruit, makes and bears fruit, and is complete in itself. See, feel, and experience together yourself as the perfection of the Perfection.

---

[62] Tree of life is the tree of unity. Tree of death is the tree of multiplicity, productivity, and profitability.

Breathe out. As this perfection, see, feel, sense, and know that nothing need be added to you, nor subtracted from you, nor can it be so that others can add to or subtract from you. Breathe out and open your eyes.

TREE OF LIFE – II

Close your eyes and breathe out and in three times slowly. See your Tree of Life. See the expanding roots.

Breathe out. Sense whether the trunk is strong. If it is not, make it strong. Make the trunk even.

Breathe out. See the tree full of faces, some familiar, some not. Ask the most knowing face a *precise* and important question and hear the answer. Breathe out and open your eyes.

TREE OF LIFE – III

Close your eyes and breathe out and in four times slowly. See yourself as a tree becoming a synthesis of earth, water, air, and light.

Breathe out. See yourself as the tree, as a dynamic life.

Breathe out. See and experience yourself as a tree growing roots into the center of the Earth, making contact with the inside water.

Breathe out. Feel, sense, and experience the water coming through your feet and into your body, cleansing each part, each organ.

Breathe out. See yourself now as the tree growing concentric circles around your calves, knees, pelvis, abdominal organs, neck, eyes, ears, feeling unified and renewed, happy about living the moment, catching the instant, having hope for the future. Breathe out and open your eyes.

RETURN TO THE ALLIANCE

Close your eyes and breathe out and in three times slowly. Be in front of a large golden door with the word *Alliance* in rainbow-colored letters in a rainbow shape on the door. Knock on it using the golden knocker. The door opens for you. There you find the guardian of the door. Ask if you are permitted to enter. He grants you entrance. When entering, the door closes behind you. Once inside, find yourself surrounded by golden light.

Breathe out. Physically sense yourself becoming very tall. Large arms and hands come from above and lift you up to become 100 times taller than you are, while your feet remain firmly planted on the ground. Physically sense and feel this new return and acceptance to the Alliance, knowing you are back in the hands of God. Now, physically sense and feel yourself returning to your usual size, firmly connected to your Source, being grateful for this acceptance. Breathe out and open your eyes.

PUTTING SELF TOGETHER

Close your eyes and breathe out and in three times slowly. See yourself in a mirror holding a tape measure in your left hand and scissors in your right hand. Cut the tape measure into 16 pieces, then burn the pieces and dispose of the ashes by burying them.

Breathe out. Into the mirror see, know, and experience the pleasures, joys, and challenges that make up a lived day.

Breathe out. See, feel, and live the scope of your possibilities — actions past and present, those that have been and are to be.

Breathe out. Live all these potentials as one. Breathe out and open your eyes.

BECOMING A TECHNICIAN OF THE SACRED

Close your eyes and breathe out and in three times slowly. See and know how you the sage carry on your business without action and give your teaching without words.

Breathe out. See and physically sense yourself in your everyday life focusing on the need to love, not to be loved.

Breathe out. See and know how knowing your faults and limitations is the means to faultlessness.

Breathe out. See yourself standing in a circle with your faults. Name them. Now, hose them down to the left, out of the circle.

Breathe out. See yourself standing now in the circle, bathed in shimmering light. Know how you feel and what you understand.

Breathe out. See and know how fortune and blessings gather where there is stillness. Be in that stillness. What happens?

Breathe out. See yourself in that stillness, listening with all your heart. What is your experience?

Breathe out and listen with your eyes. See the likeness of the speaking silence. What is the silence telling you? Know who this "you" is and to whom the speaking silence speaks.

Breathe out. See and sense your entire being becoming like the surface of calm water, reflecting the immense presence of a starry sky — knowing you are one with its indescribable harmony.

Breathe out. See, sense, and know how as you are in the center of God, God is in the center of you.

Breathe out. Recognize how as God is in the center of everywhere and everything, so everywhere and everything is in the center of God. Breathe out and open your eyes.

BURYING THE PAST

Close your eyes and breathe out and in three times slowly. You are walking along a country path. The road is cluttered with rocks that you clear to make a path, at the end of which you find a tree.

Breathe out. Sit by the tree and pick up a leaf from the ground. Having with you a stylus, use the sap on the leaf to write what has been significant and has pained you from your past, the regret, and the obstacles from that past that inhibit you from going forward. Then, have a small shovel or spade and dig a hole in the ground nearby.

Breathe out. Indicate on the leaf when you want the past to disintegrate by putting a date on the leaf. Place it in the hole and bury it with dirt; and though the personal past is still alive, it does eventually disintegrate.

Breathe out. Come quickly back to where you started from, seeing if there is anything different on the path of your return. Breathe out and open your eyes.

UNTYING THE KNOTS OF LIFE: CREATING ORDER FROM DISORDER

Close your eyes and breathe out and in three times slowly. Imagine a table in front of you on which there is a piece of rope that is very thick and has three knots in it. Imagine you are looking at each of the knots carefully to understand how they were made. They are complicated, like sailors' knots. Once you understand how one is tied, you start undoing it until you succeed and it becomes a part of the rope, perfectly straight and smooth.

Breathe out. Then look at the second knot carefully to see how it is tied. And, when you understand, start undoing it slowly. Be sure not to touch the third knot or damage the rope.

Breathe out. Check out how the third knot is tied. Undo it slowly so as not to damage anything.

Breathe out. When you finish, smooth out the rope, take it in your hands, and stretch it. When it is nice and tight, put it back on the table. Look at it, happy and satisfied to have created order from disorder. Breathe out and open your eyes.

AGONY AND THE ECSTASY

Close your eyes and breathe out and in three times slowly. Live and know what is life and death.

Breathe out. Having known and lived life and death, cast out anger, guilt, anxiety, shame, disease, and old age. Burn them, and then burn again any remaining ashes. How do you feel? After, live and know that you can do anything. Breathe out and open your eyes.

LIFE AND LIGHT

Close your eyes and breathe out and in three times slowly. See, sense, and feel yourself becoming moderate and obtaining balance in your dimensions of living. See yourself setting aside a half-minute, twice a day, for quieting imagery.

Breathe out. See yourself facing your stressful life changes with aplomb, without a feeling of "emergency."

Breathe out. See, sense, and feel that you are now able to accept your physical and emotional limitations.

Breathe out. See that you can break the spiral of distress by balancing work and play.

Breathe out. See how being less serious can break the stress-to-distress cycle.

Breathe out. See how you have fun when you are lighthearted.

Breathe out. See yourself changing perspective when an intense or painful scene is happening.

Breathe out. Know that you can use imagery as a healthy outlet — imagine walking, gardening, drinking a glass of water slowly, or washing your hands slowly — to deal with stressful situations.

Breathe out. See yourself smiling a true smile. Relax and sense the muscles of a true smile.

Breathe out and in three times slowly. Sense, feel, and know that life is your first teacher and your medium for self-expression by means of change and growth.

Breathe out. Live and know how seriousness is making you heavy, whereas your inner images make you light and alive. Breathe out and open your eyes.

THE WEAVER: THE POWER OF LIFE

Close your eyes and breathe out and in three times with long, slow exhalations: See and know your hands are sky and earth. With these hands you are able to weave the patterns of your life with the threads you choose. See and recognize the working out of the pattern that your weaving has started, and in doing so you are finding your own way for whatever you choose. Breathe out and open your eyes.

LIGHT ILLUMINATING YOUR ROAD

Close your eyes and breathe out and in three times slowly. See, know, and experience now, in the instant of creation, how obscurity is also clarity.

Breathe out. Live and feel how our function and duty is to heed these words of light: "Let Your words be the lamp that is clearing my steps, a light that radiates on my road."

Breathe out. Imagine that you say to a man who stands at the Gate of the New Year: "Give me a light that I may enter safely into the unknown," and he replied, "Go out into the darkness, and put your hand into the hand of God. That shall be to you better than a light, and safer than a known way."

Breathe out. Hear and see the injunction from the prophet Isaiah: "Get up straight into the light. The Light of God is surrounding you." "Its Eternal glory is here."[63]

Breathe out and open your eyes.

THE FOAM AND THE SEA

Close your eyes and breathe out and in three times slowly. See the sea becoming very calm and flat. See then the foam arises, sparkling with reflected light of the sun. Entering the water, swim to the horizon, to the place between the sky and the water. See, sense, feel, and experience what happens to you between sky and water as they

---

[63] From the sage Judah Halevy.

enter you from above and below simultaneously. After, swim back to the shore using the backstroke.

Breathe out. Now on the beach, kneel down and take a handful of sand and let it sift through your fingers until one grain is left in your palm. Look at it until it changes into something new. Breathe out and open your eyes.

MODERATION

Close your eyes and breathe out and in three times slowly. See, sense, and know that the remedy for the excesses for an individual and collective actions in modern life is brought to us through moderation. Breathe out. Know that to be moderate is to be in the middle, to be balanced and sober.

Breathe out. See, feel, and know that the *model* for moderation begins with your ability to *modify* your behavioral characteristics. See yourself doing that for a characteristic that needs *modification*.

Breathe out. What is your behavior now? What does it look like? What are the feelings?

Breathe out. Know that *modesty* is a virtue. How is modesty a virtue for you? Breathe out. See how modesty creates a balance for your life.

Breathe out. See, sense, and feel what is *moderate* for you. Breathe out. See, sense, and feel how being moderate brings for you your own inner medicine that makes you healthy and whole.

Breathe out. Be the moderator of your life. What message does this inner moderator have for you? Breathe out and open your eyes.

REPENTANCE: REVERSING ERRORS OF THE PAST

Close your eyes and breathe out and in three times slowly. See yourself traveling on the back of a dragon. See yourself flying through all the stages of human development by flying from the inside of the Earth to the highest mountain and from cloud to cloud above the seven skies and then return.

Breathe out and in three times slowly. See and sense the Archangel Raphael standing behind you.

Breathe out. Starting from now, see yourself reviewing your life back to earliest childhood, recollecting *significant* painful memories, especially recognizing the pain you have caused others and yourself.

Breathe out. Going forward from childhood to now, repair the damage. Repair the damage you have done to others. See yourself asking for forgiveness from those you have offended, humiliated, or abused.

Breathe out. Discover the shame and/or guilt that brings you feelings of regret. Know how by keeping them alive, you allow them to take too much space in you.

Breathe out. Repent the damage done in the past, beginning now and going back to your conception.

Breathe out. Repent honestly with your heart.

Breathe out. Sense the new well-being filling you when repenting as you return from the time of conception to now, coming back cleansed.

Breathe out and in three times slowly. Feel you are no longer blaming others or yourself. Breathe out. See a river flowing through you and cleansing you. Breathe out and open your eyes.

CLEANSING YOUR SOUL: THE LIGHT-BEARING SOUL

Close your eyes and breathe out and in three times slowly. Imagine a lake in the sky. See that it is a lake of tears.

Breathe out. A drop of water falls from a cloud above it onto the lake of tears and becomes part of this lake in the sky; this added drop becomes a tipping point stirring up pain within you.

Breathe out. Imagine that pain or difficulty ejecting from you as a flaming ball falling into the lake of tears.

Breathe out. See and know what the flaming ball becomes when it falls into the lake. Breathe out. Then see your soul going out of you to hunt in the sky for the ball of fire that faces your soul when it comes out of the lake in the sky.

Breathe out. After, see and sense what is happening as your soul reenters you. Breathe out and open your eyes.

ASCENSION EXERCISES

RAINBOW STAIRCASE

Close your eyes and breathe out and in three times slowly, counting backwards from 3 to 1, each out breath being a new number. See the number 1 as tall and bright. Breathe out. Step inside the 1, acknowledging oneness with yourself, turning inward to your inner space and your deep inner rhythm. There, see a staircase with seven steps, each step being one of the colors of the rainbow.

Breathe out and start the ascent on the rainbow staircase. See and sense the resonance or sound of each color. Notice the way each color moves through your body and the patterns or images it gives birth to. When you reach the seventh step, make a leap to the Heights and plunge into the source of the rainbow.

Breathe out. Feel and sense how all form and color emerge from formlessness and oneness. Immerse yourself into this pure clear radiance.

Breathe out and in two times slowly. See and sense yourself climbing down the rainbow staircase and bringing this highest light back into your day-to-day life.

Breathe out. Experience and know how the rainbow is the bridge between Heaven and Earth. With an out breath, open your eyes and see your soul shining in the world, giving renewed hope.

ASCENDING TO YOUR HIGHER FORM OF WISDOM

Close your eyes and breathe out and in three times slowly. See the red sun standing out against a black background.

Breathe out and in three times slowly. Now see a constellation of stars turning red against the background of an emerald-green sky dazzling your vision.

Breathe out. See your angelic intelligence leading you to the *death of death*.

Breathe out. With this new faith in God, experience the *annihilation of time*. See this heavenly angel leading you to your center where all dualities cease. Breathe out and open your eyes.

ASCENDING THE SEVEN STEPS OF THE HEART

Close your eyes and breathe out and in three times slowly. Imagine yourself ascending the seven steps of your heart starting with step one, white light. Breathe out and become this light. What is your experience?

Breathe out and ascend to the second step. Here is yellow light. Breathe out and become this light. What is your experience?

Breathe out and ascend now to the third step. Here is dark blue. Breathe out and become this light. What is your experience?

Breathe out and ascend now to the fourth step. Here is green. Breathe out and become this light. What is your experience?

Breathe out and ascend now the fifth step. Here is azure blue. Breathe out and become this light. What is your experience?

Breathe out and ascend now the sixth step. Here is red. Breathe out and become this light. What is your experience?

Breathe out and ascend now the seventh step. Here is black. Breathe out and become this light. What is your experience? Breathe out and open your eyes.

THE LIGHT OF GOD

Close your eyes and breathe out and in three times slowly. Bring the heart to the state of a perfect mirror. See in this mirror the image of God's light as that of a lamp encased in glass. The lamp has a flame reflecting the light of God. See, sense, feel, know, and live your experience. Breathe out and open your eyes.

SUPRASENSORY REALITY

Close your eyes and breathe out and in three times slowly. See yourself being carried to the heights of suprasensory reality on a beam of emerald-green light. What happens? Breathe out and open your eyes.

THE TRAIN OF LIFE
(to be done upon awakening)

Close your eyes and breathe out and in three times slowly. Imagine yourself entering your train of life. Notice what you see passing by you in the countryside. Be aware of and hear the rhythmic hum of the train's wheels. Touch the fabric of your seat.

Breathe out. Suddenly you find your train ascending. As it does, it becomes your celestial chariot taking you upwards across the divide between the waters below where we live and the waters above of the Heights to where Spirit lives. Above the waters of the Heights, there you meet Spirit, who shows you your room or place in the Heavenly Palace.

Breathe out and keep this otherworldly image for yourself.

Breathe out and in three times slowly. Return to your chariot and descend quickly the way you came: across the great divide, to the waters below.

Breathe out. The chariot becomes your train that carries you back to where you began. Come back with a new understanding, feeling, attitude, and perception toward life and note how you look. Then, leave the train, breathe out, and open your eyes, keeping the feeling of meeting Spirit and the vision of your room in the Palace. Let this image fade after a few moments. Become aware of your present surroundings, what you see and hear. Now, begin your day.

RETURNING TO THE SOURCE

Close your eyes and breathe out and in three times slowly. See and feel yourself standing in a land called "Possibility." On your belt is a small translucent pouch containing the seeds of glory, glowing with the Light of Creation through the pouch. Face to the left and examine the Garden of Past Mistakes. See the plants in the garden withering as they approach the winter, losing strength, drying up, and returning to the soil. Turn to the right and walk on.

Breathe out. Come to the cave of inner life. Breathe out and in three times slowly and enter. Dust away the webs. Dust in the interior. Decorate it with something new and different. Light a candle, be still, and hear the Great Name in any way it comes to you.

Breathe out. Gather together all your helpers under a citron tree (large yellow citrus fruit from which all other citrus fruits derive), and vow to water and weed the field so that the Glory may grow. Breathing in the scent of the citron, know the possibility is in the fulfillment of the vow to water and to weed. Slowly open your eyes, sensing the well-being of newness. Now, breathe out and open your eyes fully.

CELEBRATING THE BELOVED

Close your eyes and breathe out and in three times slowly. See yourself as the beloved, receiving the love of God. Know that you are being breathed into by the powerful presence of God, and you are breathing out loving kindness. See the King's lovingness welcoming you as the Bride or Groom of the *holy* Sabbath.

Breathe out. Create a fence of light and safeguard the place of the sacred. Gather up all the separate parts of yourself and construct them as a perfect whole in the center of the place of the sacred. Allow all you see to be bathed in a golden light of the same hue and color. Know at this instant there is one and only one God. What is your experience of this Alliance?

Breath out. See, feel, and stand before this Alliance as the palace of our nobility. The doors are very tall and grand. Stand before the doors and blow the trumpet that opens them. See the doors open, and watch the wedding procession as it enters the palace.

Breathe out, knowing the joy of welcoming the Bride or Groom of your *holy* Sabbath. Breathe out and open your eyes.

PILOTING YOUR SHIP OF NO-TIME

Close your eyes and breathe out and in three times slowly. You are piloting your ship on the arrow of no-time. With you at the helm, guide its destiny to its destination. Your ship is heading upward in a vertical direction. There are strong pulls trying to take your arrow off course in the form of mirages to your right and left. You are tempted to change direction, but resist! The name of your ship is IS.

Breathe out. Feel, physically sense, and live the exhilaration of this spiritual journey connecting you to ALL THERE IS. Be undaunted as the captain of your ship of LIFE.

Breathe out. As you come down slowly straight to Earth, guide your ship into its port here in this world, keeping what you have discovered. Breathe out and open your eyes.

DESCENT INTO THE SELF: THE BOTTOMLESS ABYSS

Close your eyes and breathe out and in three times slowly. Take a lamp and leave the zone of everyday preoccupations, occupations, and relationships, where everything seems clear by the light of day.

Breathe out. With your lamp, go down a staircase. Taking a few steps down, see a new person there who is waiting for you.

Breathe out and ask for his or her name.

Breathe out. Go to your innermost self, reaching the deep abyss where you feel deeply, from where your power of action emanates.

Breathe out. Sense and feel how it is to go further and further from the conventional certainties by which your social life is constructed. Breathe out and open your eyes.

Once more, close your eyes and breathe out and in three times slowly. Sense how it is easy to lose contact with yourself. Stay conscious and cautious.

Breathe out. See and feel at each of your steps of the descent a new person is disclosed to you. Ask for his or her name.

Breathe out. See and sense finding a new being who is no longer obeying you. You need not know his/her name.

Breathe out. Stop your exploration when your path has disappeared or faded under your feet. Breathe out and open your eyes.

Close your eyes and breathe out. See that there is a bottomless abyss out of which is arising, from the depth, what is *really* your life.

Breathe out. Sense it, feel it, recognize it, and know to contact it when necessary. Be sure to remember this experience.

Breathe out. Return to your everyday life by retracing your steps and recognizing each of your selves as you reascend.

Breathe out. Recognize the power of action this recognition now gives you.

Breathe out and with *(physically) opened eyes*, look again at the bottomless abyss and at each of your selves that you remember.

Breathe out. Imagine that you may reach this place and these beings very fast.

Breathe out. Sense and know how, every time you want to reach them, you may obtain from them the best of what they may give you in knowledge and in power of action.

Breathe out. Know and understand all this that is in you, and return peacefully to your everyday life with clarity.

Breathe out. Sense and know how enriched you are, and feel *renewed*. See yourself take decisive action now for the next future.[64]

THE POWER OF LIGHT

<u>Preamble</u>: The divine essence is clothed in the power of imagination. Now, close your eyes, breathe out, imagine, and know:

The first power is the hidden light.

Breathe out. The second power is the light comprising every color of blue.

Breathe out. The third power is green light.

Breathe out. The fourth power is white light.

Breathe out. The fifth power is red light.

Breathe out. The sixth power is composed of white and red light.

Breathe out. The seventh power is red *inclined* toward white light.

Breathe out. The eighth power is white *inclined* toward red light.

Breathe out. The ninth power is composed of white and red light together with red and white light.

Breathe out. The tenth power is composed of <u>every</u> color.

Breathe out. Experience now the divine clothed through the imagination, revealed to you.

Breathe out. Know that imagination is more important than knowledge.

Breathe out and open your eyes.

---

[64] Recall that decisions are never about right or wrong, good or bad. They are simply the behavioral actions taken in the moment to fulfill the (mental) choices we make.

PROPHETIC IMAGINATION: THE GREAT CHAIN OF BEING

<u>Preamble</u>: There are ten emanations that form the great chain of being from us to God, in *ascending* order: angels, archangels, principalities, powers, virtues, dominions, thrones, cherubim, seraphim, Ancient of Days.

Close your eyes and breathe out and in three times slowly and imagine these ten in ascending order, each with a different light and color. Be sure to breathe out one time between each level. Breathe out and open your eyes.

THE ORIGIN OF CREATION

Close your eyes and breathe out and in three times slowly. Imagine the Celestial Crown God has given to us that unites the worlds above with our world here below. Breathe out and open your eyes.

Close your eyes and breathe out. Imagine you are light and all about you is light from every direction and every side, and in the midst of the light, a stream of light, and upon it a brilliant light, and opposite that one and upon it, a good light.

Breathe out and become all those lights instantly to become a light being. Let the light replenish you. Breathe out and open your eyes.

Close your eyes and breathe out and in three times slowly. Turn to the right and find pure light; to the left find an aura that is the radiant light. Between them and above is the light of glory, and around it the light of life. Above it is the crown of light that crowns the objects of thought, illuminates the paths of ideas, and brightens the splendor of visions. This illumination is inexhaustible, unending, and out of its perfect glory come grace, blessing, peace, and endless life for those born of Spirit. Breathe out and open your eyes.

THE BLACK LIGHT OF HOLINESS: DIE BEFORE YOU DIE

Close your eyes and breathe out and in three times slowly. See and know that black light is an attribute of God's majesty that sets the spiritual being on fire. It is not contemplated, it attacks, invades, annihilates, then *annihilates annihilation* in the death of death, so you now *die before you die, that you die to death!* Breathe out and open your eyes.

Now see and understand that imagination is active contemplation.

GIFT FROM GOD

Close your eyes and breathe out and in three times slowly. Climb your favorite mountain (one you've been to, have seen personally or in pictures, on TV, or in the movies). Reaching the peak, you see it is very narrow, with only room for you to stand. Raise your arms high toward the heavens. See, physically sense and feel the heavenly rays of light come through your arms and through the crown of your skull. See God's light descending through you and around you, purifying you completely, giving you continued life and well-being.

Breathe out. Come down the mountain and as you do, you may find a clear, pure mountain stream. Disrobe and bathe in it, cleaning off any residue that may remain on your skin. Continue down the mountain to the base, finding there, for yourself, the existence you yearn for. Experience it, and come back to the chair, keeping all that you have gotten for yourself. Breathe out and open your eyes.

ILLUMINATION: FLIGHT OF THE ONE TO THE ONE

Close your eyes and breathe out and in three times slowly. See and know the universe is a huge, endlessly flowing fountain of light. The Absolute One descends as light flowing through ever lower levels of being until reaching the very lowest, that of matter. As it reaches here and contacts us, it flows from us back up to the One where we become united with the One, becoming this unity. Recognize and experience this is what we are seeking as we bring this awareness to inform our everyday life. Let this light be your light that connects you to Absolute Life as you breathe out and open your eyes. With *eyes opened*, remember what you see, letting it then fade from view after several seconds.

RESURRECTION

Now that the Ascension has been completed, we are prepared to overcome death and to be reborn.

SEVENTH CERVICAL VERTEBRA: THE VERTEBRA OF RESURRECTION, THE VERTEBRA THAT NEVER DISINTEGRATES

Close your eyes and breathe out and in three times slowly. See yourself naked in a mirror. Look at your seventh cervical vertebra. See if it is white or not. If it's not, clean it with a small golden scrub

Becoming an Imaginaut: Imagery for Discovering Eternal Life

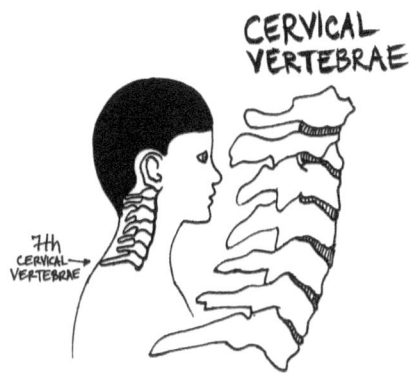

brush (like you would use for your fingernails). Clean it thoroughly, till it appears glistening white. Flick it with your thumb and forefinger or middle finger. If the sound is disharmonious, manipulate it with your thumb and forefinger little by little, till you hear a harmonious sound when it's flicked.

Breathe out and see light emanating from that seventh cervical vertebra flowing everywhere.

Breathe out and see this eternal light entering into all the other bones (including face and skull), seeing them becoming thick and glistening white. See this light flowing into the circulatory system and heart; into the digestive system from top to bottom, including the liver, gallbladder, and head of the pancreas; into all the hormonal glands: the pituitary, pineal, thyroid, pancreas (body and tail), adrenal (medulla and cortex), ovaries, and prostate; into the immune system: the lymph nodes of the groin, around the spinal column, armpits, breasts, and neck; muscles everywhere; into the nervous system: the brain, spinal cord, and peripheral nerves all over; the respiratory system: the trachea, larynx, bronchi, and lungs; the sexual organs: breasts, testicles, ovaries, penis, and vagina; sensory organs: the eyes, ears, nose, mouth, finger and toe tips; the urinary system: the kidneys, ureter, bladder, urethra; and skin.

Breathe out. Now, see your whole being in the mirror coming back to life, filled with white light as a tree of life. Know now you are the tree that is fruit, that makes and bears fruit. See and know that you need no second tree.

Breathe out. See, know, and feel you have turned from death and have come back to life. Breathe out and open your eyes.

ROUND MIRROR

Close your eyes and breathe out and in three times slowly. See yourself as a perfectly polished round mirror.

Breathe out. See the sound of your heart reflected as clearly as a sunny orb. See this sound reflected as clearly as a fountain flowing and outpouring the starry sky and golden sand.

Breathe out. See in one grain of sand all the heavens.

Breathe out. See in a drop of light all the universe.

Breathe out. See yourself now as round, then as a flying round bird soaring from star to star singing.

Breathe out. Keep this experience, knowing you are an endless part of this creation.

Breathe out and open your eyes.

THE RESURRECTION PROCESS: THE TURNING POINT FROM DEATH TO LIFE

Go to the disturbing pivotal turning point in your life; or a crossroads at the present time that you experience as a blockage; or a past trauma.

Close your eyes and breathe out and in three times slowly, counting backwards from three to one, a new number on each exhale.

Breathe out once more and see the one become a zero that grows in size and becomes a mirror. In the mirror, see, sense, feel, and live the experience at the time when it happened. Now, *correct the memory — reverse it —* so that you are returning yourself to yourself. Do whatever is necessary. This is imagination; anything can happen. You know that you are changing your past, and in doing so, you are changing your future. If you are at the crossroads in the present, imagine and know you are overcoming the hurdle. See, sense, and feel what happens. Describe it to yourself. How do you feel and what do you physically sense in your own body right here, now, as you return yourself to yourself.

Breathe out and in three times slowly. Now see the light from above enter your body through the soft spot of the skull, radiating through all the systems of the body. See, sense, feel, and experience it giving new life and energy to you. See it circulating its radiance through all 11 systems of the body (shown in alphabetic order).

- Bones — marrow brings new life.
- Circulatory (including heart and circulatory system) — all shaped as a vertical infinity sign within the body).
- Digestive — mouth, pharynx, larynx, esophagus, stomach, liver, gallbladder, small intestine, large intestine, rectum, anus.
- Hormonal — pituitary, thyroid, heart, pancreas, adrenal, testicles, ovaries.
- Immune — spleen, thymus, bone marrow.
- Lymphatic — nodes in groin, around spinal column, armpits, under chin in the neck.
- Nervous — spinal cord, brain, all the nerves (light up like a Christmas tree).
- Respiratory — larynx, trachea, bronchi, lungs.
- Sexual — breasts, ovaries, uterus, vagina, testicles, prostate, penis
- Urinary — kidneys, ureters, bladder, urethra.
- And finally, through the muscles and skin.

Breathe out. See yourself again in the mirror. See how you look and feel. Turn the mirror over and see in its other face the newly reconstructed, reborn, resurrected you.

That is your essence. Push it out of the mirror *imaginally* to the right with your right hand, knowing that you in this physical time-space existence are fulfilling that essence.

Breath out. See your soulbody bringing essence and existence together, reuniting and becoming one presence in the time-space world. Breathe out and open your eyes.

Do this exercise each morning for 21 days.

THE BLOSSOMING HEART

Close your eyes and breathe out and in three times slowly. Sensing your inner space around which your physical body forms, see and sense your heart as a blooming rose. Gaze at the center of the radiant flower of the heart. Feel its fluid light as a regenerating nectar of life.

Breathe out and physically sense a place of discomfort within your body. Imagine a luminous golden thread linking the specific area of your body with your blossoming heart outpouring the radiance of your Essence. Let the fluid light flow through the golden cord into the unbalanced body part and melt away any stagnating, solid, fixed, or darkened structure.

Breathe out, feel and experience the stream of your heart's light flowing freely through your whole being.

Breathe out and open your eyes slowly, remembering the brightness of your soul bringing healing and balance to your body, reuniting your body and soul. Experience your new absolute life.

FROM SEED TO TREE

Close your eyes and breathe out and in three times slowly. Now, bind yourself to God's will, by any means you choose.

Breathe out. Then see how the seed falls from the tree and is buried. Keeping this image, breathe out. *Die* now and after *live* again!

Breathe out. Grow like a sycamore or oak tree rooted to the Earth and growing toward the boundless sky.

Breathe out. Be blown by the wind, still strong and unbending.

Breathe out. Raise your arms to the sun. See and experience the mercy and power of God and change forever, becoming a new being of life. Breathe out and open your eyes.

OVERCOMING DEATH

Close your eyes and breathe out and in three times slowly. See how the garden of your ancestors has been weighed down. Feel and know how you are helping them by returning to your mother's womb, waiting to be born once again.

Breathe out. Sense and know that in getting our body from God and our parents, we don't dare let it be destroyed.

Breathe out. See yourself as a newborn, as an infant, as a child. Have those feelings and sensations.

Breathe out. See yourself as an adult, as an old one. Have those sensations, ideas, and feelings.

Breathe out. Feel yourself as the master of your body and of your mental life.

Breathe out. See and experience that you have become the master.

Breathe out and in three times slowly. See yourself falling into depression or sadness.

Then breathe out. See yourself light with gladness.

Breathe out. Know that it is up to you to change and choose your attitude.

Breathe out. Now, live and know what life and death are.

Breathe out. See yourself as a dead one, coming to life again as a newborn. Now live endlessly, renewed with aliveness, in a new light, in a new resurrective being in body, soul, Spirit. Breathe out and open your eyes.

DEFEATING DEATH

Close your eyes and breathe out and in three times slowly. Imagine you have taken an eternal ticket for a journey on a train that never reaches its destination.

Breathe out. See and feel how you have been born with attraction, desire, and love. Physically sense it.

Breathe out. See and feel how these privileged qualities are breaking the circles of solitude and loneliness and are bringing you a concentrated feeling of love.

Breathe out. Physically sense, know, and experience how Love is the human way to fight and shield you against *Death*.

Breathe out. See and feel how to live in the present is to resist the past.

Breathe out. Physically sense and experience in you the life of all your ancestors, your clan, and decide to accept from them only what is yours that is valuable.

Breathe out. See yourself deciphering the manuscript of the future, beginning by *catching the instant* you are living just now.

Becoming an Imaginaut: Imagery for Discovering Eternal Life

Breathe out. Feel and know how this moment is your moment. Know how it is eternity, and know how this moment of eternity need not be repeated.

Breathe out. Physically see, sense, and feel how the Light of now is the only possession you have and your only certainty.

Breathe out. Physically sense and experience how events of the past that have some value are coexisting with the present, in the same instant. See how that light of the past is the same as the light of now.

Breathe out and live your new *life of resurrection,* reborn into this instant of the present. Breathe out and open your eyes.

ISIS AND OSIRIS

Close your eyes. Breathe out and in three times slowly. Experience yourself as the dead Osiris.

Breathe out and now experience yourself as Isis, the goddess of wisdom and life.

Breathe out. As Isis, kiss Osiris on the lips, saying, "Awaken from my love to life."

Breathe out. As Osiris, experience the force of love surging through your body, awakening you and restoring you back to life. Know now that love is truly stronger than death.

Breathe out and open your eyes to this new life.

Note: For the opposite experience of man's love to woman, you may substitute the legend of Prince Charming and Sleeping Beauty.

LIFE OVERCOMING DEATH

Close your eyes and breathe out and in three times slowly. See, physically sense, feel, and become the light that surrounds you. What color is it?

Breathe out. Physically sense the way the light is alive and pulsating. What do you feel?

Breathe out. Experience the boundaries between the light and yourself blurring.

Breathe out. See, physically sense, feel, and experience how the outer becomes inner and the inner becomes outer. Know and feel now how life is everlasting and death transient.

Breathe out. Keep this feeling for yourself always. Renew it whenever you remember for a few seconds. Breathe out and open your eyes.

RE-BIRTH: A SECOND CHANCE

Close your eyes and breathe out and in five times slowly. To begin with, imagine the Eternal Essence birthing existence by generating waves of sound and emitting particles of light into emptiness. Behold! The universe appears, heaven and Earth.

Breathe out. The essence gives forth a dew spreading over the Earth, fertilizing it, and the miracle of life springs forth. Breathe out. Experience now your new birth. Feel it. Breathe out and open your eyes.

TRUMPET OF RESURRECTION

Close your eyes and breathe out and in three times slowly. Hear and feel the sound of the heavenly trumpet calling you from above to arise from the crypt of the numbing sleep of attachments to the cold, inert, lifeless grip of material existence.

Breathe out. As you wake up and become erect, strong, and alive, hear the words of love flowing to and into you from your parents who have birthed you, or any loved ones who have loved or now love you.

Breathe out. Physically sense, feel, and live how this eternal force amplifies the sound of new life coming from the Eternal Horn of life. Breathe out and open your eyes.

ETERNAL LIFE EXERCISES

THE PAST TO ETERNITY: FINDING THE MOMENT

Close your eyes and breathe out and in three times slowly. See and become one with the experience of how living in the present is the only way to stop living in the past.

Breathe out. Know how this is possible only if you pass from the horizontal plane of everyday life to the vertical Life of Spirit.

Breathe out. Now take the present moment and lift it up to Eternity seven times. Breathe out and open your eyes.

YOUR HOUSE OF BEING

Close your eyes and breathe out and in three times slowly. Imagine yourself resting in peace in the house of your own being. Sense and feel what happens.

Breathe out. Now, know and live that the angel of death cannot touch you. Keep this realization for yourself always. Breathe out and open your eyes.

NO SEPARATION

Close your eyes and breathe out and in three times slowly. See, sense, feel, and know that as much as we need you, God — You need us.

Our no-separation IS oneness — a point that increases in an unlimited space.

As we are everywhere and everything, here and now, God, You are me.

Keep that experience.

Breathe out and open your eyes.

UNBOUNDED

Close your eyes and breathe out and in three times slowly. Imagine that you are casting away your little self, making space for God.

Breathe out. Face Him when He enters, omnipresent, ever present to you as to everyone.

Breathe out. Now, know absolute freedom, nothing to fear, nothing to attain; joy unbounded as you are.

Breathe out and open your eyes.

ETERNITY

Close your eyes and breathe out and in three times slowly. See yourself grow to a greatness beyond measure. By a great bounce, free yourself from the body.

Raise yourself *above* all time. Become Eternity! Then, you will understand Truth. Know what this Truth is.

Breathe out and open your eyes.

ANTI-"AGING"

Close your eyes and breathe out and in three times slowly. See and recognize how you have already seen that aging is *only* a struggle that has to be overcome.

Breathe out. See yourself struggling with the disoriented tiger until it is changed into a cat. Be not old! Breathe out and open your eyes.

LONG LIFE

Close your eyes and breathe out and in three times slowly. Feel and know: "And if thou wilt walk in My ways, to keep my statutes and my commandments, as thy father David did walk, then I will lengthen thy days" (1 Kings 3:14).

Breathe out. "My children, forget not My law; but let thine heart keep my commandments: For length of days, and long life, and peace, shall they add to thee" (Proverbs 3:1–2).

Breathe out. "Because he hath set his love upon Me, therefore will I deliver him: I will set him on high, because he hath known My name. He shall call upon Me, and I will answer him: I will be with him in trouble; I will deliver him, and honor him. With long life will I satisfy him, and show him my salvation" (Psalm 91:14).

Breathe out. "Honor thy father and mother...with promise; That it may be well with thee, and thou mayest live long on the earth" (Ephesians 6:2–3).

Breathe out. "What man is he that desireth life and loveth many days, that he may see good? Keep thy tongue from evil, and thy lips from speaking guile. Depart from evil, and do good; seek peace, and pursue it" (Psalm 34:12–14).

Breathe out and open your eyes.

BECOMING THE WAVICLE

Close your eyes and breathe out and in three times slowly. See yourself as a dot in the center of a circle and become a moment in eternity. Then, breathe out, disappear, and become eternity. Breathe out. Be infinite space.

Breathe out. Be all that is.

Breathe out. Now become a wave of consciousness surrounding your particle.

Breathe out. As the two merge, you are becoming a wavicle (wave + particle). Now, as a wavicle, be in union with Divine Spirit. Breathe out. Leave that union to descend to Earth as a human wavicle, living the never-ending presence of God on Earth.

Breathe out and open your eyes.

Note: Do this exercise followed by Angel of Eternal Life each morning upon awakening and before bed for some seconds, for 21 days.

ANGEL OF ETERNAL LIFE: TO REPAIR THE TELOMERES

Close your eyes and breathe out and in three times slowly. See, feel, and know that your body contains the structural blueprint for generating life.

Breathe out. Enter into your body. See and experience before you the great double helix — the ladder of genetic structure.

Breathe out. Descend this ladder, experiencing and knowing its structure as the connection to your life.

Breathe out and in three times slowly. Then, imagine you and your guardian angel ascending this double-helix ladder.

Breathe out, asking your angel to brush its wings against the telomeres — the protective caps at the ends of the 23 pairs of chromosomal gene strands that make up the double helix of life within each cell.

Breathe out. See and sense the fluttering of the angel's wings emitting telomerase, the enzyme of life, painting the telomeres that become golden yellow and elongated. Know that you are reversing the breakdown of your cellular matrix of life, extending the telomere tips into the limitless energy of the universe.

Breathe out and sense the new enlivening of your body. Breathe out and open your eyes.

Do this exercise each morning upon awakening and before bed, for some seconds, for 21 days.

THE PINEAL GLAND: THE FLOW OF ENERGY FOR LIVING HARMONIOUSLY WITHIN YOURSELF

Close your eyes and breathe out and in three times slowly. See, physically sense, and feel the white flow of energy coming from the pineal gland — that absorbs and reflects the lights of the sun, moon, and stars — streaming from this gland as a radiant white light to the pituitary gland in the center of the brain.

Breathe out. See and sense this light streaming from the pituitary as a red downward flow through the body into the thyroid and thymus, down the left side of the body's arterial system, left side of the spinal column, left adrenal gland, all the way to the sole of the left foot.

Breathe out. Now, see and sense this light becoming yellow as it crosses to the right sole, where this light now becomes blue. From there it sweeps upward through the venous circulation, right adrenal gland, right side of the spinal column, thymus, thyroid, up to the pituitary, where it streams back to the pineal gland as white light. See, physically sense, and feel you are becoming a spiritual body of light. Be absorbed by it for a moment. Feel and sense your unity. Breathe out and open your eyes.

TIME FLIES/FLYING FROM TIME

Close your eyes and breathe out. See in front of you a clock with the hands set at your time of birth.

Breathe out. Now, turn your back on that clock and find yourself flying away from the clock of time.

Breathe out. Fly downward without end, then fly upward without end. Breathe out. Turn back to face the clock and see the hands are no longer there. Know that you have flown above and beyond time, beyond death. Breathe out and open your eyes.

Do this exercise every morning for 21 days.

MIDNIGHT SUN

Close your eyes and breathe out and in three times slowly. It is midnight. The sky is pitch black.

Breathe out. Now see the sun shining in all its radiance against this pure black.

Breathe out. See and experience the sun and moon unite. What happens for you? Keep this for yourself.

Breathe out. Ascend at your normal pace through the colors of a rainbow: red, orange, yellow, green, blue, indigo, violet.

Breathe out and ascend above the rainbow. Look down on all that IS. Stay for some moments.

Breathe out and in three times slowly. Then climb a ladder of stars. Each star becomes an angel as you leap up from one to another. What do you discover at the top?

Breathe out. Create a natural emptiness. Become this emptiness, becoming poor in Spirit. Now, know what consciousness IS — keep it always!

Breathe out. Know you carry a drop of the void within. Know that your freedom is the void within you. Know you are indestructible, ever living. Breathe out and open your eyes.

ETERNAL LIFE: DRINKING THE CUP OF HEAVEN

Close your eyes and breathe out and in three times slowly. Drink in the cup of heaven.

Breathe out. Drink in the Earth.

Breathe out. Drink in the light of God.

Breathe out. See the cup of forever spilling out the threads of eternity. Drink from it!

Breathe out and open your eyes.

BLISS

Close your eyes and breathe out and in three times slowly.

Become as Enoch, the one who never died, and travel into the innermost, hidden-most, centermost of your soul. This inner journey is a pilgrimage to the center of your being. Reaching the center, your pilgrim's progress is now over. So, blessed, the united you quietly rests in the core of bliss. Breathe out and open your eyes.

CHAPTER XV

The Great Sabbath of the Earth and Beyond

"He will swallow up death forever
And the Lord God will wipe tears from off all faces."
—Isaiah 25:8

AS WE HAVE SEEN, CHOOSING LIFE is a matter of progression through the minefield of this strife-torn world of exile to free ourselves from it and return to our rightful home, from which we were originally evicted. To reiterate, we are born with a trace memory of that world that ever calls us to return to the forgotten world of paradise called Eden.

This seeming impossibility is possible! The way, spelled out through GEMS, is a comprehensible and comprehensive daily practice for Living, and living to that end.

The way to transcend Life over death is both an individual and communal affair. It is something to be accomplished on both levels and is the possibility, nay, mission of the whole of humanity. The process is a progressive one, taking place in three stages: Sabbath Practices; the Great Sabbath; and the Eighth Day of the World to Come. The practice of the Sabbath in everyday life is a portal to the Great Sabbath, where we reunite body and soul, and then to the Eighth Day, where we unite with the Divine. Originally we were/are one at our inception, but we are torn asunder through the spiritual errors and the social errors of living we have participated in during the course of life. Correcting these errors, we now are able to enter into the portal of the Eighth Day, the World to Come, the world of eternal light and life, whole and holy, a receptive, unified being, in union with our Source, in this PARADISE CALLED EARTH.

Stage 1: Sabbath Practices
The first stage is the meat of this book, where we extricate ourselves from the grip of linear time, where illness and death reside. This possibility has been fleshed out through the many practices offered here to correct our spiritual and social errors. In a sense, all the practices I have described could be retitled Sabbath Practices, as they assist us in moving out of the grip of time.

The weekly Sabbath, the Seventh Day of practicing reversing the habits of the preceding six, is God's gift to prepare us for the Great Sabbath, the second stage of our evolution. Here we practice making connections with the transcendent possibility above time. In aligning ourselves with the vertical reality on the seventh day of the Sabbath, we gradually learn to extend the Sabbath Spirit out to the rest of the six days of creation. By applying even one of the practices outlined in this book consistently, we can make our habitual daily life into a Sabbath celebration. We are exiting the exile world, becoming our own personal messiahs, saving self as we master ourselves. Individually, we each climb up the rungs of the ladder of self-mastery; we begin our transformation of reuniting body and soul to evolve into a spiritual body of light. As we apply these Sabbath Practices into our collective lives, we are putting *new* information into the morphogenetic field of knowledge of humanity that death can be transcended.

The Great Sabbath of the Earth and Beyond

As indicated above, this transcendence is an individual event. We meet other transcendent souls who want to return home and take part in reshaping this glorious great creation back to the Garden of delight, pleasure, and bliss to its origin inherent in the six days of creation. As we engage more and more in this free world, transcending the enclosed time-space zone, we become part of a collaborative, shared world of peace and goodwill where we acknowledge and respect the sanctity of each other and revel in this holy sanctuary of spiritual laws of love, faith, hope, and truth.

In the traditional practice of the Sabbath etched in the 4th Commandment, to remember and observe the Sabbath, we are commanded to rest, to cease creating. This cessation has to do with our choice to stop our urge to create in the name of (horizontal) materialism and retreat from that into transcendent communion with the Origin of our existence, again to get a taste of what a no-death experience is like. Whatever degree of connection we can make in no-time is a confirmation of the possibility of the long-sought-for freedom while in a living body.

As we become spiritual beings, the Earth appears different to us. We are able to perceive it through a different frame of reference, through a different lens. As a result of this expression of self, inherent in becoming spiritually aware, we not only perceive differently, we also live differently: a simpler life, a life of love, giving, sharing, voluntary simplicity, becoming gratuitous (in its virtuous sense) — in all, a holy life of health, wholeness, and healing.

Stage 2: Great Sabbath of the Earth

What arises from this collaborative get-together and the concurrent shift created by the new information inserted in the morphogenetic field is the advent of the Great Sabbath of the Earth, the second stage. What awaits us here — no death and none of the multitude of conflicts that govern life in the dual world we find ourselves in today. Here we are now out of the grip of time: There is no duality, conflict, or new creation. It is the no-time zone, and awareness of linear time stops. The supremacy of the moment, the presence of the present, holds sway. There is no need to labor over improving what never needed improving — that is, the created world described in the six days of creation. Here the soul body and material body are rejoined, to become one unitary being of Light. Unity prevails. We are all one.

The Great Sabbath speaks to the eventual fulfillment for the hope of a personal return to our original perfection, but also to a time where the whole of humanity's destiny will establish a wholesale turn toward Spirit.

As a person of faith, in its multifaceted meaning connected with knowing God, I have no doubt that this Great Sabbath shall dawn, nay, is dawning upon us. The seemingly impossible becomes possible.

We've had beings scattered throughout the flow of human history who have modeled what a Sabbath being looks like. Now the time has come to begin to imitate these models, and the ripple effects of such imitation will flow out to others.

Stage 3: Eighth Day of the World to Come
By our universal acts of redemption and repentance, and our return to our divine progenitor, we take ourselves to the doorstep to enter into the Eighth Day, the World to Come. We return as prodigal children coming home. As my then three-year-old daughter Sarah would constantly remark, "I want to go home!" I knew what she was talking about. She was not alone in this desire: It is the worldwide desire shared by all of us to want to "return home."

The Eighth Day of the World to Come is the world of higher transcendence, of eternal life and timelessness in repose with God. Here we become one with the One. This is the world of indescribable bliss waiting to be redeemed for us. This is not a utopian vision but a spiritual vision! Here there is nothing but experience of harmony, love, faith, hope, bliss, and eternal life, where we mingle as one in the vertical spiritual reality among all the realms of eternal beings (e.g., angels, archangels, etc.). Going through this evolutionary process of navigating through stage 1 to 2 to 3, we fully evolve into spiritual beings of light. The rest is left up to all of us to discover.

In sum, the purposeful practices contained in this book embody our seeking to reunite body and soul, bringing us to an existence of transcendence subsuming and including those two while choosing the path of life instead of the path of death. These practices are all about living a Sabbath existence in everyday life as well as making it an exclusive practice on the Seventh Day. Everything said throughout this book is part of an educational process to remind us to remember ourselves, to choose life; to cleanse and purify our two natures; to live freely; and to exit from enslavement, idolatry, and the grip of death.

The world of the Great Sabbath and beyond is hard to fathom through the lens of our everyday existence. We can catch glimpses of it that grow to a fuller vision and experience as we apply these GEMS practices in our lives to live a Sabbath existence to rise above the grip of linear-time, attachment to three-dimensional space, illness and death. Here are some closing imagery exercises to give a taste of that blissful time we once knew and can know again:

GREAT SABBATH IMAGERY EXERCISES

ENTERING THE WORLD TO COME: CELESTIAL ORGASM

Close your eyes and breathe out and in three times slowly. See, physically sense, and feel the orgasmic experience of cessation of awareness of ordinary time and space.

Breathe out. Know, understand, and experience now what it is to die to death, and, by extension, to die to time and space.

Breathe out. Come back now to a new life full of new meaning and purpose. Breathe out and open your eyes.

TRANQUILITY: THROUGH THE PORTAL OF THE GREAT SABBATH INTO THE WORLD TO COME

Close your eyes and breathe out and in three times slowly. See, feel, know, and experience the tranquility that existed at the beginning of the world, and at the end of time. Be absorbed in that rest. Breathe out and open your eyes.

IN THE WORLD TO COME

Close your eyes and breathe out and in three times slowly. You are in the New World, coming back home to your celestial Father and Mother.

Breathe out. See the Great Chain of Beings all descending toward you — angels, archangels, principalities, powers, virtues, dominions, thrones, cherubim, and seraphim.

Breathe out. Join with them, reuniting as one with them and as One with yourself, reuniting with the Absolute One Mind.

Breathe out one time. Know and experience the bliss of Eternal Life, rejoicing in the fulfillment of what we all are yearning for in Paradise regained.

Breathe out and return now to this life, knowing that you return with the Good News that you have united the Tree of Life and Tree of

The Great Sabbath of the Earth and Beyond

Knowledge within yourself, to share gratuitously with the fellowship of humanity. Breathe out and open your eyes.

> Love, and may God bless us all,
> Dr. Jerry

We Are Not *Meant* to Die

Glossary

Absolute — Unerring truths not subject to relative concepts or debate. Not subject to doubt. A matter of certainty, such as faith. Spiritual, not religious, doctrine consists of absolutes that are either accepted or not. If not, then one simply has not chosen a spiritual path of life.

Acausality — That without cause. Experiences happening to us that seem unusual, as they are not explainable by the physical laws of cause and effect that are easy to determine. In contrast to the everyday physical world where an immediate cause can be found to account for the effect you are perceiving.

Adultery — Weakening by mixing, polluting, contaminating; serving two masters at the same time. Can occur in *many different* levels of experience.

Agape (*ag-a-pay*) — Unconditional love — to be distinguished from parental, sexual, friendship/sibling love.

Analogy — Thinking by seeing relationships between things; perceiving wholeness through such relational thinking rather than thinking by reaching conclusions; mirror reflection; perceiving and/or conceiving points of similarities *and* points of differences in such thinking; otherwise known as acausal thinking (not by linear cause leading to effect, or one-to-one thinking, viz., this causes that).

Apostasy — In spiritual terms, assuming an attitude of utter rejection of the existence, or truth, of an Invisible Reality by whatever terms used to describe that reality.

Atomization — A central effort of materialist thinking to break down experience into bits, pieces (atoms) — and by this method to arrive at truth.

Chaste — Faithful to one; opposite of adultery; pure, undefiled.

Coincidence — Two seemingly unrelated things happening together.

Conditioning — Dependency training serving to keep one attached to something or someone outside of oneself for worth, survival, legitimacy of thinking, feeling, and behaving.

Contingent — Dependent upon outside circumstances.

Decision — To take action; erroneously conceived of as having to distinguish between right and wrong, good or bad.

Determinism — The belief that all behavior is caused by preceding factors and is thus predictable. The causal laws of determinism form the basis of the [natural] sciences (Saul McLeod, B.Sc. Psychology, University of Manchester, U.K., 2013).

Dyad — Two people in relationship to/with each other.

Ennobling — Raising or raised to a higher status of character.

Faith — Taking action without regard for the outcome or result; making up one's mind; verb form of trust; belief in the existence of an Invisible Reality or God.

Five Dimensions of Experience — Physical, Emotional, Mental, Social, and Moral/Spiritual.

Glossary

Glory — Light of God emanating from God.

God — The conversationally used term as a shorthand to describe and denote the indescribable, ineffable Absolute. Absolute One Mind; One; That Without End; Invisible Reality; Divinity, Absolute Source of Light, Source of Creation, Universal Oneness; Spiritual Father/Mother; Indivisible Wholeness.

Hologram — the whole message = holo/whole + grams/messages; the part containing and reflecting the whole; made in the image and likeness of God (One) (Gen. 1:26).

Imagery — Mental exercises to create transformative shifts in oneself. The divine, invisible language conveyed from Invisible Reality to visible reality, mediated through the mind (see definition). It is a mental hieroglyph, analogous to the written language of the Egyptian Pharaonic tradition. The ordinary term for such language experience is symbol, pointing to visible and Invisible Reality at the same time.

Intention — Aim toward; direction toward; purpose toward. It is to be distinguished from goal. Intention is a process-laden activity, while goal is product- or end point–driven.

Intuition — A form of thought that withdraws from materialistically based logical thinking and attends to subjective receipt of thoughts, feelings, and inner sensory impulses by attending squarely to the present moment. Intuition provides a continuous flow of "knowing in the moment" not readily available to us through logical thought.

Linear Thinking —Deterministic or "cause to effect" conclusionary thinking. Thinking in a straight line along the arrow of time from past to future, where past events determine the future and what happened in the past must happen again; projecting a thought into the "future," a time, place, and circumstance that doesn't exist.

Mind — The channel of communication between invisible to visible reality. The inner informational superhighway along which images travel from what is not immediately perceptible to what becomes perceptible.

Reify — To make an idea or thought that is abstract by nature into a thing that appears to exist for you. A prime example is the "future" that becomes perceived as a concrete thing that by its nature as a thing is perceived to literally exist. This perceptual twist is the basis for mental idolatry.

Remember — To put oneself together again. Can be done physically, as in surgery; mentally, as in recollecting; socially, recalling relationships; emotionally, loving.

Renouncing — To relinquish, sacrifice; detach from; withdraw from.

Repent — Literally, to think again. In spiritual terms, to think again in a new way.

Reversing — To relinquish, sacrifice; detach from; withdraw from. Turn about, turn around. To return. To change around. To make holy.

Socio-genetic — The social, emotional, and behavioral tendencies passed down from generation to generation, not through our physical genetic characteristic inheritance but by a separate channel.

Soul — The infused essence of Spirit housed in our human body (*Nefesh*). There are two levels of essence above the bodily one in the monotheistic tradition: One is called "wind" or "oversoul" (*Ruach*); the other is "highest soul" (*Neshama*), which has descended to Earth when Creation took place.

Space — In everyday reality, thought of as comprising three *measurable* dimensions: height, width, and depth, forming the boundary of all physical objects; precisely called "three-dimensional space."

Spirit — God.

Stopping-Pause — For spiritual practice, putting a wedge between a stimulus and its response as a way to dehabituate or reverse a habit.

Glossary

For intuitional practice, stopping future thoughts and impulsive behaviors.

Synchronicity — Two things happening together as one in time; simultaneous occurrence of events that appear significantly related but have no discernable causal connection. These events are sloughed off as coincidence or chance in the natural sciences, as the phenomena cannot be explained through linear thought. Extending this further, events may not occur simultaneously yet have an analogic relational connection to each other that I term "the law of unity."

Time — In everyday reality, ascribed in *linear* terms as past and future, denoted by a horizontal line or arrow from these two points, connecting them as a sequence from one to the other; precisely called "linear time."

Transformation — Change of form, as in human development from infancy → toddler → child → adolescent → adult, or in the growth of a tree: seed → seedlings → sapling → tree.

Transmutation — Change of one form that is present to another form that wasn't there before, such as caterpillar to butterfly or moth. In alchemy (the parent of chemistry), the changing of lead into gold.

Tzimtzum — A contraction specific to God beginning creation by contracting itself in giving birth to the world.

Unconditional — A term denoting freedom from dependencies, strings, influences, contingencies; otherwise free of conditioning or habituation.

We Are Not *Meant* to Die

Index

Aboulker, Henri, 60
Aboulker-Muscat, Colette, 16, 34, 72, 149, 223-224, 359
  Absolute One Mind
    philosophy of, 40
  climatic disturbances and, 106
  clinical stories from, 32, 343, 373-374
  meeting Dr. Epstein, 42-43, 186, 225, 245-246, 332
  mental imagery and, 235
  reversing and, 202
  Seven Divine Forces and, 210
  social errors and, 179
  Ten Commandments and, 247-250, 253
Absolute One Mind (AOM), 85, 117, 238
  God concept and, 40, 73
  Theater of Life and, 112, 114
  Three Virtues and, 298
  See also God, Invisible Reality
agape, 209, 311
Allen, Woody, 40-41, 180, 261, 280, 313
Alliance, The, 187-188, 210-211, 298, 315
  faith and, 218

American Institute of Mental Imagery (AIMI), 25, 43, 368
analogous thinking. *See* intuitional thinking
Atlan, Henri, 51-52
attachment, 32, 33, 71, 208, 298, 354
  dark currents of will and, 171
  death and, 29-30
  definition of, 140-141
  effort and, 310
  entropy/ectropy and, 47
  exercises for reversing, 37-38
  Law of, 251
  reversing, 115, 313-315, 363, 364, 369
  Ten Commandments and, 252, 254
  See also detachment, reversing
Attachment, Insufficiency, and Doubt (AID), 114, 137, 202, 287
  definition, 139-142
  See also attachment, doubt
Barrett, Elizabeth, 86
Berman, Morris, 34
Bible, Hebrew, 196
  Book of Deuteronomy

Deut. 6:5, 115, 193, 208, 246
Deut. 28:66), 220
Deut. 30:15 &19, 23, 30, 52, 53, 56, 176, 206, 255, 346
Deut. 32:35, 169
Book of Ecclesiastes, 171, 210
Book of Exodus, 246, 323
Ex. 6:6, 118
Ex. 15:26, 257, 260
Book of Ezekiel
Ezek. 1:1-28, 382
Ezek. 37:1-11, 59
Book of Genesis, 69, 70, 281
Gen. 1:6, 73
Gen. 1:26, 335, 369, 433
Gen. 2:11, 233
Gen. 5:24, 60
Gen. 5:27, 60
Gen. 12:1, 377
Book of Isaiah
Isa. 1:6 & 2:4, 90
Isa. 25:8, 47, 59, 423
Isa. 26:18, 381
Isa. 58:13, 261
Book of Leviticus
Lev. 19:18, 208, 246, 274
Book of Proverbs, 35
Prov. 3:1-2, 418
Prov. 3:35, 241
Book of Song of Songs
Songs 8:6, 21, 30, 37, 59, 176, 273
Bible, New Testament
Book of Corinthians
Cor. 15:26, 18
Book of John
John 3:8, 357
John 3:16, 59
Book of Luke, 334
Luke 14:33, 202
Book of Mark
Mark 12:31, 246
Book of Matthew, 334
Matt. 5:37, 346, 351
Biblical figures
Abraham, 187-188, 246, 257, 269
Adam and Eve, 49, 53-55, 140, 259, 288, 322, 349, 351, 354
Cain and Abel, 269, 287
Daniel, 376
Esther, 254, 272
Ezekiel, 59
Isaiah, 90
Jacob, 188
Jeremiah, 316
Jezebel, 254
Job, 224
King David, 223-224
King Solomon, 21, 37, 59, 209-210, 301
Maimonides, 59
Miriam, 88-89
Moses, 31-32, 79, 88-89, 210, 218, 228, 341
Nachson, 218, 367
Noah, 60
Satan, 57, 224-225
See also Jesus Christ
Biblical stories
Genesis/Creation, 69, 70, 237, 239, 366-367
Great Flood, 60, 237, 261
Tower of Babel, 233, 235, 257-258
See also creation, Garden of Eden
Bhagavad Gita, 48
bios, 48
"Blue Zones," 44

Index

brain (spiritual concept), 80
Buddhism, 29, 32, 33, 278
Byrd, Randolph, 342
chastity. *See* Three Virtues: chastity
Chinese medicine, 60
Christianity, 78
    symbols, 77, 323
    See also Bible, Hebrew; Bible, New Testament; Biblical figures; Biblical stories; Jesus Christ
climatic disturbances and health, 103-107
cloning, 60-61
concentration, 310-316, 320-321, 358
    mental imagery exercises for, 317-320
creation, 69, 73. *See also* Biblical figures: Adam and Eve; Garden of Eden
Coué, Emile, 221, 318
dark and light currents of will. *See* attachment, will
Day of Atonement, 58, 284-285
Death Path, 30, 38
death penalty, 267-268
"Death Thou Shall Be Defeated" (essay), 57
"Death Thou Shalt Die" (poem), 59
de Chardin, Teilhard, 59
de Grey, Aubrey, 62-63
DePinho, Ronald, 62
detachment, 31, 34, 354
    Alliance and, 315
    grammar and, 363
    Law of, 32, 251, 297, 308
    mental imagery exercise for, 37-38
    poverty and, 306-307
    practices for, Chapter XII
    reversing and, 314-315
    Seven Divine Forces and, 115

detached intellect, 229, 231, 312-314, 321
Dickinson College, 40
dis-emergency state, 131-133. *See also* false emergency state
Divine Source. *See* God
Donne, John, 59
Dossey, Larry, 89, 222, 342, 372
doubt, 85, 144, 175, 275, 283, 358, 359, 367
    GEMS and, 101
    faith and, 186, 203, 215, 219, 221
    yes or no phenomenon and, 345-355
    See also Attachment, Insufficiency, and Doubt
dreams, 289
    imagery phenomenon of, 234-235, 326-327
    reversing and, 353-355
    subjective reality and, 20
ectropy, 50-51, 52, 358
    love and, 209
    reversing and, 314-315
    war and, 195
Einstein, Albert, 94, 228
Egypt, 39, 68, 191-192, 233, 246
entropy, 49-50, 52
    reversing and, 314-315
    war and, 195
Epstein, Max, 16
etzem, 61
faith, 79, 133-134, 221-222, 301, 302, 303, 359-360
    mental imagery exercises for, 227-228
    Seven Divine Forces and, 215-226
    stopping exercises and, 366-367
    yes and no phenomena and, 354

false emergency state, 120
    Attachment, Insufficiency, and Doubt (AID) and, 137-138
    clinical examples of, 102, 103, 133
    faith and, 134
    fight, flight, or freeze response and, 122-123
    physiology of, 122-125
    practice reversing, 137-138
    source of, 126
    Theater of Life and, 113-114
    true emergencies and, 121-122
false selves, 112-113. *See also* inner terrorists
fight, flight, or freeze response, 122-123
five dimensions of experience, 89, 102, 104, 210, 325
F.M. 2030, 43-44, 90
Fool, the (tarot), 35, 37
forgiveness, 168-169, 193, 221, 281, 285
    mental imagery exercise for, 170, 395
FoxO gene, 62
Freud, Sigmund, 42, 288, 326-327
futurizing, 152, 356, 358, 360. *See also* pasturizing
Garden of Eden, 38, 49, 53-55, 209, 218, 221, 259, 287-288, 322, 349
    See also Biblical figures: Adam and Eve, Tree of Death, Tree of Life
Gerald Epstein Medical System (GEMS), 15-21, 85
    attachment and, 99
    dimensions of experience and, 86-87
    essence to existence and, 77
    intuition and, 99-100
    practices, 187-203, 243
        Alliance, The, 187-188
        remembrance, 189-196
        reversing, 202-203
        watching, 196-202
        will, 189
    sacred medicine and, 98
    science of disease model versus, 94-95
    spirituality and, 185-187
    spiritual science and, 81
    whole health system of, 96-97
ghost organ, 64
Gibson, Robert Rondell, 17, 95, 114, 156
God, 187-188, 229, 240
    conversing with, 341-345
    emulating, 369-370
    etymology of, 73
    imagery exercises for connecting with, 240-241
    See also Absolute One Mind, Alliance, Invisible Reality
Gödel, Kurt, 353
grammar of self, 355-364
greed, 55, 93, 116, 143, 149, 171, 208, 248, 278, 288, 292, 308
    exercise for, 292
Gronowicz, Gloria, 61
guilt, 140, 169
Hadassah Hospital/Medical School, 41, 51
Hafiz, 59
Hawking, Stephen, 313
healing, 22, 35, 36, 76, 92, 180
    Biblical, 89, 209
    GEMS and, Chapter VI, 321, 324, 359, 364, 425
    health-care and, 371-377
    imagery and, 91, 130, 146, 234, 235, 329, 343, 381
    mental imagery exercise for, 91, 131
    science and, 87

Index

spiritual, 82, 89, 202, 342
    See also GEMS, mental imagery, Ten Commandments
health-care archaeology, 152
heart (spiritual concept), 80, 87, 269
HeartMath Institute of California, 65
Hillel, Rabbi 175
Hitchens, Christopher, 313
Holocaust. *See* World War II
holy (concept), 186, 297
    etymology of, 75-76
    GEMS and, 96, 98
    healing and, 21
    See also kailo
hope, 236-238
    mental imagery exercises for, 238
horizontal world, 76-77
    symbols, 77-78
    See also vertical world
immorality concepts, 60
impermanent reality, 71-72. *See also* permanent reality
inner terrorists, 54, 112, 113, 115, 118, 136, 309, 361
    social errors and, 139, 142, 155, 167, 168, 169
    spiritual awareness and, 196-202
    See also false selves
intuition, 228-232
    mental imagery exercises for, 232
intuitional thinking, 321-329
Invisible Reality, 73, 177, 189, 193, 246, 369
    faith and, 134, 186, 218, 301
    imagery and, 336, 338, 339
    intuition and, 99, 229-230
    Neter Principle and, 69, 222
    prayer and, 222
    spiritual gifts and, 114, 115
    spiritual science and, 20, 67
    Ten Commandments and, 248, 251, 252, 255, 264, 273, 376
    Western spirituality and, 30
    See also God
Isis and Osiris, 191-192
    mental imagery exercise, 413
Islam, 59, 233, 367, 368.
    Sufism, 223-224, 367
    See also Hafiz
Izutsu, Toshiro, 233
Jantsch, Eric, 51
Jesus Christ, 59, 70, 78, 202, 296, 346.
    See also Biblical figures
Journal of Psychiatry & Law, 41
Judaism, 57, 59, 284-285
    symbols, 77-78, 323
    Talmud, 268, 366
    See also Bible, Hebrew; Biblical figures; Biblical stories; Sabbath
kailo, 21, 76, 87, 95
    GEMS and, 98, 186
    Theater of Life and, 117
    See also holy
Kaplan, Ulas, 85
Konigsberg, Alan. *See* Allen, Woody
Kook, Abraham Issac, 57
Kook, Zvi Yehuda, 34-35
Kurzweil, Ray, 63
Lacey, John and Beatrice, 80
ladder of self-mastery, 45, 72, 101, 118, 187, 188, 243, 300, 424
Law of Unity, 199-201, 321
Lawrence, D.H., 220
Levin, Jeffrey, 341-342, 372
Life Path, 30, 38
Longevity, Immortality, Freedom, and Ectropy (LIFE), 381-382
    ascension exercises, 396-406
    eternal life exercises, 415-422

prepatory exercises, 385-396
resurrection exercises, 406-415
longevity philosophies, 60-66
love (from Seven Divine Sources), 208-211
    mental imagery exercises for, 211-214
Man Against Himself, 40
Master of Christianity. *See* Jesus Christ
McClelland, David, 82
meditation, 98, 206, 262, 354, 368
memory, 189-190, 190-196
Menninger, Karl, 40
mental imagery, 235-236
    ascension exercises of, 396-406
    clinical examples of, 91, 102, 130, 335-340, 372-373
    eternal life exercises of, 415-422
    instructions for practice of, 24-25
    levels of, 382
    mirror neurons and, 338
    neuro-physical phenomena of, 336-337
    placebo and, 146
    preparatory exercises of, 385-396
    resurrection exercises of, 406-415
    See also greed: exercise for; stopping exercises; Index of Mental Imagery Exercises
Methuselah, 60
Mind As Healer, Mind As Slayer, 40
mind (spiritual concept), 80
Nashel, Howard, 41
Neter Principal, 68-70
New Wave of Consciousness, 28, 34
New York Psychoanalytic Institute, 41

nocebo, 35-36, 144, 146, 284, 331, 358, 375
    definition, 145
    See also placebo
Nomadic Spirituality, 34
Nova (show), "Can We Live Forever?," 65
"On Beginning the Analysis" (paper), 42
one-minute life repair, 91, 92, 334-335
"On the Creativity and Reversibility of Time" (paper), 51
pasturizing, 152, 356, 360. *See also* futurizing
Pelletier, Ken, 40
Pentateuch. *See* Bible, Hebrew
permanent reality, 71-73, 242. *See also* impermanent reality
physiology of death, 53, 125
placebo, 35-36, 331, 374
    components of, 144
    mental imagery as, 146
    See also nocebo
poverty. *See* Three Virtues: poverty
prayer, 334
    faith and, 222-223
    healing power of, 89, 372
    reversing practice of, 203, 341-345
purpose of living, 45
regret, 152-153
    mental imagery exercise for, 154
religious symbols, 77-78
resurrection, 60
    mental imagery exercises, 406-415
reversing, 98, 115, 137, 202-203, 424
    imagery exercise for, 395
    practices, Chapter XII
Sabbath, 423-427
    holiness and, 76
    mental imagery exercises, 263, 427-429

Index

prayer L'cha Dodi, 383
    Ten Commandments and, 248, 261-262
    Ten Laws Life Plan and, 247
    sacred medicine, 98
science of disease, 94-95
secrets, 283, 285-286
Self-Mastery Through Conscious Auto-Suggestion, 221, 318
SENS Research Foundation, 63
Seven Divine Forces (Chapter XI), 79-80, 118, 204
    hope, 236-238
    imagination, 232-235
    intuition, 228-232
    Law of Detachment and, 308
    light, 238-240
    love, 208-211
    Theater of Life and, 114-115
    will, 205-208
Shakespeare, William, 23, 44-45, 111, 137, 287
Sheldrake, Rupert, 344-345
social errors, 142-143
    1st (suggestion), 144-146, 361
    2nd (future and past talk), 150-154
        expectations, 154-155, 361-362
        futurizing, 152
        pasturizing, 152
        regret, 152-153
    3rd (five dual false beliefs), 159-162
    4th (institutional/cultural standards), 162-164
    5th ("what ought to be"), 165-166
    6th (dominate others/subjugate self), 167-168, 363-364
    7th (accounts receivable and payable), 168-169
    8th (will, greed, and vanity), 171-172
    9th (enslavement), 32, 173-178
    10th (seriousness), 179-182
    mental imagery exercises for, 154
    See also forgiveness, futurizing, guilt, health-care archaeology, pasturizing, regret
Sons of the Prophets (school), 186
"Spiritual Body of Light," 72, 241, 331, 420, 424
Spiritual Constitution, 21
spiritual gifts, 114-115
spirituality, history of, 20
spiritual materialism, 275
spiritual science, 20, 48, 201, 215, Chapter IV
Steinsaltz, Adin, 57, 58
stem cell replacement, 64
stopping exercises, 364-369
suicide, 36, 269-271, 283
Sullivan-Smith, Anne, 85
Talmud. *See* Judaism: Talmud
Tanakh. *See* Bible, Hebrew
tarot. *See* Fool, the
Ten Commandments, 22, 244-247, Chapter XII: The Laws
    1st, 251
    2nd, 149, 169, 177, 252-255, 376
    3rd, 169, 255-261
    4th, 261-263
    5th, 263-266
    6th, 36, 88, 169, 266-273
    7th, 273-278
    8th, 278-281
    9th, 88, 149, 151-152, 162, 281-286

10th, 169, 286-290, 303, 356, 359
charting the, 292-296
conscience and, 244-245
dark currents of will and, 248
Law of Detachment and, 308
linguistically re-framed, 247
love and, 81-82
memory and, 194-195
Theater of Life and, 114-115
Ten Laws. *See* Ten Commandments
Theater of Life, 112
Absolute One Mind and, 112
Attachment, Insufficiency, and Doubt and, 114
developing spiritual awareness and, 196
false emergency state and, 113-114
spiritual gifts and, 114-15
The Power of Now, 357
Therapeutic Touch, 61
The Self-Organizing Universe, 51
thinking by analogy. *See* intuitional thinking
Three Virtues, 297-300
Absolute One Mind and, 298
chart of, 308
chastity, 114, 297-298, 302-304, 306, 308
Law of Detachment and, 308
obedience, 300-302
opposites of, 116
poverty, 114, 116, 223, 231, 297-298, 306-308
renunciation and, 296-297
Theater of Life and, 114-115

Tree of Death, 49-50, 54-56. *See also* Biblical figures: Adam and Eve; Garden of Eden; Tree of Life
Tree of Life, 49-50, 54-56. *See also* Biblical figures: Adam and Eve, Garden of Eden, Tree of Death
Tolle, Eckhart, 357
Torah. *See* Bible, Hebrew
truth, 281-286
United States Army, 41
vertebra physiology, 346-348. 350-351
vertical memory, 189-190
vertical world, 76-77, 117, 187, 427
reversing and, 242-243
symbols of, 77-78
See also horizontal world
watching (concept as GEMS practice), 196-202, 357-358
Watson, Lyall, 344
Weinreb, Friedrich, 369
will, 54, 158
dark and light currents of, 171, 207-208, 223, 229, 248, 260, 278, 307, 370
GEMS practice of, 187, 189
Seven Divine Forces concept of, 79, 204-206
See also GEMS: practices; Seven Divine Forces
World War II, 128, 223-224, 244, 285
yes or no phenomenon, 345-346, 351-353
Yom Kippur. *See* Day of Atonement

Index of Mental Imagery Exercises

A Sabbath Exercise: The Cessation of Time, 263
About Love, 212
Agony and the Ecstasy, 391
Altar of Idolatry: For Coming Out of Enslavement, 178
Angel of Eternal Life: To Repair the Telomeres, 419
Anti-"Aging," 417
Ascending the Seven Steps of the Heart, 397-398
Ascending to Your Higher Form of Wisdom, 397
Becoming a Technician of the Sacred, 389-390
Becoming Moderate, 306
Becoming One with your Soul Self, 319
Becoming the Wavicle, 418-419
Bliss, 422
Burying the Past, 390
Celebrating the Beloved, 400-401
Cleansing Your Soul: The Light-Bearing Soul, 396
Come to Your Light, 240
Confessing the Truth, 286
Crossing the Red Sea, 102, 227
Crystal Vase, 241

Defeating Death, 412-413
Descent into the Self: The Bottomless Abyss, 401-403
Developing Ennobling Love in our Relationships, 213
Eternal Life: Drinking the Cup of Heaven, 422
Eternity, 417
Exodus: Crossing the Red Sea, 227
Forest of Forgiveness: To Forgive Others, 170
From Seed to Tree, 411
Frustrated Love, 214
Gift from God, 405-406
Illumination: Flight of the One to the One, 406
Isis and Osiris, 413
Life and Light, 391-392
Life Overcoming Death, 414
Light- Glory, 241
Light Illuminating Your Road, 393
Light of the Heart/Light of the Brain, 240
Long Life, 417-418
Love, 211
Midnight Sun, 421
Mistake in Love/Mistaken Love, 212

We Are Not *Meant* to Die

Moderation, 394
No Separation, 416
Obedient Ears, 302
One-Minute Life Repair, 91, 92, 334-335
Overcoming Death, 411-412
Pillar of Salt: for Removing Regret, 154
Piloting Your Ship of No-Time, 401
Prophetic Imagination: The Great Chain of Being, 404
Putting Self Together, 388-389
Rainbow Staircase, 396-397
Re-Birth: A Second Chance, 414
Repentance: Reversing Errors of the Past, 395
Return to the Alliance, 388
Returning to the Source, 399-400
Road of Love, 212
Room of Detachment: For Becoming Free, 37-38
Round Mirror, 407
Seeing Straight: Sobriety, 305
Seventh Cervical Vertebra: The Vertebra of Resurrection, The Vertebra that Never Disintegrates, 406-407
Stillness of Mind, 320
Suprasensory Reality, 398
Swallow the Rainbow: For Nausea, 176
The Ark of Safety, 227
The Black Light of Holiness: Die Before You Die, 405
The Blossoming Heart, 410
The Color of Your Life, 385-386
The Foam and the Sea, 393-394
The Guest House, 385

The Lake of Inner Knowing to Develop Intuition, 232
The Light of God, 398
The Origin of Creation, 404-405
The Past to Eternity: Finding the Moment, 415
The Pineal Gland: The Flow of Energy for Living Harmoniously Within Yourself, 420
The Power of Light, 403
The Rainbow Bridge of Hope, 238
The Resurrection Process: The Turning Point from Death to Life, 408-410
The Sinai Desert, 228
The Tightrope Walker, 318
The Tornado, 130, 131
The Train of Life, 399
The Weaver: The Power of Life, 392-393
Time Flies/Flying from Time, 420-421
To Know Yourself, 320
To Learn Concentration without Effort, 317
To Learn Focused Concentration, 317
Tree of Life - I, 386-387
Tree of Life - II, 387
Tree of Life - III, 388
Trumpet of Resurrection, 415
Tunnel of Love (clinical reference), 102
Unbounded, 416-417
Untying the Knots of Life: Creating Order from Disorder, 390-391
Visibility and Ennobling Love, 214
Your House of Being, 416

About the Authors

Gerald Epstein, MD (1935-2019) was a pioneer in the field of integrative medicine and a leading expert in the therapeutic use of mental imagery for healing physical and emotional ailments. Initially trained as a Freudian analyst, he shifted his focus in 1974 to study under Mme. Colette Aboulker-Muscat, becoming a major catalyst in using the Western spiritual tradition in healing. Dr. Jerry (as he was affectionately known) directed The American Institute for Mental Imagery (AIMI) in New York City until his death in 2019. There, he facilitated group practices, trained healthcare professionals, and taught courses on the Gerald Epstein Medical System (GEMS), a therapeutic treatment that uses one's inner wisdom to balance and repair mind, body, and spirit. In addition to his teachings and private practice, Dr. Jerry authored numerous books and audios, including the seminal Healing Visualizations: Creating Health through Imagery.

We Are Not Meant to Die is his final opus — a collection of 83 years of wisdom and an offering of love and healing for the future.

Rachel Epstein, JD, LAc, is co-founder and director of the American Institute for Mental Imagery (AIMI) in New York City and is a holistic health coach. With over 30 years of experience, Rachel helps clients heal from physical illness and emotional trauma. She teaches the core GEMS (Gerald Epstein Medical System) curriculum and is Editor-in-Chief of ACMI Press. As AIMI's academic director, Rachel continues to evolve the core curriculum to meet the current needs of human transformation and personal development. She received her training in mental imagery from internationally recognized authorities Mme. Colette Aboulker-Muscat and Dr. Gerald Epstein, her late husband and co-author. In addition to *We Are Not Meant to Die*, Rachel co-authored *Reversing the Trauma of War: PTSD Help for Veterans, Active-Duty Personnel and Their Families* (2019), and edited seven major works on mental imagery, healing, and the Western spiritual tradition.

Contact Rachel at:
rachel@aimi.us or visit
REheals.com for self-healing services, courses, publications,
blog or to book a session.

Visit aimi.us to explore the American Institute for Mental Imagery.

Visit drjerryepstein.org to learn more about
the life and work of Dr Jerry Epstein.